Ascot

THE HISTORY

Ascot
THE HISTORY

Sean Magee

with Sally Aird

With a foreword by Sir Peter O'Sullevan

methuen

1 3 5 7 9 10 8 6 4 2

Published in 2002 by Methuen Publishing Ltd
215 Vauxhall Bridge Rd, London SW1V 1EJ

Copyright © Ascot Racecourse Limited 2002
The right of Sean Magee to be identified as the author of this work has been
asserted by him in accordance with the Copyright, Designs and Patents Act 1988.

Methuen Publishing Limited Reg. No. 3543167

A CIP catalogue record for this book is available from the British Library

ISBN 0 413 77203 9

Design by designsection, Frome, Somerset
Printed and bound in Great Britain by Butler and Tanner Limited, Frome and London

Endpapers: The field for the 1993 King George VI and Queen Elizabeth Diamond Stakes at the home turn. The winner Opera House (Michael Roberts) is third from the right.

Title spread: The field for the 1991 King George VI and Queen Elizabeth Diamond Stakes at the home turn. The winner Generous (ridden by Alan Munro) is the chesnut on the right of the leading trio, with Luchiroverte (Frankie Dettori) on his inside and the white-faced Saddlers' Hall (Lester Piggott) on the left.

CONTENTS

INTRODUCTION

MARQUESS OF HARTINGTON CBE

This is the first official history of Ascot Racecourse. Its publication in this Golden Jubilee Year is particularly appropriate, given Ascot's connection with the Royal Family since 1711.

My particular thanks go to Paul Roberts, who has driven this project, to his small team of Sally Aird and Emily Hedges, and to Sean Magee, who has written a history worthy of its subject. Numerous organisations and individuals have helped us by allowing access to their archives, including those of the Royal Collections at Windsor Castle, Weatherbys and the Jockey Club. David Oldrey has wisely guided us, whilst Peter Tummons and Methuen have produced a book of high quality to a very tight deadline. Finally, many members of Ascot's staff have been involved in the production of the book.

This is a particularly exciting time as Ascot Racecourse plans its next redevelopment and the celebration of its tercentenary in 2011. In the meantime, we look forward to welcoming you at Ascot Racecourse to enjoy racing, the landscape and the jollity of a day out, all of which I believe Queen Anne would have appreciated. We owe her and her successors a great debt for their patronage: none more than Her Present Majesty.

Hartington

May 2002

FOREWORD

SIR PETER O'SULLEVAN CBE

Ascot racecourse has commanded a special place in my affections for the best part of six decades.

When in October 1944 I applied for my first job in journalism with the Press Association, the entrance exam was to write a piece previewing the first October meeting on the royal heath. Amazingly, three of my four suggestions obliged – including winners at 20–1 and 13–2 – and the job was mine.

Since then my love of Ascot has grown ever deeper, helped along by Scobie Breasley on Be Friendly winning the King's Stand Stakes in 1967 and the privilege of calling home so many of the great Ascot horses – Ribot, Nijinsky, Brigadier Gerard, Mill Reef, Sagaro and Shergar among them.

Modern Ascot is comfortable with its history but constantly looking for ways to improve, and has distilled a unique blend of tradition and innovation. At which other course could a major sponsorship deal such as De Beers' support for the King George VI and Queen Elizabeth Stakes have been handled with such discretion that the self-effacing sponsors did not even add any hint of their product to the race's title until the fourth year of their support?

Ascot has long been fortunate in the vision and imagination of the people directing its destiny – men like Sir John Crocker Bulteel, who founded the 'King George' in 1951 and put Ascot firmly on the international racing map; the Duke of Norfolk, who with the skill of a practised organiser brought the course into the modern age; and, more recently, the Marquess of Abergavenny, who succeeded the Duke as Her Majesty's Representative, and the current incumbent of that role, 'Stoker' Hartington.

Published in the year of the Golden Jubilee of Her Majesty the Queen – whose own input into the development of Ascot during her reign has been immense – this new history provides a delightful and appropriate celebration of the world's most famous racecourse.

Peter O'Sullevan

May 2002

Ascot

THE HISTORY

PROLOGUE –
A HUNT IN THE FOREST

By the summer of 1711 Queen Anne had grown prodigiously fat.

At the age of forty-six she was far from healthy. Her marriage to Prince George of Denmark – 'I have tried him sober, and I have tried him drunk,' complained Charles II, 'and there is nothing in him' – had produced some eighteen pregnancies but numerous miscarriages and no child who survived beyond the age of eleven. She suffered from gout so badly that at her coronation in 1702 she had to be carried into Westminster Abbey in a sedan chair. She had been widowed in 1708, and she was (in the words of Ascot historian Dorothy Laird) 'self-indulgent at the table to the point of gluttony'. Reputedly tipping the scales at around twenty stone, she could scarcely walk.

Yet the commonly held notion that Queen Anne was dull can hardly be sustained in one area of her life – a devotion to hunting and racing which bordered on addiction.

Horses were in her blood. Her great-grandfather James I was deeply devoted to hunting and established Newmarket as a sporting centre in the early seventeenth century. Her uncle Charles II was passionate in his love of racing. He rode in races and built himself a palace in Newmarket (with a handy underground tunnel to Nell Gwyn's house across the street) as a base from which to pursue that passion. His hack Old Rowley gave the King his popular nickname, perpetuated in the Rowley Mile at Newmarket. Anne's father, James II, was not on the throne long enough to make much of an impact on any area of public life, let alone horse racing, but his successor William III – William of Orange – was an enthusiastic breeder of racehorses, and won a £500 match race at Newmarket.

Queen Anne's own racing interests were established well before she succeeded to the throne. A keen racegoer and a notable benefactress of the

Previous pages: Henry
Bernard Chalon, *Unkennelling
the Royal Hounds on Ascot
Heath*, 1817.

sport, she inherited from William III a 'Keeper of the Running Horses' named
Tregonwell Frampton (whose role was akin to that of a racing manager today),
a stable at Newmarket (where she paid £1,000 to have the town's streets paved)
and the Royal Stud at Hampton Court. She was the first monarch to race her
horses at York, where in 1711 she presented a gold cup worth £100. At several
other racecourses she inaugurated the running of Queen's Plates, each worth
£100 to the owner of the winning horse.

In the second decade of the eighteenth century horse racing in Britain was
a very different affair from the organised sport we know today – indeed, a very
different affair even from the semi-ordered world of the Turf which had come
into being by the end of that century. The founding of the Jockey Club was
some forty years off; the races we now know as the Classics would not be
thought of for another sixty-five years; and the variety of venues at which the
sport took place reflected the haphazard nature of its development over the
previous two centuries.

While there are records of horse racing in England since the twelfth century,
it was not until the sixteenth that public races became regular events, often
held as an adjunct to town fairs. There were races at Chester early in the reign
of Henry VIII; Elizabeth I was known to have enjoyed the sport; and James I
instituted race meetings at Richmond in Yorkshire and Enfield Chase in
Middlesex as well as attending Epsom. He played a major role in the development of racing at Newmarket, where his first recorded attendance at a race was
in March 1619. This momentum was maintained by James's son Charles I.

Oliver Cromwell put a stop to racing in 1654 and 1655, but the Restoration
signalled a surge of support, with Charles II's devotion to Newmarket the
engine for rapid growth. By the turn of the eighteenth century racing was
again a thriving – if unregulated and not always well organised – activity.
Meetings were held all over the land, with Newmarket leading the way.
Epsom and Salisbury staged well-run meetings in the south, and Yorkshire
had already established itself as a major racing county with big meetings at
Black Hambleton, York and Doncaster. It was in this atmosphere that Ascot
was founded.

Queen Anne's passion for riding could not keep up with the expansion
of her girth. Her growing obesity caused her to forsake the saddle, but she
continued to indulge her enthusiasm for following hounds through the

ingenious use of a specially designed two-wheeled horse-drawn carriage, which she drove herself to follow the Royal Buckhounds.

The Buckhounds had been founded in the fourteenth century, and their fortunes waxed and waned according to the inclinations of the monarch of the time. Under Anne they thrived, and in order to fuel her passion she had built new kennels at Swinley Bottom – close to where the Ascot water jump is today – so that she could follow hounds when the Court was at Windsor Castle. In this pursuit she was memorably described by Jonathan Swift to Esther Johnson (the 'Stella' of his journal) on 31 July 1711:

> The queen was abroad to-day to hunt, but finding it disposed to rain she kept in her coach; she hunts in a chaise with one horse, which she drives herself, and drives furiously, like Jehu, and is a mighty hunter like Nimrod.

A few days later Swift wrote:

> The queen was hunting the stag till four this afternoon, and she drove in her chaise above forty miles, and it was five before we went to dinner.

Queen Anne.

It was probably during one of these breakneck charges through Windsor Forest in the summer of 1711 that it dawned on the Queen that Ascot Heath, where the Buckhounds were kennelled, was the ideal place to race horses. In this simple way was conceived the most famous racecourse in the world, whose founder is remembered every June with the running of the Queen Anne Stakes as the opening race of the Royal Ascot meeting.

The name Ascot was first recorded in 1177 as 'Estcota' ('east cottage'). It was referred to as 'Ascote' and 'Achecote' in the thirteenth century and

'Astcote' in the fourteenth, and the Heath itself, although having a reputation as a wild and desolate place, was located in an area already steeped in horse racing tradition. Henry VIII had raced horses in Windsor, while Charles II raced at nearby Dorsett Ferry in 1684 and at Datchet Mead – where Anne and her husband, apparently taken aback by the level of gambling at Newmarket, organised a fixture in 1705, causing the royal-watcher Narcissus Luttrell to note that 'the royal couple seemed mightily given to racing'. A Queen's Plate was run at Datchet in 1709.

Although the exact date and circumstances of Queen Anne's impulse to construct a racecourse on Ascot Heath are not known, the hard evidence that her plan was being realised appeared in the *London Gazette* on 12 July 1711:

> Her Majesty's Plate of 100 guineas will be run for round the new heat [course] on Ascott Common, near Windsor, on Tuesday August 7th next, by any horse, mare or gelding, being no more than six years old the grass [spring] before, as must be certified under the hand of the breeder, carrying 12st, three heats, to be entered the last day of July, at Mr Hancock's, at Fern Hill, near the Starting Post.

That was not all:

> A plate of 50 guineas to be run for on Monday August 6th, by any horse, mare or gelding, that had never won the value of £40 in money or plate. Each animal to carry 12st, in three heats. To be entered on preceding Wednesday, at the Town Hall, New Windsor, or with the Town Clerk or his Deputy, paying two guineas, or at the time of starting 6 guineas to the said Clerk or Deputy. The entrance money to go to the second horse in the race.

Back on the Heath, preparations for the inaugural meeting proceeded.

Charles, Duke of Somerset, Master of the Horse, instructed Sir William Wyndham, who had become Master of the Royal Buckhounds in June 1711, to have the racing ground cleared of scrub and gorse in preparation for a race meeting on the next occasion the court was at Windsor Castle, and the Duke's Account Books record payments to the workmen who constructed the course:

£558.19s.5d to the principal contractor William Lowen for paying 'sundry workmen employed in making and perfecting the round Heat on Ascot Common in the months of July and August 1711'; £15.2s.8d to the carpenter William Erlybrown 'for setting up posts and other carpenter's work on the said common'; £2.15s.0d to Benjamin Culchott for painting the posts; £1.1s.6d to John Grape 'for engrossing the Articles for Her Majesty's Plate run for at Ascot Common' – that is, copying out the race conditions.

Preparations seem to have hit a problem, for on 28 July, nine days before the first day's racing was due to take place, the *London Gazette* announced a short postponement: the Queen's Plate would now take place on 11 August, four days later than originally planned.

On the eve of that historic day Jonathan Swift was again in the area:

> Dr Arbuthnott, the queen's physician and favourite, went out with me to shew me the places: we went a little after the queen, and overtook Miss Forester, a maid of honour, on her palfry, taking the air; we made her go along with us. We saw a place they have made for a famous horse-race tomorrow, where the queen will come. We met the queen coming back, and Miss Forester stood, like us, with her hat off while the queen went by … Much company is come to town this evening, to see to-morrow's race. I was tired with riding a trotting mettlesome horse a dozen miles, having not been on horse-back this twelve-month. And Miss Forester did not make it easier; she is a silly true maid of honour, and I did not like her, although she be a toast, and was dressed like a man.

Miss Forester's mannish behaviour in doffing her hat to the queen rather than curtseying suggested an unorthodox nature, which was to be confirmed by her dress at the races: a long white riding coat over a full-flapped waistcoat and a habit skirt; on her head, over a white-powdered periwig, a small three-cornered cocked hat, bound with gold lace, the point placed exactly in front.

Royalty, high fashion and horse racing – already the unique brew was being stirred that was to make Royal Ascot both the most famous race meeting and the most stylish fashion event in the world.

ASCOT IN THE EIGHTEENTH CENTURY

The first race meeting at Ascot took place on Saturday 11 August 1711. According to a contemporary source:

> The Queen, with a brilliant suite, drove over from Windsor Castle to Ascott Common on 11th August 1711, to inaugurate Ascott races and attended Ascott again on the following Monday ... Her Majesty proceeded along the common with her long train of courtiers and other attendants.

Jonathan Swift was still in the area, but did not get to join in the fun:

> I intended to go to the race to-day, but was hindered by a visit ... I dined to-day at the green cloth [the dining room for guests of the court at Windsor], where everybody had been at the race except myself, and we were twenty in all; and very noisy company ...

Seven horses were entered for the fifty-guinea Plate:

> The Duke of St Albans' chesnut horse Doctor
> Mr Erwell's grey horse Have-at-all
> Mr Smith's grey gelding Teague
> Mr William Hall's bay stone horse Dimple
> Mr John Biddolph's bay brown horse Flint
> Mr Charles May's grey gelding Grey Jack
> Mr Merrit's iron-grey stone horse Grim

Previous pages: Thomas and Paul Sandby, *Ascot Heath Races*, *c.* 1765 (detail). (See pages 30–1.)

The fixture's major event, the £100 Queen's Plate, was run two days later on Monday 13 August, when four runners went to post:

> Lord Raylton's brown bay
> Lord Craven's grey horse
> Sir William Goring's brown bay
> Mr Orme's bay horse

The sport again took place without Jonathan Swift:

> I miss'd the race to-day by coming out too late, when every body's coach
> was gone, and ride I would not; I felt my last riding three days after.

It is Ascot's loss that Swift managed to attend neither of those historic days' racing, as we could do with an eye-witness account: the names of the winners have not been passed down, and we have little in the way of detail about the nature of the races themselves. No map of the course from that time survives, so we do not know, for instance, exactly where the starting post or the winning post were – though from the first map of the course, published over a century later, we can make a reasonably informed guess that the winning post was about halfway up the straight as we know it today. Nor do the race conditions as advertised in the *London Gazette* mention the distance over which the 'three heats' on each day would be run, though it can be safely assumed that the distance of each race was four miles, since that was the standard distance for horse races at this period.

The heats system produced a day's racing very far removed from the programme of several individual and distinct races that we know today. To take the first Queen's Plate run at Ascot as an example: all four entered horses would run in the first heat, twice round the two-mile course; they would then run in a second heat; then a third. A horse that won two heats would be declared the winner, but if the first three heats were won by different horses, the sport would continue to a fourth – for which only horses who had won one of the first three would qualify. A horse who had not passed the 'distance pole', 240 yards from the winning post, by the time the winner passed the winning post, was judged to have been 'distanced' and could not run in the next heat; a horse who did not win but was inside the distance pole as the winner passed the post was said to have 'saved his distance'; if horses tied for first place, that heat was held to have died – it was a 'dead heat', and would be rerun.

It will be obvious from such details that races at these first Ascot fixtures, where runners could race for as much as sixteen miles in one day with only a short rest between each heat, placed much more emphasis on stamina and endurance than on the factor of speed so sought after today. So it must be borne in mind, when trying to picture how those early races at Ascot would have appeared, that in physical terms the horses who raced then were a far cry from Nijinsky, Dubai Millennium or other famous names who have graced the Ascot turf in recent years, and in appearance would have looked something like a cross between an English hunter and a modern Thoroughbred. The development of the purpose-bred racehorse which became the English Thoroughbred had been steadily carried on through the import of Eastern bloodlines from the time of Richard I, but in the early years of the eighteenth century was only beginning to reach its peak through the influence of the Darley Arabian, the Byerley Turk and the Godolphin Arabian, Arab stallions imported around the turn of the eighteenth century. That the first Ascot meetings attracted 'real' racehorses is another indication of their prestige.

The first Ascot fixture in August 1711 must have been a success, for it was followed by a second in September – a two-day affair consisting on Monday 17 September of a Plate of fifty guineas for any horse carrying ten stone 'that never won in money or Plate the value of £20', which attracted three entries, and on Tuesday 18 September a £20 Plate which attracted four entries.

The identity of the owners of the horses in these early races offers an important clue to the nature of these events. One of the runners in the initial fifty-guinea Plate was owned by the Duke of St Albans, an illegitimate son of Charles II; one of the trio who ran on the September Monday belonged to the Duke of Somerset, Master of the Horse; and one of the quartet on the September Tuesday was owned by Sir William Wyndham, Master of the Buckhounds. These horses were owned by courtiers or by those closely connected with the court or the hunt, and the sport was essentially entertainment for the court and its adherents, rather than a public spectacle. (This was not the case with other race meetings at the time, many of which were closely linked to local social events.) The connection with the Royal

Buckhounds is emphasised by the overall responsibility for Ascot racing having remained with the Master of the Royal Buckhounds from its very inception until the death of Queen Victoria in 1901, nearly two centuries later: thereafter the responsibility fell to the appointed representative of the monarch.

Ascot seemed set for a long and successful life as a venue for horse racing, and the meeting as one of the great social events of the year. In 1712 the nobility and gentry flocked to the Heath for the running of the Queen's Plate on 25 August: the Duke of Beaufort was there, and the Duke of Hamilton, and Lord Chancellor Harcourt, and numerous Members of Parliament, High Sheriffs, Justices of the Peace and 'other gentlemen and freeholders'. That year the Queen's Plate attracted six runners, four of whom were distanced in the first heat, and this time we have the name of the winner – or at least of the winning owner: 'Robert Fagg, Esq., son of Sir Robert Fagg, Baronet of Sussex'. Another fixture was held in September 1712, when a £50 Plate was run, while the following year saw the Queen's Plate contested in August, and the Windsor Town Plate – twenty guineas, open to any horse carrying ten stone – was run the same month.

In 1714 the Queen's Plate was advertised to be run on 13 August, but Anne's health was fast giving up the unequal struggle. On 31 July her horse Star won a £40 Plate at York. Even as news of this royal victory was hurried to London, the Queen lay dying at Kensington Palace, and she was never to hear of her final victory as a racehorse owner. The last of the Stuart monarchs died on the morning of 1 August 1714 at the age of forty-nine – her Vice-Chamberlain Thomas Coke noted ungraciously that 'she died monstrously fat, so much so that her coffin was almost square' – and the Ascot fixture scheduled for later that month was cancelled.

Anne had no living children, and the Crown passed to her nearest eligible blood relative, the Elector of Hanover, who became George I and whose comparative lack of interest in horse racing (he visited Newmarket just once) seems to have brought about a hiatus in the history of Ascot. While it is impossible to be certain that there were no races at the course during the early part of his reign, no record of fixtures survives, and it must be significant that from 1715 until after George's death in 1727 there was no appointment to the position of Master of the Buckhounds. It was not until August 1720 – some seven years after the last recorded meeting – that two days' racing were held at Ascot, both featuring Plates of thirty guineas run for not by true racehorses but by hunters 'used in hunting 12 months last past'. The entrance fee for each runner was two guineas, or four guineas if entered at the starting post (an early version of the method of 'supplementing' for big races that we know today), or just one guinea for 'contributors' to the prize fund. The owner of the winner took the thirty guineas, and the owner of the second horse collected the pool of entrance money.

Further meetings followed in 1722 (when one day was confined to horses that had stag-hunted in Epping or Windsor Forest with the King's hounds), 1724 (when a Stag-Hunters' Plate was won by the delightfully named Clubfoot) and 1726.

Our knowledge of Ascot races increases significantly from 1727, as it was in that year that John Cheny published *An Historical List, or Account of all the Horse-Matches Run, and of all the Plates and Prizes run for in England (of the Value of Ten Pounds or upwards)* – the prototype form book which evolved into the *Racing Calendar*. The first Ascot entry is for 31 July 1727, in the records of racing in Berkshire:

ASCOT-HEATH

On the 31st of July, a 40 Guineas Purse was run for at Ascot-Heath in this County, by such Horses &c. as had the same Season carried the Owners of them to the Death of a Leash of Stags in Windsor-Forest, Weight 12 st.

The purse was won by Mr Walter with his grey horse Hobbler, who won both of the first two heats from his five opponents – who included horses named Slouch and Sober-sides.

The interesting aspect of this fixture is its date, since at the end of July 1727 the court was in mourning for George I, who had died of apoplexy in Osnabrück the previous month, and there would have been no royal presence at the sport – further evidence that the racing of horses at Ascot was at this time inextricably linked with the hunt rather than simply with the court. The post of Master of the Buckhounds had been revived when one of the first acts of the new King, George II, had been to appoint Colonel Francis Negus, and it was Negus, a keen hunting and racing man, who staged that 1727 fixture.

The royal presence at races had been restored by 1730 – when, significantly, the race conditions included the stipulation:

> The Manner and Rules for running to be according to the Rules used in running for the King's Plate at Newmarket; and if any Dispute or Difference about entring [*sic*] or running arise, the same to be determined by the Judges of the Course, who shall be appointed Judges by the Duke of St Albans.

Two decades before the founding of the Jockey Club, Newmarket was already exerting influence on the sport.

For all the enthusiasm of the Master of the Buckhounds, Ascot as a racing occasion was dependent on the interest and commitment of the sovereign, and with George II showing no more interest in the sport than his father, Ascot hiccoughed its way through the 1730s, with racing taking place only intermittently.

Then in 1740 came a serious blow – the passing of an Act of Parliament 'to restrain and prevent the excessive Increase of Horse Races' because horse racing for 'small prizes or sums of money had contributed very much to the encouragement of idleness, to the impoverishment of many of the meaner sort of the subjects of this kingdom and the breed of strong and useful horses hath been much prejudiced thereby.' It ordered that all horses were to be entered for races by their real owners, and nobody was to start more than one horse for the same Plate, under pain of forfeiting the horse. It was declared illegal to run for a Plate of lower value than £50, under a penalty of £200 to the owner and £100 to the advertiser. Every race must begin and end on the same day, the second horse should recover his stake, and gifts left for annual races were not to be altered. Five-year-olds must carry ten stone, six-year-olds eleven stone, seven-year-olds twelve stone. The owner of any horse carrying less weight had to forfeit £200, and the entrance money was to go to 'the second best horse'. The Act did not apply in Scotland or Ireland, and Newmarket and Black Hambleton were exempt from the £50 condition.

Unfortunately the Act failed to take account of genuine races such as those run at Ascot and elsewhere by horses owned by staghunters and hunt servants, and these suffered along with the races that had been made the target. Ascot was too poor to raise sufficient money to take every race up to the £50 level, and consequently the course dropped out of the records of the Turf for the next four years.

But in 1744 an official notice of the Ascot races reappeared, with the terms and conditions much more involved than had previously been the case:

> To be run for on Ascot Heath, in Windsor Forest, on Monday the 7th of September, Fifty Pounds, by any horse, mare or gelding, that is at this Time in the Possession of Huntsmen, or one of the Yeoman Prickers of his Majesty's Buck Hounds, or in the Possession of the Keepers of the said Forest, or Windsor Great Park in the said County; to carry twelve Stone, Bridle and Saddle included, as never started for Match or Plate, and has been hunted in the said Forest between Lady-Day last and Michaelmas-Day. All Disputes for this Plate, relating to Entering or Running, to be determined by Ralph Jennison Esq; or whom he shall appoint.

> And on Tuesday, the 18th Instant, Fifty Pounds by Hunters, that never won either Match, Plate or Stakes, and that never started for any Thing except a Hunter's Plate, to carry twelve Stone, Bridle and Saddle included. No less than three deem'd Hunters to start, and if only one comes, to have Twenty Guineas, and the Plate not run for; and if two only, to have Ten Guineas each. No Person to enter two Horses.

> All horses that run for the first Plate must be enter'd on Monday next, the 10th of this Month, between the Hours of One and Six in the Afternoon, at Sunninghill Wells in Windsor Forest, by the Clerk of the Course, paying Half-a-Crown to him, Entrance Fee.

> And for the second Plate to enter at the same Time and Place, paying if a Subscriber One Guinea Entrance, if a Non-Subscriber Three Guineas, or at the Post Two Guineas if a Subscriber; if a Non-Subscriber Five Guineas, to go to the second best tho' distanced.

> All Horses to be kept from Time of Entering to the Time of Running, at some Publick House within three Miles of the said Course; and all Horses &c to be plated by some Smith that lives within that Distance.

Ralph Jennison, Master of
the Buckhounds 1737–44
and 1746–57.

All Disputes for this Plate, relating either to Entering or Running, to be determin'd by the Majority of Subscribers there present.

There will be Ordinaries each Day, at Sunninghill Wells at One o'Clock.

The first race was a Hunters' Plate organised and judged by the Master of the Buckhounds or his associates. Ralph Jennison, described in these race conditions as the man who would arbitrate in disputes, had become Master of the Buckhounds in 1737 and was to remain in the post – with one brief interval – for twenty years. He clearly knew how to entertain, being described as 'a thorough representative of the excessive conviviality of the age, "a five-bottle man" who would not let his friends walk away from the table'. Furthermore, he presided over the period when Ascot races blossomed, giving the course the benefit of his prominence as a patron of the Turf who became involved in the wider developments occurring in racing at the time. Jennison owned and bred some good horses, and numerous entries in the *Racing Calendar* demonstrate that he was keen to compete with them. He was also the last commoner to fill the office of Master of the Buckhounds, perhaps suggesting that his qualifications for the post were so great that a title was not a necessary aid. Jennison's name in the 1744 race conditions underlines the degree to which that position had become central to the Ascot Races.

The second race appears to have been a more local event, organised by local 'subscribers' who used the Town Hall to enter their horses and managed the race themselves, agreeing that any dispute would be determined by the majority of the subscribers present. (The 'Yeomen Prickers' mentioned in the race conditions were employed by the Master of the Buckhounds, and their place in the history of racing at Ascot is acknowledged by the livery of the course's gatemen at the Royal Meeting: their forest green coats with gold facings are derived from the livery of the Yeomen Prickers.)

An Act of 1745 revoked the weight stipulations in the 1740 Act, acknowledging that:

> The thirteen Royal Plates, of one hundred guineas each, annually run for, as also the high prices that are constantly given for horses of strength and size, are sufficient to encourage breeders to raise their cattle [*sic*] to the utmost size and strength possible …

and the course was properly back in business.

Enter the second great figure in the early history of Ascot: William Augustus, Duke of Cumberland.

Third son of George II, he was born in 1721 and created Duke in 1726, and by the time of his appointment as Ranger of Windsor Forest in 1745 had

The legacy of the Yeomen Prickers lives on in the livery of Royal Ascot gatemen, photographed here with Lord Hartington, Her Majesty's Representative.

Jan-Baptiste Loo, *William Augustus, Duke of Cumberland.*

already made a considerable reputation for himself as a soldier: the year after his appointment as Ranger he defeated the Jacobite army led by Bonnie Prince Charlie to earn himself the soubriquet of 'The Butcher of Culloden'. This did not make Cumberland universally popular: Richard Onslow, the most recent historian of Royal Ascot, notes that 'the flower the English named Sweet William after him was known as Stinking Billy in Scotland'. Cumberland was named Governor of the state of Virginia in America (though he never went there), and gave that state's name to Virginia Water, the artificial lake he constructed two miles east of Ascot.

The Duke of Cumberland was passionately interested in horse racing – a passion closely linked to his love of wagering. Described as 'like both the prodigal son and the fatted calf', he was a compulsive gambler. Horace Walpole told how even when out hunting the Duke and the Earl of Sandwich took dice along so they could gamble when the action in the field was quiet. Having taken up residence in Windsor at Cumberland Lodge, the Duke made it his mission to revive the fortunes of Ascot. Race conditions were framed to attract 'proper' racehorses again. Three-day meetings became the norm, and in 1749 the course staged its first four-day fixture – Tuesday, Wednesday, Thursday and Friday of the first week of August – which brought it into line, at least in terms of the duration of its meetings, with the principal courses in the land, notably Newmarket, Epsom and Doncaster.

In line with its growing status, Ascot racecourse was now being run on more organised and professional lines than hitherto. In 1751 a 'clerk of the course' is mentioned for the first time (though not named), and the same year each owner had to pay contributions – in addition to the entrance fee for the race – to the clerk towards course maintenance. That year is also notable for the first recorded warning off at Ascot:

> No horse, mare or gelding that was on the 7th Day of April last the Property of Mr Prentice (who was then the Owner of Trimmer), or shall belong to him at the Time of these Races, shall be admitted to start for any of these Plates.

Another first from this period came in 1752: the first recorded accident at Ascot. Two horses named Little Driver and Johnny Armstrong faced each other in a Weight-For-Age Plate, and as they passed the winning post at the end of the second heat Johnny Armstong was felled 'by a Man's being in the Way'. The jockey was unharmed but it was reported that the unfortunate horse 'is believed will die' – and he was put down a day later.

The following year, 1753, saw reference to the 'Ascot Heath new course', probably indicating the part of the course now known as the Old Mile.

On the social front, this period affords plenty of evidence that Ascot was already fashionable in London society. A Mr Rigby wrote to the Duke of Bedford on 13 August 1752 to complain that when he arrived in London, everyone was at Ascot Heath races 'and I could find no soul to dine or sup with': he had heard via Lord Waldegrave that 'there was much company' at Ascot. In 1760, it was reported that 'a large assemblage of the nobility and gentry attended this meeting', and although etiquette applied at Ascot as it did elsewhere, there were those who would act at Ascot as they would not dare to do in London. In 1764, the Duke of Grafton took his mistress Nancy Parsons to Ascot Races: their appearance together met with stern disapproval, especially as rumours abounded that he had picked her up in the street.

By the 1760s the status of Ascot was such that it could attract some of the very best horses in the land.

King Herod, bred by the Duke of Cumberland, won there in June 1764 and went on to become a very influential sire under the name Herod, while Gimcrack, the diminutive grey colt whose name is immortalised in the great two-year-old race run at the York August Meeting, won a £50 Plate at Ascot in June 1767. (An indication of the racing map of England in those days is that his last race before Ascot was at Wisbech, and his next three races that year were at Marlborough, Wells and Wantage.) Gimcrack returned to Ascot to win a second £50 Plate in 1768.

Most notable of all was Eclipse, arguably the greatest racehorse of all time. Bred, like King Herod, by the Duke of Cumberland, Eclipse was foaled at the Duke's stud in Windsor Forest on 1 April 1764, the day of a total eclipse of the sun. The chesnut colt was the offspring of the Duke's sire Marske and his broodmare Spiletta. He was thus a great-great-grandson of the Darley Arabian, and his exploits were to demonstrate that the influence of the three stallions imported from the Middle East was now beginning to be felt in earnest. Eclipse did not race until the age of five in 1769, but soon became one of the most fabled of racehorses. He won no fewer than eleven King's Plates, in eighteen races was never stretched, let alone beaten, and he gave rise to one of the most famous of all racing phrases. After his initial race, in a four-mile heat at Epsom in 1769, an Irish gambler named Denis O'Kelly (later the horse's owner) bet that he could predict the result of the next heat: 'Eclipse first, the rest nowhere' – that is, all the other runners would be 'distanced' by Eclipse. They were. As a stallion Eclipse proved just as sensational as he had as a racehorse, siring three of the first five Derby winners.

Eclipse's single appearance at Ascot came on 29 May 1769, the month

George Stubbs, *Eclipse*, 1770.

after that initial race at Epsom: carrying 9 stone 3 pounds and starting at 8–1 on, he won a £50 Noblemen's and Gentlemen's Plate.

But the Duke of Cumberland did not live to see his greatest horse run on the course he had done so much to sustain. He had died in 1765 at the age of forty-four, having the week before gone to Newmarket to win a 500-guinea match against the Duke of Bridgwater.

The artist Thomas Sandby was made a Deputy Ranger of Windsor Great Park in 1746, and his famous painting of Ascot Heath, probably a joint effort with his brother Paul, greatly enhances our knowledge of Ascot races in the 1760s. It shows a course marked out by a rail on the inner – stretching from the distance post – but not the outer; behind this rail carriages are drawn up, with a huge throng of people, some on horseback, watching the race.

Previous pages: Thomas and
Paul Sandby, *Ascot Heath
Races, c.* 1765

Another throng watches from the outer side of the course. In the shade of a
large tree is located a covered stand, a small and flimsy erection with about six
rows of terraces, each apparently accommodating twenty or so men; beyond
this, further down the course, is a similar stand. These early stands were not
permanent buildings but portable and mobile facilities: a notice in 1777 asked
'those having booths not to begin building until the horses are entered, except
for the booth for the Grand Stand, which is not to be appropriated to the
benefit of the plates, and is to be built a fortnight before the races.' Behind
these stands are tents for refreshment and entertainment.

As the course developed, so did the structure of the racing. In 1772 the
new Duke of Cumberland (nephew of Eclipse's breeder) provided the first
Gold Cup – not a lineal precursor of the two-and-a-half-mile marathon that
forms the showpiece of the Royal Meeting today, but none the less a
significant move towards giving the racing programme a more distinct shape.
The race was confined to five-year-olds whose owners each paid five guineas,
and eleven subscribers entered their horses – including Sir Charles Bunbury,
one of the towering figures of racing administration at the time. Despite that
healthy entry, the Gold Cup turned into a walkover for the Duke of
Cumberland's own mare Maria, and the event did not survive.

In the history of horse racing, the second half of the eighteenth century
was a period of remarkable advance.

The Jockey Club, founded around 1752, was initially concerned with
arranging match races (one horse against one other) and settling betting
disputes, but found itself being referred to so frequently by those who ran
other courses that it began to publish rules – its first recognizable order was
published in 1758 – and generally to exert influence over the way in which
races were run. Other developments were designed to bring more order to the
sport, such as the first use of racing colours in 1762 (which did not become
mandatory for another two decades), ordered by the Jockey Club 'for the greater
convenience of distinguishing the horses in running, as also for the prevention
of disputes arising from not knowing the colours worn by each rider'. In 1773
James Weatherby, Keeper of the Match Book (the book of record for match
races), was authorised by the Jockey Club to publish a racing calendar – thus
paving the way for the Weatherby family's position as the secretariat of horse
racing in Britain.

Match races themselves and races run in heats started to give way to the sort of race we know today, and the races we call the Classics first appeared in this period (though the five-race sequence was not referred to as 'The Classics' until the 1880s). The St Leger was first run at Doncaster in 1776, the Oaks in 1779 and the Derby in 1780 at Epsom. (The two Guineas races at Newmarket followed in the early nineteenth century.) Horses were growing bigger, maturing sooner and racing younger: two-year-old racing was established by the 1780s, with the July Stakes at Newmarket, the oldest juvenile race in the calendar, first run in 1786. (Yearlings were also first raced in 1786, but competition between infants never achieved any great level of popularity and ceased in the mid-nineteenth century.) Shorter races were being run: it is significant that the Straight Mile at Ascot was constructed in 1785.

As the eighteenth century neared its close, Ascot was not yet the most important racecourse in the land, but it was closing the gap on those ahead of it in prestige. Newmarket held pre-eminence; in the north, York was the leading course, with Chester, Richmond and Doncaster steeped in racing tradition (Black Hambleton was on its last legs and barely survived into the new century), and Newcastle and Manchester were starting new courses. In the south, Epsom was gaining in popularity, with Salisbury and Winchester still well supported. In addition, towns all around the country staged races on a less regular basis: for example, in 1780 – the year of the first Derby – the *Racing Calendar* records races in Berkshire at 'Ascot-Heath, Windsor', Reading, Lambourn, Abingdon and Maidenhead.

With a new century dawning, Ascot's drive towards the top of the tree was about to receive a major push from the third influential character in its history.

PRINNY

George II died at Kensington Palace in October 1760, to be succeeded by his grandson. George III's sixty-year reign saw momentous events – including the American War of Independence, the French Revolution and the Napoleonic Wars – but as an individual he is doomed to be remembered more for the episodes of mental instability that in 1811 finally forced Parliament to appoint his son George as Prince Regent. It was 'Prinny' – described by racing historian John Tyrrel as 'the most colourful royal character ever to grace the Turf' – who brought Ascot to a place of pre-eminence, for its racing and its social cachet.

Born in 1762, George was brought up in strict seclusion with his brother Frederick Augustus, but still managed to get himself versed at an early age in the ways of dissipation and intrigue that would lead Charles Greville to declare that 'a more contemptible, cowardly, selfish, unfeeling dog does not exist'. Wedded to gambling and extravagance (he had the Brighton Pavilion built for his use as a palace in 1784), he took a keen interest in the Turf, and started owning racehorses as soon as he reached the age of twenty-one, having his first runner at Ascot with a four-year-old bay filly named Rosaletta in 1785. She finished second to Colonel O'Kelly's Soldier for a £50 race over four miles, but three days later was successful in a three-heat two-miler, thus recording Prinny's first Ascot victory.

Young George's flamboyant lifestyle did nothing to foster good relations with his more sober-minded father, from whom he was becoming increasingly estranged, and when his racing fortunes hit a turbulent patch he was forced to sell nine of his horses, amid rumours that his stables at Newmarket would be closed. In 1787 an understandably hesitant Parliament gave him £161,000

Previous pages: James Pollard, *Ascot Heath Races*, *c*. 1818 (detail). (See page 52.)

to redeem his debts – most of which were attributable to his racing – and he cheerily returned to the sport and built up a string of thirty-nine horses, prompting a correspondent in *The Times* in 1791 to write:

> The Prince of Wales is acknowledged to be in possession of the finest racing stud in the kingdom, and yet how seldom it is that his Royal Highness wins a match. This circumstance serves but to prove what has so often been said, that a man of generous mind and noble conduct, whatever advantages he may possess in the mere way of business, can never be successful on the Turf.

The Prince of Wales had registered the first royal victory in the Derby when his colt Sir Thomas won at Epsom in 1788 (at 6–5 on the first odds-on favourite in the history of what is now the premier Classic), but his greatest racing moment of this period came in the 1791 running of the Oatlands Stakes – Ascot's first really big race.

The Oatlands had been first run in June 1790, and marks a highly important moment in the history of horse racing in Britain. It was the first handicap, where the weights of the runners were adjusted according to their form to give them (at least in theory) equal chances, and thus make the race a livelier medium for betting than a race where the horse with the greatest ability can be expected to win.

In the inaugural Oatlands Stakes (for which the weights were allotted six months in advance), the Prince of Wales's horse Escape was runner-up to Seagull, owned by the Whig leader Charles James Fox, who owned many racehorses and gambled in considerable proportions. It is a measure of the growing status of Ascot that the 1791 Oatlands Stakes attracted so many entries at 100 guineas each that the prize to the winner was 2,950 guineas – over £160,000 in today's money.

Prinny was so determined to win this huge sum that he entered four horses: Escape, Baronet, Pegasus and Smoker. Five days before the big race, the four were tried at Epsom at the Oatlands distance – two miles – and weights. Enter the diminutive figure of Samuel Chifney, 'riding groom' to the Prince of Wales – or, as we would say today, the royal jockey.

Chifney was not a sportsman overburdened with low self-esteem. Not

only did he entitle his autobiography (published in 1792) *Genius Genuine*, but
he described his achievements when only eighteen thus:

> In 1773, I could ride horses in a better manner in a race to beat others,
> than any person I ever knew in my time; and in 1775, I could train
> horses for running better than any person I ever yet saw.

Given his undoubted talents, he expected to have the pick of the royal horses,
and when he travelled to Epsom to meet Warwick Lake, the Prince of Wales's
trainer and a man on whom Chifney's bravado wore very thin, he firmly
anticipated being on Escape, best and highest weighted of the quartet. The
story is well told in Chifney's own words:

The finish of the 1790
Oatlands Stakes – Seagull
beating Escape and Highlander
– painted by J. N. Sartorius.

Early on that morning I came from Mickleham, and met Mr W. Lake at the stable gate on Epsom Downs, before day-light. I observed that I had made myself nine stone ten lbs, thinking he would have me ride Escape. 'No!' said he in a sharp tone, 'I meant you to ride Pegasus; but I don't care what you ride.' ... I then made myself ready to ride Pegasus ...

As soon as it was light enough, the horses ran two miles, at the same weights they were to run for the Oatlands, on the Tuesday following, at Ascot Heath. Escape won this trial; he beat Baronet about a neck; Pegasus was beaten a great way, and I think Smoker was beaten more than a hundred yards from Pegasus.

When Escape and Baronet had about three hundred yards to run, they were going by themselves in a very severe manner, and very fast, and Baronet was then running at his utmost, and he could not lay nearer than within about two lengths of Escape; but from Escape's making so very free with himself in most parts of the race, it made him come back to Baronet. I think Escape would have beaten Baronet three lengths or more if Escape had waited.

In those days jockeys were allowed to bet, and Chifney asked Lake to go to Tattersall's – where bets were struck – and wager fifty guineas on his behalf on Escape.

On the next day the horses set out for Ascot, and on Sunday afternoon Gaskein, His Royal Highness's groom at Carlton House, went with me to see them ... I [went] into Escape's loose stable. I found him stripped, and the lad brushing him over. I instantly saw Escape was not well to run, and I was very certain that his chances for the Oatlands Stakes were all done away, and entirely so from mismanagement. I then went up to Escape, I coaxed him, kissed him, then left him ...

I then proceeded to Baronet's loose stable, and I also found him stripped, and brushing over. I saw him very well, and I thought he was likely to run for the race as he had done for his trial; and I immediately made up my mind to ride him for the Oatlands.

Chifney made straight for Egham to find a bookmaker named Sykes, and laid a bet of £500 to £30 that Baronet would win, then wrote to Warwick Lake forbidding him to bet any money on his behalf on Escape. On the Monday Chifney went to Tattersall's himself and bet another £500 to £27 about Baronet.

Tuesday was the day of the race:

I was the next morning on the race ground to wait for His Royal Highness, who came on it with Mr Lake on horseback. I immediately placed myself in sight, and His Royal Highness called to me, saying, 'Sam Chifney, come this way.' I immediately got to the side of His Royal Highness and Mr W. Lake, and His Royal Highness said, 'Sam Chifney, I shall run Escape and Baronet only, which do you ride? Ride which you please – say which you ride – I am in a hurry.'

Chifney answered he would like to ride Baronet. 'I thought you intended to ride Escape?' the Prince asked, having bet money on that horse. When Chifney stated that he believed Escape to be unwell, the Prince said that Warwick Lake thought him very well. The Prince then asked him if he thought he would win upon Baronet, to which Chifney replied that he was fearful as there was a very great field to run against, but he thought he had a good chance. The Prince revealed to Chifney that he would be glad if Baronet won, as he had money on this horse as well. Chifney took the liberty of asking how much, and received the reply: 'I think I shall win seventeen thousand.'

An alternative account, described by the racing writer 'The Druid' (Henry Hall Dixon), has it that on the Monday the Prince of Wales ordered Chifney to meet him at the stables, where the four horses were looked over. As soon as the sheets were taken off Escape, Chifney begged the Prince's permission to ride Baronet instead, declaring that it was impossible to win with Escape. Brushing aside Lake's protests, the Prince not only decided that Chifney should ride Baronet but added, 'Whenever I have two horses in a race, I wish you, Sam, to ride the one you fancy most on the day, without consulting us about it.'

Unaware of these behind-the-scenes shenanigans, a huge crowd was flocking to the biggest occasion in the course's history to date. 'The immense concourse of people that attended this race, even from the most remote parts of England, exceeds belief,' wrote *The Sporting Magazine:* 'It was calculated that not less than forty thousand people were present.' Ascot had never seen anything like it.

The first event on the card was a King's Plate of 100 guineas for hunters, run in two four-mile heats, and then came the Oatlands.

A field of nineteen – very large in those days, but reflecting the huge prize on offer – went to post. The betting was feverish – £100,000 was reportedly staked on the race – with the Earl of Barrymore reputedly putting £20,000 on his horse Chanticleer, who started at 9–1. Favourite at 3–1 was Vermin, a three-year-old by the great horse Highflyer who had run second when favourite for that year's Derby and now carried just 5 stone 3 pounds. Baronet, who carried 8 stone 4 pounds, started at 20–1.

Who better to describe a famous race than the winning jockey?

This was a very hard race with Baronet and Express together till within a few yards of the end. My very favourite horse Escape was beaten a great way; for when these horses had near half a mile to run, Baronet at that time was about four lengths behind the front horse. Baronet was there by choice. Escape was at that time about two lengths behind Baronet; but I saw him clearly beaten, and the man getting very severe upon him. I was about to call to the rider to pull Escape up but thought better of it, because Escape was not only behind me, but wide from me, and there were horses between us, and I was fearful of keeping my head turned till the rider should hear me, lest my horse's fore legs should get entangled with the other horse's hind legs. I very much wished Escape to be pulled up, that he might not be abused after being so much beaten. I saw no more of him in this race, but from the situation I left him in, and the front horses renewing their pace, he must have been beaten a very great way … A short distance before coming to the winning-post Express' and Baronet's heads were even with each other and both horses at their utmost. Express tired first in this severe run, which flung Baronet clear before him just before getting to the winning-post.

The two horses, wrote *The Times*, 'were almost equal in coming in, but by the superior skill of the rider, Baronet outstripped the other just half a length', and *The Sporting Magazine* reported that 'the judge could only place the first four, for not only those, but four or five others, might have been nearly covered *with a blanket*'. (In fact the judge placed only three.)

Report has it that George III, his disapproval mellowed by the great victory, wryly commented to his son: 'Your baronets are more productive than mine. I made fourteen last week, but I get nothing by them. Your single Baronet is worth all mine put together.'

A great victory can also mean great losses, and the phenomenal level of betting on the 1791 Oatlands Stakes left Ascot Heath reeking with the smell of burned fingers. An unknown contemporary source wrote of the effects of the aftermath of the race: 'Horses are daily thrown out of training, jockeys are going into mourning, grooms are becoming EO [roulette] merchants and strappers are going on the highway.'

That Oatlands victory began an unbeaten season for Baronet, who then walked over for King's Plates at Winchester and at Canterbury, won a four-mile race at Lewes in just two heats, and then won the King's Plate at Newmarket in October. He was later exported to America.

The Prince's other runner in the Oatlands went on to achieve notoriety in the annals of the Turf as the centre of 'the Escape Affair' at Newmarket later in 1791. On 20 October, Escape started at 2–1 on and after what has been called an 'unenterprising' ride by Chifney finished last. The following day he ran again: starting at 5–1, he won easily. The ensuing unease about whether Escape had been running on his merits in the first race led Sir Charles Bunbury, Senior Steward of the Jockey Club, to warn the Prince that 'if Chifney were suffered to ride the Prince's horses, no gentleman would start against him'. This threat so incensed the Prince that he chose to forsake Newmarket rather than sacrifice his jockey, and Prinny and the Turf parted company – for the time being, at least.

The Prince of Wales's father George III might have lacked the public appeal of his wayward son, but 'Farmer George' – so named on account of his fervour for improving farming methods – played his own part in the development of Ascot racecourse, notably in the provision of better viewing facilities for the public.

David Morier, *An Equestrian Portrait of King George III Wearing Order of the Garter.*

In 1793 he had George Slingsby, one of his favourite master bricklayers, build the first permanent stand at the course. The Slingsby Stand – or Old Betting Stand – provided accommodation for some 650 people.

Generally the viewing facilities were improving. Apart from the Slingsby Stand, there was 'a row of towering booths, thirty or forty in length, each containing two or three hundred females, amongst whom may be seen beauties of the first distinction'; these booths were exclusive and frequented only by 'the rank and beauty of the land'.

Those unable to afford such luxuries stood where they could to see the races. A racegoer of the time remembered:

A wood just opposite the distance post made a semicircular opening of considerable extent, which was filled with spectators chiefly of the female sex, who, from the obliquity of the ground rising one above another in a kind of theatrical order, covered the slope quite up to the trees, that were also loaded in the front with boys clustering upon the branches as they judged they should best see the horses run.

When the horses had started and passed the stands for the first time, many people dashed to find a better viewing position:

> Every person's spirits seemed to be on the wing, while men, women, horses, chariots, phaetons and coaches hoping to better their stations, flew over the field in a hundred different ways, and crossed each other, with that precipitance and disorder as made me apprehensive lest one half of the company should be trampled down by the other; but to my great joy, as well as wonder, not a single person was hurt.

In 1785 a spur was added to the east of the round course to form a straight mile – in reality a distance slightly short of one mile.

Through the late 1780s the running of the meetings was becoming more regulated. In 1788 the Master of the Buckhounds, the Earl of Sandwich, issued a notice that 'no person do bring dogs on the course, as there will be proper persons appointed to destroy them', and a notice in 1790 asked that horses 'are not allowed to start until the course is clear'. The management also succeeded in obtaining money towards the race fund from the farriers, 'No smith to plate any horse but who subscribes 10s 6d [half a guinea] towards the plates, and if two smiths acted jointly 10s 6d each.' Other new regulations included that all disputes were to be determined by the Stewards, and that no stalls or gaming tables could be erected between the Betting Stand and the winning post. Riders wearing colours other than those declared had to pay 10s 6d forfeit for the benefit of the race fund, and if they defaulted the rider was to be excluded from riding for any of the plates at the Ascot Races the following year. If a groom neglected to bring his horse out in time for a race, he had to pay 10s 6d for each horse towards the race fund.

It is clear from such stipulations that money was a constant worry, and then, as now, a significant source of income for the racecourse came from sponsorship – local gentry and merchants would be encouraged to donate towards the prize fund – and by renting out facilities to the suppliers of refreshment and other entertainment. In 1793, according to *The Sporting Magazine*:

> An absolute town of near two hundred booths, erected in a fortnight (and many possessing the convenience of comfortable habitations) upon the middle of a heath, some miles from the nearest market town (and for permission to do so which, the owners pay from three guineas to five) affords ample proof what an incredible multitude must be assembled daily on such sport to reimburse the adventurers for their expenditure.

As the nearest market town was safely out of reach, the refreshment booths offered the only source of food and drink available to the racegoers, and often charged exorbitant prices – though the aristocracy brought their own picnics and had spectacular luncheons by their carriages or in their own private tents (*plus ça change ...*).

An example of particular extravagance occurred in 1791. Before the Ascot meeting, the Earl of Barrymore had fallen out with the Prince of Wales, and in an attempt to remove the unpleasantness offered Prinny two banquets to be prepared in his Ascot marquee. He gave *carte blanche* to the caterers to provide everything 'in or out of season, and of the best' with no consideration to cost, and the feasts were rumoured to have cost him 1,700 guineas – all to no avail, as the Prince, doubtless aware that there is no such thing as a free lunch, failed to attend. At the first banquet the Earl sat down with just one friend, and at the second with two.

As at other racecourses, there was much entertainment and gambling on offer apart from the equine sport – notably 'EO', an early version of roulette (so called because the wheel consisted of twenty compartments marked 'E', twenty marked 'O', plus two for the operator's margin). Ten marquees at Ascot were given over for 'the Paragon of Equity, an EO table', each containing three or four tables. (A less ordered medium of wagering was 'thimble-rigging', a version of the three-card trick involving three large thimbles and a pea.)

The proprietors of EO booths and other gambling games were not above a little underhand improving of the odds in their favour, and sometimes the victims' sense of grievance boiled over. In 1799 a gentleman's servant lost all his money and his watch, causing him to denounce the proprietors as rogues and thieves. A fight ensued, owners of other booths came to support their companions, and soon the mayhem was such that a party of the Light Horse Brigade had to be summoned from Windsor to quell the riot. Many were arrested but only three men convicted, and sentenced to long terms of imprisonment.

The gambling atmosphere of Ascot had long encouraged bizarre bets. A contemporary recorded in 1768 that one of the leading ladies of fashion undertook, for a wager of £5,000, to ride a hundred miles in ten hours. The bet appears to have been made by her husband, who had offered to hold £5,000 more that she would eat a leg of lamb and drink two bottles of claret into the bargain. Frustratingly, history does not relate the outcome of the bet.

From the 1790s to the 1820s, cockfighting was the chosen amusement of the Ascot race mornings and evenings. A German visitor to England described the preamble to a fight –

> When it is time to start, the persons appointed to do so bring in the cocks hidden in two sacks, and then everyone begins to shout and wager before the birds are on view. The people ... act like madmen ... Then the cocks are taken out of the sacks and fitted with silver spurs ...

– and the *Reading Mercury* for June 1798 ran the advertisement, 'during Ascot Races will be fought the great main of Cocks at the Crown Inn, Egham, between the Gentlemen of Surrey and Middlesex against the Gentlemen of Kent and Sussex, for 5 guineas a battle and 50 the odd'.

Another entertainment to be found at Ascot was prizefighting. In 1768 a bout on the heath caused such a riot that troops were sent from Windsor to calm things down, while on the last day of the 1777 races a weaver named Woods fought a sawyer named Selway for 500 guineas. After a savage encounter, Woods was declared the winner and Selway left the ring with the loss of an eye.

With all this going on in addition to the horses, it is hardly any surprise that Ascot races became a magnet for pickpockets, conmen and other petty criminals from London, but they could expect to suffer rough justice if caught on the racecourse. Their pigtails might be cut off to mark them out on future occasions, and in 1791 a pickpocket died after being ducked, beaten and shaved. Apparently, having been caught on the Tuesday, he 'had the audacity of visiting Windsor on Thursday and was present at that day's Friday's and Saturday's sport with a piece of crepe and a handkerchief round his head to conceal his amputated tail'. The beatings, however, had already taken the toll and 'the same poor wretch is since dead from the severe whipping the jockey boys gave him'. Swindlers and cheats could be hauled to Englemere Pond and 'well ducked', and a local rumour that persisted into Victorian days related that, as a culminating degradation, a small piece of the culprit's ear was cut off so that he might be recognised in the future.

Away from the mayhem and beatings, fashion was gaining in importance at Ascot in the 1790s, with *The Sporting Magazine* noting that:

> during the intervening spaces of time between the running of the heats a great part of the company descend from the stands and, intermixing in the Grand Parade between the starting and the distance post, form an absolute incorporation.

Balls and dances in Windsor and Egham provided entertainment for the racegoers in the evenings. However, in 1795 new taxes and duties had been imposed on the public to pay for the efforts of the military, with the result that Mr Graves, who arranged the balls at the Assembly Rooms in Egham, was under the 'disagreeable necessity of raising his charges owing to the high prices of provisions and the new duty on wines'. Prices went up to 'Gentlemen's tickets 12s, ladies' 9s'.

Although Ascot Races were most certainly aristocratic affairs, the gentry did not dissuade the locals and working men from joining in, and the nobility mixed casually with the masses. Moreover, at Ascot observers could see 'the unprincipled determined desperate gambler assume the dress and dignity of a peer, whilst the peer is exultingly imitating the manners of his stable-boy'.

The royal party had a particular misfortune in 1794. The crowd, imbued with an even fiercer patriotic fervour than usual on account of the defeat of the French fleet off Ushant, clamoured for a glimpse of the royals, who, in the report of *The Sporting Magazine*, 'displayed their accustomed benignity and mingled with that degree of affability among all ranks and descriptions'. The enthusiastic subjects cheered so loud that the horses drawing the carriage of the King's daughter Princess Elizabeth took fright, bolted and overturned the carriage – from which the Princess and her two companions were extricated without damage.

'His Royal Highness the Prince of Wales with a Lady of Quality driving to Ascot Races' – an early nineteenth-century engraving.

For all the social throng, the standard of racing at Ascot was for the most part fairly moderate, with heats and private matches still providing most of the sport. But changes were afoot in the shape of racing elsewhere. Horses were being raced younger, and shorter races were much in vogue: the Derby, confined to three-year-olds, was run over one mile from 1780 to 1783, the first four years of its existence, and its sister race the Oaks was run over a mile and a half. Stakes races – a single event between several horses – were growing in appeal, match races lessening.

Many of these changes were being driven from Newmarket, now the acknowledged engine room of the sport's progress, and in 1805 the Jockey Club made a concerted attempt to patch up its differences with the Prince of Wales. Sir Charles Bunbury and Lord Darlington, Stewards of the Jockey Club, wrote to Prinny:

> From various Misconceptions or Differences of Opinion which arose formerly relative to a race, in which Your Royal Highness was concerned, we greatly regret, that we have never been honoured with Your Presence there since that period, but experiencing as we constantly do, the singular Marks of your Condescension and Favour, and considering the essential benefit not only that the Turf will generally derive, but also the great satisfaction that we must all individually feel from the Honor of Your Presence, we humbly request that Your Royal Highness will bury in oblivion any past unfortunate Occurences [*sic*] at Newmarket and that You will be pleased to honor us there with your Countenance and Support.

But the appeal fell on stony ground. As prince or king, George would never return to Newmarket.

At Ascot, the quality of the sport took a significant step upwards in 1807 with the first running of the Gold Cup, oldest of the races that form today's Royal Meeting. This Gold Cup, instituted by George III's queen, Charlotte, was no relation to the Gold Cup run in 1772, but more in the tradition of the Doncaster Cup, first run in 1766 and the oldest race under Rules to have survived to the present day. The conditions for the first Gold Cup read:

> A Gold Cup of 100 guineas value, the remainder in specie, [i.e. in cash] a subscription of ten guineas each, for three-years-old 6st 12lb, four-years-old 8st 2lb, five-years-old 8st 12lb, six-years-old and aged [i.e. over six] 9st 4lb, mares allowed 3lb. The owner of the second horse to receive back his stake. Distance once round the course.

That 'once round the course' distance – two miles – was increased to the present two and a half miles the following year, 1808, when the race was started on the spur of the Straight Mile.

The royal family was out in force for this signal Ascot occasion. A pavilion and two marquees were erected for the Queen and Princesses near what we would call the home turn, with another opposite the judge's box for the Prince of Wales – dressed in 'bottle-blue' – who was accompanied by his younger brothers, the Dukes of York, Kent and Cumberland. (The pavilion was in effect the first permanent Royal Stand at Ascot. Entry was subject to the King's invitation and was restricted to his family, guests and Household. The rule of the King's consent was so strong that during the 1810s Queen Charlotte was unable to enter without her son's – the Regent's – consent. Immediately upon the Regency commencing in 1811, the stand was known as the Queen's Stand, but this lasted only a short period, and it soon became known as the Prince Regent's Stand.)

The three-year-old Master Jackey was the first horse to inscribe his name on one of the most distinguished rolls of honour in all racing, beating Hawk by half a length in a stirring battle – and just twenty-four hours after he had won another race at Ascot. It is significant that the first Gold Cup was won by a three-year-old (an age group not eligible for the race today): this was an

Opposite: 'Plan of the allotments in the parish of Sunninghill in the County of Berks – as set out under the Act of Inclosure and referred to in the Award, 1817', which includes the oldest extant map of Ascot racecourse – in the upper left-hand part of the map, just under the words 'Crown allotment'. The Buckhounds' kennels are located just above the same words.

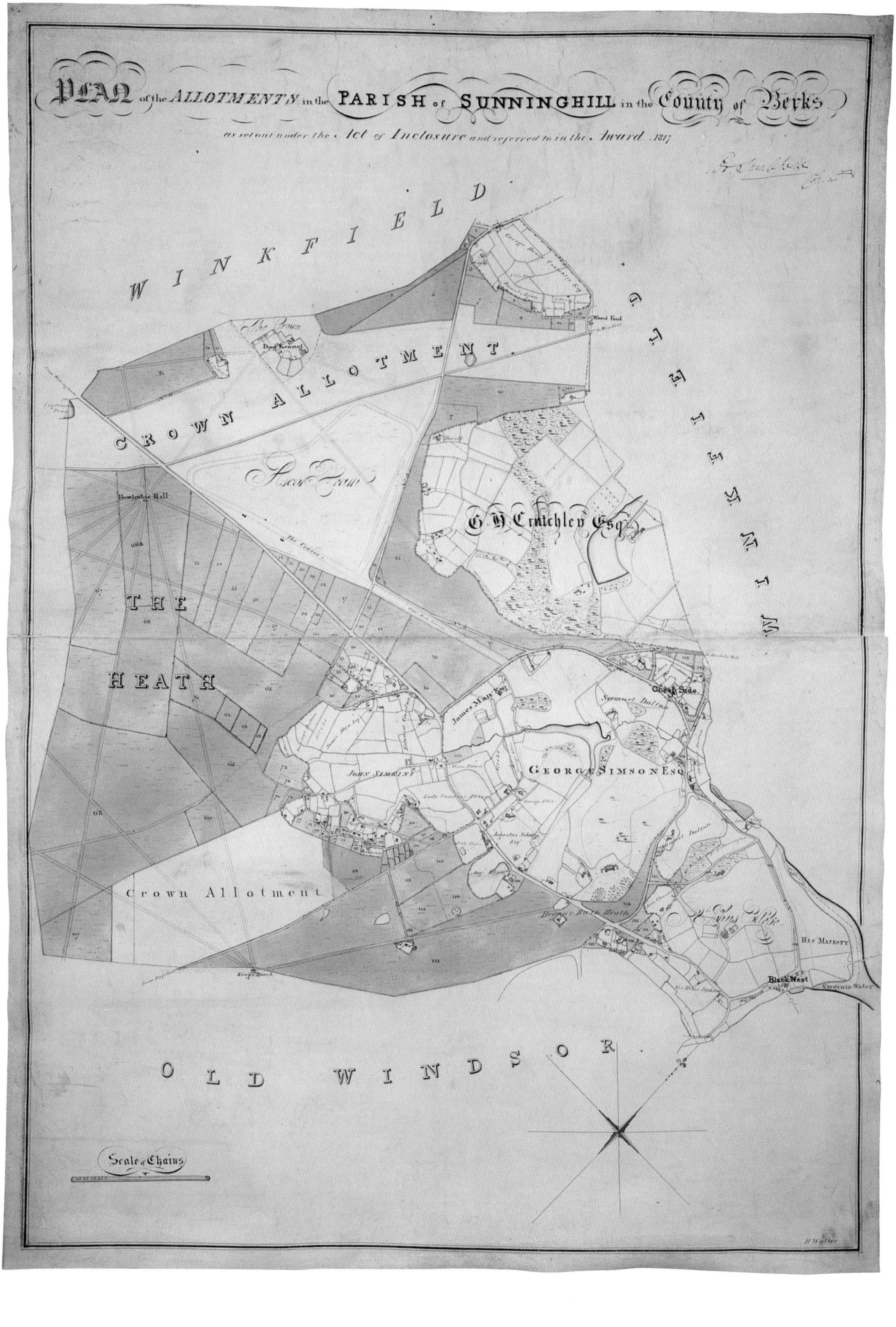

PLAN of the ALLOTMENTS in the PARISH of SUNNINGHILL in the County of Berks

as set out under the Act of Inclosure and referred to in the Award. 1817

WINKFIELD

CROWN ALLOTMENT

THE

HEATH

G. H. Critchley Esq.

Cheap Side

James May Esq.

Samuel Dalton

JOHN SIMKINS

GEORGE SIMSON Esq.

Crown Allotment

HIS MAJESTY

Black Nest

Virginia Water

OLD WINDSOR

Scale of Chains

event designed to attract horses being bred to compete much younger than had been the case the previous century.

In 1813, six years after the first Gold Cup, Ascot saw the first running of another big event very familiar to modern racegoers: the Wokingham Stakes, named after the town not far from the course and the oldest extant handicap race in Britain. The initial winner was Pointers, owned by George III's second son the Duke of York (the self-same Grand Old Duke of York who marched his men to the top of the hill and marched them down again), who was as enthusiastic about horse racing as his elder brother. He had his own stand at Ascot (where he had first attended the meeting in 1789), and the Oatlands Stakes had been named after his residence.

A few weeks after the inaugural Wokingham, on 21 July 1813, an Act of Enclosure placed Ascot Heath, together with wide expanses of Windsor Forest, into the ownership of the Crown, under the management of the Office of Woods, Forests and Land Revenues (which became the Crown Lands in 1924 and later still the Crown Estate), the culmination of a process which had begun in 1806 when an Act of Parliament appointed commissioners for inquiring into the state of Windsor Forest. This commission strongly recommended enclosure, but they estimated the Crown rights at so high a rate that it was impossible to pass the scheme through Parliament, so in 1813 a compromise was reached whereby the Crown secured 6,665 acres in compensation for a variety of rights. The 1813 Act referred specifically to the racecourse:

> And be it further enacted that such parts of the said Commons and Waste Lands as are hereinafter particularly mentioned and described, shall form and be considered as Part of the said Allotment, and shall be accordingly set out and allotted by the said Commissioners to and for the exclusive use of His Majesty, His Heirs and Successors ... and in the said Parish of Sunninghill, all that Piece or Parcel of Open Common or Waste Ground appropriated for, and used a long time past as a Race Ground, being Part of the Heath called Ascot Heath, with proper Avenues thereto, and an Area or Space of Ground on the Boundaries and round the Race Courses there, as the same are now set out with Stakes, and containing by Admeasurement Two hundred

and six Acres Three Roods and Three Perches, and all Erections and Buildings, Posts, Rails and Fences of every Description thereon, which Piece of Ground shall be kept and continued as a Racecourse for the Public Use at all times, as it has usually been.

The clause ensuring the future of racing at Ascot was of central importance. Although the Regent was likely to continue racing there, people could not be sure that his successors would be so accommodating. Enclosures had been occurring throughout the country since the final decades of the eighteenth century and, as Robert Slanely noted, 'owing to the inclosure of open lands and commons, the poor have no place in which they may amuse themselves in summer evenings, when the labour of the day is over, or when a holiday occurs'. Matters had become so bad and so many traditional local pastimes had already been lost that in 1845 an Act was passed to preserve the remaining village greens expressly for this reason.

George IV at Ascot – pencil drawing by John Doyle.

As a precaution against lawsuits being taken in the King's name, the ownership of the existing racecourse and its buildings was transferred by lease into the name of the Stewards of the Ascot Races, which duly separated the ownership of the course from the land upon which it stood, and placed independent responsibility for the races in the hands of the Stewards. The Stewards were appointed for a year at a time only, and as a consequence the Master of the Buckhounds continued to manage the races and the racecourse.

Enclosure did not mean that any physical barrier was erected, and public access to Ascot Heath continued – though at the 1814 meeting there was more attention paid to visitors from overseas than to those who could get in for free. Earlier that year Napoleon had abdicated as Emperor of the French and gone into exile (which proved temporary) on Elba, and among the royal party at Ascot were dignitaries from allied countries who had joined together to overcome him: King Frederick William III of Prussia and his famous general Marshal Gebhard von Blücher, along with Tsar Alexander I with *his* general Platoff. Triumphalism was short-lived as Napoleon escaped from Elba in March 1815, and it took the battle of Waterloo in June that year to remove him finally from the scene.

George III died in January 1820 at the age of eighty-one, having spent the last nine years of his troubled life ravaged by porphyria, and the Prince Regent finally acceded to the throne as George IV.

At Ascot, the new King ordered 'alterations' to be made to the Royal Stand by John Nash, one of the most famous architects of the age, whose work in London included the glories of Carlton House Terrace, Regent's Park and Trafalgar Square, and who had worked for George on the Brighton Pavilion. Building operations on the Royal Stand went over budget by £100 and amounted finally to 'about £1,100', but still the alterations did not satisfy the monarch. So in 1822 Nash designed a brand new Royal Stand, erected in just

James Pollard, *Ascot Heath Races*, c. 1818.

five weeks by Mr Perkins, clerk of works, and his 'able assistants', and described by *The Times* as 'a light tasteful building, with fluted pilasters of composition supporting the roof, in imitation of a Greek portico'.

The square, stuccoed building was of two storeys, with each floor measuring twenty-seven feet by seventeen. Sides and front were composed of white Doric columns, between which were five high sash windows, with a further window at each end, affording the upper floors 'an admirable view of the whole course'. All the windows were hung with spotted muslin draperies. The columns supported a flat roof from where the races could also be watched by 'nearly a hundred people', and the upper floor was divided into two rooms: 'One of these is elegantly furnished for the use of his Majesty and the Royal family, and the other is also handsomely furnished for the attendants.' At ground level the floor space was divided into two apartments, one for the ladies and one for the gentlemen of the Royal Household, while the basement contained two rooms 'designed as a permanent habitation for the servants who take charge of the building', including a kitchen and offices. The basement was faced with compo,

Drawings for building a balcony on the Royal Stand.

resembling smooth porphyry stones. A circular, eight-foot-high wall enclosed a gravelled yard at the rear for the reception of carriages, while around the other three sides was a lawn, admission to which on race days was strictly reserved for the personal guests of the King. This was the precursor of the Royal Enclosure.

The Duke of York's Stand was moved next to the Royal Stand in 1826, and following the death of the Duke of York in early 1827 that stand was appropriated by the Jockey Club.

From the early 1820s, seven large wooden grandstands, in a line with and to the right of the Royal Stand, would be 'crammed full of ladies, for the most part, even to suffocation, water being exhausted as fast as the carriers could come up, and not a drop of cyder remained at three o'clock'. They might have been uncomfortable to the inhabitants,

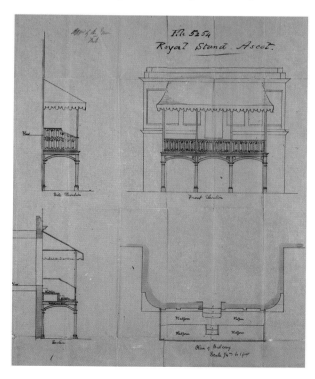

but they were lucrative for the race fund: in 1822 tickets to these were estimated to have brought in some £600. Then in 1827 a 'very commodious and excellently planned betting stand' was erected midway between the distance and winning post, thus adding to the range of wooden stands.

Ascot was hugely popular and hugely fashionable – in the words of *The Sporting Magazine* in 1825, 'unquestionably the first of all provincial sporting places'. Pierce Egan gave a graphic account of the course's popularity in 1827:

> The attraction of Ascot Races is so great, that, by six o'clock, every body within five counties round is awake, and getting breakfast as fast as possible; and Windsor's Merry Wives, with the consanguinities, are all alive again, and as merry as ever. By nine o'clock, Park-street is lined with embowered wagons, filled with glowing lasses, and buxom dames, and ancient dames, and fathers and brothers, and husbands, and sweethearts to match; and off they go, drawn by sleek, fat-haunched, flower-bedecked horses, driven by sun-burnt youths, each with a nosegay in his Sunday vest, as proud as army-inspecting emperors, and doubtless much happier. Meanwhile, post-chaises, and stage-coaches, and gigs, and open landaus from London, and glittering barouches dash in from every quarter, bringing lords and ladies, and knights and squires, in gay and splendid activity; and all roll blithely along, through sunny lanes, bordered with rose-covered cottages, towards the fields of the day. For hours, the roads, and the forest walks, and the by-field-paths, leading to Ascot Heath, are thronged with troops of jocund beings, converging towards 'the great centre of attraction'. The Heath itself presents a scene of gallant bustle. Long lines of snow-white tents, surmounted by ensigns of all sorts – 'bandroll, and scroll, and pennant there, o'er the pavilions flew,' – betokening – not war and bloodshed – but ham sandwiches, and London particular Madeira.

If that was the throng on the road to Ascot, the course itself was no less teeming. In June 1829 *The Times* reported:

When all had assembled, which was not the case till nearly the commencement of the races, the spectacle was such as no words of ours can describe. The betting-stand was crowded with rows of heads, tier above tier. The sides of the course were lined with double and triple lines of spectators on foot; behind whom, on the side opposite to the royal stand, were ranged carriages, as before-mentioned, clustered over the human beings standing on and clinging from every part of them. So dense was the crowd, that it was utterly impossible for three-fourths of the persons present to obtain a view of the running, or know any thing of the result of the races, except by report.

The greatest legacy George IV left to the Royal Meeting is the Royal Procession. Although versions of a grand royal arrival at the racecourse had been witnessed before, it was in 1825 that the royal party first made a formal procession in carriages up the Straight Mile. The diarist Thomas Creevey described that first procession in a letter dated 3 June 1825:

Contrary to his former practice, [the King] drove up the Course to his stand, in the presence of everybody – himself in the first coach and four, the Duke of Wellington sitting by his side. There were three other carriages and four, and a phaeton after him, and I sh'd think 20 servants in scarlet on horseback, and as all his horses are of the greatest beauty, the whole thing looked very splendid; in short, quite as it should be.

The procession was also described by *The Sporting Magazine*, which recorded that it took place on the second day of the meeting:

His Majesty (I understood for the first time) adopted the plan of his revered father, by coming up the New Mile Course with his splendid retinue, thus giving to all a full view of his person. The gratification was, I am sure, mutual to the Sovereign and his people – as the most enthusiastic huzzas hailed him in his arrival and departure.

The Times described how the King arrived with

> a more numerous train of outriders than we ever recollect observing: in fact the whole of his Majesty's stud, by his express command accompanied him ... His Majesty came on the course up the Straight Mile, thus giving a full view of his person and procession to all present.

And later Creevey wrote of the procession:

> Prinney came as before, bowling along the course in his carriage and four. In passing the young Duchess of Richmond's open landau he played off his nods and winks and kissing his hand, just as he did to all of you 20 years ago on the Brighton racecourse.

The difference in style of arrival before this date is neatly shown by two records of the arrival of the reigning monarch by the diarist Charles Greville. Recording the arrival of George IV in 1820, he wrote:

> The King was at Ascot every day; he generally rode on the course and the ladies came in carriages. One day they all rode. He was always cheered by the mob as he went away.

Eleven years later came the contrast of William IV's arrival in 1831:

> The Royal Family came to the course the first day with a great cortège – eight coaches-and-four, two phaetons, pony sociables, and led horses – Munster riding on horseback behind the King's carriage, Augustus (the parson) and Frederick driving phaetons. The Duke of Richmond was in the King's calèche and Lord Grey in one of the coaches.

The Royal Procession provided the most enduring image yet of the connection between royalty and Ascot racecourse – an image that abides to the present day – and it also formed a focal point of a key aspect of the meeting in the first half of the nineteenth century, the idea of 'king-seeing'. In an age before photographs in newspapers and long before television, at Ascot the Royal Family were on display, and the meeting provided an important opportunity for the King's subjects to look at him. Pierce Egan wrote in 1832:

> It is at Ascot, delightful Ascot races, where the public have the opportunity of beholding his Majesty, and of hearing his remarks without the least reserve … Ascot may be deemed the rallying point for all the nobility and gentry, for miles round Windsor, to pay homage to their beloved monarch. It is also truly interesting to view the king at his ease, divested of the paraphernalia and etiquette of the court, habited like a private gentleman, easy of access, and conversing with the utmost affability and attention to all his auditors.

With the monarch vital to the well-being of the country, his health – and indeed the nature of the company he was keeping – was of crucial importance to his subjects. Thomas Creevey was not reassured by what he witnessed in 1824:

> Our old acquaintance Prinney was at the races each day, and tho' in health he appeared perfect, he has all the appearance of a slang leg – a plain brown hat, black cravat, scratch wig, and his head cocked over one eye. There he sat, in one corner of his stand, Lady Conyngham [his mistress, who found racing dull] rather behind him, hardly visible but by her feathers. He had the same limited set of jips about him each day, and arrived and departed in private. I must say he cut the lowest figure; and the real noblesse – Whig and Tory – were with his brother York.

But the following year Creevey reported the King as 'looking quite well and nearly as merry as we have seen him in his best days'.

For some – then as now – the royal-watching was more important than the racing. In 1829 the *Windsor and Eton Express* wrote that 'the popularity of these races arises more from the sanction afforded them by His Majesty, than from the mere running. Horses may be seen every day, but Kings are scarce.'

This scrutiny could work against the sovereign when word of his behaviour at Ascot got back to London. In 1829 Mrs Arbuthnot noted in her diary how the King had reacted to the presence of the Home Secretary, Robert Peel:

> I found all the town talking of the King's conduct at Ascot … He gave a bad reception to all the friends of the Government who went into his stand, and said to Mr Peel he should have as soon expected to see a pig in a church as him at a race!

What of the catering arrangements at this time? Among the many refreshment tents of the early decades of the nineteenth century was a 'temporary tavern' immediately adjoining the course: the gentlemen who frequented it were particularly rough and made a 'terrible uproar'. While the farmers might have drunk bottled ale, the gentry brought on their coaches an 'ice-house with cases of champagne, sixteen of cigars'. The royal party had somewhat better fare, dining on potted meats and fruit at the meeting of 1824.

In 1826 ice cream was introduced for wealthy racegoers. 'However difficult any commodity is of production, it would seem that a demand is all that is necessary in this country – there was absolutely "ice-cream" to be had on the course,' drooled *The Times*. 'The amount of "cream" (or ice) was perhaps not very considerable in their composition; but they were cooler than any other material at hand.'

The races were interrupted for an hour's luncheon between the first and second race – a practice that continued up to the Second World War. (In 1939, for example, the first race was run at 1.30 and the second race at 2.30.) Magnificent picnics were laid out beside carriages, with 'a boundless profusion of cold viands, with hock or champagne to keep up the ladies' delicate frames'.

In 1826 the Duke of York attended Ascot for the last time. His health had been steadily declining, but was perked up during race week, as Charles Greville reported:

> From that moment he grew worse till the time of the Ascot races. We went to Frogmore two days before the party began, and for those two days he led a quiet life. When the party was assembled he lived as he had been used to do, going to the races, sitting at table, and playing for hours at whist. He slept wretchedly and seldom went to bed, but

passed the greatest part of the night walking about the room or dozing in his chair.

His death in 1827 seems to have prompted his brother George IV to take up again the mantle of nurturing the royal family's racing interests, though his horses raced in the name of his friend Delmé Radcliffe rather than that of the King himself.

George's enthusiasm for Ascot was at its peak in the final years of his life, and in 1828 he instituted a second meeting at the end of June: this meeting took place over three days, and the highlights included His Majesty's Plate of 100 guineas, and a Gold Cup subscription race.

By now the Ascot Gold Cup, after a fairly stuttering start to its life – several two-horse races, and a walkover for the Duke of York's Banker in 1821 – was gaining in prestige, a process accelerated by the victory of the 1825 St Leger winner Memnon in 1827, and George IV was determined to win the Ascot showpiece in 1829, perhaps knowing that this would be his last chance. According to Charles Greville: 'The King has bought seven horses successively, for which he has given 11,300 guineas, principally to win the Cup at Ascot, which he has never accomplished.' One of these horses was The Colonel, his most expensive purchase at 4,000 guineas, but the horse who was to make the head that wore the crown lie uneasy was called Zinganee.

Owned and trained by Will Chifney, son of Sam (who had died in a debtors' prison in 1807), Zinganee was a top-class three-year-old who had been forced to miss the 1829 Derby after contracting a virus. A few days before the Gold Cup, in which Zinganee was to be ridden by Chifney's brother Sam junior, the owner–trainer was asked by Lord Darlington for his opinion of the forthcoming contest. His response was a masterpiece of early nineteenth-century race analysis:

Sunninghill Wells, Monday morning, 8 o'clock
My Lord – I lose no time in answering your lordship's note, desiring me to remit my opinion of the horses in the Ascot Cup.
Cadland and Mameluke are good horses; the latter, at times, shows temper, and will require the most skilful management to make him run his best form amongst a field of horses, and the slightest

mistake in this respect will be fatal to him for the race. The Colonel is badly shaped; his ribs and quarters are much too large and heavily formed, and will cause him to tire and to run a jade; independent of this defect, the course, of all others, is especially ill suited to him, and will cause him to fall an easy victim. Still his party are so exceedingly fond of him as to think no horse can defeat him, and they have backed him for an immense sum. In the face of all this, I entertain the most contemptible opinion of him, for the distance of ground, and I fear nothing whatever from him. Lamplighter is not sufficiently good to cope with the company he will have to meet; and neither Green Mantle nor Varna, although good mares, can have a chance with the old horses over this strong course.

I have the best horse in England at this moment in Zinganee; and if the race is desperately run, which I hope and anticipate it will be, and my brother sends him out the last three-quarters of a mile, to keep the pace severe, I shall be very much surprised and greatly disappointed if I do not see him win the Cup on Thursday without the slightest degree of trouble, notwithstanding the powerful field of horses he has to contend against.

I am your Lordship's most obedient servant
William Chifney.

Lord Chesterfield shared Will Chifney's view of Zinganee and made an offer for the colt after he had won the Trial Stakes at Ascot on the Tuesday. The Chifneys had already turned down 3,000 guineas from a betting man as they feared it was intended 'to square him', but after the Tuesday victory, and still smarting from recent Derby losses, they decided to sell when they could and accepted 2,500 guineas from Chesterfield, with the stipulation that in the likely event of Zinganee's winning they would receive the £340 stake and his lordship the cup. Knowing George's burning desire to win the Gold Cup, Chesterfield mentioned this deal to him at Windsor Castle that evening, expressing his willingness to break off the arrangement if the King wished to purchase the horse himself. 'The Druid' wrote that the King replied: 'Buy the Chifneys' horse by all means; if you don't beat me [his runner was The Colonel] with him, Gully [owner of Mameluke] will; and I don't mind being beaten by you.'

It was an exceptional field for the Gold Cup. Mameluke had won the Derby in 1827, and Cadland (after a dead heat and a run-off against The Colonel, not yet in the King's ownership) the same race in 1828; The Colonel had won the 1828 St Leger; Bobadilla the Gold Cup the previous year; and Green Mantle that year's Oaks; Lamplighter was destined to be the sire of Derby winner Phosphorus, and of two One Thousand Guineas winners, Mayday and Firebrand.

'There was such a crowd to see the Cup run for as never was seen before,' wrote Charles Greville, while another contemporary noted:

> Thursday was considered by all as the grandest day ever seen at Ascot, both as to number of people, elegance of dress, and rank in life and what they came to see was never equalled in the memory of the oldest man, nor recorded in history, apt as old men are to fancy what wonderful things were done in their younger day.

The race itself proved the ancestor of so many titanic struggles at Ascot, even if the details are sketchier than those surrounding Grundy and Bustino or Galileo and Fantastic Light. After three false starts, George Edwards made the running on Bobadilla until beyond the Swinley Post (in what is now Swinley Bottom), with Zinganee and Mameluke playing cat-and-mouse a few places behind. Whenever Sam Chifney eased his horse for a few strides, William Wheatley on Mameluke instantly followed suit. Half a mile out, Chifney – aware that Mameluke possessed the superior turn of foot – pushed Zinganee through the field and sent him on, with Mameluke straining to stay at his quarters. A furlong out Mameluke weakened, and Zinganee forged clear to win by two lengths.

Contrary to accounts of his pre-race affability about the prospect of buying Zinganee, George IV did not, according to Greville, take the defeat kindly and 'complained the horse was not offered to him. He is not extravagantly fond of Chesterfield, who is

Jockeys Sam Chifney jnr, Jem Robinson, William Wheatley and William Scott.

pretty well bit by it.' Victory for his mare Maria in a £500 match over two miles provided some pleasure for the King at the last Ascot meeting he would ever attend.

Shutting the stable door after the horse had bolted, the King then purchased Zinganee for 2,500 guineas soon after the 1829 Gold Cup victory, but it was too late: when the horse ran in the following year's race, the Royal Stand was closed and the bloated King lay dying six miles away in Windsor Castle. Still desperate to win the Gold Cup, he sent his servant Jack Ratford across the park to Ascot to discover the result of the race, but the news he received on Ratford's return did not allow him to die happy: Zinganee had run last of four in the Gold Cup behind Lucetta, and it was scant consolation that The Colonel had finished runner-up.

In one way Zinganee's defeat served the King right. In an act of vindictiveness he had altered the conditions of the 1830 Gold Cup to prevent John Gully — famous pugilist who became a major racehorse owner and an MP — from having a runner. Gully's offence, according to the *Observer* in March 1830, was that he had failed to take his hat off when passing the Royal Stand at the 1829 meeting, and to punish such impertinence George IV stipulated that the 1830 Gold Cup would be confined to horses 'bona fide the property, at the time of starting, of a member of the Jockey Club, of a member of the Upper or Lower Rooms at Newmarket, or of those clubs in London whose members may be admitted into the above clubs without ballot' — that is, Brook's or White's. This ruling understandably attracted criticism: *The Sporting Magazine* insisted that:

> A man must have possessed bad taste and worse feeling to advise His Majesty to exclude all but Members of the Jockey and certain other Clubs, as it is well known that there are many wealthy, honourable, noble and amiable characters who from health, station and many other circumstances cannot possibly belong to these Clubs.

The ruling got the response it deserved with that paltry four-runner field, and worse was to come with a field of two in 1831. By the time of the next running George IV was no longer in a position to insist on its observance, and the restrictive rule was quietly dropped.

The King died at Windsor on 26 June 1830, succeeded by his oldest surviving brother the Duke of Clarence, who became William IV. Horse racing seems not to have been high on the new King's list of priorities, but by now the royal presence at Ascot was as much to do with the obligations of monarchy as with the sport, and William duly appeared at the 1831 meeting – where Charles Greville noted that 'William was bored to death of the races, and his own horse broke down.' Nor did William get a better press from 'The Druid', who wrote that the King, 'in the very year of his accession, cared so little about it, that he was often seen to turn his back on the horses while they were running at Ascot'. His wife Queen Adelaide affronted the racing nobility by sewing between races.

No doubt such churlish behaviour would not have endeared King or Queen to racing fanatics, but it hardly justifies what happened to William IV after the first race on 19 June 1832, when a stone hurled by a one-legged ex-seaman named Dennis Collins struck him on the head.

'Oh God! I am hit!' screamed the King, but the stone – a large flint with jagged edges, hastily retrieved to be produced as evidence in court – had merely dented his hat and did not draw blood. 'It made very little sensation on the spot, for he was not hurt,' reported Greville: 'It however produced a great burst of loyalty in both Houses, and their Majesties were loudly cheered at Ascot.' The indignation of the Ascot crowds 'was loudly and unequivocally expressed. His Majesty's appearance at the window two or three minutes after was most enthusiastically cheered by all classes.'

Having appeared at the window to reassure his subjects that he was unharmed, the King spotted a poor gipsy woman, and tossed a sovereign to her. But in the scrum to retrieve the coin the intended beneficiary was pushed aside, so William, seeing her distress, sent one of his servants down to give the woman a £5 note – at which she insisted on being admitted to the Royal Stand so that she could shower blessings upon his head.

By coincidence the Duke of Wellington had been assaulted in London the day before, but 'so far the outrages have done rather good than harm'. Many people believed the attack was politically inspired. The Duke of Buckingham described it as 'a forcible commentary on the "No king" doctrine'. He believed that the culprit 'probably read some of the appeals to physical force that were in circulation', and that the two attacks within

ASCOT HEATH RACES, 1831.

TUESDAY, MAY 31.

HIS MAJESTY'S PLATE OF ONE HUNDRED GUINEAS,

For Horses of all ages; four years old, 10st. 7lb.; five, 11st. 7lb.; six, 11st. 12lb.; and aged, 12st. Four Miles

The OATLANDS STAKES of THIRTY SOVEREIGNS each, 20 ft.; for Horses of all ages (two years old excepted.) Two Miles and a Half.

	Age.	st.	lb.
HIS MAJESTY's *The Colonel*	6	9	6
Duke of RUTLAND's *Oppidan*	6	8	12
Lord EXETER's *Augustus*	4	8	0
———— *Mahmoud*	4	8	0
Mr. MILLS's *Mouche*	4	7	5
Lord VERULAM's *Whip*	4	7	4
Mr. SADLER's ch. f. *Design*	4	7	4

Lord JERSEY's *Juryman*, 6 years, 8st. 6lb. and Mr. COSBY's *Hindoo*, 5 years, 8st. 2lb, having declared forfeit by the time prescribed, to pay 10 sovereigns each.

SWEEPSTAKES of ONE HUNDRED SOVEREIGNS each, h. ft.; for colts, 8st. 7lb, and fillies, 8st. 4lb. New Mile.

Mr. ROGERS's c. *Exploit*, by *Partisan*, out of *Corinne*
Mr. THORNHILL's b. c. by *Emilius*, out of *Mercy*
Mr. UDNY's b. c. by *Emilius* out of *Antiope*
Lord EXETER's ch c. *Anthony*, by *Tramp*, out of *Augusta*
Lord VERULAM's c. *Vestris*, by *Whalebone*, out of *Varennes*
Duke of RICHMOND's c. *Elvas*, by *Whalebone*, out of *Leopoldine*
Duke of GRAFTON's c. *Æneas*, by *Emilius*, out of *Pastille*
Gen. GROSVENOR's b. c. *Sarpedon*, by *Emilius*, out of *Icaria*
———————— gr. c. *Sedan*, by *Gustavus*, out of *Blue Stockings*
Mr. SCOTT STONEHEWER's f. *Lioness*, by *Tiresias*, out of *Emma*
Mr. DELME RADCLIFFE's c. by *Whalebone*, out of *Electress*

SWEEPSTAKES of ONE HUNDRED SOVEREIGNS each, h. ft.; for three years old colts, 8st. 7lb.; those by untried stallions, or out of untried mares, allowed 3lb. Old Mile.

Sir J. SHELLY's by *Middleton*, out of *Cressida* (horse untried)
Duke of RUTLAND's *Clansman*, by *Partisan*, dam by *Andrew*—*Quiz*—*Selim's* dam (mare untried)
Lord JERSEY's *Riddlesworth*, by *Emilius*, out of *Filagree*
Mr. THORNHILL's by *Emilius*, out of *Mercy*, by *Merlin* (mare untried)
Mr. DELME RADCLIFFE's by *Whalebone*, out of *Electress*
Mr. NOWELL's by *Bustard*, or *Aladdin*, out of *Camelina*, sister to *Camel* (mare untried)
Lord G. H. CAVENDISH's by *Partisan*, out of *Barrosa*
Mr. SOWERBY's b. or br. *Sir Thomas*, by *Abjer*, out of *Lady Henry*, by *Orville*
Mr. ROGERS's *Despatch*, by *Partisan*, out of *Nina*
Duke of GRAFTON's b. *Pertinax*, by *Emilius*, out of *Pawn*
Lord VERULAM's by *Whalebone*, out of *Tredrille*
Lord TAVISTOCK's by *Middleton*, out of *Lyrnessa* (both untried)
Mr. VANSITTART's ch. by *St. Patrick*, out of *Slight*
Mr. L. CHARLTON's b. by *Master Henry*, out of *Liberty*, by *Clavileno*—*Allegretta* (mare untried)
Lord GROSVENOR's br. *Damascus*, by *Whisker*, out of *Bombasine*

twenty-four hours 'displayed the spirit that political agitation had excited'.

Whether there was any political motive for the Ascot assault is unlikely, as suggested by *The Times*:

> The author of this brutal and daring outrage is a low profligate gaol-bird, a discharged Greenwich pensioner, who has been repeatedly committed from the police-offices of the metropolis as a rogue and vagabond, and it was an imaginary personal wrong which induced the reckless miscreant to the commission of so heinous an offence.

Collins had served as a cook on *HMS Kangaroo*, whose captain J. Baker wrote to Viscount Melbourne on 22 June 1832 to state that he remembered Collins and that 'his general character was that of a drunken, worthless, quarrelsome person … I have thought it my duty at the present particular moment to make this statement to your Lordship feeling with every Loyal subject the utmost horror and abhorrence at such atrocious conduct.'

At his trial on a charge of High Treason, Collins 'appeared but little affected by his situation', and was sentenced at the Berkshire Assizes at Abingdon – where, to mark the occasion, he had fitted himself with a new wooden leg – on 22 August 1832 to 'be drawn on a hurdle to the place of execution, hanged, decapitated, quartered etc. etc.'. But the King immediately reprieved him and his sentence was commuted to transportation. He died in exile many years later.

A less sensational feature of the 1832 meeting was the first running of the Eclipse Foot – a race for the prize of a gold-plated mounted hoof of Eclipse, which had been donated by the King to the Jockey Club earlier that year: members of the Club contributed £100 to the stakes, with William himself adding another £200. The first winner was Lord Chesterfield's Priam (who had won the 1830 Derby when owned by Will Chifney), but the race was short-lived: after only one member put up a runner for the Foot in 1835, the event was discontinued, and this curious relic is now kept as the centrepiece of the dining table in the Jockey Club Rooms in Newmarket.

Despite the assault in 1832, William returned to Ascot in 1833, when *The Times* paid tribute to 'the warm and personal interference of His Majesty, who has lately expressed a desire to place Ascot, if not first, at least inferior to

Opposite: The front page of the racecard for 1831 – printed before the entries for 'His Majesty's Plate of one hundred guineas' over four miles are known. (The races shown are not given in order of their running: they were in fact fourth, second, fifth and third respectively on an eight-race programme.)

none amongst the stations of racing celebrity'. The same year Charles Greville, however, complained of the deteriorating standards of the King's party at Ascot: 'His household is now so ill managed that his grooms were drunk every day, and one man (who was sober) was killed going home from the races. Goodwin [William Goodwin, Inspector of the Stables to William IV] told me nobody exercised any authority, and the consequence was that the household all ran riot.'

Either Greville's dyspeptic attitude was very much the minority view or rapid changes took place before the next meeting, for in 1834 *The Times* reflected:

> During race time, especially on the Cup day, the characteristics of Ascot are altogether distinct from those of any other meeting. Newmarket, as a place of business, stands by itself. Epsom for horses, crowd, dust and confusions surpasses it. Goodwood and Doncaster boast many and varied attractions, but in the beauty of the surrounding scenery, the numberless delightful rides to the heath, and its proximity to the seat of Royalty, added to other local and artificial advantages, there is a fascination which we in vain look for elsewhere, and which rarely fails of bringing together a brilliant assemblage of the highest rank in the country.

The same year saw the introduction of two races that now form major elements of the Royal Meeting: the St James's Palace Stakes over the Old Mile for three-year-olds (there had been an identical but unnamed race in the 1833 programme), and the Ascot Derby – now the King Edward VII Stakes – for three-year-olds over a mile and a half.

Ascot's showpiece Gold Cup was going from strength to strength. The 1835 renewal was won by Glencoe, who the previous year had won the Two Thousand Guineas and run third in the Derby, and the 1836 running went to Touchstone, who as a three-year-old in 1834 had won the St Leger. His rider at Ascot was John Day, whose great-great-great-grandson was to win the Gold Cup an astonishing eleven times: Lester Piggott.

Touchstone won the Gold Cup again in 1837 – the third dual winner, after Anticipation in 1816 and 1819 and Bizarre in 1824 and 1825 – and went on to prove an outstanding success at stud, siring three Derby winners.

Yet the mid-1830s also saw a clamour for reform at Ascot. Not for the last time, the going became a bone of contention. In 1831 *The Sporting Magazine* reported:

> Generally if one half of [the track] is sufficiently soft, the other half (the lower part) is a mire; and if this is sufficiently dry, the upper part becomes as hard as a brick-field.

The Clerk of the Course, Thomas Jenner, tried to improve the turf by rolling and bush-harrowing it, but by 1835 the condition of the ground was worse, and *The Sporting Magazine* had more cause for complaint:

> The Race-course at Ascot is radically bad. Mr Jenner had done all for it that care and attention could effect: rolling and bush-harrowing had been liberally bestowed upon it; but literally you cannot make a silk purse out of a sow's ear.

There were other causes for complaint – criticisms of the approach roads, the stands, the gambling, the beggars and the mismanagement of the homebound crowds. On one occasion, the racegoers had to contend with 'an immoderate quantity of Irish beggars, in the utmost apparent state of misery and destitution, who annoyed by their unceasing importunities everyone within their reach … Every carriage, as it arrived, was beset by a mob of vagabonds, forcing their services upon the occupants, and, in many instances, using the most disgusting language if their aid was refused.'

On 4 June 1836, *The Times* published a long analysis of possible remedies at Ascot:

Suggestions for Reconstituting Ascot

> In our notice of Tuesday we took occasion to advert to the poverty of the sums given as compared with those collected; the moderate character of the races on that and subsequent days prove to demonstration that unless something be done towards their improvement, or rather regeneration, they will come to nothing. Our

remarks, we believe, have excited attention to the proper quarters, and an illustrious personage has been heard to express his surprise that the list should have been so unproductive of sport on the first day!

It is not too late to restore it to that pre-eminence which it formerly boasted, and, as we are quite satisfied that the disposition exists, we venture to throw out the following hints:

(1) The ground should be let by tender, the renter being allowed to take a small fee for each carriage placed in an enclosed space, next the rails: £500 or £600 at least might be obtained in this way, and there would not be any question as to the amount collected.

(2) An 'Ascot Club' should be formed on the basis of those at Goodwood and Heaton Park, the Master of the Buckhounds for the time being officiating as President. Of a club of this description His Majesty would no doubt condescend to become Patron, and we are convinced that there are many distinguished individuals who would willingly become members.

(3) There should be a free Handicap of 100 sovereigns each, half forfeit, three or four miles (as might be resolved upon) with 200 sovereigns added, the horses to be handicapped, and the acc. declared, in the month of March.

(4) And the Oatlands might again be made a sporting race by adding to it £100 or £200 …

(5) Under the present regulation the Eclipse Foot can never become a race of importance, but as His Majesty wishes it to be select, would not the exclusion of objectionable people be secured by confining it to horses nominated by members of the Jockey Club? Or, if no alteration be deemed advisable, would not the £200 so generously offered by His Majesty, be more judiciously bestowed on the Oatlands?

(6) There should be a Plate each day, and the entrance money, if exacted at all, be given to the owner of the second horse, as is required by the Act of Parliament.

(7) The Cup articles should be altered so as to give inferior horses a chance.

(8) And the course, at present in a wretched state, kept in proper order.

(9) Should a club, or failing that, a racing committee be formed, and measures taken, embodying the spirit of our suggestions, we are convinced that Ascot, now twenty years behind the times, may regain its popularity; one thing, however, is certain – viz, that unless the axe is laid to the root of the evil, it will be better not to touch it at all.

(10) King's Plate. His Majesty has been graciously pleased to give a free Plate of 100 guineas to the Egham races. Would it not be as well to withdraw the one from Guildford, where it is completely thrown away?

(11) The want of accommodation for the ladies at Ascot has suggested the idea of a Grandstand, on the same lines as that of Goodwood; if placed between the Royal and betting stands, it could not fail to answer. The profits might go to a race fund.

This was a major turning point for Ascot. Within the space of less than five years, it had descended the ranks of the nation's racecourses and was deemed to be some twenty years behind. Radical and urgent reform was needed, and now events, driven along by a concerned William IV, moved swiftly – so swiftly that on 9 August 1836 *The Times* was able to report the effect of its earlier declaration:

We are very happy in being able to state that means will be adopted to restore Ascot races to that magnificent prosperity which marked their progress under the warm, invigorating, and influential patronage of George IV. Indeed, when His Majesty learned that they languished under bad management and the lack of exalted countenance and support, he invited the members of the Jockey Club to dine with him and expressed an earnest desire that Ascot races should experience the requisite revivification as soon as possible.

The result was an entire renewal of personnel at Ascot in 1836. William Hibburd of Egham was appointed as Clerk of the Course in place of Jenner, and the Earl of Erroll had already been appointed as Master of the Buckhounds in 1835. Together they rapidly improved the track, filling in holes, levelling uneven rough ground and re-laying the turf in many parts.

R. G. Reeve, *Ascot Heath Races*, 1837 – William IV's last Ascot.

It was announced that Erroll had commenced the reformation of the races 'with a determination that cannot fail to be productive of the best results'. One of the first acts was to construct a second line of rails and posts for carriages between the distance and winning post. Then in August, a programme for the 1837 races was published which showed 'Lord Errol has carried out his intentions into effect with a rapidity, vigour and effect altogether without precedent.' Such vigour was to continue, for by the start of Queen Victoria's reign Ascot was transformed, and rather than trailing behind other racecourses, it became the leader.

By the 1837 meeting, *The Times* was able to report that 'the turf has been very much improved and in some places it has been newly laid down, and it now presents an appearance of smoothness and evenness almost equal of the surface of a billiard-table'.

But the races themselves that year were overshadowed by the King's illness. On the Wednesday, it was announced for the first time that he was alarmingly ill, and the account on Thursday was no better. Nevertheless, the Royal Family were keen to maintain appearances, and Queen Adelaide attended the races by herself on the Tuesday and stayed at the course for an hour before leaving to entertain an immense party at Windsor.

On 20 June 1837, two weeks after Touchstone's second Gold Cup victory, William IV died at Windsor Castle – and Ascot entered the Victorian age.

QUEEN VICTORIA AT ASCOT

Tuesday 12 June 1834 was a busy day for the fifteen-year-old Princess Victoria.

I awoke at 7 and got up at a $\frac{1}{4}$ to 8. At $\frac{1}{2}$ past 9 we breakfasted, with the King, the Queen, Feodore, Ernest, George Cambridge, the Duchess of Northumberland, and Lady Clinton. All the other ladies breakfasted together. We then went to the Queen's room. At a $\frac{1}{4}$ past 12 we went to Ascot Races with the whole company in 9 carriages. In the first went the King, the Queen, Mamma and I. In the second Feodore, the Duchess of Richmond, the Duchess of Northumberland and Lady Clinton. In the third Lady Flora, Lady Sophia Sydney, the Duke of Richmond, and the Duke of Cleveland. In the fourth Lehzen, Miss Hope Johnston, the Duke of Grafton and the Duke of Dorset. How all the others went I do not know. At about 1 we arrived on the race course and entered the King's stand with all our party. The races were very good and there was an immense concourse of people there of all ranks. At about $\frac{1}{2}$ past 2 we had luncheon. At a little after 6 we left the stand and returned to the castle in the same way as we came except that, as it rained very hard, we came home in shut carriages. At 7 we arrived at the castle. At $\frac{1}{2}$ past 7 we dined. The company at dinner were the same as yesterday with the exception of Lord and Lady Conyngham not dining here, and a few other gentlemen having dined here. We went in in the same way. I sat between the King and the Duke of Cleveland. I stayed up till a $\frac{1}{4}$ to 11. I was very much amused indeed at the races.

James Pollard, *The Ascot Gold Cup 1834*. The winner was Lord Chesterfield's Glaucus.

Previous pages: Queen Victoria arrives at Ascot, 1840.

The first appearance of Princess Victoria at Ascot with her uncle William IV had a very special significance, as by 1834 she was next in line to the throne, Queen Adelaide's two children both having died in infancy. So the future queen was being exposed to her subjects – and they to her.

In June 1838 Victoria paid her first visit to Ascot as sovereign, accompanied by the Prime Minister Lord Melbourne (who confessed to the new queen that he had not been to Ascot since leaving Eton forty-two years earlier). She wrote in her diary:

Precisely at a quarter past twelve we set off for Ascot … It was very bright and fine when we got there, and such myriads of people there – more than ever were there, they say. Lord Melbourne found

Ascot much changed of course since he was there. He never left the stand, and stood near me near the window in the beginning. I was so happy that he should be seen with me, on such Public Occasions. He does not care the least about the Races, but yet was amused and pleased. I stayed five races. The first race, the Windsor Town Plate, was won by Fulwar Craven's Doncaster; the 2nd by Lord Jersey's Ilderim; the 3rd (the St James Palace Stakes), a most interesting race, by the Duke of Portland's Beotian; the 4th (for the Cup), also very interesting, by Lord George Bentinck's Grey Momus, and the 5th by Lord Exeter's Mecca. Between the 2nd and 3rd race we took luncheon. I sat between Lord Anglesey and Lord Melbourne. Unfortunately it came on to rain after the 2nd race, and went on raining … We came home at a quarter past five. I was much amused. Wrote my journal. At half past seven we dined … I sat between Lord Anglesey & Lord Melbourne. I asked Lord Melbourne if he was tired. He said not. Spoke of the races, and of betting. I said I had not betted this day as it bored me. He replied, 'It's much better not', for that spoilt the grandeur of the race. He admired the races & was amused with them, he said. I said I feared he had been rather bored part of the time. He said not: 'I was rather tired, I slept for half an hour when I came home' … I then asked him if he thought it would be well, if, on occasions like the Races I should wear my Star & Ribbon; he said yes … Lord Anglesey said that he had felt the draft in the stand in the morning, upon which Lord Melbourne said, 'You should have asked Her Majesty's leave to put on your hat', which is quite true, but Lord Anglesey would not allow …

To mark her first Ascot as monarch, the Queen inaugurated a new race over one and a half miles, with a gold vase worth £200 added to a £25 sweepstake for three-year-olds. (Nowadays the Queen's Vase, the race's distance was increased to its present two miles the following year.)

The nature of the new sovereign's reception seems to depend on which chronicler you choose to believe. Charles Greville, subject as so often to a bout of dyspepsia, wrote:

A great concourse of people on Thursday; the Queen tolerably received; some shouting, not a great deal, and a few hats taken off. This mark of respect has quite gone out of use and neither her station nor her sex procures it; we are not the nearer a revolution for this, but it is ugly. All the world went on to the Royal Stand, and her Majesty was very gracious and civil, speaking to everybody.

Bell's Life in London went for the fashion angle:

The Queen was dressed in a pink silk slip, over which was a lace dress or frock; she wore a white drawn gauze bonnet, trimmed with pink ribands, and ornamented with artificial roses, both inside and out … She repeatedly during the day conversed with great liveliness with those around her, and surveyed the races through a double opera glass; and, if we are not misinformed, occasionally entered into the spirit of the scene, and indulged in a few bets – not infrequently proving her attention to passing events by choosing the favourites, and making up her 'book' to advantage.

The Times reported that the Queen had appeared at the window and 'courtesied [*sic*] with great elegance and condescension to the numerous company assembled in front'; she was cheered several times and 'was in excellent health and spirit, appearing to enjoy the scene and to enter into the sport of racing'.

A new sovereign was in place, but old habits die hard, and at the same meeting *The Times* reported goings-on at the other end of the social spectrum:

The amusements of the day were diversified by the performances of crowds of conjurors, indeed the wise men yesterday almost exceeded the simpletons in number; herds of jugglers, itinerant rope-dancers, almost as good as those who are sometimes engaged to support the legitimate and illegitimate theatres of the metropolis; swarms of swarthy sibyls, of whom there was an encampment on the heath, and groups of ballad singers a little husky with unmitigated practice and Berkshire beer.

Grey Momus, winner of that year's Gold Cup under just 6 stone 10 pounds after finishing third in the Derby, was owned by Lord George Bentinck, one of the great men not only of the Turf in the nineteenth century but of all racing history. In 1838, at the age of thirty-six, he had already made a considerable mark on the sport, having owned the winners of three Classics, including the 1838 Two Thousand Guineas with Grey Momus himself. But it was as an administrator and member of the Jockey Club that he left a lasting legacy to racing, bringing order to the sport and ruthlessly taking on the crooks and defaulters who blighted the Turf.

Minor improvements in the running of Ascot itself continued. In 1838, horses were numbered on the racecard, and in 1839 at the end of every race the judge hoisted the number of the winner onto a large blackboard erected at the side of his box, thus putting an end to disputes over which horse had won. Ascot led the country in this respect, explaining the process thus: 'The list contains nine races, each horse having a number affixed to his name in the card; as the jockeys weighed, the numbers were exhibited on a black board placed conspicuously on the judge's chair, and on the termination of each race, the number of the winning horse, much confusion and trickery being thus prevented.'

A much less formal sort of 'race-card' was that purveyed by card-selling tipsters, for decades – depending on your point of view – either a menace to innocent racegoers or all part of the rich social tapestry of racing at Ascot.

The trade had begun in the 1830s, and by the middle of the century some card-sellers had become notorious Turf characters, with Ascot their natural habitat. They had names like 'Fair Helen' and 'Big Ann', or 'Jerry', who dressed 'as a Broadway dandy with a huge straw hat, or enacting the captain in a red coat, a spy-glass, and a beaver "cock and pinch".' That description comes to us from 'The Druid', who also described a curious character named 'Donkey Jemmy', whose particular skill was imitating a donkey:

At the Ascot meeting he, of course, wore his huge yellow wig; and as we counted at least forty distinct brays during the Cup afternoon, and as his tariff is sixpence per bray, he did not go far amiss. Those people who are not in carriages, he looks down upon with supreme contempt – 'I do the donkey to please the aristocracy, not the common people,' was his withering remark in our presence, about a

The Royal Stand in the early years of Queen Victoria's reign.

quarter to three that afternoon, when two or three Berkshire Lubins indulged at some elephantine pleasantries at his expense.

Other tipsters attracted their clients in different ways. 'Minstrel poets' wrote ballads which commonly began:

You sportsmen all, both great and small, one moment now attend,
And listen with attention to these verses I have penned

– and then launched into a rhyming series of tips.

Ascot as an occasion was now growing relentlessly, and the month after the 1838 Royal Meeting a decision was taken to construct a Grand Stand between the Betting Stand and the Royal Stand.

The principal reason for building a new stand was to raise money for the race fund and thus improve the quality of the racing. A second reason was to provide better facilities to racegoers and 'for the purpose of affording additional accommodation to all Classes of Her Majesty's Subjects attending the Races at Ascot Heath'. Better facilities would entice more racegoers to attend and spend more money, and if a Grand Stand were provided, the authorities could charge admittance at a higher rate. The new stand would be administered by the Grand Stand Trust, established in June 1838.

Construction began in July 1838, the contract stipulating that the work had to be complete by 20 May 1839 under a penalty of £500. In the event, everything bar some iron fencing was completed by 25 May, just three days before the meeting opened.

There are several detailed contemporary accounts of the new Grand Stand written immediately it was opened in 1839. Racing historian J. C. Whyte wrote that the new Grand Stand is

situated between the Queen's and the old betting stand, occupying the spot formerly taken up by several wooden stands. Its elevation from the ground is fifty-two feet, its length ninety-seven and a half feet, or, including the balcony which extends beyond the building, a hundred and twenty-one feet. The drawing-room, or grand floor, is ninety feet in length and is provided with ten rows of benches placed above each other; both in front and at the ends of the room the windows extend from the ceiling to the floor, and slide up and down. The ground floor will hold about twelve hundred persons, and the roof, which is leaded, will accommodate nearly eighteen hundred persons. There are several refreshment, retiring and play rooms; in fact, the conveniences are more numerous than at any other building of the kind in England.

A very handsome balcony, supported by Corinthian pillars, extends the whole length of the building, and the colonade [*sic*] beneath it affords a sheltered promenade. The entrance is at the back of the building, under an elegant portico, the carriage approach to which is by the great Reading road. To prevent confusion there are two distinct staircases to the grand floor and the roof. The Grand Stand is placed well back, and as the straight course in front has been carried out about thirty feet, the turn from the old mile into the straight running is greatly improved. A space of fifty-five feet from the railing to the colonnade has been enclosed in front of the building, for the use of betting men and others who have paid for admission to the stand; here the ring is formed, and the betting is carried on without the least inconvenience. A spacious room on the basement floor is appropriated for their use, in case of bad weather. Judging from the attendance of company at the recent meeting, there can be no doubt that, the Grand Stand at Ascot is highly acceptable to the public, and will fully answer the objects sought by its projectors.

The press warmly welcomed the new Grand Stand. The *Mirror* wrote on 8 June 1839:

It has long been a subject of surprise and regret, that while Epsom, and almost every other provincial race-course in the kingdom, was provided with a grand stand, Ascot should have been until now without one. However, 'better late than never' the Stand is now erected, and a very handsome and commodious building it is.

And *The Times* declared: 'The extent of patronage bestowed upon the new building yesterday proved that we were right in looking at it as a desideratum; the ground floor was full of well-dressed females, the leads were patronized by hundreds, and the betting and play rooms were as full of animation as the mania for gambling could make them.' There were some complaints, such as the seats on the roof and the principal floor were not sufficiently inclined to permit a good view; that situation was rectified before the 1840 meeting. The distemper used inside the building also rubbed off on the racegoers' clothes and the entrance hall was so crowded 'that many elegant females were compelled to seek accommodation elsewhere'. This 'evil and annoyance' was remedied the following year 'by having the walls painted in oil'. The Grand Stand and its enclosure had an enormous effect on the Ascot races. Less than twenty years later 'The Druid' was to write of 'those primitive days when the Grand Stand enclosure was unknown', and in 1846 the *Illustrated London News* wrote that Ascot's stands 'form a little city of Olympian palaces'. However, the same journalist was less impressed by the lack of facilities for members of the press: 'The only place to which they are accorded resort was a spot appropriated to the use of stable-boys, on the roof of one of the stands, in which there were rooms wholly unoccupied!'

Another new building erected in 1839, although on a rather different scale, was the first proper box for the judge.

That year's meeting saw the first running of the Windsor Castle Stakes, now a five-furlong sprint for two-year-olds, then a mile race for three-year-olds, and the Ascot Stakes, the two-and-a-half-mile handicap which today provides one of the best betting heats of the royal fixture. The inaugural Ascot Stakes was won narrowly by an unnamed three-year-old filly (later named Marchioness), ridden by a diminutive young jockey named Bell, whose performance occasioned a royal summons. According to J. C. Whyte:

The excellent riding of little Bell, a mere child, only four stone, and who rode the winner, excited general wonder and admiration, and even attracted the notice of Her Majesty, who was pleased to have the juvenile jockey brought before her after the race, and graciously

presented him with a ten-pound note. It is said, that, upon being asked his weight by the queen, he answered, to the no small amusement of the royal circle, 'Please, ma'am, master says as how I must never tell my weight.'

Gradually the Royal Meeting as we know it was taking shape. The following year, 1840, saw the first running of one of today's highlights, the Coronation Stakes over one mile for three-year-old fillies – a rather belated celebration of

Saddling up for the 1839 Gold Cup (won by Caravan) in front of the new Grand Stand.

Queen Victoria arrives at Ascot in 1840 with Prince Albert, whom she had married earlier that year.

Queen Victoria's coronation, which had taken place in Westminster Abbey in June 1838.

But although the supporting programme was gradually improving in quality, Gold Cup day remained the high point of the meeting. In 1842 *The Times* reported of the Thursday that:

> The attendance of the race-course has been more than usually numerous, and amongst the company have been an immense muster of the nobility and the most distinguished fashionables ... We do not remember ever to have seen the course so well or so brilliantly attended.

Distinguished fashionables or undistinguished unfashionables, a great many of the throng that day would have been excited by the prospect of seeing, in the Gold Cup itself, the great northern mare Beeswing.

Now nine years old, 'The Flower of the North' had run third behind St Francis in the Queen's Vase on the first day of the meeting. But neither horse was favourite for the Gold Cup, that honour going to the 1841 winner Lanercost. For a five-runner field the betting read:

5–6 Lanercost
7–2 St Francis
9–2 The Nob
7–1 Beeswing
20–1 Eringo

The story of the race is well told in the spare, form-book prose of *The Times* the following day:

> Eringo was first from the post, and kept in front for a quarter of a mile; the mare then overpowered her jockey, and went away with a good lead, followed by Eringo, Lanercost lying third, The Nob fourth, and St Francis last. In making the top turn the pace became severe, but no

alteration in the places was observable until they reached the brick kiln [the turn out of Swinley Bottom], where Lanercost was beaten, and at the turn he was last in the race. Eringo held the second place to the stand, where The Nob passed him, and challenged the mare. For a moment he headed her, but 'The Pride of the North' resumed her position in a couple of strides, and after a fine race won by half a length. Lanercost pulled up lame. The race came off at half-past 3.

The Sporting Magazine called it 'one of the most beautiful races for the Ascot Cup on record'.

In all Beeswing won fifty-one races (including the Doncaster Cup four times) from sixty-four starts, and despite an arduous racing career went on to become a successful broodmare. Her matings with another Gold Cup winner Touchstone (1836 and 1837) produced two Classic winners: Nunnykirk (1849 Two Thousand Guineas) and Newminster (1851 St Leger).

The sight of great horses in action – more and more a feature of the Royal Meeting – was enough for many Ascot racegoers, but for others the whole point of the fixture was royal-spotting. Victoria had married her first cousin Albert, second son of the Duke of Saxe-Coburg-Gotha, in February 1840, and the Prince Consort became a new star in the Ascot firmament – although there is no evidence that he had any enthusiasm for racing itself. He had first attended Ascot the June following their wedding, and at the 1842 meeting – which took place a short time after an attempt by a man named John Francis to shoot Victoria had been thwarted – *The Times* wrote:

> The great attraction to the course this day was not so much the racing, though it must be admitted there was no want of that, but the presence of Her Majesty and her illustrious Consort. The recent dastardly attempt of the wretched assassin who now lies awaiting the fiat of a jury had awakened a spirit of loyalty which everybody was anxious to testify on all occasions of the appearance of Her Majesty and Prince Albert in public.

Internal problems raised their head in 1843, and as so often politics was at the root. Lord Rosslyn, Master of the Buckhounds, decided that the printing of the racecards for Ascot could no longer be undertaken by the usual printer, one Mr Oxley of Windsor, and henceforth the work would go to another printer, Mr Brown. Oxley, convinced that he had lost the job because he published a Whig newspaper and Lord Rosslyn, a Tory, wanted a Tory printer, petitioned the Jockey Club, who took Lord Rosslyn's line that he simply wanted a different printer. The stubborn Oxley then printed his own racecard for the 1843 meeting in competition with Brown's card, and with the situation unresolved the following year the rivalry became more bitter. In 1844, by which time Brown had himself been ditched in favour of another printer, handbills denouncing Oxley's card were distributed around the racecourse, and the Great Western Railway prohibited his card from going on sale at Slough station. Despite such obstacles market forces won the day for Oxley. His racecard had consistently been more popular with the racing public than those of his rivals, and in 1846 he was reinstated as printer of the official racecard.

Whichever card they were consulting, racegoers in 1843 would have seen two more significant additions to the programme. The Royal Hunt Cup, named after the Royal Buckhounds and run in its early years over the Old Mile, was then – as now – a fierce betting medium; and the New Stakes for two-year-olds – renamed the Norfolk Stakes in 1973 – was first run over 5 furlongs 136 yards. The first running of the New Stakes was won by Ratan, owned and bred by William Crockford – 'The Father of Hell and Hazard' who founded Crockford's gaming club in St James's, London.

In 1844 Alice Hawthorn, a racemare who rivalled Beeswing in popularity and durability – she won fifty races outright, plus one dead heat, from sixty-eight outings between 1841 and 1845 – won the Queen's Vase in such a facile manner that one observer was moved to remark, 'so hollow a race was never seen before' (and winning at Ascot became a family tradition when her son Thormanby won the 1861 Gold Cup).

But that year attention was less on the track than on the Royal Stand, graced by no less a dignitary than the Emperor of Russia.

Nicholas I, on a brief and unexpected visit to England, paid his first visit to Ascot on the Tuesday, and was rewarded with the sight of Alice Hawthorn's victory. Whether the distinguished visitor had laid the odds of 3–1 on the great mare is not recorded, but he clearly knew his horseflesh. *The Times* described how:

At the conclusion of the race for the Queen's Cup or Vase, which was won very easily by Alice Hawthorn, the Emperor of Russia, the King of Saxony and Prince Albert left the Royal Stand and, without any warning, came down upon the turf to examine the winner, with whose points the Emperor seemed particularly pleased. On this occasion the police had much ado, from the suddenness of the visit, to keep back the public. The Emperor was loudly cheered, and evidently enjoyed the scene and the struggle of the spectators to get a close view of him … The Emperor patted Alice Hawthorn with obvious satisfaction.

Nicholas I, Emperor of Russia, with the King of Saxony and Prince Albert in the Royal Procession, 1844.

Nicholas I must have had a good day that Tuesday, as before he left Ascot it was announced that he was endowing the Gold Cup with £500 – not in cash but in the form of a plate that would bear the Russian coat of arms – and from 1845 until 1853 the Gold Cup was run as the Emperor's Plate, to revert to the Gold Cup in 1854 when the Crimean War soured relations. The Emperor returned to Ascot on the Thursday of the 1844 meeting, when he saw the Gold Cup won by an unnamed chestnut colt owned by Lord Albemarle, who promptly and appropriately named the horse The Emperor. (In those days – indeed, until 1946 – it was possible for a horse to race before it had been named. It would be identified by its breeding.)

The hubbub surrounding the royal party's descent to the enclosure to see Alice Hawthorn clearly concerned the authorities, and in 1845 – the year The Emperor won his second successive Gold Cup – it was decided to enclose the area in front of the Royal Stand: it would not only become the second most exclusive part of the racecourse (the most exclusive being inside the Royal Stand), but would also be used for the saddling and unsaddling of runners. It was acknowledged by the authorities that such an enclosure

will be a great addition to the comfort of Her Majesty's Stand by keeping at distance of 16 or 17 yards from Dancers and Balad [*sic*]

The first running of the Gold Cup as the Emperor's Plate in 1845: The Emperor, winning the race for the second year running, beats 1844 St Leger winner Faugh-a-Ballagh and the great mare Alice Hawthorn.

Singers and other musicians with which a Race Course is infested and will afford an opportunity for the Prince or any of Her Majesty's Guests to inspect any of the horses without being annoyed by the pushing of a Mob, or protected by Police Officers.

Thus was born the Royal Enclosure.

The Emperor of Russia and the King of Saxony were by no means the only overseas grandees to frequent Ascot during the early part of Victoria's reign. One particularly exotic visitor was the Indian potentate the King of Oude, whose valet gave an exclusive interview to 'The Druid':

'I trust his Majesty has enjoyed the races?'
　'Oh! Very mush – most beautiful!'

'Where were you?'

'We did come so late by that train; and we go into the Queen's Stand below; but dat was full, and there was luncheon laid out – ham!' (and here the excellent Mahometan paused).

'His Majesty would like the sight?'

'Oh, yes! But the King, he say to me, "What for the people stare so? Do you take me for wild beast?" And I say, "Oh! No, your Majesty: it is the ladies, your Majesty; they all look at you, because they lov [*sic*] you."'

But the lower orders did not always behave well, and there was no character who attracted more opprobrium on the racecourse than the welshing – that is, defaulting – bookmaker. The Victorian bookmaker Dyke Wilkinson described Ascot welshers in the 1850s in his candidly titled autobiography *A Wasted Life*:

Welshers were not only thieves, they were composed of the very residuum of thievery. No such blackguards and irredeemable ruffians

Sketch plan proposing the Royal Enclosure, 1845.

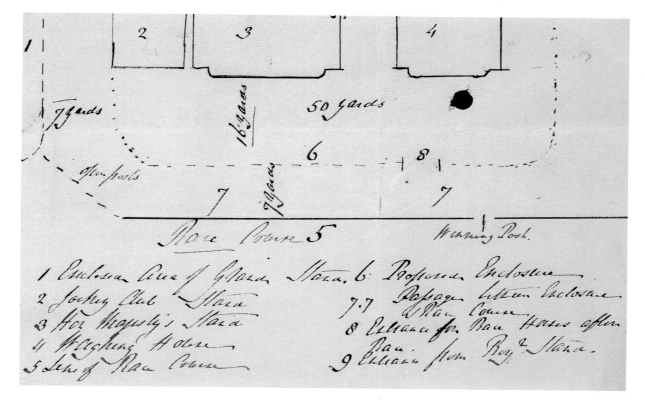

would ever have been permitted to follow their nefarious occupation, for such a length of time, in any other civilised country under the sun … It was only when it menaced the very existence of a noble sport that steps were taken to check it, and all honour is due to the magistrates at Ascot who so construed an Act of Parliament as to warrant them in sending welshers to prison, which aforetime had never been done, thus creating a precedent which many magistrates have since followed, to the purification of the Turf in a remarkable degree.

Not only was the on-course magistrates' court expanded; a new, purpose-built court was added to it.

In 1848 *The Times* reported how an unnamed man had pursued one Mr Dell around the racecourse, calling him 'the most opprobrious names'; he then 'attacked him in the pugilistic style and struck him on the mouth'. This was too much for Dell, who struck the man back and ruptured his jugular vein. Verdict? Justifiable homicide.

Less dramatic but more pervasive was the habit of smoking. In 1833 *The Times* wrote: 'One annoyance there was that the ladies must have felt particularly – the smoking of cigars, which was indulged in to excess by a set of young men, who evidently were not and could not be mistaken for gentlemen.' In 1855 there were 'numerous complaints' about smoking, and the Grand Stand Trustees appointed two men – at £4 a day each – 'with authority peremptorily to prevent the same beyond a certain line'. The Ascot Minute Book records that 'They did their utmost to carry out the orders of the Trustees both as related to the smoking, which was considerably checked, and to the system of bringing private seats and benches into the enclosure which they found is impossible to prevent.'

Ascot picnic, 1844.

Charles Greville, who served as Clerk of the Council in Ordinary (i.e. secretary to the Privy Council) from 1821 to 1859 and whose acerbic observations provide such a barbed commentary on the political and royal life of this period, is best

The road to Ascot, 1846.

remembered in racing circles for the accuracy with which he summed up the essence of the Turf in 1838:

> Racing is just like dram-drinking – momentary excitement and wretched intervals, full consciousness of the mischievous effects of the habit and equal difficulty in abstaining from it.

In 1846, eight years after that grizzled *aperçu,* Greville's horse Alarm won the Gold Cup – or rather, Emperor's Plate. How did it feel to win the big race, Mr Greville?

> It was a moment of excitement and joy when I won this fine piece of plate, in the midst of thousands of spectators; but that past, there returned the undying consciousness of the unworthiness of the pursuit, and the self-reproach that I permit it to exercise the pernicious influence which it does over my mind, filling my thoughts, hopes, and wishes to the exclusion of all other objects and occupations, agitating me, rendering me incapable of application, thought, and reflection, and paralysing my power of reading or

busying myself with books of any kind. All this is very bad and unworthy of a reasonable creature.

It can be safely assumed that Lord Eglinton, owner of 1850 winner The Flying Dutchman, had a less grumpy attitude to the sport, for his mighty colt had won the Derby and St Leger in 1849, and when beating Canezou by eight lengths at Ascot became the first Derby winner to land the Gold Cup (though strictly it was still the Emperor's Plate). The Flying Dutchman's most famous moment came in May 1851 when he beat Voltigeur (to whom he was conceding eight and a half pounds) in the famous match race in front of 100,000 spectators at York.

The weights for that match – Flying Dutchman 8 stone 8½ pounds, Voltigeur 8 stone – were drawn up by 'The Great Master of Weights' Admiral Henry Rous, who had drawn up the first weight-for-age scale and who became Public Handicapper in 1855. At Ascot, Rous would watch races through a naval telescope and make meticulous notes on individual horses, but the results of his observations did not please everybody. On one occasion Lord Ribblesdale (father of the Lord Ribblesdale who served as Master of the Buckhounds in the 1890s) sought out Rous to protest at the weight given to one of his two-year-olds, at which the Admiral consulted his notebook, found his comment on that horse, and declared: 'Fat, Ribblesdale, fat.' Rous's ability as a handicapper was legendary, and rarely better exemplified than in the 1856 Royal Hunt Cup, where the twenty-eight runners approached the finish so closely bunched that they were described as like a line of cavalry charging: Forbidden Fruit won by a head.

Rous was less successful at Ascot, though, when he tried his hand as a starter. Before the introduction of the starting gate to the course at the end of the nineteenth century, races were started by flag, and dispatching the field could be a haphazard business, especially with big fields over short distances. *The Times* reported that in 1860 the Royal Hunt Cup was seriously delayed, 'not owing to the fractiousness of any particular horse, but principally attributable to the perversity of certain jockeys, who obstinately refused to listen to the directions or obey the commands of the starter'. Rous wrote to *Bell's Life*:

It is an extraordinary fact that the art of starting racehorses on fair terms for short courses should be considered an arduous task. They are not ridden by sailors, or tailors, but by the most accomplished jockeys, who are assisted by well-paid officials, under the superintendence of stewards. Forty-nine horses out of fifty come to the starting post like sheep. It is not until they have been ill-used and wantonly spurred that they become, like their riders, inclined to be mischievous.

At the 1861 Royal Meeting *The Times* reported that after a succession of false starts 'even the most industrious speculator, who seldom likes to omit an opportunity of "laying", closed his book in sheer weariness, while the patience of that portion of the spectators who were indifferent to the mere racing was quite exhausted'. An exasperated Rous decided to show the starter how it should be done and insisted on taking over. *The Times* noted that 'his starting was not so successful as his handicapping, and when he gave the signal, the horses were not in line. Buccaneer was in front when the flag fell' – and remained in front to win.

Despite the occasional difficulty of that nature, racing in the mid-nineteenth century was generally becoming more professional. At about this time was appointed Ascot's first official Clerk of the Scales, James Manning (whose family stayed in the post until 1970, latterly working for the Jockey Club), and while the Clerk of the Course often acted as starter, it was becoming more usual for courses to engage a person (ideally not Rous) whose sole duty was to start the races – a duty whose difficulties the *The Sporting Magazine* did not exaggerate:

> With a little practice and attention it is easily accomplished. If properly managed jockeys will start themselves. The only thing requisite on the part of the starter is to prevent any from obtaining a great advantage over others. When he sees they are all prepared and well together, he has nothing more to do than ask, 'Are you all ready?' – which is intended as a note of final preparation and seeing that they are, to give the word 'Off!' It will seldom be necessary to call them back.

Although Lord Melbourne had not been a great devotee of the Turf, a later nineteenth-century premier certainly was. William Temple, third Viscount Palmerston, was Prime Minister from 1855 to 1865 (apart from a brief hiatus when the Earl of Derby held that office), and in 1853, two years before he entered Downing Street, his Buckthorn won the Ascot Stakes at 20–1.

Gratifying as it was to win at Ascot, Palmerston had weightier matters on his mind: gaining support for his drive to counter Russian aggression in the Near East. In early 1854 he convinced the Prime Minister, the Marquess of Aberdeen, of the need to take military action, and by the spring Britain was at war with Russia and the Crimean campaign had started – with the knock-on effect that Nicholas I was hardly a personage whose commemoration at Ascot was appropriate. The Emperor's Plate was no more, and the Gold Cup had returned – though its value dropped to £300.

That 1854 running went to West Australian, who the previous year had landed the Two Thousand Guineas, the Derby and the St Leger to become the first winner of the English Triple Crown. Horses could run very frequently in those days, and West Australian won a two-mile race at Ascot on the eve of the Gold Cup to put him straight for the main event. Ridden by Alfred Day and starting at 6–4 on, he engaged in a furious home-straight battle with Kingston before scraping home by a head.

That same meeting witnessed a curious incident in the Royal Stand. The finish of the New Stakes was so close that Queen Victoria, watching with mounting excitement in her box, forgot that the window had been closed on account of the rain, leaned forward suddenly and smashed the glass with her head. She was uninjured, and *The Times* reported that the incident 'produced a great deal of merriment in the royal party'.

In 1856 the opening of the Staines to Wokingham line brought the railway to Ascot. (Previously rail travellers from London could get only as far as Windsor, from where they would make the 'long walk' to the course, while some chose to travel to Maidenhead and to make their own way from there.)

There was a mixed reaction to making Ascot readily accessible by rail. Many of the rich felt that the trains did 'considerable damage by adding to the quantity and diminishing the quality'. Sportsmen such as Pierce Egan had particularly enjoyed Ascot races before the railways because 'the distance of Ascot from London gives it also a preference over Epsom: the set out and return to the Metropolis is too long a journey for a single day' and protected it from 'the pollution of sheer cockneyism'. *The Times* complained:

> The opening of the Staines and Wokingham Railway has destroyed to
> a certain extent the 'glories' of what racing men call 'Aristocratic

West Australian, first winner of the Triple Crown in 1853 and winner of the Gold Cup in 1854.

Ascot'. It occasioned the display of carriages on the Heath to be considerably diminished, and altogether it caused the meeting to assimilate in character to the Epsom gathering. The attendance was immense, but the muster of pleasure folk comprised perhaps an unusual number of that class of persons who are popularly denominated 'roughs'.

The *Sporting Life* observed in 1859 that 'the hilarious cockney is as much out of his element at aristocratic Ascot as a duck on a turnpike lane'. The same year the *Reading Mercury* bemoaned the loss to local trade:

> The trade of the town has been very flat during the race week, in fact visitors have been very scarce, and the principal Inns even but little patronised. The majority of the private lodgings have remained unlet, and the direct communication to Ascot per rail, appears every succeeding year to have a more injurious effect on the town, which except on Thursday, had more the appearance of a deserted village.

Those roughs who crowded onto the trains for the 1856 Royal Meeting were rewarded with brilliantly fine weather and a view of one of the all-time great Ascot horses: Fisherman. Owned and trained by Tom Parr, Fisherman must

Fisherman, winner of the
Gold Cup in 1858 and 1859.

have had a constitution rarely equalled in racing history, running in 121 races and winning sixty-nine – of which five were at Ascot. He won the Queen's Vase as a three-year-old in 1856 (when his twenty-three victories in one season formed a British record which still stands), then in 1858 and 1859 returned to the course to land both the Gold Cup and the Queen's Plate. *The Times* reported his 1858 Gold Cup victory thus:

In accordance with custom, the horses were paraded round the enclosure in front of the Royal Stand before proceeding to the starting post ... When the flag was dropped Princess Royal went off into the lead, which she increased to a hundred yards before reaching the grandstand, the rest headed by Arsenal and Warlock running in a cluster. On rounding the top turn Princess Royal was still further ahead, and on descending the Swinley Hill Commotion drew into second place, Arsenal and Warlock, nearly side by side, coming next, Glidermire going on fifth, and about three lengths in the rear was Fisherman. No further change occurred until reaching the Brick Kiln Turn, when Princess Royal gradually 'came back' to her pursuers, Arsenal taking second place ... and Fisherman well laid up. On entering the straight, Princess Royal was beaten ... Before reaching the distance, Sunbeam was disposed of, and Fisherman soon afterwards took his place at Arsenal's quarters. At the half distance, Wells called upon the old horse, who cleared Arsenal without any perceptible effort, and won by a length and a half.

Another famous horse to have appeared at Ascot at this time – 'raced' would be the wrong word – was Blink Bonny, who came to the course in 1857 having won both Derby and Oaks at Epsom the previous month (one of only four fillies ever to do so). Unsurprisingly her reputation frightened off all the opposition for a sweepstake and she walked over: she was then paraded in front of the royal stand so that the Queen and her party could admire her.

The old Betting Stand was demolished in 1859, and the following year was erected the 'Iron Gazebo', or Iron Stand, a men-only club for subscribing members – mostly owners who could not obtain entry to the Royal Enclosure because of Court rules (the most common bar to that august location being that they were divorced) and were too self-regarding to join the masses in the Grand Stand. (The Iron Stand has survived as an interesting and yet popular minor anachronism in a small discrete area of the Grandstand to this day.)

Another significant new Ascot building at this time was the Royal Ascot Hotel, near the western extremity of the course (where the roundabout by No. 1 Car Park is now situated) to provide accommodation for horses and their connections. The hotel eventually had 150 boxes, with dormitories above for the stable lads, and became the focus for post-racing gatherings when owners, trainers and jockeys would get together to ruminate on the day's sport and look forward to the following day. (The Royal Ascot Hotel stood for just short of a century before being demolished in 1961.)

In 1860 the race that became the King's Stand Stakes was first run as the Queen's Stand Plate, but the Royal Stand itself was closed the following year: the Queen was in mourning for her mother the Duchess of Kent, who had died in March 1861. The following year, 1862, it was still closed following another death, one from which Victoria would not recover. Prince Albert had died of typhoid fever on 14 December 1861, and his widow never again visited Ascot.

BERTIE

An anxious mother writes to her son on a delicate matter:

Dearest Bertie,

Now that Ascot Races are approaching, I wish to repeat earnestly and seriously and with reference to my letters this spring, that I trust you will … as my Uncle William IV and Aunt, and we ourselves did, confine your visits to the Races to the two days, Tuesday and Thursday and not go on Wednesday and Friday, to which William IV never went, nor did we …

If you are anxious to go on those two great days (though I should prefer your not going every year to both) there is no real objection to that, but to the other days there is. Your example can do much for good and do a great deal for evil, in the present day.

I hear very true and attached friends of ours expressing such anxiety that you should gather round you the really good, steady, and distinguished people.

But the son replies with some exasperation:

I fear, dear Mama, that no year goes round without your giving me a jobation on the subject of racing. You know how utterly and entirely I disapprove of what is bad about them; and therefore I think much may be done in trying to elevate what has always been the great national sport of this country. If it was not national it would long have ceased to exist.

The betting ring, 1866.

Previous pages: The Prince of Wales arriving on Gold Cup day 1882. (See page 113.)

Should we shun races entirely we should no doubt win the high approval of Lord Shaftesbury and the Low Church party, but at the same time the racing would get worse and worse, and those pleasant social gatherings would cease to exist …

The Tuesday and Thursday at Ascot have always been looked upon as the great days as there is the procession in your carriages up the course, which pleases the public and is looked upon by them as a kind of annual pageant. The other days are, of course, of minor importance, but when you have guests staying in your house they naturally like going on those days also, and it would, I think, look both odd and uncivil if I remained at home, and would excite comment if I suddenly deviated from the course I have hitherto adopted.

If I went to most of the small race meetings, people might have a right to complain; but as I do not do so, and only go to Epsom, Ascot and Goodwood (and certainly not every year to the latter), I do not think my example in that respect could be disapproved.

I am always most anxious to meet your wishes, dear Mama, in every respect, and I always regret if we are not quite *d'accord* – but as I am past twenty-eight and have some considerable knowledge of the world and society, you will, I am sure, at least I trust, allow me to use my discretion in matters of this kind.

Albert Edward – known to his mother and to the population at large as 'Bertie' – was certainly right in declaring to Queen Victoria in this exchange of letters in 1870 that he had 'some considerable knowledge of the world and society'. Indeed, he displayed a particular liking for that version of society afforded by race meetings.

Born in November 1841, the eldest son and second child (after Victoria, the Princess Royal, born a year earlier) of Victoria and Albert, Bertie had shown from an early age that he preferred the distractions of music, theatre and sport to serious study. Growing up in comparative isolation from other boys, he developed a love of dogs, and especially of horses. His mother considered him too unreliable to be allowed to become closely involved with serious affairs of state, which left Bertie in effect killing time until his accession to the throne upon her death.

The principal pursuits that sustained him through four decades of kicking his heels in the green room of monarchy were travel, women, and the Turf – and the last-named was to benefit considerably from his support. A magisterial volume entitled *The British Turf and the Men Who Have Made It*, published in 1906, five years after he had eventually ascended the throne, declared:

> It is impossible to over-estimate the good service that our Monarch has rendered to the King of Sports during the thirty-five years that his colours hath [*sic*] adorned both flat and steeplechase courses. When the progress of racing in the past fifty years is analysed, and when the causes of the evolution from the narrow grooves of fifty years ago to the more popular methods of this year of grace come to be inquired into, it will be found that the example of King Edward – the lead that he has given to his people – has had enormous influence, and it will be found, too, that the strengthening of the hold that he has over the English nation, in spite of violent and unreasoning attacks, is due to the fact that His Majesty's imprimatur has been put to the Meetings under the control of the Jockey Club and the National Hunt Committee.
>
> The Royal patronage which, at any rate since the Restoration, has been extended to the Turf, and which had been practically withdrawn by Queen Victoria in consequence of her great bereavement, was given in full measure by King Edward, then Prince of Wales, who restored to Ascot the pageantry which had been hitherto, and which has been since, one of its glories.

George Fordham, who won 99 races at Ascot between 1855 and 1883, including the Gold Cup five times (Lecturer 1867, Mortemer 1871, Henry 1872, Doncaster 1875 and Tristan 1883).

Bertie made his first visit to Ascot at the age of twenty-one in 1863, the year after a new race at the meeting had been named in his honour: the Prince of Wales's Stakes, forerunner of today's Group One ten-furlong highlight and first run over thirteen furlongs in 1862.

The Prince's first Ascot came three months after his wedding to Princess Alexandra of Denmark, and he enjoyed a better view of the sport from the Royal Box than his mother had experienced on her last visit: hundreds of trees and shrubs that hid the lower reaches of Swinley Bottom from the stands had been removed in 1861. The return of the royal presence gave Ascot a major

Trophies in 1863 for (*from top*) the Gold Cup, Gold Vase and Royal Hunt Cup.

boost at a time when the absence of the Queen might have undermined the special nature of the occasion. A huge crowd turned out to see the Prince and his young bride, and *The Times* reported:

> The Princess, who now wears half mourning, took her place at the window of the Royal Stand, and with a little book of the races in her hand, gave herself up to the enjoyment of the scene with the most vivid interest – an interest apparently as great in its way as that of the Prince himself, who stood beside her.

The couple returned regularly over the next few years. In 1864 a new race over approximately three miles was named the Alexandra Plate in honour of the Princess, and the same year a wooden construction down the course from the grandstand was named the Alexandra Stand. In 1866 the Prince and Princess provoked some comment by attending on all four days of the meeting, highly unusual royal behaviour at the time, and the following year saw the revival of the Royal Procession. Ascot – despite the continued absence of the monarch herself – was getting back to normal.

Back in Windsor Castle, however, the Queen was becoming increasingly unamused. She refused to let her son use the castle as a base for his racegoing activities, and started carping at his enthusiasm for the Turf. In July 1867 she complained about his attendance at Goodwood, and two years later, following a similar barrage of complaint, he wrote back that it was important for the family to be at Ascot: 'It is an opportunity for the Royal Family to show themselves in public – wh. I am sure you much desire – & after all Racing with all its faults still remains, I may say, a National Institution of the Country.'

A year later the Queen was still making her views felt – in the exchange with which this chapter opened – and the Prince was still steadfastly defending his position, and gradually Victoria seems to have given up the unequal struggle. Had her view prevailed, the Ascot we know today might never have come about.

One of the most prominent Ascot personalities of the 1860s was Henry Chaplin, a long-standing friend of the Prince of Wales. In 1864 his name was repeatedly linked with that of Lady Florence Paget, 'The Pocket Venus' whose grandfather the 1st Marquess of Anglesey – nicknamed 'One-Leg' – had

commanded the cavalry at Waterloo. Lady Florence had numerous other admirers, among them Henry Hastings, who had become Marquis of Hastings, and hence possessor of a huge fortune, at the age of eight. By the time he went to Oxford – where at Christ Church he reputedly breakfasted on mackerel fried in gin, caviar on toast and a bottle of claret – he had developed a taste for racing, and for gambling on a prodigious scale, and on coming down he built up a string of racehorses in training with the leading betting trainer of the age, John Day, at Danebury.

In June 1864 Lady Florence Paget appeared on the opening day of Ascot on the arm not of Henry Chaplin but of Harry Hastings, who was running a horse named after her – Lady Florence – in a maiden plate. The filly finished unplaced, though Hastings had winners on the next two days of the meeting. Any notion that Hastings was usurping Chaplin in the Pocket Venus's affections

The Grand Stand in the mid-1860s.

was soon quashed by the announcement of her engagement to Chaplin: they would marry in August. A few weeks before the wedding the bride-to-be declared that she needed to visit Marshall and Snelgrove's in Oxford Street for some of those essential pre-nuptial purchases. Alighting from her carriage at the main entrance, she strolled into the store ... then nipped out of a side entrance straight into another carriage, which took her at once to St George's Church in Hanover Square, where she was married to Harry Hastings.

The devastated Chaplin sought solace in the Turf – he was said to have 'bought horses as if he was drunk and betted as if he was mad' – and the rivalry between him and Hastings (fuelled, it must be said, more by Hastings than Chaplin) spilled over onto the racecourse. At Ascot in 1866 Chaplin's two-year-old Hermit (for whom as a yearling Hastings had been the underbidder) won a Biennial Stakes and his colt Breadalbane a Triennial. (The Biennial and Triennial were, as their names suggest, events staged over two and three years respectively, with the same horses eligible to run over longer distances as they got older: for example, a Triennial would involve a race over five furlongs for two-year-olds, then over a mile for three-year-olds, and over two miles for four-year-olds.) At the same meeting Hastings lost so heavily on The Duke in the Queen's Stand Plate that he was compelled to bring the horse out again later the same day in the Gold Vase and recoup the losses – to no avail, as The Duke finished second.

Lecturer, ridden by George Fordham, winner of the 1867 Gold Cup.

The following year Hermit's bid for the Derby became the focus for the rivalry. Chaplin punted heavily on the colt and Hastings invested heavily against, and after Hermit had come with a late run to win by a neck, Hastings found himself £120,000 to the bad – which by the following Monday he had settled by selling his Scottish estate of Loudoun. When he appeared in the betting ring at Ascot two weeks after the Derby the bookmakers showed their heartfelt appreciation with the cry: 'The Markis – Gawd bless 'im!'

Hastings's aim at that meeting was to recover what he had lost on Hermit, and he had exactly the means: his colt Lecturer in the Gold Cup, and the unbeaten Lady Elizabeth in the New Stakes the same day. Lecturer, ridden by the great George Fordham, duly won, and Lady Elizabeth did her part by winning the New Stakes by six lengths. Lecturer won again on the last day of the meeting, and Hastings had recovered most of his losses on Hermit – who was himself in action at Ascot in 1867, winning the St James's Palace Stakes (at 20–1 on) and a Biennial.

By the spring of 1868 Hastings was deep in debt again, and decided that the best way out was to back Lady Elizabeth for the Derby. He had reckoned, however, without the unscrupulousness of his trainer John Day. As Hastings lumped on the bets, so Day, aware from her home trials that Lady Elizabeth was losing her form, laid against her. The filly ran unplaced in the Derby, and

Hermit, winner of the St James's Palace Stakes and a Biennial in 1867.

Inside the Royal Box in 1868.

Hastings was ruined. Shortly before his death at the age of twenty-six in November 1868 he declared to one of his very few remaining friends: 'Hermit's Derby broke my heart, but I didn't show it, did I?'

The shenanigans surrounding the triangle of Chaplin, Hastings and the Pocket Venus had scandalised society and outraged Queen Victoria, who was appalled that a scion of the aristocracy like Hastings should have been brought so low by horse racing. Given such goings-on, it is hardly surprising that the Queen should have disapproved of her son and successor becoming involved in the Turf.

But luckily for Ascot, her repeated admonitions fell on deaf ears.

Of all the horses that Bertie saw race at Ascot in the 1860s, the greatest was undoubtedly Gladiateur, the first French-bred Derby winner, who was dubbed 'The Avenger of Waterloo' after winning the 1865 Triple Crown. A notoriously unsound horse, Gladiateur faced just two opponents in the 1866 Gold Cup: Regalia, winner of the 1865 Oaks, and Henry Chaplin's Breadalbane, winner of the 1865 Prince of Wales's Stakes. This extraordinary contest has been graphically described by Richard Onslow in his book *Royal Ascot*:

> The short-sighted Harry Grimshaw, [Gladiateur's] regular jockey, was instructed to lie up with the other two until the Paddock bend, nurse him down the hill to put the minimum strain on the unsound leg, then kick on along the level ground on the run to Swinley Bottom. These instructions

Agreements for match races at Ascot in the late nineteenth century. **Left**: Lord Huntly's Lowlander against Lord Rosebery's Controversy for £1,000 on the Friday in 1876. **Above**: A match in 1881 between Lord Rosebery and the banker Leopold de Rothschild, who each nominate three horses. (Note that the forfeit for defecting from this match includes 'a hogshead of claret'.)

Gladiateur – 'The Avenger of Waterloo'.

Grimshaw elected to interpret in a singularly eccentric manner, so that Breadalbane had set up a lead of 20 lengths from Regalia, who was 10 lengths clear of Gladiateur as they passed the stands. Racing down the hill, Grimshaw rode the big horse so tenderly that he was tailed off, and by the time he reached Swinley Bottom he was actually 300 yards behind the other two. Then, with a little less than a mile to travel, Grimshaw gave Gladiateur his head. Those in the stands could hardly believe the evidence of their eyes, as the big, lanky bay went in hot pursuit of the pair so far ahead of him, in a manner that made a mockery of the old dictum that a good horse can give away weight, but not start. Almost before some people had realised that the uninteresting sight of a straggling procession of three was fast being transformed into a spectacle fraught with tension, Gladiateur had made up a furlong, and then, as he continued to devour the ground with his remorseless stride, the suspect leg totally impervious to the almost bone-hard going, he passed Breadalbane and ranged upsides of Regalia, who had nothing left with which to answer him. Having come from a seemingly impossible position so far behind her, Gladiateur reversed the picture, as it were, so it was she who was tailed off, and he galloped away to win by 40 lengths. Nobody had ever seen a horse win in quite such a magnificent manner. Regalia, a classic winner, had just been galloped into the ground, as she finished totally exhausted, her tongue hanging out like that of a tired dog. As for Breadalbane, he had completely given up the ghost and pulled himself up just after the turn into the straight.

Sydenham Dixon, who wrote for *The Sportsman* under the pseudonym 'The Vigilant', called it 'the most remarkable race I have ever seen, or ever expect to see … The style in which the great horse closed up the gap when he was at last allowed to stride along was simply incredible.'

Gladiateur is commemorated by a huge statue just inside the main gate of Longchamp racecourse in Paris, and his Gold Cup victory opened the gates to other French challengers for the Royal Meeting's principal race: within twelve years Mortemer (1871), Henry (1872), Boiard (1874) and Verneuil

(1878) had also taken the Gold Cup across the English Channel. (Verneuil performed the remarkable feat of winning three races at the meeting in 1878 – Gold Vase, Gold Cup, and Alexandra Plate.) In much the same way that the Hungarian football team's 6–3 victory at Wembley in 1953 destroyed notions of English football supremacy, so Gladiateur's exploits in the Classics, and particularly in the Gold Cup, jolted the idea that English-bred racehorses were pre-eminent.

The parade before the 1878 Gold Cup, with eventual winner Verneuil in front.

Richard Lawrence St Edmund Boyle, ninth Earl of Cork and Orrery, served as Master of the Buckhounds in 1866 and then from 1868 to 1874 and 1880 to 1885. In 1870, during the second of these stints, the Earl, who was also a director of the Great Western Railway, asked that company's telegraph superintendent Mr Spagnoletti to design an electrically driven telegraph board for use on Ascot racecourse. Operated from the weighing room and the judge's box, the major object of the Spagnoletti Board was to display the names of the riders before a race and the result after, and in that way 'cure the highly inconvenient practice indulged in by racegoers of flocking to the winning post in large numbers to ascertain the results and lingering thereafter round the grand stand gazing upon its occupants'.

The road to Ascot through Windsor Great Park on Gold Cup day 1871.

Another major course improvement at this time was the creation of a 'saddling paddock' at the western end of the stands, 'where the animals before starting can be carefully looked to by their trainers and owners, instead of, as heretofore, saddled anywhere on the course in the midst of the crowds'.

In 1873 Ascot witnessed for the first time a victory for the riding phenomenon who in his tragically curtailed career achieved enough to be recognised as the greatest jockey of the nineteenth century: Fred Archer. Born in Prestbury, Cheltenham, in 1857, Archer rode his first winner at the age of

Fred Archer, as depicted by 'Spy' in *Vanity Fair* in 1881.

The Sultan of Zanzibar at Ascot in 1875.

twelve, and his first Ascot winner came at the age of sixteen when Merodach won the 1873 Wokingham Stakes. In all 'The Tinman' – as he came to be nicknamed in recognition of his appreciation of the money his talents accrued to him – rode eighty winners at the course over fourteen years (though never the Gold Cup), including an astonishing twelve at the Royal Meeting in 1878, and ten in both 1881 and 1883. Champion jockey for thirteen consecutive seasons between 1874 and 1886, he rode twenty-one Classic winners but constantly fought a fierce battle against the scales, and in November 1886 his obsessive wasting brought on a bout of typhoid fever which triggered a fit of depression and delirium, in the throes of which he shot himself.

If Archer was the riding star of the 1870s, the equine hero at Ascot was Prince Charlie, winner of twenty-five of his twenty-nine races and probably the greatest sprinter of the nineteenth century. He won the All-Aged Stakes (later the Cork and Orrery) three years running from 1872 to 1874, the Fern Hill Stakes in 1872 and the Queen's Stand Stakes in 1873.

Along with restoring the Royal Procession, the Prince of Wales was enthusiastic about reviving the custom of taking visiting overseas potentates to Ascot, and among the spectators of Fred Archer's victory on Ladylove in an 1875 Triennial Stakes was the Sultan of Zanzibar. In 1877 there were two new faces in the royal party: the twelve-year-old George – the future George V – and his elder brother Prince Albert Victor. But missing that year was Admiral Rous, who had fallen seriously ill in London just before the start of the meeting and died on 20 June at the age of eighty-two. In his memory Ascot staged the inaugural running of the Rous Memorial Stakes in 1878 – won by Fred Archer on Petrarch.

New to the racing programme in 1879 was the Hardwicke Stakes, named after the 5th Earl of Hardwicke, Master of the Buckhounds from 1874 to 1880, who was afforded this glowing testimonial by Sir George Chetwynd, Jockey Club member and one of the big racehorse owners of the late nineteenth century:

Everybody connected with racing ought each year to feel grateful to Lord Hardwicke, who, when Master of the Buckhounds, added more money and created fresh races, to him alone being due the fact that Ascot is the best meeting in the world.

Hardwicke suffered serious injuries when his horse fell while out with the Buckhounds in March 1878 and subsequently had to resign his post. The Hardwicke Stakes was first run in his honour in 1879.

New races such as the Hardwicke were continually upgrading the standard of racing, but the Gold Cup remained the highlight of the meeting and continued to attract the best horses. Isonomy, trained by the legendary John Porter at Kingsclere, won the 1878 Cambridgeshire (his only race that season) and on the opening day of the 1879 Ascot meeting beat the 1877 Derby winner Silvio in the Queen's Vase, then two days later was out again to win the Gold Cup, beating Insulaire by two lengths. Isonomy went on to win the Goodwood Cup and Doncaster Cup, and thus the 'Stayers' Triple Crown', as well as the Brighton Cup and Ebor Handicap. In 1880 Isonomy returned to Ascot to beat Chippendale

The Earl of Hardwicke, Master of the Buckhounds 1874–80.

Isonomy wins the 1880 Gold Cup from Chippendale and Zut.

William Powell Frith,
The Road to Ruin:
No. 2, Ascot, 1879.

by a length and become the seventh dual Gold Cup winner.

The 1881 meeting witnessed some remarkable antics from a horse named Peter, owned by the indefatigably affable Sir John Astley, whose own accounts can never be improved upon:

As there were only some rips in the Queen's Vase on the Tuesday, I thought Peter might canter with them, and place that piece of plate on my sideboard. But there must be two to any bargain, and Peter didn't fall in with my views, for when he got to the stable turn he pulled up and began kicking, and eventually returned to the paddock. That looked bad for the Hunt Cup on the morrow; but, notwithstanding his foolish pranks on Wednesday morning, I found he was first favourite, and I had to take 5 to 1.

I warned Archer, when about to mount, to treat him kindly, and, if he felt like stopping, to pat his neck and coax him. I also sent 'Farmer' Giles [another jockey] on my cob down to the post with a hunting-whip, being afraid that Peter might turn back and try what the iron gates were made of, at the start of the new mile. All who were there, know what a wonderful animal Peter proved himself that day. Soon after he started he began to scotch, and was on the point of stopping to kick, as he had done the day before; but Archer patted him (according to my orders) and though at the half-mile he was a long way last, he suddenly took hold of his bit, and, coming up hand over hand, he won quite cleverly, and that with 9 st. 3 lbs. on his back. When Giles returned on my cob he could not believe it possible the horse had won; for he declared he was so far behind at the half-mile post when he went over the hill, that he felt certain he would be last at the finish. However, he realised the fact when I gave him a 'pony' [£25]; and he bought a black pony with it, which he afterwards rode constantly at Newmarket.

On the Friday, Peter looked good (if in the humour) for the

Hardwicke Stakes, worth over three thousand, and here Archer's wonderful forethought came in useful. Before the races began he said to me: 'I have been thinking over this race, Sir John. You know the start for the mile and a half we run to-day is just below the spot where Peter stopped to kick on Tuesday, and it is very likely, if I canter up past it with the other horses, he may take it into his head to repeat his Tuesday's performance. If you will get leave from the stewards, I will hack canter him round the reverse way of the course, and arrive at the starting-post just as the other horses fall in; by so doing, he may jump off and go kindly.'

'A brilliant idea, my lad,' said I, and Peter was seen to emerge from the paddock some minutes before the other horses. Luckily, they were off at the first attempt, and he literally walked in, eight lengths ahead. I didn't bet till I saw Peter was fairly off, but was fortunate to have two good bookies, hungry to get back some of the Hunt Cup money I had won of them, and so I landed some £1,500 at evens.

The same year Fred Archer won both the Prince of Wales's Stakes and the St James's Palace Stakes on Iroquois – who two weeks earlier had become the first American-bred winner of the Derby – and a Biennial on Voluptuary. Bred by Queen Victoria (who although she would not attend race meetings continued to maintain the royal bloodstock breeding at Hampton Court), Voluptuary went on in 1884 to achieve the highly unusual feat for an Ascot winner of landing the Grand National. (The same year The Scot, owned by the Prince of Wales, was the first royally owned runner in the National: he fell at the Canal Turn second time round.) After his unorthodox racing programme was over, Voluptuary had an equally unorthodox second career: he became an equine actor at the Theatre Royal, Drury Lane, carrying his new owner over a stage water jump in a play named *The Prodigal Maid*.

Several other notable horses raced at Ascot in this period. Bend Or won the 1880 St James's Palace Stakes soon after beating Robert The Devil in a furious finish for the Derby (when his jockey Fred Archer rode with one arm out of action after being savaged by a horse): at Ascot he was ridden by George Fordham. Robert The Devil himself, who had won the 1880 St Leger, landed the the Gold Cup and the Alexandra Plate in 1881. Foxhall, winner in

William Manning, Clerk of the Scales from 1875 to 1919.

Robert The Devil, winner of the Gold Cup and Alexandra Plate in 1881, with Tom Cannon up. Note the double bridle – common with racehorses in the nineteenth century but unheard of in modern racing.

1881 of both Cambridgeshire and Cesarewitch at Newmarket (an unusual but not unique double), won the Gold Cup in 1882. And in 1883 the unbeaten Barcaldine won the Orange Cup over the Old Mile, with the £600 gold cup donated by the King of the Netherlands.

But the two greatest Ascot heroes of the 1880s have to be St Simon and Ormonde.

Trained by Mathew Dawson – the fabled trainer who between 1853 and 1895 trained twenty-eight Classic winners – and bought by the Duke of Portland as a yearling for 1,600 guineas, St Simon was a legend of the Turf by the time he lined up for the 1884 Gold Cup, despite the fact that he had not run in any Classic: all his entries had become void on the death of his first owner Prince Batthyany. As a two-year-old he won his first race by six lengths and ended the season with a tally of five out of five. In the Gold Cup he faced four other runners: Tristan (winner the previous year, and a horse St Simon had slammed in a trial race at Newmarket earlier in 1884), Faugh-a-Ballagh (not the 1844 St Leger winner), Friday, and the Duke of Portland's other runner Iambic. St Simon's regular jockey Fred Archer could not do the weight, and the ride went to Charlie Wood. According to one witness, 'St Simon came with such an easy swing up to the leaders that when the line for home was fairly reached, he was fairly treading on the heels of Tristan. From this point the race was virtually over, as St Simon in his own inimitable style strode gaily to the front, and won easily by twenty lengths.'

A measure of the form of this Gold Cup is that Tristan reappeared at Ascot the following day and won the Hardwicke Stakes (for the third year in a row), beating Harvester, who had dead-heated for the Derby.

Although comparisons may be odious, Richard Onslow, doyen of Turf historians, cannot be far off the mark when he observes that St Simon was 'arguably the greatest of all Gold Cup winners'. But greatness is not everything, and many of those close to St Simon found his temperament

The Prince and Princess of Wales arrive at the course on Gold Cup day 1882, as depicted in an engraving in *The Graphic*, whose reporter noted that the royal couple arrived 'amid the acclamations of the public, who are never tired of looking at the procession, which, indeed, forms one of the chief attractions of the Ascot Week.'

almost impossible to cope with. His lad Charlie Fordham remarked with feeling: 'Talk about the patience of Job! Job never did no St Simon!' And spare a thought for the cat that was put into St Simon's stable in an effort to calm him down: he picked up the unfortunate feline in his teeth, hurled it against the ceiling of his box and killed it. It is little consolation to the cat to note that St Simon went on to become one of the greatest sires of all time.

The Duke of Westminster's Ormonde, a son of Bend Or trained by John Porter, first ran at Ascot as a three-year-old in 1886. Ridden by Fred Archer at what would be his last Royal Meeting, Ormonde lined up for the St James's Palace Stakes already the winner of that year's Two Thousand Guineas and Derby, and he won the Ascot race without undue difficulty. At the same meeting Ormonde won the Hardwicke Stakes, but for that race Archer was claimed by trainer Mat Dawson to ride the previous year's Derby winner Melton. George Barrett rode Ormonde to beat Melton by two lengths, though Archer was back in the saddle when Ormonde won the St Leger – and thus the Triple Crown.

Scenes from St Simon's Gold Cup victory in 1884.

Queen Victoria celebrated fifty years on the throne in 1887, but not even the Golden Jubilee would persuade her back to Ascot. In the continuing absence of the monarch, the horses remained a prime attraction – though racegoers also had the newly opened tunnel between the grandstand and the Paddock to marvel at – and a massive crowd gathered on the Thursday to witness the seasonal reappearance of the greatest horse in the land: Ormonde, running not in the Gold Cup but the Rous Memorial Stakes. With Fred Archer departed, the ride on Ormonde went to another of the great jockeys of the age, Tom Cannon, who had what today's riders would call a 'steering job' in getting Ormonde home by six lengths from Kilwarlin – who went on to win that year's St Leger – despite conceding him twenty-five pounds.

'Ascot Races – Horses passing the Royal Box on their way to the starting post', engraving in *The Graphic* in 1887.

Ormonde had started at odds of 4–1 on for that stroll on the Heath, and his price of 5–4 on for the following day's Hardwicke Stakes suggested a much more arduous task. His three rivals were Minting (7–4), favourite for the previous year's Two Thousand Guineas and a top-class horse, Bendigo (100–8), winner of the inaugural Eclipse Stakes the previous year, and Phil (100–7) – who although the outsider of the quartet was ridden by George Barrett, still smarting at not having come in for the Ormonde ride himself. *The Times* told the story of the race:

At the first attempt Minting shot to the front and showed the way to Ormonde, who, in turn, was clear of Phil on the outside, with Bendigo lying at the latter's quarters. On settling down Minting slightly increased his lead and went down the hill clear of Ormonde, who was still in front of Phil. With little alteration they raced through the bottom, but as they passed the brick kilns the pace materially improved. Minting was now striding along with a length and a half lead of Ormonde, at whose heels lay Phil, while Bendigo, who was pulling hard, was still last. Rounding the bend closer order was taken, and as they entered the line for home the pace told its tale on Phil, who was here beaten, and Minting, on the rails, came into the straight attended by Bendigo, who here deprived Ormonde of second place, but the latter, on the outside, directly afterwards drew up to Mr Barclay's horse's [Bendigo's] quarters. For a few strides Bendigo flattered his supporters, but at the distance he faltered and again resigned second place to Ormonde, who drew alongside Minting, the pair coming on almost locked together, until 50 yards from home, where Minting got in front, but Ormonde, answering gamely to Tom Cannon's call, again drew level, and, getting the best of a magnificent finish, won by a neck, amid great excitement. Bendigo was third, three lengths behind, and Phil last.

Ecstatic at this heroic victory – Ormonde had gone in his wind – the Duke of Westminster could not bear to be parted from his great horse, himself leading Ormonde twice round the paddock and halfway back to the stables before handing him back to the care of his stable lad.

The 1890 meeting saw the first running of the Coventry Stakes for two-year-olds – named after George, 9th Earl of Coventry, who had become Master of the Buckhounds in 1886 – but the Prince of Wales was still without a winner in his own colours, a fact he lamented when recording the defeat of his horse The Imp:

> Alas! The Imp was beaten – but it is sure to win a Race on a future occasion – as there are such good horses running at Ascot that it is not easy to win.

Class distinction on Gold Cup day 1889.

Such realism was rewarded in 1891, when The Imp, ridden by George Barrett, won the High Weight Plate over a mile and a quarter to give Bertie his first Ascot victory.

The 1894 Gold Cup went to the great mare La Flèche. Purchased by Baron de Hirsch at the Hampton Court Yearling sale for the then astronomical sum of 5,500 guineas, she soon proved a bargain. In 1892 she won the Fillies' Triple Crown of the One Thousand Guineas, the Oaks and the St Leger, as well as the Cambridgeshire. Standing at 15 hands 3 inches, Flèche was hardly an imposing individual and she rarely carried much condition. But handsome is as handsome does, and the more ragged and thin she looked, the better she would run. In the Gold Cup she beat Callistrate by three lengths, but she had had a harder race than appeared the case in the immediate aftermath, and the following day was beaten half a length in the Hardwicke Stakes. She did, however, go on to win the 1894 Champion Stakes.

Another triple Classic winner landed the Gold Cup in 1895: Isinglass, who had won the Two Thousand Guineas, the Derby and the St Leger in 1893 and the Eclipse Stakes in 1894, and now became the third Triple Crown winner to take the Ascot showpiece, following West Australian and Gladiateur. He started at 11–2 on in a field of three and won as he liked.

The following year the Ascot skyline underwent a dramatic alteration with the erection of the clock tower over the grandstand – described by *Racing Illustrated* as 'very handsome'. The tower was some forty-five feet high, built of white bricks with Bath stone dressings and supported from the main walls on steel girders, and the turret was surmounted by a weathervane depicting a horse and jockey, while the clock itself was made and fixed by Messrs Joyce and Son of Whitchurch, Shropshire, and 'admitted to be a very superior and highly finished piece of mechanism'.

Queen Victoria celebrated her Diamond Jubilee – sixty years on the throne – in 1897 at the age of seventy-eight, and what was always going to be a special Ascot turned out to be one of the very best.

Centre of attention was the Prince of Wales's great colt Persimmon, who had won the Derby and the St Leger the previous year and was now going not just for the Gold Cup, but for a very timely royal victory: if the Queen herself was not in a position to win the showpiece of the Royal Meeting, who better than her son?

Persimmon, who had been bred by the Prince and was trained by Richard Marsh, had made his mark on Ascot two years earlier when easily winning the

The home turn in the three-runner Gold Cup in 1895: Kilsallaghan (third) leads from the winner Isinglass and runner-up Reminder.

Persimmon, ridden by
Jack Watts.

Coventry Stakes, and now returned to the course as a four-year-old without a previous outing that season. The colt's work at home made owner and trainer brimful of confidence, and shortly before the race the Prince's racing manager Lord Marcus Beresford wrote to Marsh informing him that if he thought Persimmon was sure to win the Gold Cup, Queen Victoria might come to see the race. Marsh replied that he thought Lord Marcus 'might safely invite Queen Victoria to see the race and Persimmon win it!' – but in the event Victoria did not attend.

The Prince and Princess of Wales did, though, and with them – in glorious sunshine the whole week – came a panoply of foreign dignitaries, including the Duke of Saxe-Coburg, Prince Albert of Schleswig-Holstein and the Crown Prince of Denmark.

Persimmon instantly caught the eye on entering the paddock, where he was mounted by jockey Jack Watts. The trainer George Lambton, in his famous memoir *Men and Horses I Have Known,* wrote:

> When Persimmon was stripped for the Ascot Cup he stands out in my memory as the most perfectly trained horse I ever saw, and on that day he could have given my two heroes, St Simon and Ormonde, as much as they could do to beat him.

Persimmon's rivals included the 1896 winner Love Wisely and Winkfield's Pride, a good Irish handicapper hotly fancied by connections to turn over the royal colt. 'Even his most enthusiastic admirers scarcely expected that he would treat them as though they had been a field of selling-platers,' wrote Sydenham Dixon – and *The Times* takes up the story:

> Persimmon, like Gladiateur in 1866, lay last for the greater part of the way, only coming to the front at the last turn. Directly, however, his jockey sent him going he won his race in a few strides, and sailed home the easiest of winners by eight lengths from Winkfield's Pride, who could make no sort of impression on him.

It was a great performance and if Persimmon had belonged to the humblest of racehorse owners he would have been loudly cheered as he passed the post, so that it was easy to understand the enthusiasm which his victory in the Prince of Wales's handsome colours evoked. The demonstration was, in its way, as remarkable for its spontaneity and its warmth as that which attended his Epsom triumph, for the whole of the vast multitude turned, as with one accord, to the Royal Enclosure, cheering, for several minutes. The Prince came forward to acknowledge the compliment, and the cheering was continued until Persimmon had been led back to scale and his jockey duly weighed in.

The royal colours worn by Jack Watts on that great occasion had evolved gradually over the years. Purple and black had been the chosen colours of the Duke of Cumberland back in the mid-eighteenth century. George IV had never seemed to settle on colours, and changed his regularly: in 1783 they were recorded as crimson and purple, which by 1827 had shifted to 'crimson body, gold lace, purple sleeves and black cap' – very close to the royal colours with which we are familiar today. It was Queen Victoria who introduced velvet as the material for the headgear, and her son the Prince of Wales who added the 'gold fringe'. (Bertie's first success under Jockey Club Rules in his own colours had come when Counterpane won at Sandown Park in 1886.)

When the heat of battle had died down the Duke of Portland wrote that 'Persimmon when he won the Ascot Gold Cup as a four-year-old was the most splendid specimen of a thoroughbred horse I ever saw … I was intensely proud of him as a son of St Simon.' Persimmon went to stand at Sandringham Stud and he became sire of many good horses, notably the extraordinary mare Sceptre (of whom more shortly). He was the last horse to have won the Derby at Epsom and the Gold Cup at Ascot, completing a distinguished line of ten that had started with The Flying Dutchman in 1850 and continued with Teddington (1853), West Australian (1854), Thormanby (1861), Gladiateur (1866), Blue Gown (1868), Cremorne (1873), Doncaster (1875) and St Gatien (1885).

But one unsatisfactory aspect of Ascot in the late nineteenth century was the state of the going. Trainer Richard Marsh described the ground when Persimmon won as 'in fact like nothing so much as a macadamised road, for in those days I am sure it was not given half the attention that was bestowed on it in later years'. Eleven years later the racing writer A. E. T. Watson mentioned that 'scarcely a year passes in which some animals do not permanently injure themselves by running here', and *The Times* demanded that the course be watered and kept free of people, adding scathingly of the Ascot management that 'If they do not realise how easily this might be done, they have only to send their manager over to France, where he would soon learn how simple a matter it is.'

That need to keep the course free of people was a sensitive issue, for the 'promenade' had been a feature of Ascot for much of the nineteenth century. In 1823 *The Times* related how 'numbers of fashionable persons of both sexes promenaded up and down the course between the races attired in dresses of all hues and textures', and in the late 1830s 'Nimrod' – Charles Apperley – described how 'the charms of Ascot, to those not interested in the horses, consist in the promenade on the course between the various races, where the highest fashion, in its best garb, mingles with the crowd, and gives a brilliant effect to the passing scene'.

The promenade was obviously incompatible with providing the best possible racing surface, but the problem really lay in the soil. Ascot's turf was of poor quality, and beneath it was Bagshot Sands, sitting on top of London clay. In the 1890s, Lord Ribblesdale commented that 'The soil is sand and gravel; rain silts away through it like a filter … The course is regenerated common land, and the grass, especially the New Mile, is peevish haggard stuff and hardly honest.' Various methods were attempted to improve the turf. New seeds were sown every year, irrigation systems were tried out, various sorts of manure were applied, and sheep were allowed to graze on the course. Ribblesdale commented in 1897: 'No better illustration can be given of [the turf's] hostility to the best intentions than the fact that the sheep have been tried both on the course and on the lawns, but owing to the thinness of the turf and the dry and thirsty subsoil, they did so little good and stained the land so unbecomingly that much had to be re-turfed.'

In 1900 the 9th Earl of Coventry, Master of the Buckhounds before and after Ribblesdale, led a party of experts (including leading trainers Richard Marsh and John Porter) to consider the ground, and various measures were taken, including treating the grass with 'a top dressing consisting of good rotten stable manure or road scrapings and good loam or rotted turf' before sowing new seeds, and by 1906 improvements in the surface were being widely praised.

But the promenade along the course had to be sacrificed in the interests of the ground, and the fashion parade was gradually relocated to the paddock area. In 1912 *The Times* reported that 'The Paddock is Ascot's promenade, and most of the distinguished people in the Royal Enclosure were to be seen there in the intervals between the races.' As has occasionally happened in the history of Ascot, the interests of horses and the interests of the fashion parade did not always accord. General Owen Williams found his path blocked by a well-known actress's large red parasol. At that moment an excitable two-year-old passing by reared, causing the lady to leap back and stab the general in the cheek with the tip of her parasol. She exclaimed indignantly: 'It's perfectly scandalous that horses should be allowed in here!'

The 1899 Gold Cup was won by eight lengths by the brilliant Cyllene (who went on to sire four Derby winners), and the Coventry Stakes at the same meeting saw the racecourse debut of the Prince of Wales's Diamond Jubilee, a full brother to Persimmon foaled at Sandringham in Jubilee year. Given his breeding and his ownership, much was expected of the colt, and he started favourite for the Coventry despite his behaviour deteriorating throughout the preliminaries: he lashed out while being saddled and hit a bystander on the hand, and at the start tried to grab his jockey's boot with his teeth, then – having been disappointed in that – took to rearing and bucking. After such a mulish display Diamond Jubilee could finish only fourth in the Coventry Stakes and never ran again at Ascot, but he matured into a brilliant horse, winning the Triple Crown in 1900.

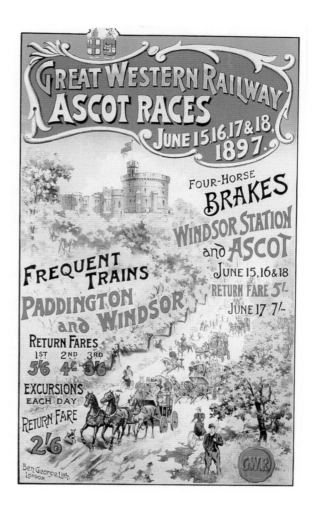

Great Western Railway poster, 1897. Half a century earlier the company had become the first commercial sponsor in racing history. In 1845 GWR gave £300 to the Ascot race fund, and the Great Western Stakes was inaugurated at the course in 1846. The prize money was reduced to £100 in 1852, and withdrawn altogether in 1856.

The Royal Enclosure in the late nineteenth century.

Winner of that Coventry Stakes was Democrat (in later life Lord Kitchener's ceremonial charger), partnered by the riding sensation of the time, the American jockey Tod Sloan – whose 'monkey-on-a-stick' style in the saddle revolutionised race-riding, and whose skill at controlling a race from the front gave rise to the rhyming slang 'on your tod'. Sloan rode three winners at Ascot in 1899 – his first visit to the course – but the same meeting landed Sloan in hot water. One evening after racing he was dining in the racecourse restaurant, having changed out of his riding gear into a white yachting suit with white braid and a peaked yachting cap, an outfit he later conceded was 'a curious get-up on Ascot Heath'. This is Sloan's own version of what happened:

There was only one waiter about. Two tables away from me there was a man sitting who kept on glaring at me and presently he called the waiter over and they had a loud whispered conversation, part of which, I got the idea, was to the effect that the man sitting down would give the waiter five shillings if he would upset the table and the champagne over me – and my suit! I could not make out then, nor have I been able to since, whether he was annoyed with me personally or that my 'costume' got up … Shortly, an accident did happen; our table was upset, and I caught the bottle before it had got to the ground. Having it in my right hand as the waiter lurched towards me I made a light jab at him with the neck of it, meaning just to give him a reminder.

The waiter's lip was cut, and the next day the papers were awash with the story that Sloan had been drunk and had 'heaved' the bottle at him. Advised by his friends to calm matters down with a fiver to the stricken waiter, Sloan obliged – only for a blood-stained £5 note to be returned to him later with a note to the effect that the waiter's silence would not be bought. The more the story was reported in the press, the more brutal became the attack by this upstart American on an innocent British worker just doing his job. Sloan's patron

Lord William Beresford tried to hush the story up by paying the waiter several hundred pounds, but still the story grew – to the extent that four years later Sloan overheard a policeman declaring:

> Wasn't I at Ascot when Sloan slung that magnum of champagne at the waiter and split his skull? Hot stuff, I tell you. Yes, that there Sloan is mustard. What he don't know isn't worth picking up, but he can ride – I'll give him his due. He's a fire eater, that there Sloan.

Whatever actually happened in the Ascot restaurant was never tested in court, but the incident did little to enhance Sloan's already controversial image in England. He was leading jockey at the Royal Meeting in 1900 with six winners, but in December that year the Jockey Club found against him following an investigation into his betting on the Cambridgeshire, and, in the words of the Club's official statement, 'informed him that he need not apply for a licence to ride' for the following year. Sloan was deported from England in 1915 for running an illegal gaming house, and died in the charity ward of a Los Angeles hospital in 1933.

Tom Cannon on the weighing chair – the forerunner of the weighing scales. Cannon rode the winners of seven Gold Cups, and has the unique distinction of having won four consecutive runnings of the race – on Isonomy in 1879 and 1880, Robert The Devil in 1881 and Foxhall in 1882. His other three Gold Cup winners were Blue Gown (1868), Petrarch (1877) and Althorp (1886).

The century turned with the eighty-year-old Victoria still on the throne, and the Prince of Wales's racing fortunes at their peak: in 1900 he won the Grand National with Ambush II and the Triple Crown with Diamond Jubilee – and although he did not enjoy a winner at the Royal Meeting, there was plenty of sport to watch. In 1900 Ascot had a programme of seven races a day, as opposed to the usual six: twenty-eight for the whole meeting. To show how far the Royal Meeting we know today had taken shape by 1900, it is instructive to list those twenty-eight races:

Tuesday

Trial Stakes [now the Queen Anne Stakes] over the New Mile (7 furlongs 166 yards): value £640.

Prince of Wales's Stakes over about 1 mile 5 furlongs: £2,100.

Coventry Stakes over the Two-year-old Course (5 furlongs 136 yards): £1,809

Ascot Stakes over 'about 2 miles': £1,655

43rd Biennial (first year, for two-year-olds) over the Two-year-old Course: £1,232

Gold Vase [now the Queen's Vase] over 2 miles: £620

46th Triennial (third year) – 'once round and in, starting opposite the Grand Stand' [about 1 mile 6 furlongs]: £658

Wednesday

Visitors' Handicap over the Swinley Course (1½ miles): £435

42nd Biennial (second year, for three-year-olds) over the Old Mile: £1,196

Royal Hunt Cup over the New Mile: £2,490

Fern Hill Stakes over 5 furlongs 136 yards: £620

Coronation Stakes for three-year-old fillies over the Old Mile: £2,750

48th Triennial (first year, for two-year-olds) over the Two-year-old Course: £759 10s

Ascot Derby [now the King Edward VII Stakes] over the Swinley Course: £1,750

Thursday

37th New Biennial (second year, for three-year-olds) over the Old Mile: £1,060

St James's Palace Stakes for three-year-olds over the Old Mile: £2,000

Gold Cup 'to start at the Cup Post and go once round' [about 2½ miles]: £3,360

New Stakes [now the Norfolk Stakes] over the Two-year-old Course: £1,928

Rous Memorial Stakes over the New Mile: £970

All-Aged Stakes [later the Cork and Orrery Stakes] over 6 furlongs: £355

38th New Biennial (first year, for two-year-olds) over the Two-year-old Course: £880

Friday

Ascot High Weight Stakes over 1¼ miles: £565

Windsor Castle Stakes for two-year-olds over the Two-year-old Course: £732

Queen's Stand Stakes [now the King's Stand Stakes] over the Two-year old Course: £930

Wokingham Stakes over 'the last three-quarters of the New Mile': £865

Hardwicke Stakes over the Swinley Course: £2,421

Alexandra Plate [now the Queen Alexandra Stakes] 'to start at the New Mile Post and go once round (about three miles)': £1,480

47th Triennial (second year, for three-year-olds) over the New Mile: £770

Of those twenty-eight races in 1900, no fewer than sixteen were won by American jockeys: Tod Sloan 6; Lester Reiff 4; Johnny Reiff 3; Skeets Martin 3.

Sloan's principal Ascot success that year was in the Gold Cup on Merman, owned by a 'Mr Jersey', *nom de course* of the actress and celebrated beauty Lillie Langtry – 'The Jersey Lily' who in the late 1870s had been Bertie's mistress; by the time Merman won at Ascot she was Lady de Bathe (having married Sir Hugo de Bathe in 1899). Although overshadowed in fame by his owner, Merman must have been quite a horse: he had won the Caulfield Cup in Australia, and was an eight-year-old when landing the Gold Cup.

During the latter part of 1900 Queen Victoria's health was steadily declining, and by early January she was clearly dying. On 21 January her eldest son travelled from London to Osborne, her home on the Isle of Wight. On seeing him the bedridden Queen flung out her arms and exclaimed 'Bertie!', and he broke down after embracing her.

Victoria died at 6.30 p.m. on 22 January 1901, having reigned for over sixty-three years. The same evening Bertie's private secretary Sir Francis Knollys wrote to the Prince's friend, the Duke of Devonshire: 'He desires me to say that he would propose to call himself Edward 7th.'

EDWARDIAN ASCOT

'Black Ascot': the first Royal Meeting of the Edwardian Age reflected the mood not just of the Court – still in the official period of mourning – but of the country at large following the death of Victoria.

In 1901 racing took place in a sombre atmosphere. The Royal Stand was closed entirely, but in order not to cause disappointment to those who usually received Royal Enclosure tickets, the new King commanded that only a portion of the lawn immediately in front of the stand should be railed off. Dressing in black, 'or some hue almost as sober', was *de rigueur,* and the racecard sported a black border. On the Wednesday *The Times* reported there was 'scarcely a touch of colour' but on Gold Cup day 'a number of ladies who were in black on the first two days had assumed a more modified form of mourning, as there were many dresses of white, lavender and mauve, although not enough to impart any colour to the scene'.

The new monarch himself was absent, not because the Court was in mourning but on account of illness. The previous weekend he had started feeling violent pains in his stomach while at Aldershot to review the troops, and on the Monday – the eve of Ascot – he was back at Windsor but very feverish. By the opening day of the race meeting the worst seemed to have passed, and Queen Alexandra went to provide a royal presence at the racecourse, returning on Gold Cup day. But the following weekend the King's condition worsened, and his coronation – scheduled for less than a fortnight later – was postponed. Edward was operated on for appendicitis – and made a rapid recovery. (Despite his absence from the course, the King did in fact have a winner at the 1901 meeting: Lauzan, who won the St

James's Palace Stakes in the straw colours of Edward's friend the Duke of Devonshire.)

In the early years of the reign of Edward VII there were changes afoot at Ascot. In 1901 the Royal Buckhounds were disbanded, and hence there was no Master of the Buckhounds to be responsible for control of the meeting. So a new position was created to fulfil that role: the King's Representative. The first man to act as the sovereign's representative was Viscount Churchill, who had served as a Page of Honour under Victoria and took his new function at Ascot very seriously. He is reputed to have taken personal charge of vetting applications for entrance into the Royal Enclosure, sorting the letters into three baskets, marked 'Certainly', 'Perhaps' and 'Certainly Not'.

More visible to the Ascot racegoer were new stands. The old stands were reported as having become 'an eyesore to King Edward', who involved himself closely in designs for replacements and the effect these would have on the layout of the course itself. In August 1901 a letter from Lord Churchill mentioned that 'His Majesty has decided to have the bend of the course altered.' Churchill then requested the King's approval of the new plan to place all of the new stands at an angle rather than just the new Royal Enclosure Stand, 'in view of its being of such great advantage ever after', and added: 'Please point out to His Majesty that I am bearing in mind the absolute necessity of not spoiling the view from the Iron and Grand Stands – as I think it would be extremely unfair for us to do anything in the Enclosure which would deteriorate the value of their property.'

All three stands in the Royal Enclosure were demolished in August 1901, as were the old police barracks and the stabling for the royal carriages and horses. In effect, everything to the west of the grandstand enclosure was removed, with the exception of the Metropolitan Police office and the post office.

The scheme was given royal approval, and work on the foundations began in early September 1901, with the contractors Messrs John Allen & Sons of Kilburn to be paid £28,350 for two stands and the weighing room, with a further bonus of £7,950 provided the whole of the work was completed by 1 May 1902. John Allen was paid a further £27,636 for the third stand and the Otis Elevator Co. received £5,740 for the lifts – the first time such devices had been installed on a British racecourse. In order to have the work

Previous pages: The Royal Meeting, 1904.

completed by May 1902, some five hundred men were employed on the task, working day and night shifts. It was impossible to accommodate all the workmen at Ascot, so a special train was run twice daily from Reading. By April 1902 the work was almost complete.

The three new stands were, running from east to west: the Jockey Club Stand, the Royal Stand and the Royal Enclosure Stand, all set at an angle to the course to give a better view of the racing. The Jockey Club Stand had a frontage of fifty-seven feet and was designed along the same lines as its more elaborate neighbour, the Royal Stand: there were separate entrances for members and visitors, and it included Otis elevators. The Royal Stand or 'Pavilion' was erected on the site of the old Royal Stand and part of the old Master of the Buckhounds Stand, and had a frontage seventy feet long and a height of forty feet. The Royal Enclosure Stand to the west of the Royal Stand was the largest of the three at 148 feet long, with capacity for 2,000 people: the ground floor contained cloakrooms, the first floor luncheon rooms, and at the top there were tiered terraces facing the course. At its east end were rooms for the Lord Chamberlain and the Clerk of the Course, each with its own luncheon room and a balcony above. At its west end was the owners' stand on the principal level, with a stand for trainers and jockeys in the middle and the press at the top. Behind the stands a new weighing room was built with facilities for the racing professionals, including the jockeys' dressing room and rooms for the Clerk of the Course and the Clerk of the Scales. This building remains, having been cut in half during the 1960s redevelopments.

Of particular interest in the history of the buildings at Ascot is the 'Five Shilling Stand' – later the Silver Ring Stand. This was constructed in 1908 at a cost of £30,000 on the instructions of the King, as was acknowledged by a report in *The Star* in January 1915, nearly five years after Edward's death:

> The public owe its existence entirely to the kindness of our late Sovereign King Edward. His Majesty always thought that not quite enough was done for the comfort of the ordinary public at Ascot.

The Ascot Authority Act 1913 recorded that the Five Shilling Stand had been built because 'it would be for the benefit of Ascot Races that a new stand at lower prices of admission should be provided for the accommodation of the public at Ascot Races', and the *Sporting Life* acclaimed the stand as a sign of 'progressive Ascot'. Over the next few years various additions were made, including the relocating of the bandstand on the lawn, 'away from the noisy asphalt where the movement of thousands of hurried footsteps drowned out the band', according to the *Windsor and Eton Express*. Further alterations to the stand itself in 1913 gave 'a most perfect view of the races'.

All the new stands were enthusiastically received: *The Gentlewoman* was particularly taken with the replacing of the old Royal Stand with 'the present stately structure with its beautiful spacious balcony', while *Horse and Hound*

William The Third (ridden by Morny Cannon) being led in after winning the 1902 Gold Cup.

declared the new buildings 'excellent, and put at an angle which enables one to see all the races perfectly'. And in 1903 *The Times* wrote:

> Everywhere are to be seen signs of a desire to move with the times, and to make Ascot as attractive socially as it is interesting from the racing point of view.

Certainly there could be no complaints about Ascot being 'interesting from the racing point of view' in the first decade of the twentieth century, for this period brought to the course some of the greatest names the Turf has known.

In 1902 the star was the redoubtable filly Sceptre. By the time of her first appearance at Ascot on 18 June she was already well on the way to iconic status, and by the end of that year she had become the only horse in history to win four Classics outright. By Persimmon out of a full sister to Ormonde – two great horses who had already written their names large in the history of Ascot – Sceptre had been bred by the 1st Duke of Westminster, and on his death in 1899 was sold at public auction as a foal to Robert Sievier, a notorious gambler. As a two-year-old she won two races (including the July Stakes at Newmarket) before running third in the Champagne Stakes at Doncaster. Her Classic potential was apparent, but when her trainer Charles Morton was appointed private trainer to J. B. Joel at the end of 1901, Sievier decided to train Sceptre himself. Before preparing her for the Classics he thought he'd have a tilt at the Lincoln Handicap in March, but his hopes of pulling off a hefty touch with what must have been the highest-class horse ever to run in that handicap came to nothing: overtrained by Sievier's assistant, Sceptre finished second, beaten a head by St Maclou.

She then won the Two Thousand Guineas in record time, and the One Thousand Guineas two days later (despite losing a shoe at the start). She started at even money for the Derby but could finish only fourth behind Ard Patrick, then had a day off before reappearing to win the Oaks. Next stop Longchamp for the Grand Prix de Paris, in which she was beaten, and then, just three days later and after an arduous return by train and boat, Ascot.

Her first race at the Royal Meeting was the Coronation Stakes. At the starting post she worked herself up into a state and threw jockey Herbert Randall into a blackberry bush, and when the race got under way she was left

Sceptre (ridden by Frank Hardy) after winning the St James's Palace Stakes in 1902.

so far that some spectators thought she must have broken down. Sceptre managed to get back into the race, but the weight she was conceding to her rivals proved too much, and she finished unplaced.

Randall had come in for criticism after some of Sceptre's earlier races – notably the Derby, where he had ridden the filly too hard to make up ground in the early, uphill part of the race – and for Sievier his being dumped in a blackberry bush was the last straw. So it was the apprentice Frank Hardy who got the leg-up when she reappeared the following day for the St James's Palace Stakes, which she won easily.

But Sceptre was not the only top-notch horse on view at the 1902 meeting. The Prince of Wales's Stakes went to the Derby winner Ard Patrick, but only after an objection to first-past-the-post Cupbearer for interference. It then transpired that Ard Patrick had strained a tendon in the race, and he was confined to walking exercise for a long period, thereby missing the St Leger. And the 1902 Coventry Stakes was won by Rock Sand, who the following year would win the Triple Crown.

Sceptre was back at Ascot in 1903. The great filly's extraordinary achievements in 1902 had done no more than temporarily alleviate Sievier's chronic money troubles, and after another abortive attempt at the Lincoln Handicap he had sold her for £25,000 to William Bass, who sent her to be trained at Manton by Alec Taylor. At the 1903 Royal Meeting she won the Hardwicke Stakes before going on to Sandown Park for the famous Eclipse Stakes duel with Ard Patrick (which she lost by a neck).

Rock Sand (who would run third in that Eclipse) was back at Ascot too, in the wake of his Derby victory, to win the 1903 St James's Palace Stakes at 100–7 on, and the same year the Coventry Stakes went to St Amant, who would go on to win the Two Thousand Guineas and the Derby in 1904. But perhaps the most memorable Ascot race that year was the Prince of Wales's Stakes won by Mead, owned by Edward VII himself and ridden by Herbert Jones (who ten years later would achieve permanent fame as the rider of Anmer, King George V's horse brought down in the Derby by the suffragette

Emily Davison). Mead's victory was the first at Ascot in the royal colours since Edward had acceded to the throne, and was rapturously received: the journalist J. B. Booth recalled how a respectful rendition of 'God Save The King' by a loyal group in the Royal Enclosure was drowned out by the Tattersalls' men, who in no time had the stands and enclosures united in a less stately 'For He's A Jolly Good Fellow'.

For all the emotion of such rousing royal successes, there can be little doubt that the very finest horse to run in this period at Ascot was the filly who made her first appearance at the Royal Meeting in 1904: Pretty Polly.

Bred in Ireland and foaled near The Curragh at the stud of her breeder Major Eustace Loder, she was sent into training with Peter Purcell Gilpin at Newmarket, and astonished connections by winning her first race as a two-year-old at Sandown Park by ten lengths. She went through her juvenile career unbeaten in nine races and made her three-year-old début when winning the One Thousand Guineas at 4–1 on, going on to land the Oaks in a canter at 100–8 on (the shortest price ever returned in an English Classic).

So she came to Ascot for the Coronation Stakes with a tally of eleven wins from eleven races, cloaked in the aura of equine invincibility and wildly popular with the racing public. She coasted home by three lengths at 5–1 on.

Pretty Polly and Sceptre – two outstandingly brilliant fillies foaled within two years of each other – never met in a race, but the latter also ran at Ascot in 1904, her third successive year at the meeting. She had won the Champion Stakes and the Jockey Club Stakes (beating Rock Sand) at Newmarket the previous autumn but now, at the age of five, it seemed that her gruelling programme was taking its toll. She had been beaten in the Coronation Cup at Epsom, and in the Gold Cup – in which she was ridden by Otto Madden – had to give best to Throwaway, ridden by Billy Lane. Sceptre then came out for the Hardwicke Stakes on the Friday and was beaten again, finishing third behind Rock Sand. Word was that she had become a very finicky feeder by this time, and the announcement that the Hardwicke had been her last race came as no surprise.

Sceptre might have been defeated, but her presence in the Gold Cup field that year ensured her a special place not only in sporting but in literary history, as 16 June 1904 was to become immortalised as 'Bloomsday', the single day on which the action of James Joyce's novel *Ulysses* (published in 1922) is set. Otto

Madden's approximate namesake O'Madden Burke and his friends Lenehan and Phyllis have backed Sceptre:

> Madden had lost five drachmas on Sceptre for a whim of the rider's name: Lenehan as much more. He told them of the race. The flag fell and, huuh, off, scamper, the mare ran out freshly with O. Madden up. She was leading the field: all hearts were beating. Even Phyllis could not contain herself. She waved her scarf and cried: Huzzah! Sceptre wins! But in the straight on the run home when all were in close order the dark horse Throwaway drew level, reached, outstripped her. All was lost now. Phyllis was silent: her eyes were sad anemones. Juno, she cried, I am undone. But her lover consoled her and brought her a bright casket of gold in which lay some oval sugarplums which she partook. A tear fell: one only. A whacking fine whip, said Lenehan, is W. Lane. Four winners yesterday and three today. What rider is like him? Mount him on the camel or the boisterous buffalo the victory in a hack canter is still his. But let us bear it as was the ancient wont. Mercy on the luckless! Poor Sceptre! he said with a light sigh. She is not the filly that she was. Never, by this hand, shall we behold another.

Two years after Throwaway's victory, 1906 produced one of the most famous Gold Cups of all.

Since winning the Coronation Stakes on her first Ascot appearance two years earlier, Pretty Polly had established herself as one of the all-time greats. She had gone on from Ascot to win the Nassau Stakes at Goodwood, the St Leger (thus taking the 'Fillies' Triple Crown') and the Park Hill Stakes, then met her first defeat in sixteen races when beaten by 66–1 outsider Presto II in the Prix du Conseil at Longchamp. Her jockey that day was the American rider Danny Maher, who was to be champion jockey in 1908 and 1913 and who was not convinced of Pretty Polly's stamina. But she ended her three-year-old career on a winning note in the Free Handicap, and went through her four-year-old season unbeaten, winning all her four races including the Coronation Cup, the Champion Stakes and the Jockey Club Cup (in which she beat Bachelor's Button, ridden by Maher, by half a length); her other victory that year was against a solitary opponent in the Limekiln

Stakes at Newmarket, for which Pretty Polly started at 55–1 on. Kept in training at five, she won at Newmarket at 1000–35 on, then took the Coronation Cup for the second year running.

Pretty Polly was now more than a great racehorse: she was a national heroine, and the crowds who packed Ascot on 21 June 1906 pressed to catch a glimpse of her before the race. Many who succeeded did not much like what they saw, for she was clearly not at her best – agitated and sweating, she fretted her way around the paddock area. It was well known that Pretty Polly had been suffering from the effects of a suppurating wart on her belly, which would have gone some way to explaining her present state, but none the less those who put their money where their hearts were and sent her off 11–4 on favourite cannot have done so without the odd flutter of trepidation.

She faced four rivals. Bachelor's Button was owned by Solly Joel and trained by Charles Peck, and while apparently not in the same league as Pretty Polly had won the Champion Stakes in 1904 and the Hardwicke Stakes and the Doncaster Cup in 1905; on his most recent outing he had won the Manchester Cup under nine stone, and he started 7–1 joint second favourite at Ascot with the 1905 Derby winner Cicero (who had won the Coventry Stakes in 1904 to give that Ascot race three future Derby winners in a row).

Edwardian Ascot from the centre of the course.

Three-year-old Achilles was a 40–1 chance, and the field was completed by St Denis, whose odds of 500–1 reflected his role as Bachelor's Button's pacemaker – though he was a good horse in his own right, having run third in the 1904 Derby, and the same year winning the Princess of Wales's Stakes.

The presence of St Denis as pacemaker provided a clue to the tactics being planned to overturn the great mare, for Bachelor's Button was being ridden by Danny Maher, who when partnering the same horse to finish runner-up to Pretty Polly in the Jockey Club Cup over two and a quarter miles the previous autumn became even more convinced of the chink in her stamina. Pretty Polly herself was ridden by Bernard Dillon (known outside racing as the third husband of the music-hall star Marie Lloyd), who had kept the ride since winning the Limekiln Stakes on her.

Then, as now, trainers of the leading fancies for big races were pestered by the press for their pre-race opinions, and Gilpin fielded in measured tones the umpteenth question about whether Pretty Polly would prove unbeatable:

> Do not be too sure about that. The Bachelor's Button people are cocksure of beating us. He has been doing wonderfully well in his gallops and from what I hear won the Manchester Cup the other day in spite of being nearly knocked over in some scrimmaging. We hope to beat him, of course, but he is a formidable opponent.

Pretty Polly showed a marked disinclination to leave the paddock, and there were even rumours that she might at that late stage be withdrawn, but such fears came to nothing, and as the runners came past the stands first time round, with St Denis setting the pace as expected, she was last of the quintet but going comfortably enough. On the run down to Swinley Bottom the order was St Denis, Achilles, Cicero, Bachelor's Button and Pretty Polly, but with three-quarters of a mile still to race St Denis started to weaken, and it was Achilles who led the field up the hill towards the home turn. Cicero fell away beaten, and once in the straight Achilles tired rapidly and edged towards the stands – seeming to take Pretty Polly with him. Once straightened up she looked set to go on and win, but Maher on Bachelor's Button, having gained the inside rail, would not be shaken off. A hundred yards out Dillon went for his whip, but to no avail. Proving Maher completely right in his assessment of the mare's stamina,

Bachelor's Button wore her down and went on to win by a length.

The crowd was stunned. *The Times* reported:

> Not a cheer was raised for Bachelor's Button when he came back to scale, though he had run a gallant race and well deserved recognition. But the defeat of Pretty Polly was regarded as something like the shattering of an idol, and Bachelor's Button was looked upon as the perpetrator of the deed.

'Alas, and again Alas!' – Pretty Polly fails to peg back Bachelor's Button in the 1906 Gold Cup.

The racing writer J. Lechmere observed that 'I have seen many races and many sensational results, but nothing to equal the absolute silence as Bachelor's Button passed the post the winner of the Ascot Gold Cup in record time.' William Allison in *The Sportsman* tried to put the catastrophe in perspective: 'It is too much to write that the defeat of Pretty Polly was a national calamity but it is quite certain that it cast a gloom over the proceedings.' The *Sporting Life* made no such attempt at balance, wailing:

> Alas, and again Alas! Pretty Polly beaten! Lamentations as sincere as they were loud were heard on every hand after the race was over.

Rather unfairly, some ladies in the Royal Enclosure who should have had better manners were reported to have called Bachelor's Button 'a brute' and 'a detestable thing', while George Lambton, reflecting on this famous race nearly twenty years later, noted that after Pretty Polly had beaten Bachelor's Button in the 1905 Jockey Club Cup, Maher had told him that 'if these two met in the Ascot Cup the following year, Bachelor's Button would be certain to win'. Lambton observed of Bachelor's Button: 'He was a sterling good horse, especially at Ascot, but he was not a Persimmon, and if a real good jockey had been on Pretty Polly I think she might just have scrambled home.'

Pretty Polly did not race again. She jarred a leg while being prepared for the Doncaster Cup and was retired, the 1906 Gold Cup her only defeat in England. She has the unusual distinction of current races being named after her at two major racecourses – Newmarket and The Curragh – and her Ascot connection continued when her great-great-great-grandson Brigadier Gerard won five races at the course in 1971 and 1972.

When Edward VII ascended the throne, he made the Royal Enclosure more exclusive and élite than it had been in the Victorian age, ruling that no one was eligible for admission unless eligible also to receive invitations to Court. The number admitted to the enlarged enclosure was restricted to 1,200, and it is perhaps this change of policy that earned the King's Representative Lord Churchill the reputation of being a tyrant over the distribution of the tickets. Whereas Lord Ribblesdale had contended that it was impossible to remember all the people who could and could not enter the Royal Enclosure without making a lifelong career of it, Viscount Churchill succeeded in doing just that, and became notorious for recognising faces in the enclosure and challenging those who should not be there. In 1912 he saw a lady in the Royal Enclosure to whom he had refused a voucher. After an enquiry, an interim injunction was granted restraining a certain Miss Meadows from selling vouchers. 'It was a grave social impropriety that persons who had applied for and had obtained invitations to the Royal Enclosure, should seek to make money out of them, and sell the privilege that had been extended to them,' fulminated *The Times*, but the *Liverpool Post* took a different tack, running an article headed 'Snobs at Ascot and elsewhere' which criticised 'this nauseating snobbishness and worship of mere wealth' and wondered at the 'comment on the aspirations of the idle rich that such scheming and dodging and deviation from right should be thought worth while for so trivial an object'.

The essential and immutable qualification for entry was to have been presented at Court, but not every would-be entrant understood this. An American lady once enclosed a blank cheque and, it was reported, invited Lord Churchill to 'fill it in for any old sum he liked, so long as tickets came along sure.'

Although Edward VII tightened entry to the Royal Enclosure, he did informally relax one rule, namely Queen Victoria's order 'that no actor or actress should be eligible to the Enclosure'. When the King asked the actor Charles Hawtrey – father of the Charles Hawtrey who became a regular in

Carry On films – whether he would be seeing him at Ascot, Hawtrey explained that the rules prevented it, whereupon the King took it upon himself personally to send Hawtrey the necessary badge. Come the day, Hawtrey entered the enclosure to the consternation of Lord Churchill, who was adamant that he had not sent him a badge. Hawtrey explained that Churchill had indeed not sent one: 'King Edward did.'

The worst sin that an applicant could have committed was to have been involved in a divorce, since there had long been a rule that guilty parties to divorce suits or persons whose suits were pending came under the banner of people 'of an undesirable character' and should not be admitted to the Royal Enclosure. In 1913 Lord Churchill asked the solicitor John Withers to assist him in his task of examining the applications for vouchers for the Royal Enclosure: 'Many attempts have been made in the past by undesirable persons to obtain access to the Royal Enclosure and many people still make application for tickets who, although they are aware of the rules governing the right to make application, are not qualified to do so.' Together Churchill and Withers set up a system whereby a dossier was kept by the Ascot Office on every applicant, and the London Divorce Lists for each term were sent to be checked against that list. The partners of Withers & Co. would then attend at the Ascot Office to go through the lists again, and if there was an element of doubt an extra search was made at the Divorce Registry Office. Information obtained from the Divorce Registry was always treated with the greatest secrecy: the general public did not have access to such information, but Ascot's use of it was justified in order 'to see that only those persons shall be admitted to whom objection could not be taken by His Majesty'.

Divorce remained 'the principal bar to candidates for vouchers' until 1955, and it is more than likely that the rule had been established as far back as 1845 when the Royal Enclosure first came into being, as the rules on admittance to the Royal Enclosure were in accordance with Court rules.

Applying the rules of entry was arduous enough, but spare a thought for the Clerk of the Course at this period. In 1905 Churchill outlined the clerk's duties to the King:

During the meeting he has to run messages for me all day long, and has to be at the racecourse for 5 a.m. to personally direct the labourers in their work. He has also to sleep in a stuffy little office in the Stand, to look after the money, and to be on the spot in case of Heath fires, or any other emergency.

He has to go round the Police on duty late at night and come and report to me the last thing, and he has ever to superintend the Stewards of those who have luncheon rooms being in food or we should have them wandering all over the enclosure! And he is hardly ever able to be in his office for a moment, ever to see a race, unless he is sent by me on official business. For a month before the meeting he has personally to bargain with all the gipsies and other blackguards who hire land for their booths and 'merrygrounds' and to constantly keep an eye on them during the race week; and has to meet various club secretaries and peg out the ground for all the luncheon tents, and see they are erected properly – as well as many other menial duties.

During the rest of the year he must always be on the spot, as he acts practically as Bailiff on the farm connected with the course and has a large staff of workmen to personally give orders to.

He has also many duties connected with Ascot Heath House for as your Majesty is, I think, aware in order to make as much money as possible I frequently let it for a few weeks at a time.

In 1905, Lord Marcus Beresford had written to the King (whom he served as racing manager), asking if he might be considered for the position of the Clerk of the Course following the death of the incumbent, Major Reynold Clement. However, Lord Churchill advised against the proposal because 'I do not think it at all advisable to appoint a gentleman of so high a social standing'; there were 'too many things that I could not possibly ask Marcus, or a gentleman of that sort, to do.'

In 1907 The White Knight won the first of his two Gold Cups, but that year the drama was more off course than on. During the race the trophy itself, which had been made by Garrards, was on display behind the grandstand, guarded by two policemen and two gatemen. Responding to the ringing of the bell as the horses turned for home – or, in another version, to the cry of 'Here they come!' as the runners came up the straight – the quartet looking after the cup dropped their guard as they tried to get a glimpse of the finish. When they turned back the cup had vanished, and was never found – though later that summer the King was highly amused when at Kempton Park a racegoer called across to him: 'What've you done with the cup, Teddy?' (Dorothy Laird, author of a history of Royal Ascot, was told by an elderly gateman who had been present that day that at the crucial moment a lady nearby had fainted, or pretended to faint, and the policeman and gatemen had dropped their guard by going to her assistance.)

Had the policemen and gatemen managed to catch the finish of the 1907 Gold Cup they would have witnessed an exciting race. After a fierce tussle The White Knight and Eider ran a dead heat, but William Halsey on The White Knight lodged an objection against George Stern on Eider. The Stewards rejected the suggestion that Stern had put out his hand to stop The White Knight or unseat Halsey, but found him guilty of not keeping his horse straight, and awarded the race outright to The White Knight.

Remarks were made in the press about the 'bad taste' of objecting at Ascot, repeating reservations aired a few years earlier with Cupbearer and Ard Patrick in the Prince of Wales's Stakes. But gradually this notion of not objecting at Ascot faded away as the course became less associated with the gentlemanly conduct of lords and nobles, and more with professionals participating in a professional sport. As the journalist J. C. Booth wrote, 'If there is one place more than another at which the strictest observance of the rules should be insisted on, surely it is Ascot.'

The same meeting saw the first Ascot appearance of a young jockey named Donoghue, who before long would have the familiar cry 'Come on, Steve!' echoing around the Ascot stands and would be champion jockey every year from 1914 to 1923.

Edward VII's own racing fortunes scaled another peak in 1909 with the victory of Minoru, trained by Richard Marsh, in the Derby, and although the King had won the premier Classic twice as Prince of Wales – with Persimmon in 1896 and Diamond Jubilee in 1900 – Minoru's Epsom victory was especially significant, as it was the first time that the Derby winner had been owned by the reigning sovereign. Minoru's next race after Epsom was the St James's Palace Stakes, which he won easily from two decidedly inferior opponents. (After a brief stud career in Ireland, Minoru was exported to Russia, where during the Revolution one story had him hitched to a cart together with another Derby winner in the shape of Aboyeur, 100–1 winner at Epsom in 1913, and another story had the horse executed as a royalist!)

It is widely accepted that the Edwardian age was characterised by a delight in the social whirl in a way that the later part of the Victorian era certainly was not, and this brought about a reinvigorated fashion scene at Ascot.

In 1902 George James Cawthorne and Richard S. Herod, early historians of Ascot, wrote that 'the dresses and parasols of the ladies upon the Lawn have all the appearance of a gaudy bed of flowers', but also acknowledged that 'the dresses at Ascot are a characteristic feature, for it would not be Ascot were not the lawns and enclosures filled with graceful women in beautiful costumes'. In 1904 Lady Violet Greville wrote of Ascot, 'It is frocks, frocks everywhere.'

In general the Edwardian era was an opulent age when ladies' fashions achieved new heights of femininity and Edwardian milliners enjoyed designing extravagant and frivolous hats. A young lady was expected to look fashionable and beautiful while retaining a demure, conservative aspect, and since an hour-glass figure was demanded by fashion, so corsets dominated the design of dresses. Edwardian ladies also had a passion for jewels: pearls, rubies and diamonds were used to complement outfits. Even shoes could be encrusted with gems, especially on the fashionably large buckles.

In 1909 *The Times* noted:

Such fragile materials as muslin, laces, nets and soft silks were the only wear … Fine net or ninons, embroidered in filoselle very handsomely worked in bold raised patterns and long coats were among the successes of the day.

Eccentricities were noticed in some of the fantastic tunics and in one dress of willow-patterned blue girdling the waist and hips and tied in a bow at the back, but in front giving a corselet effect. Hats were trimmed with feathers, ospreys, flowers or merely a bow of lace, white, black or metal …

Princess Daisy of Pless, an English lady who had married a member of one of the minor German royal families, was invited at short notice to stay with Edward VII at Windsor Castle for Ascot, and her response to this invitation indicates how – for some Ascot racegoers at least – clothes had become the overriding preoccupation: 'I have no clothes! I can't go to Vienna now … I really can't get Ascot dresses in Breslau; and we cannot arrive in London before Sunday the 13th and have to be in Windsor on the 14th.' Yet in the event she coped perfectly well: 'All my clothes have been a great success and Hans said I was the best dressed woman at the races. All very simple and draped; one day a big bunch of pink lilies and my scarab turquoises. Then I twice wore Fritz's gold coat which made a great effect and looked lovely.'

But black was again the order of the day in 1910, for Edward VII had died on 6 May at the age of sixty-eight. In one of his last conscious moments he was informed that his filly Witch Of The Air had won the Spring Two-Year-Old Plate at Kempton Park by half a length. 'I am very glad,' Edward whispered, before lapsing back into a coma.

He was succeeded by his second and oldest surviving son, who became George V.

While in strict terms the Edwardian age was at an end, its mood lingered, and it was entirely in keeping with Edwardian spirit that the 1910 Royal Meeting managed to display, even in black, the style that had characterised the whole decade. The *Daily Mirror* wrote of the opening day:

'Black Ascot' – the Royal Meeting in mourning for Edward VII, 1910.

Strange and striking were the contrasts at Ascot. The most splendid fête of the year usually had now its dominant note in mourning. No member of royalty was present, the King's pavilion had drawn blinds and closed doors, and the occupants of the royal enclosure were in black, unrelieved save where ladies wore white flowers or had strings of pearls as the only ornament.

The bandstand, 1910.

But even on such an occasion, for many who attended Ascot the horses were more important than the clothes, and in 1910 the big attraction was Bayardo. He had won the New Stakes at the course on his two-year-old début in 1908 and the Prince of Wales's Stakes in 1909, after which he had gone on to land several big races, including the Eclipse Stakes, the St Leger and the Champion Stakes. Now he was running in the Gold Cup, for which there was an unusually large field of thirteen runners, including Bronzino, winner of the 1910 Doncaster Cup, Carousel, winner of the 1909 Goodwood Cup, and Sir Martin, winner of the 1910 Coronation Cup. These were good horses, but Bayardo's main rival appeared to be the French challenger Sea Sick II, who had dead-heated for the Prix du Jockey-Club (French Derby) in 1908 and behind whom there was a great deal of stable confidence – confidence that doubtless increased when Bayardo dropped his jockey Danny Maher on the ground just before the start. Horse and rider reunited, Bayardo won easily, and the Gold Cup was the first of four races Danny Maher won that afternoon. He followed up in the St James's Palace Stakes on the Derby winner Lemberg, then the 47th New Biennial (second year) on Mustapha and 48th (first year) on Sunder.

Third behind Lemberg in the 1910 St James's Palace Stakes was the future St Leger and Eclipse Stakes winner Swynford, who made a second Ascot appearance that year to win the Hardwicke Stakes – another example of how in those days even top-class horses would run in (and occasionally win) two (or even three) races at the meeting.

But some doubles are more unusual than others, and mention must be

made of the good stayer Willonyx, who in 1911 won the Ascot Stakes on the Tuesday and the Gold Cup on the Thursday. That year he also won the Chester Cup, the Jockey Club Cup, and the Cesarewitch (under 9 stone 5 pounds).

Bayardo, ridden by Danny Maher, wins the 1910 Gold Cup.

The same year brought an edict against a pestilence that was becoming more and more aggravating for Ascot racegoers: photographers. A stir had been caused back in 1895 when during the meeting the Master of the Buckhounds Lord Ribblesdale had been informed that 'an individual with a Kodak was loose in the enclosure' photographing the royal party, and 'when last seen was actively engaged upon a group of duchesses'. The offender was rapidly tracked down, and turned out to be 'a distinguished visitor to our shores, accredited by the embassy of one of the great Powers, and a relative of an ex-crowned head'. The man's rank clearly stood him in good stead, as after delivering 'a wordy reprimand' Ribblesdale invited him to lunch.

By 1911 the plague of photography had grown worse, and the racecourse noted that 'A good many complaints have indeed been received by the authorities from people who resent being "snapped" at unexpected moments by the camera fiend', though there was more tolerance shown towards moving pictures, with Ascot announcing just before the 1912 meeting that it would provide 'special facilities to take bioscope pictures, from the most advantageous points, of all the principal races next week, together with scenes of the paddock and a full view of the Royal Procession.'

In 1919 George V insisted that no photographers be allowed in the Royal Enclosure as he had 'a rooted objection to being snap-shotted and feels sure that the people in the Enclosures and Paddock and even the Grand Stand

'Ascot Sunday' – also known as 'Show Out Sunday' – at Boulters Lock on the Thames early in the twentieth century. The tradition whereby on the Sunday before the Royal Meeting the local population would don its Sunday best, sample some of the entertainments being installed on the racecourse and generally enjoy an *al fresco* summer party, lasted until the Second World War.

would equally object to it.' The following year a formal prohibition was introduced, and the rule banning cameras from the Royal Enclosure still applies today.

Given that attitude, we can only speculate what would have happened had any rogue photographer fallen foul of Gordon Carter, who became Clerk of the Course in 1910.

Of all the major Ascot characters from the Edwardian period, none seems quite so rooted in a different age from our own as Carter, who served as Clerk of the Course until his death in 1941, and whose singular contribution to Ascot is acknowledged by the running of the Gordon Carter Handicap at the September Meeting.

It is easy to make fun of a man who was so fastidious that every night he had his shoelaces washed and ironed, but Carter's correctness and military discipline – he had risen from trooper to Lieutenant Colonel in the 1st Life Guards and took part in the relief of Kimberley – brought Ascot no end of benefit. He took great pains to improve the racing surface, and behind the scenes his meticulous attention to detail made the racecourse an exceptionally well-lubricated operation. Dorothy Laird described Sir Gordon's schedule during the race meeting itself:

During Royal Ascot Sir Gordon would be on the course, in riding kit, at seven in the morning. Later he would change into a lounge suit at his office. At noon he crossed the road to his home, to change into morning dress. When the Royal Procession came down the course, he stood always at the gate where the Procession left the racecourse. It was at this spot that his ashes were scattered after his death.

After the first race, which was one thirty p.m., there was a break of one hour for luncheon. Sir Gordon Carter and his house party always took luncheon in a private dining-room on the course. After the racing, his valet brought another lounge suit over to the office into which Sir Gordon changed. He changed again, for the fifth time that day, into evening dress for dinner, an eight-course affair of iced melon, soup, fish, entrée, water ice, saddle of lamb, sweet, savoury and dessert, followed by coffee, liqueurs and cigars.

An appropriate mark of Gordon Carter's tenure as Clerk of the Course came in 1939, two years before he died, when the *Yorkshire Post* remarked that his 'arrangements each year for Ascot are so good that it is a pity that he cannot also have charge of the weather'.

The death of Edward VII in 1910 did not immediately transform the nature of racing at Ascot, but a change was detected in the royal arrangements away from the course, and while George V and his consort Queen Mary continued the tradition of Windsor Castle house parties during Ascot week, the ceremonial protocol was even more demanding than that of their predecessors.

Listening to the band, 1910.

Each evening before dinner the ladies were lined up by the Lady of the Bedchamber in a quarter circle in the Green Drawing Room, in strict order of precedence, while the men were lined up by the Master of the Household on the other side of the room. At precisely 8.30 the King and Queen arrived, whereupon the Master of the Household bowed and backed across the threshold. The Queen shook hands with the curtseying women before the man who had been commanded to sit on the Queen's right bowed to her, offered her his arm and escorted her to the dinner table, to the strains of 'God Save the King' played by a Guards string band concealed behind a grille in the dining-room, where the food was served on silver services by pages in blue livery and footmen in scarlet. At the end of the meal the Queen left the room with the ladies, who curtsied to the King as they withdrew. The King and the men then partook of port, coffee and liqueurs while discussing the day's racing and current politics. 'My father never sat more than twenty minutes,' recalled the King's oldest son, later Edward VIII and Duke of Windsor: 'Abruptly, as if controlled by a hidden time-clock, he would rise and lead his guests back to the Green Drawing Room to join my mother.' The guests would then play cards until 11 p.m., when the company would resume their places in the two quarter circles and the King and Queen would bid their guests goodnight. The evening was officially over, but once the King and Queen were safely out of the way, their sons – Edward, Prince of Wales, and his brother George, Duke of York – returned to the Green Drawing Room, where they rolled back the rugs and invited the younger guests to join them in dancing.

After Lady Elizabeth Bowes-Lyon (later Queen Elizabeth the Queen Mother) had married the Duke of York in 1923, she introduced the singing of folk and popular songs, playing the accompaniment herself on the piano.

On a less giddy rung of the social ladder, the suffragette movement was at full throttle. On 4 June 1913 Emily Davison threw herself under the King's horse Anmer in the Derby, sustaining injuries from which she died four days later. Two weeks after that sensational Derby, on the evening before the Gold Cup, Steve Donoghue was having dinner at a Maidenhead hotel with a group of fellow jockeys, including Albert 'Snowy' Whalley, who in the following day's big race was to ride Tracery – a horse who in 1912 had run third in the Derby before winning the St James's Palace Stakes and the St Leger.

> We were all dining together and talking and exercising our wit on each other, as is the way with jockeys, and the conversation came round to the subject of suffragettes, who at that time were very much to the fore and just beginning to do some of those really violent things which they thought would cause Parliament to take their cause more seriously and give them the votes to which they felt they were entitled.

The carriage stand on the inside of the course, 1912. The carriages, which stretched all the way up the straight and could number nearly two hundred in the front rank, provided a major vantage point. The Five Shilling Stand, built in 1908, is at the far end of the stands on the right.

All of a sudden Whalley, a fine jockey, remarked:

'I have a feeling that some suffragette is going to be there for the Gold Cup to-morrow. I tell you fellows, if one of them happens to get in front of me, I will ride straight at him or her. I have a feeling in my bones that it is going to happen.'

It was a remark made in the course of the evening, and I dare say most of us forgot it among an awful lot of other remarks.

But the next day, as we were coming round the turn in the race for the Gold Cup, and just as the leaders were getting into the straight, a man walked down with a gun in his hand, shouting: 'Stop! Stop! Stop, or I'll shoot ...'

Donoghue's credentials as an eye-witness ('as we were coming round the turn') are somewhat undermined by the fact that he did not ride in that Gold Cup. For a more measured account of this sensational incident – which took place approximately where the third last steeplechase fence now stands – we turn to *The Times*:

Many wild rumours were afloat, but what actually occurred is that a man, subsequently identified as Mr Harold Hewitt, carrying a suffragist flag in one hand and a revolver in the other, issuing almost unnoticed from the bushes on the outside of the course, had planted himself directly in front of the leading horse and had been thrown down and, as appeared later, very seriously hurt. The horse fell and threw its jockey, Whalley, who was not badly injured, and was able to walk back to the paddock, while the horse galloped home abreast of the last competitor in the race, riderless.

The police rushed to the scene and found a fully loaded six-chamber revolver. Even as they were discharging the bullets into the turf, investigative reporters from *The Times* were getting on the case. It turned out that Hewitt was a zoologist who lived at Hope End in Herefordshire, and had reportedly been at the funeral of Emily Davison on the Monday of Ascot week. The base from which he sought to emulate Davison was a hotel in Bloomsbury, where he had left his luggage:

A Bible and a considerable quantity of writing were among Hewitt's possessions. Of late he had apparently been attending lectures by Mrs Besant [the theosophist and socialist free-thinker], and he was also interested in the views of Miss Hageby, the anti-vivisectionist. The fly-leaves of the Bible found on him are full of quotations, and he kept a diary up to within an hour and a half of the outrage. In this there was an entry as late as 1.30, as follows:– 'Oh! the weariness of these races. If I fail in my intention to stop the Gold Cup, I hope I shall not hurt any of the jockeys. Oh! the weariness of these races, and the crowds they attract. They bring out all that is worst in humanity.' In other entries he speaks of life no longer being sweet to him. He adds:– 'There are plenty of pretty girls, but none for me.'

The Minute Book in the Ascot archives contains a letter from the King's secretary Lord Stamfordham to Lord Churchill dated 20 June 1913 declaring that: 'His Majesty appreciates the extra strain and anxiety which has been cast upon all the responsible authorities owing to the suffragettes ... He heartily congratulates you and all those who have worked with you on the most happy results which have been achieved.'

Not so happy, though, for Harold Hewitt, whose fractured skull pressed so tightly down onto his brain that, according to *The Times* at the time of his trial over seven years later, 'his mind became unhinged, and later he was confined in several asylums, from one of which he escaped'. Hewitt made for Canada, where he made a new life for himself as a farmer in Victoria, British Columbia. He returned in 1920 to give himself up, and in January 1921 was charged with causing grievous bodily harm to Whalley. Mr Justice Darling, summing up, declared that:

> No matter what the prisoner's opinions were on horse racing, drinking water, and other matters, that was no justification for his seeking to injure perfectly innocent people. He had, like many others, about the period in question, been carried away in a wave of folly and had become really crazy.

Hewitt was sentenced to two days' imprisonment.

It is almost incidental to record that the 1913 Gold Cup was won by the previous year's winner Prince Palatine – he broke the existing course record for two and a half miles – and that back in fifth place was a good stayer named Jackdaw, whose son Brown Jack made such an impact on Ascot two decades later that he merits a whole chapter to himself later in this book.

A far happier feature of the 1913 meeting was the Coventry Stakes on the opening day of the meeting, when for the third time in little over a decade Ascot was the place to see one of the all-time greats. Unlike with Sceptre or Pretty Polly, who were both three-year-olds when first appearing at the royal course and enjoyed well-established reputations, the hero of 1913 was a two-year-old having only his third race in public.

His name was The Tetrarch, fabled not only for his racing achievements, but also for his highly distinctive colour, well described in the *Biographical Encyclopaedia of British Flat Racing*:

> When a foal, The Tetrarch was chestnut with black splodges. As he grew older, he became grey with white splodges, rather as if some joker had shaken a brush dipped in whitewash at him. At first he was known as 'The Rocking Horse'; later, when his outstanding merit was apparent, he was called 'The Spotted Wonder';

SOME WINNING HORSES AT THE ASCOT MEETING.

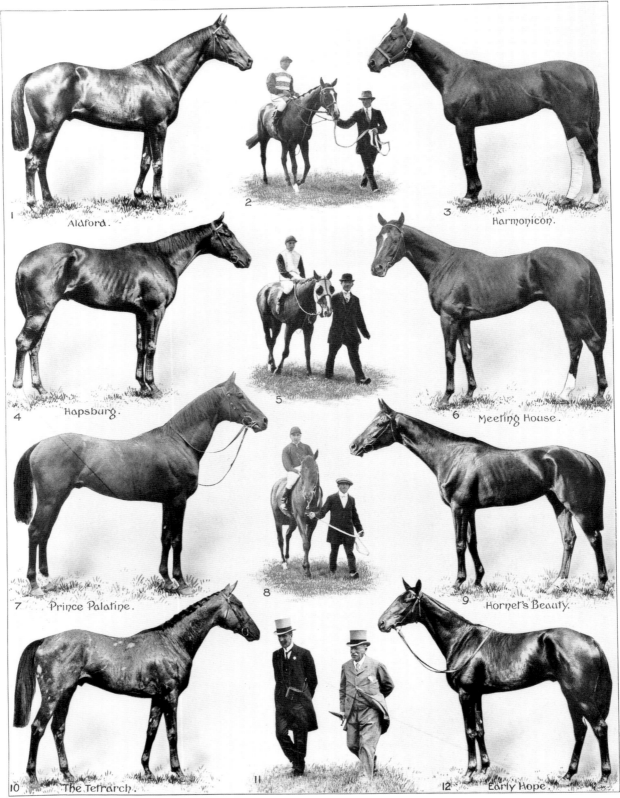

1. Aldford.
2.
3. Harmonicon.
4. Hapsburg.
5.
6. Meeting House.
7. Prince Palatine.
8.
9. Hornet's Beauty.
10. The Tetrarch.
11.
12. Early Hope.

1. Mr. W. C. Waugh's Aldford, by Maurezin—Mangalmi, winner of the 61st Triennial Stakes of £798.
2. Mr. A. Basset's Roseworthy (D. Maher up), after winning the St. James's Palace Stakes of £2,400.
3. Mr. H. P. Whitney's Harmonicon, by Disguise—Harpsichord, winner of the 50th New Biennial Stakes of £1,395.
4. Sir E. Cassel's Hapsburg, by Desmond—Altesse, winner of the New Stakes of £1,936 10s.—his first public appearance.
5. Harmonicon (O'Neill up), after winning the 50th New Biennial Stakes.
6. Mr. H. P. Whitney's Meeting House, by Voter—Noonday, winner of the 51st New Biennial Stakes of £1,230.
7. Mr. T. Pilkington's Prince Palatine, by Persimmon—Lady Lightfoot, winner of the Gold Cup of £3,620. (The same horse won in 1912.)
8. Mr. J. Joel's Spanish Prince (F. Wootton up), after winning the Rous Memorial Stakes of £910.
9. Sir W. Cooke's Hornet's Beauty, by Tredennis—Hornet, winner of the All-Aged Stakes of £430 and the King's Stand Stakes of £810.
10. Mr. D. McCalmont's The Tetrarch, by Roi Herode—Vahren, winner of the Coventry Stakes of £1,843.
11. Mr. Alison and Mr. Willoughby (the starter) off to the gate.
12. Mr. J. Kenney's Early Hope, by Earla Mor—Ishallah, winner of the Visitors' Handicap of £570.

schoolboys passing through an awkward phase were liable to be nicknamed 'The Tetrarch'.

Trained at Stockbridge by Atty Persse, The Tetrarch had shown enough in home trials before ever seeing a racecourse to suggest that he was something a long way out of the ordinary, and it is a tribute to the highly disciplined lines along which Persse's stable was run that he started at 5–1 for a maiden two-year-old race at Newmarket's Craven Meeting. He won by four lengths without breaking sweat. Then Epsom, for the Woodcote Stakes on the day before that notorious Derby: The Tetrarch easily beat Parhelio (then unnamed), whose trainer Charles Morton remarked after the race: 'Well, I'm jiggered. The Tetrarch's a marvel and no mistake. He went past my horse as if he was going past a tree.'

Steve Donoghue, who rode 'The Spotted Wonder' in all his races, takes up the story:

> Next came Ascot. Once more he shot from the gate like a bullet, and though I saw the advance flag The Tetrarch's speed was so terrific that in a short while I could neither see nor hear anything near me and I thought there might have been a false start. I won by a tremendous margin and was actually in the paddock when the others were finishing their race.

The Tetrarch's ten-length victory in the Coventry Stakes was an awesome performance, one of the very greatest ever seen at Ascot (though the *Times* correspondent took the 'Yes, but what did he beat?' line, then as now an easy refuge for the killjoy).

The grey went through the rest of his two-year-old career unbeaten, going on from Ascot to win the National Produce Stakes at Sandown Park, the Rous Memorial Stakes at Goodwood, the Champion Breeders' Foal Stakes at Derby (where racing was held until the Second World War) and the Champagne Stakes at Doncaster – and, after just seven races, that was the last seen of him on a racecourse. Although it was impossible to conceive of this wonder horse ever being beaten, an injury sustained in training brought about his premature retirement.

Opposite: Ascot fashions
1913, as displayed in
The Sphere.

Considerably less awesome, but in the long run more important for the
future of Ascot racecourse, was the passing in 1913 of the Ascot Authority
Act, which replaced the Grand Stand Trustees with a single trust named the
Ascot Authority, 'to hold and manage the Ascot Racecourse and Races'.
The overall objective of the Act was cited as:

> An Act to constitute Trustees for the purpose of holding and
> managing Ascot Race Course and the stands buildings and property
> held or used in connection therewith and to vest in them all property
> now held or used for the benefit or purposes of Ascot Races and to
> confer all necessary power on the Trustees so constituted and for other
> purposes …

The Ascot Authority was to be made up of three Trustees: the sovereign's
Representative, the Keeper of the Privy Purse and 'one other person appointed
by His Majesty in writing', and the first Trustees in these respective categories
were Viscount Churchill, Sir William Carrington and Sir Henry Brassey.
The Trustees, although still appointed by the monarch, were empowered

> to further and promote the welfare and prosperity of the Ascot Races
> and to that end the Ascot Authority shall have and may exercise as
> they shall in their absolute discretion from time to time think fit (but
> subject always to any direction which may from time to time be given
> to them by His Majesty) the powers hereinafter specifically set forth.

Those powers included control over all financial affairs of the racecourse, the
leasehold of all property and the maintenance of that property, managing the
races and making any regulations or byelaws with reference to visitors or
buildings, the ability to take on lease or acquire property in the name of the
Authority, the ability to let premises vested in the Authority, and finally to
operate 'in any other manner which in the opinion of the Ascot Authority will
be calculated to promote the success, welfare or prosperity of Ascot Races'.

On a more immediately practical level as far as the racegoer was
concerned, the still fairly newfangled contraption called the motor car had
started to make its presence felt at Ascot, and in 1912 cars had for the first

Graceful Modes and Millinery at Ascot.

A STUDY IN LACE AND SATIN

Showing the newest phase of the Bayadère sash

VISITORS TO ASCOT HAVING A LITTLE CHAT BETWEEN THE RACES

THE VOGUE FOR WHITE

Depicting the slit-up skirt and draped corsage

ALLIANCE OF RIBBON AND LACE

These divide honours in the coat, the crêpe skirt being draped

THE REVIVAL OF THE CLASSICAL COTHURNE SHOE

Accompanied by a distinctive costume of black charmeuse and new winged hat. Lace and crêpon are happily mingled in the toilette on the right

THE NEW COATEE

Of brightly-coloured taffetas with V opening

THE CHARM OF SIMPLICITY

Two delightful toilettes in which the simplest ideas are expressed

THE SCENE OPPOSITE THE ROYAL STAND AT ASCOT

The day was a truly glorious one for the display of the variegated costumes which are such a feature of this great social function

ELABORATE MODES

Of lace and charmeuse (on left) and of broché and lace (on right)

King George V and Queen
Mary arrive at the Royal
Meeting in 1914.

time been allowed on to the Heath. The same year George V, it was reported,
'displayed his interest in modern manners and customs by authorising the
formation of a motor enclosure just below the grand stand lawns, and next to
the old carriage enclosure. This will enable motorists to view the racing from
their own vehicles just as if they were four-in-hands, and the innovation will
do much to popularise the meeting.'

Racegoers who motored to Ascot and availed themselves of this facility in
1914 saw the first running of the Bessborough Stakes, now the Duke of
Edinburgh Stakes. They also witnessed the last Ascot victory of a real course
specialist in Hornet's Beauty, who, when giving jockey Freddie Fox his first
Ascot winner in the All-Aged Stakes, was registering his sixth course win:
he had won three races at the fixture in 1911 (when he went through the year
unbeaten in fifteen starts in Britain), including the King's Stand Stakes, and
two (including a second King's Stand) in 1913.

The Royal Meeting in 1914 ended on Friday 19 June, having been
acclaimed as a highly successful occasion. One social correspondent reported:

If this is necessary, as seems to be the custom, to give every event of
the Season a nickname, this was emphatically a Parasol Ascot. Pink

and blue, yellow, scarlet, mauve and apricot – with every intermediate shade and combination of tints – to look down upon the sunshades from an upper tier in one of the stands was like gazing down on a gorgeous flower garden where every flower was mushroom-shaped.

Gold Cup day 1914, as seen by *London's Social Calendar*.

Nine days later, on 28 June, Archduke Franz Ferdinand's driver took a wrong turn into a narrow street in Sarajevo. As he reversed the car a nineteen-year-old Bosnian Serb, who by chance was standing nearby, fired two shots, killing the Archduke and his wife. On 4 August, Britain declared war on Germany. Field Marshal Sir John French predicted that it would be all over by Christmas.

1914 TO 1945

By Christmas 1914 the war was far from over, and early in 1915 rumours started going round that the Royal Meeting would not take place that year – or, bizarrely, that it might be held on another course. In March *The Times*'s racing correspondent loftily passed on that 'I have the highest authority for stating that the meeting fixed for June 15th and three following days will take place', but the following month a leader in the same newspaper made the case for abandonment:

> We are convinced that any attempt to hold the great popular racing festivals, such as Epsom, and above all Ascot, will make a deplorably bad impression upon our neighbours, and lead to a misconception in this country which we should try to prevent. We should like to see them abandoned altogether for this year. The Ascot meeting falls on a date when the war may be at its climax. Can it be seemly to hold it when millions of men, including great numbers of our own people, will be at death-grips?

Straight talking – but positively namby-pamby compared with the views forcibly expressed by Colonel Henry Knollys, who had served with the Royal Artillery:

> Is it unreasonable to hope that in 1915 the upper classes of men and women will forbear from assembling in their tens of thousands, say, at Ascot, peacocking in their plumes and and prattling their puerilities, eating plentifully and drinking still more so, semi-intoxicated with the

Previous pages: Passing the stands on the first circuit of the Ascot Stakes, 1936.

splendour and spangle of the gaudy scene, yelling with enthusiasm because one favourite has galloped a few inches in advance of the nose of another favourite, while thousands of our countrymen … are enduring every description of pain, peril and privation and may indeed, at the exactly coincidental moment, be moaning their agony or gasping out their lives to save their country from annihilation?

But others took a different view. Lord Rosebery, who served as Prime Minister for less than sixteen months between March 1894 and June 1895 and in that short period managed to own two Derby winners, invoked the spirit which saw the Derby and Ascot continue during the time of the French Revolution and Napoleon:

All through that score of bloody years the Epsom and Ascot meetings were regularly held, nor indeed does it seem to have occurred to our forefathers that it was guilty to witness races when we were at war.

Admiral of the Fleet Sir Hedworth Meux tried an unusual slant:

The best horses in the world and the prettiest women are seen on the Royal Heath. We racing men go to Ascot to see the horses, non-racing men, such as Lord Curzon and Lord Robert Cecil and Mr Cust, go to look at the women – and very good judges too. The incomparable beauty of English women is the real cause of the envy and hatred of their country that has been growing up for many years in Germany.

With an end to the war looking ever more remote, those in favour of Ascot continuing were rapidly losing the argument. In April, even as the spring offensive was being stalled at Ypres, it was announced that the Tuesday of the Royal Meeting would be cancelled, and the fixture last only three days, and the following month came the inevitable news that the whole meeting would be abandoned. Some of the major races – including the Gold Cup and the Coventry Stakes – were transferred to Newmarket.

Ascot itself would not see another horse race until June 1919, but the course played its part in the war effort.

A recruitment office was set up in the grandstand, proving so effective that a local reporter was soon noting that 'there are no young men left in the district, which speaks highly for the patriotism of Ascot'. Another part of the grandstand was converted into a hospital for fifty wounded soldiers, with the Five Shilling Stand (or Silver Ring) used as a depot for medical supplies; the long bar in that stand became a workroom for bandage parties. Wounded soldiers organised their own version of Ascot races around the Tattersall's ring (sometimes on crutches) or even on the course itself. In 1917 the hospital in the grandstand was shut down, and the building taken over by the Royal Flying Corps. A cinema for servicemen – open to the public every evening – was opened on the Heath.

After four years of the war to end all wars, the Armistice was signed on 11 November 1918. Later the same month *The Times* reported that 'Ascot house agents are already receiving enquiries as to what houses will be available for the race week.'

The Royal Meeting resumed on Tuesday 17 June 1919 and provided what turned out to be a memorable meeting – not least for the ease with which the meeting seemed to put the unspeakable horrors of the Great War behind it and effortlessly resume the frivolity of the fashion parade. *The Times* wrote of dresses displaying

> lightness and flimsiness, predominately black and white, shading away into cream, dove-colour and grey, lit occasionally by grand splashes of blue, or by pink and yellow … a wonderful sunshade decked with pink ostrich feathers … an almost equally remarkable hat with ostrich feathers of brightest yellow, a cloak of Lincoln green which Maid Marion might have worn … a black and white chessboard lady, and a brown and white spotted lady …

It was almost as if Ypres and Mons and the Somme had had no more substance than a bad dream.

In celebration of the war victory it was intended that the Royal Procession should for the first time take place on all four days of the meeting, rather than just Tuesday and Thursday as had been the case before. But in the event heavy rain caused the procession to be cancelled on the Friday, and it was not until

1920 that, as a document in the Ascot archive records, 'for the first time in the annals of Ascot Their Majesties came every day in procession up the Racecourse and received a splendid reception from all quarters'.

Less grand ways of getting to the meeting in 1919 were not affected by the weather. *The Times* carried details of road routes to the course, and some four thousand cars were estimated to have carried racegoers to Ascot in 1919.

On the racing front, the 1919 meeting had many highlights, notably the two victories of the great mare Diadem, who as a two-year-old in 1916 had won the substitute Coventry Stakes at Newmarket, and the following year had won the One Thousand Guineas. Owned by Lord D'Abernon, Diadem was trained by George Lambton and ridden by Steve Donoghue, both of whom were unstinting in their praise of her. Lambton described her as 'the sweetest and most gallant little mare that ever was seen on a race-course', and Donoghue waxed even more lyrical:

She was the strangest little creature that I ever rode. Before a race she was like a pony, so small, so insignificant, with nothing but her beautifully intelligent head to distinguish her. When you mounted her to ride her down to the post she began to grow bigger and bigger with each stride and when you faced the starter all her lassitude and quietness had gone; all the littleness of her had vanished, and from the saddle she seemed like a sixteen hand horse full of mettle and vitality. She was on her toes ready when the tapes went up, and whatever the distance she ran the race out to a finish, dead game.

When the race was over she relaxed again and became once more the gentle pony.

The close relationship between horse and jockey was observed by George Lambton:

Stephen is a great lover of horses, but I am sure Diadem held first place in his affections and she thoroughly reciprocated it. I have seen her after a hard race, as he unsaddled her, turn round and rub her nose against his hands, more like a dog than a horse.

Diadem was a five-year-old when she first ran at Ascot in 1919. On the Thursday she won the Rous Memorial Stakes, and she was out again the following day to win the King's Stand Stakes. This was not the last that Ascot would see of her.

The other great horse on view in 1919 was Irish Elegance, the strapping chestnut who landed a huge gamble for his financier owner Jimmy White (described by Richard Onslow as 'this cold, grasping egotist, whose ruthlessness was masked by an earthy geniality') when, ridden by Fred Templeman and backed from 50–1 a few days before the race to 7–1 at the off, he made all the running and cruised to victory in the Royal Hunt Cup under the crushing burden of 9 stone 11 pounds. Later that season Irish Elegance turned in another stupendous performance when winning the Portland Handicap at Doncaster under 10 stone 2 pounds.

Jimmy White admitted to having 'won a bundle' on Irish Elegance in the Hunt Cup, but even for the biggest punters winnings are often only on loan from the bookmakers, and in due course the empire he had built out of nothing started to crumble. When his financial problems became apparently insoluble in the summer of 1927, he solved them with prussic acid and chloroform.

A much more attractive personality was the genuinely genial Lord Glanely – nicknamed 'Old Guts and Gaiters' – who had a particularly memorable Ascot in 1919 by owning seven (or, strictly, six and a half) winners: that year's Derby winner Grand Parade (St James's Palace Stakes), Dominion (Prince of Wales's Stakes), Scatwell (Wokingham), Bright Folly (Windsor Castle), Lady Juliet (Granville), Sky-Rocket (dead-heated for the Visitors' Handicap) and He (walked over for the Churchill Stakes). Five of those were ridden by Arthur Smith, still an apprentice to Glanely's trainer Frank Barling.

Sir Gordon Carter (left) with Lord Glanely.

Also noteworthy in 1919 were the absence of Biennial and Triennial races (these categories of race did not survive the war); a terrible pile-up in the Coronation Stakes, when three fillies fell; a frustrating Gold Cup for Steve Donoghue, who bred the winner By Jingo! but rode runner-up Air Raid; and George V's first post-war Ascot winner, Viceroy in the Waterford Stakes. New races in 1919, familiar to modern racegoers, were the Chesham Stakes, Jersey Stakes and Ribblesdale Stakes. Nowadays the Ribblesdale is for three-year-old fillies over a mile and a half but originally it was run over a mile for three- and four-year-olds of either sex, and named after Lord Ribblesdale, the Master of the Buckhounds whom we last met chasing after the unwelcome photographer.

Diadem was back in 1920 to take both the Rous Memorial Stakes and the King's Stand for a second time – though the magnitude of that achievement is compromised by her having a walkover in the Rous Memorial – and for good measure she beat her only rival Tetrameter in the All-Aged Stakes. The following year, at the age of seven, she returned again to try for a third Rous Memorial Stakes in what would be her final racecourse appearance. She had been beaten at Epsom earlier that June and, as George Lambton chronicled, Ascot was not to provide a happy farewell:

> I had some trouble with her near fore-joint after she had run at Epsom, where she had made a gallant fight, carrying 10 stone. This had been got over, but that year the going at Ascot was terribly hard, and I had some doubts about running her. However, she moved so freely and well, the morning before the race, that I told Lord D'Abernon that she could run and would win. Starting with three to one laid on her she was beaten easily by Monarch, and pulled up very sore, not on the leg that had been giving the trouble, but, as is so often the case, saving that one had put too much pressure on the other.
>
> I don't think I have ever felt a defeat more, for not only was my favourite beaten, but I had let her owner down badly. Tragedy as it was to him, he had not a word of reproach for me, although I deserved it. A curious thing happened in connection with this race. After Diadem's first victory Lord D'Abernon had given my wife a very pretty brooch with the mare's name in diamonds. She, like the rest of us, was devoted to Diadem, and always wore it. On going into the Paddock to see the mare saddled, she suddenly realized that the brooch was gone; she never told me at the time as she thought it was such a bad omen, and it was. It never was found.

Although not noted for any great fondness for racing, Queen Mary had a race named after her in

Major and Mrs Hedges – she sporting an unusual stole – set heads turning in 1922.

1921: the Queen Mary Stakes, now the highlight of the meeting for two-year-old fillies, and worth a handsome £2,680 to the winner on its first running.

The third running of the Queen Mary Stakes in 1923 attracted another of the great horses whose names illuminate the history of Ascot: Mumtaz Mahal, a daughter of The Tetrarch who had inherited from her sire such blistering speed that she (like he) is often described as one of the fastest two-year-olds ever seen. She was bought as a yearling at Doncaster Sales by George Lambton on behalf of the Aga Khan, grandfather of the present Aga Khan (owner of Shergar) and between the wars a racehorse owner on a huge scale: he won the Derby three times in that period (Blenheim (1930), Bahram (1935) and Mahmoud (1936)), adding two more after the Second World War (My Love in 1948 and Tulyar in 1952).

Mumtaz Mahal scorched through her first race at Newmarket, breaking the track record, then started 4–1 on for the Queen Mary. The *Daily Mirror* reported:

> The real stir of the afternoon was Mumtaz Mahal. This flying filly – with the spots of her famous 'rocking-horse' sire – literally lost her rivals in the Queen Mary Stakes … After standing as quiet as a sheep at the gate she went off with the same wonderful burst of speed she had shown when making her record-breaking debut at Newmarket, and before a furlong had been covered she must have been at least half a dozen lengths clear.

Above: Straining for a better view from the carriage stand, 1923.

Below: Smiler the clown plying his trade, 1924.

At the post she was ten lengths to the good – a remarkable winning distance in a top two-year-old race, and the most extraordinary juvenile performance at Ascot since that of her sire a decade earlier. (Mumtaz Mahal's great-great-granddaughter Petite Etoile was to make her own, controversial impression on Ascot in 1960.)

The same meeting saw a royal double, with Knight Of The Garter winning the Coventry Stakes and Weathervane the Royal Hunt Cup in the colours of George V.

Through the 1920s the course was constantly being improved. In 1922 (the year that Golden Myth became the only horse in the twentieth century to win the Gold Vase and Gold Cup in the same year) the eye of the *Evening*

Standard's correspondent was caught by the horticultural arrangements:

> … ornamental bamboos, Japanese maples, and other sub-tropical plants, a great bed of rhododendrons, and many tubs with brilliant geraniums, marguerites and Canterbury bells, while all along the balconies and approaches will be hung baskets with ivy-leafed geraniums, lobelia and many other gaily coloured flowers.

A couple of years later the eye of *The Times*'s correspondent was caught by something else. 'Ascot is notoriously the best place in England to see beautiful women in beautiful clothes,' he wrote, adding acerbically, 'and also less beautiful women in very odd clothes. I do not hold vaccination marks to be beautiful.'

In November 1925, at a time of great economic hardship with a general strike looming, the *Evening Standard* noted with approval that 'Unemployment in the Ascot area is being considerably relieved by alterations now in progress at the racecourse property.'

Distinctions between classes were becoming blurred, and the social spread of those in the Royal Enclosure was widening – not to everybody's satisfaction. In 1925 Sir Frederick Ponsonby, a Trustee, suggested to Viscount Churchill that the charge for entrance to the Enclosure be reduced as many young people, however well bred, could not afford the cost: 'There is also the consideration that we may be letting in all the Mosensteins and leaving out the gentlemen of England.'

It was also becoming more difficult to distinguish class by clothes. Dresses became more casual, and the hemline could hardly keep still. In 1920 it was just a few inches below the knee, then through the 1920s it crept further up: legs came into their own, with shoes and stockings important fashion points. Furthermore, the term 'Ascot hat' started to come into use in the 1920s. *The Times* wrote in 1923: 'Above all it was a day for the Ascot frock and especially for the Ascot hat.' In 1928 it was announced that Bradleys boutique was 'showing a delightful collection of hats for Ascot', and by the 1930s entire fashion advertisements were given over to Ascot hats.

There were changes in gentlemen's fashion, too. Bow ties and cravats gave way to ties, and buttonholes began to be worn, a fashion led by the Aga Khan who bought his flowers each day from Frank Markey.

Testing the weighing chair, 1924.

One of those characters who provide important footnotes in the history of Ascot, a history not just as a racecourse but as an occasion – like 'Donkey Jemmy' in the nineteenth century or the flamboyant 'Abyssinian' tipster Ras Prince Monolulu in the twentieth – Frank Markey first went to Ascot races in 1919 to sell flowers for buttonholes outside the Royal Enclosure, thereby beginning a family tradition that continues to the present day: in 1952 Frank's son Martin started helping out his father and later took over. Frank, who had lost a leg at the age of seven and was known as 'Long John Silver', had sold flowers at Epsom and Doncaster before the First World War and was asked to extend his operation to cover Ascot, where there was no flower-seller.

His routine was gruelling. Each morning of the meeting he woke at 4.30 a.m. and went to the old Covent Garden market, where he bought

Above: Sir John Lavery, *The Gold Cup, Ascot – The Royal Enclosure*, 1922.

Below: Frank Markey selling flowers in Jermyn Street.

Raoul Dufy, *Ascot*, 1930.

three or four boxes of flowers. These boxes, stacked some two feet high, were then carried on his head until, on arrival at Ascot by road, he arranged the flowers in two old gherkin cans and set up his stall in what is now No. 1 Car Park. This was where the cream of racegoers would set out their lavish picnics, and although provided with a chair Frank stood all day from nine in the morning until the last race.

In Markey's early days at Ascot the stall was dominated by carnations, with a few roses and gardenias, and while women very occasionally would buy a flower, his prime customers were men. The traditional colour was clove – dark red – but on Gold Cup day the preferred colour switched to yellow in honour of the big race, and men would often wear a yellow tie or waistcoat to match. Others would choose their colour for sentimental

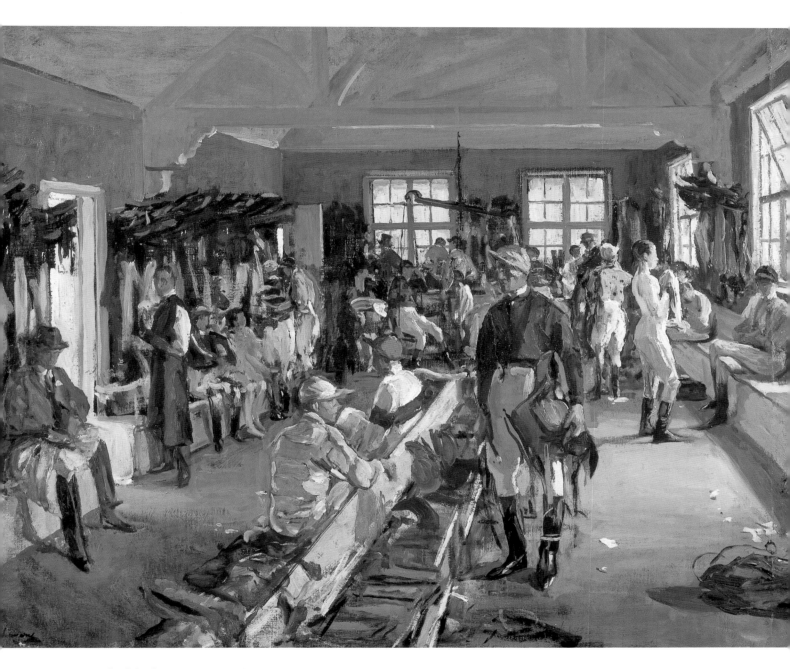

Sir John Lavery, *The Jockeys'*
Dressing Room at Ascot, 1923.

Picnic in the car park, 1920s.

reasons: for example, old boys of Harrow School were the only ones to ask for blue, in the form of a cornflower. Some men always had the same buttonhole – the Duke of Marlborough, for instance, sported a white carnation – and it was traditional that the buttonhole be entirely devoid of leaves and trimmings.

Some racegoers were superstitious. If they had backed winners while wearing a certain flower, they would ask for the same sort and colour of flower the next day; if they had lost, they would ask for a different one. Others insisted that a particular member of the Markey family secure the flower on their lapel. If a gipsy had given them a flower, they would ask the Markeys to remove and replace it, fearing to touch it themselves.

Frank Markey's final Ascot was in 1971, when the Ascot Heath fixture on the Saturday was called off following torrential rain: the flowers that year were given to the local hospital. When shortly afterwards he died, a local newspaper reported the death of 'The King of the Flower Sellers'.

In 1925 Queen Mary commissioned Sir Alfred Munnings to paint her a scene of the Royal Procession crossing the park, and did her best to make his task as painless as possible. Each morning a chauffeur called at his Chelsea home in a Daimler and drove him to Windsor Castle to see the horses being harnessed, and then into the park to watch the procession pass by. Munnings recalled the experience in his autobiography:

> Nearer and nearer came the Procession, a long, glittering line of moving scarlet and gold. Two scarlet-coated outriders on white horses were in the lead; next the King's carriage, drawn by four greys; then came two more scarlet-coated outriders on bay horses. The next carriage was drawn by bays, followed by more outriders on bays, and so the Procession of ten carriages went by. One may well imagine the length of it, with outriders between each carriage, and outriders

bringing up the rear. For me the glorious part of this Procession were the colours of the royal livery worn by the postillions – too magnificent to describe. Short, tight-fitting, dark-blue jackets with rich frontage of gold braiding, gold belts, scarlet, gold-braided sleeves, black velvet caps worn over short, white-powdered wigs, tight-fitting white leather breeches, and boots with flesh-coloured tops. Above all, the gorgeous display of large red rosettes on either side of the horses' heads. These lovely rosettes gave an indescribable beauty to the whole Procession.

How shall I write of the beautiful movement of the two leading grey steeds as they came along, ridden by the outriders? ... The outriders wore silk hats with gold bands and cockades, scarlet coats with gold braiding, white leathers and boots with flesh-coloured tops. ...

After leaving Duke's Lane, with the King and Queen and Royal Family and guests seated in their respective carriages, the Procession

Sir Alfred Munnings, *Their Majesties' Return from Ascot*, 1925.

Above: Gordon Richards, who rode 178 winners at Ascot between 1925 and 1954.

Below: Charlie Smirke, whose Royal Ascot career spanned riding generations from the 1920s to the 1950s.

assumed its right look. Parasols, ladies' hats and dresses gave a fresh gaiety to the scene. Also on either side of the royal carriage were two mounted gentlemen of the Royal Household, in top hats, black morning coats and tight, striped trousers strapped beneath their boots.

The 'Duke's Lane' mentioned by Munnings was the spot in Windsor Great Park where the royal party would be disgorged from the Daimlers, which had driven them from the castle, into the carriages, which would then take them from there through the Golden Gates and up the New Mile.

On that occasion witnessed by Munnings, neither the royal party nor the watching artist would have known that the 1925 meeting was to see the first Ascot victory for a young jockey who was to become the most successful rider in British Turf history.

Born in Shropshire in May 1904, Gordon Richards (who had gained his early riding experience on pit ponies) was twenty-one years old when riding Lord Glanely's Sunderland to win the Trial Stakes, opening race of the 1925 meeting, and well on the way to landing the first of his twenty-six jockeys' championships. By the time of his retirement in 1954 he had ridden 178 winners at Ascot.

If Richards was already a riding legend in the making, the equine star of the 1925 meeting was Diomedes. Unbeaten in six races as a two-year-old, he came to Ascot with a huge reputation and proceeded to win both the Granville Stakes on the Thursday and the King's Stand Stakes the following day. He returned to Ascot in 1926 and won the Cork and Orrery All-Aged Stakes, ridden (as in all his races) by Jack Leach, who in his autobiography *Sods I Have Cut on the Turf* described the colt: 'Free, but not too free, quick and alert, he was a beautiful ride … He was truly an epoch-making sprinter.'

At the 1925 meeting the Ascot Derby (which the following year became the King Edward VII Stakes) went to Solario, whose easy defeat of Manna reversed Epsom form: Manna had won the Derby by eight lengths, with Solario back in fourth after being caught up in the tape at the start. Having won the 1925 St Leger, Solario went on to win the 1926 Coronation Cup at Epsom by fifteen lengths, then returned to Ascot for the Gold Cup. Ridden by Joe Childs, he started 6–4 on in a field of six, with the French colt Priori II second favourite at 7–1. *The Times* described how Solario led the field out of

Swinley Bottom towards the home turn:

> He went on making his own pace, followed by Priori II and Warminster, and came into the Straight with a clear lead, still galloping resolutely and easily. Half way up the Straight Priori II made his effort and drew up to Solario and then actually got his head in front. For an awful silent moment there were visions of Solario's defeat. Childs shook him up and actually showed him the whip, but never used it. Solario seemed at once to realize that he was to make a final effort, and he made it, sailing away to win in the style of a great horse.

Solario was not the only top-notch horse on view in 1926. Coronach, who had that year's Derby by five lengths, strolled home in the St James's Palace Stakes by twenty lengths, while the Queen Mary Stakes went to Book Law, who scored an Ascot double when landing the Coronation Stakes as a three-year-old in 1927 *en route* to winning the St Leger. Book Law's additional claim to fame is as paternal granddam to a horse whose own Ascot moment in 1966 was the final victory in the greatest of all steeplechasing careers: Arkle.

Above: Brownie Carslake, who won consecutive Gold Cups on Foxlaw in 1927 and Invershin in 1928.

Below: Joe Childs won the Gold Cup three times at Ascot.

The 1926 meeting saw the Royal Enclosure buildings extended and a new Iron Stand erected by the Enclosure lawn, and during the same year the course began to install a new watering system, with the facility to dispense around two million gallons of water onto the turf through 5,000 nozzles, an innovation warmly welcomed by owners and trainers. Less popular was the grandstand clock – at least to one local lady, who wrote to Gordon Carter and told him forcibly that the clock was a 'sauce' [*sic*] of annoyance to her at night, and that it 'threw the whole neighbourhood out of gear by being a quarter of an hour wrong' one Sunday.

In 1928 trainer Cecil Boyd-Rochfort had his first Ascot winner with Royal Minstrel in the St James's Palace Stakes, and for the next forty years 'the Captain' enjoyed one of the most glittering careers of the twentieth century, winning thirteen Classics (each of the five at least once) and numerous races for members of the Royal Family, including 57 for King George VI (whose trainer he became in 1943) and 136 for Queen Elizabeth II.

Another notable first in 1928 came in the Ascot Stakes: the first course win for a young horse named Brown Jack (on whom, see pages 197-217 below).

The unsaddling enclosure, 1926.

Somewhat above Brown Jack in class was Fairway, who in 1929 returned to the course where he had won the Coventry Stakes two years earlier. In the meantime he had won the 1928 Eclipse Stakes, the St Leger and the Champion Stakes to pronounce himself one of the best colts of the 1920s, and could well have won the Derby but for being mobbed on the way to the start by his adoring public and boiling over. In 1929 he won the Rous Memorial Stakes at Ascot, and in the autumn scored a notable double at Newmarket, winning a second Champion Stakes and the Jockey Club Cup.

That year there was no Royal Procession at Ascot as George V was absent, still suffering the effects of a streptococcal infection that had struck him down the previous November. He was not even completely recovered when attending a service of thanksgiving for his recovery in St Paul's Cathedral three weeks after Ascot.

The Royal Procession was resumed in 1930 (when the Trial Stakes was renamed the Queen Anne Stakes), but after two races on Wednesday 18 June a more appropriate mode of transport at Ascot would have been Noah's Ark, as the course was ravaged by a storm of Biblical intensity.

John Hislop – later a noted journalist and amateur rider, and a man who would earn the lasting gratitude of the racing world by breeding Brigadier Gerard – was allowed time off from Sandhurst to go racing:

Gipsy flower sellers, 1925.

> When we got to Ascot the sky was the colour of charcoal and before long a storm of almost tropical violence broke over the racecourse, a bookmaker was killed by lightning and, after The Macnab, ridden by Gordon Richards, had slopped through the mud to win the Royal Hunt Cup, the intensity of the rain making it appear that the runners were galloping through an interminable series of curtains made of glass beads, racing was abandoned. We were on the Heath, and, to shelter from the rain, went into the tunnel leading under the course. At first all went well, but as the rain continued the depth of the water began to rise and those in the middle, visualising being drowned, tried to get out, while those outside were trying to get in. For a few moments it seemed probably that a watery Black Hole of Calcutta was about to result, but thanks to the phlegmatic nature of the English character and the rain eventually stopping, disaster was avoided. The scene afterwards was remarkable: everyone and everything was drenched, miniature lakes seemed to have sprung up all round and women were driving home half-naked and wrapped in newspapers, which they had exchanged for their soaked dresses.

The finishing touches, 1927.

Also at the meeting was a thirteen-year-old boy named Doug Smith – soon to make his own mark on Ascot as five times champion jockey:

> All the course and the enclosures were awash, and I was perched on my father's shoulders to keep my feet out of the floods. I have a

vivid recollection of the smartly dressed ladies, their Ascot hats drenched and drooping, sadly leaving the Club marquees that stood on the heath side of the course in those days, and picking their way disconsolately through the floods towards the car parks. My own reaction was philosophical. The storm broke a long dry spell. My first thought was: 'Well, at least I won't have to water the garden this evening.' But when we got home we found that not a drop of rain had fallen, though the farm was only six miles from Ascot, so local was the storm.

The *Daily Herald* painted a graphic picture of chaos:

In some of the tents women fainted. Four collapsed together in one small tent. Word sped that a man had been killed by lightning in Tattersall's. The real terror showed then. Men went pale. Women gazed on the storm with fascinated horror, deadly white. Gradually the density of the rain became lesser. The air became lighter, the thunder less like the crash of a battery of guns. The frigid stare of terror, incongruous in painted eyes, melted. Women pinned up their frocks in the manner of charwomen and trooped out. It was almost impossible to find their motor-cars. Once-smart men and women jostled, ran, searched. Those who set off down the tunnel to the station found two feet of water. They went across the field ankle deep in mud. Their clothes? They were past caring for them.

Another newspaper gave a rather sexist report of 'women drenched to the skin, women all but knee-deep in water, women left shoeless in the mud,

Opposite: The calm before the storm, as racegoers make their way from Ascot station in 1930.

Below: Making the best of it.

women blown or pushed off their feet or slipped off the improvised bridges of chairs and boxes and falling full length into the lakes which once were grass – before a thought can be spared to their clothes', but far more serious than ladies' clothes being ruined was the day's fatality. He turned out to be a bookmaker named Holbein, who had been sheltering under an umbrella in the betting ring.

Despite the bombardment, racing was resumed on the Thursday, with Wednesday's abandoned races added to that card and Friday's.

The Totalisator – a novel form of betting that involved putting all stakes into a pool which was then shared out among the winners – was introduced to British racing in 1929, though its benefits were not immediately understood. A cartoon in the *Sporting and Dramatic News* showed a groom discussing with a yokel this newfangled way of betting:

COUNTRY LAD (GOT IN TO HELP IN STABLES): 'Wot's this 'ere Tote they're talking about, penny in the slot kind o' thing, ain't it?'
GROOM: 'Yes, like one that's out of order, it is. You puts your penny in, and you may get a bit o' toffee – mostly you don't.'

After a stuttering start – difficulties with building caused delays – the Tote became fully functional at Ascot in 1931. The Ascot Authority had constructed the Tote buildings between 1929 and 1930 in the Paddock, the grandstand and the Six Shilling Enclosure (as the Five Shilling Enclosure had become with inflation), the designs having been agreed in consultation with the Racecourse Betting Control Board, the authority overseeing betting at this time. It was not until 12 June 1930, just four days before the race meeting began, that the first three Tote buildings were completed, but the RBCB was not able to install all the necessary equipment in time for the meeting so the new form of betting was not properly operational in that year. Installation of the electrical equipment did not commence until January 1931. It was used that June, and the RBCB report stated that the Ascot facility was 'the largest of its kind yet erected and worked most efficiently during this important meeting'.

There were 156 windows for selling tickets and 163 for paying out (unlike now, the two operations used different windows), as well as eighteen for

The inner workings of a Tote display board, 1929.

betting on the Daily Double and nine for exchanging tickets. There were three synchronised electric-light indicator boards, each large enough to accommodate the numbers of forty runners. The ticket-issuing machines were portable and had previously been in use on other racecourses.

An RBCB officer controlled all the betting throughout the course from the central control room, using a control switchboard with facilities for locking or freeing all ticket-issuing machines, a miniature indicator, plugging-down rack for arranging the disposition of the horse numbers on the indicators, a dividend-display panel, and a power switchboard for controlling the electricity supply that operated the equipment and indicators. Some 1,000 staff worked for the Tote at Ascot that first year, and the RBCB thanked the Ascot Authority 'for the valuable assistance given to the Board in their difficult task of organising the operation of the Totalisator at the Ascot Meeting, a task which demanded the closest attention to detail and the co-operation of all connected with the management of the Meeting'.

The new Tote buildings dramatically transformed the environment of the racecourse, and the *Windsor, Slough & Eton Express* stated that 'the thousands who will attend the meeting in June next will scarcely recognise some parts of it'. (During the construction of the buildings, George V insisted that no tree should be removed, due to his 'marked affection' for the plants.)

Moreover, the Tote developments led to the greatest change to the paddock area since the beginning of the century. As the old loose boxes were converted into the Paddock Tote, new boxes were constructed further to the west outside the previously developed racecourse area: this range of buildings stands in its original form today. Two rings were created, the first the pre-parade ring and the second the parade ring – the first time that actual designated parade areas were provided within the Paddock.

The Tote was an immediate success at Ascot in 1931, total turnover for the meeting being announced at £227,711 – of which the largest amount bet on a single race was the £9,236 Win Pool and £7,781 Place Pool for the Royal Hunt Cup: indeed, this was the largest Tote pool for any one race in Britain that year. The largest turnover for a single day was the £66,808 wagered at Ascot on Gold Cup day.

It soon became apparent that the Tote as a means of betting made particular appeal to women, nervous of the hustle and bustle of the

The Tote display board at Ascot, 1933.

bookmakers' ring. Sidney Galtrey, 'Hotspur' of the *Daily Telegraph*, wrote in his book *Memoirs of a Racing Journalist*, published in 1934:

> Why have women come racing in such vastly greater numbers in recent years? They are expected at Ascot. They may be excused for thinking the meeting is run for them and not primarily for the horses and their owners. It is their show ground. The Totalisator came to them as their special godsend. Incidentally, the Racecourse Betting Control Board can regard women as their godsend. The Tote would languish without the interest of women. They will offend against the unwritten law of the Royal Enclosure at Ascot if they make personal contact with the bookmakers on the rails. What they may do at Newmarket, Goodwood, and indeed, anywhere else they must not do at Ascot lest great indignity befall them. The Tote saves

The Royal Procession enters the Royal Enclosure, 1932.

them from their men friends and from total abstention from wagering at the royal meeting.

Not being able to have direct contact with bookmakers was not the only 'unwritten law' which fettered women in the Royal Enclosure: in 1922 Gordon Carter had made it clear that they were not to smoke. But there were ways round the betting restriction, most notably the simple strategy of getting the men to place bets on the ladies' behalf. In June 1925 Sir Frederick Ponsonby had written that, 'Young men complain that they are made into messenger boys and have to run up and down between the races for their women friends taking tickets to Pickersgill [a bookmaker].' One man suggested that a box should be placed in the Enclosure into which women could put their notes for bookmakers, but for legal reasons this was not possible.

This problem for ladies wishing to place a bet had caused Mrs Helen Vernet to set up as a bookmaker immediately after the First World War, and she became a familiar sight at Ascot. The daughter of a Scottish nobleman, she had squandered much of her fortune betting, and after being advised to lead an outdoor life following a bout of tuberculosis decided that she would be much better off as bookmaker than punter. At first she took small bets from a circle of friends – mostly female – who would slip their instructions to her on

Preparations in the 1930s. **Above:** Getting the Royal Box ready. **Below:** Watering the course.

pieces of paper. Such informal betting was strictly illegal, but her client base gradually grew, with lady racegoers finding her a more congenial medium for betting than the bookies in Tattersalls ring. As soon as the ring bookmakers were aware of her activities they lodged a complaint, and Ascot was witness to the undignified spectacle of her being bustled out of the ring by officials.

The romantic novelist Barbara Cartland leaving the Highland Brigade enclosure, 1930.

Agreement between employer and employee, 1934.

GENERAL CONDITIONS

Smoking during working hours is strictly forbidden. Any one caught disobeying this order will be immediately discharged.

Smoking is permitted in the Bothies during the time allowed for meals, but at no other times or in any other buildings.

Men working with horses will arrange for their meals according to work in hand.

Men are expected to work overtime, if required, at the rate of 1/- per hour.

Painters will be allowed to leave work 5 minutes earlier in order to enable them to wash their hands before partaking of their meals.

Signature of Employee

Signature of Employer
Lt.-Colonel.

6th October 1934

The upshot of this unseemly exit was that she was offered a position with Ladbrokes, and became the first official lady bookmaker in Britain. She became a director of Ladbrokes, and stayed with the firm until 1955, the year before her death.

Whether on the Tote or by the more traditional means of taking the odds with a bookmaker, plenty of Ascot bets in 1932 and for the next two years would have been on one of the most bonny and popular horses to race between the wars, Lord Derby's diminutive chestnut colt Hyperion.

Trained by George Lambton, Hyperion had been so small as a foal that serious thought was given to having him put down. But he grew sufficiently to be reprieved, and made his racecourse début when finishing fourth in a small race at Doncaster in May 1932. The twenty-two-runner New Stakes at Ascot was a considerable step up in class, but Hyperion astonished connections by winning by three lengths from the very highly regarded Nun's Veil, and later that year won the Dewhurst Stakes at Newmarket. His two-year-old career had been very good but not earth-shattering – two outright wins and a dead heat from five outings – but he excelled as a three-year-old, winning the Chester Vase and the Derby (by four lengths) before returning to Ascot for the Prince of Wales's Stakes, which, starting at 2–1 on, he won easily by two lengths from Shamsuddin. 'Hyp-hyp-hyperion!' cheered a leader, no less, in *The Times* the following morning. He then won the St Leger.

George Lambton and Lord Derby parted company at the end of the 1933 season, and Hyperion came under the care of Colledge Leader for a four-year-old campaign geared towards one major race: the Gold Cup. But Leader did not seem

to understand that Hyperion was a lazy horse who needed a great deal of work to get him fit, and shortly before the big race rumours were in circulation that all was not going to plan. Connections of his main rival Felicitation accordingly worked on a strategy, instructing their jockey Gordon Richards to set a strong pace from the start to test Hyperion's fitness. To the dismay of the crowd, the plan worked brilliantly: the blinkered Felicitation made all the running and kept going to win by eight lengths from Thor II, with Hyperion and his regular jockey Tommy Weston a very weary third. 'It was sad to see him beaten,' lamented *The Times*'s man before adding philosophically, 'but it must be admitted that he was beaten fairly and squarely by a better colt, and that is all there is to it.' Lord Derby's colt ran once more – beaten in the Dullingham Stakes at Newmarket – and was then retired to pursue a highly successful career as a stallion.

Hyperion was only one of a succession of famous horses to run at Ascot in the 1930s. Leaving Brown Jack until the next chapter, we think of Trimdon, Gold Cup winner in 1931 and 1932; the brilliantly fast sprinter Myrobella, a

Hyperion wins the Prince of Wales's Stakes in 1933 from Shamsuddin and Belfry.

Trimdon, on the right, beats Singapore in a desperate finish for the 1931 Gold Cup.

granddaughter of The Tetrarch, who won the five-furlong Fern Hill Stakes in 1933 by five lengths; the 1935 Triple Crown winner Bahram, who won the St James's Palace Stakes that year; and Mid-day Sun, winner of the Hardwicke Stakes in 1937 after winning the Derby two weeks earlier.

But in terms of famous races rather than just famous horses, the high point of Ascot between the wars – and one of the most fêted races run anywhere in the twentieth century – was the 1936 Gold Cup duel between Quashed and Omaha.

Like Grundy and Bustino, the names of Omaha and Quashed are destined to be inextricably linked in Turf history: you can't have one without the other. But they were very different types of horse.

Omaha was the first winner of the US Triple Crown to have run in Europe, let alone at Ascot. After winning the Kentucky Derby, the Preakness and the Belmont Stakes in his native land in 1935 he had gone lame, and early in 1936 his owner William Woodward sent him across the Atlantic to Captain Cecil Boyd-Rochfort's Newmarket stable to be prepared for an audacious attempt at the Gold Cup.

A large and powerfully built chestnut, the four-year-old Omaha certainly had the physical credentials for the race, but there was concern that in the USA he had done all his racing on left-hand tracks, so to get him used to going 'the wrong way' he had his first two outings in England at a course with a similar shape to Ascot, Kempton Park. He won both his races there, and became favourite for the Gold Cup.

The four-year-old filly Quashed was Omaha's principal rival but could not match him for physique. She was altogether more leggy, and as a yearling had looked so like a late developer that it was even suggested she might one day make a Grand National horse. But a highly encouraging two-year-old campaign in 1934 had put paid to that sort of idea and led owner Lord Stanley and trainer Colledge Leader to aim her for the 1935 Oaks, which despite starting at 33–1 she won by a short head.

In the autumn of that year her obviously increasing strength pointed towards the big staying races at Newmarket: she ran third in the Cesarewitch under 8 stone 9 pounds, and won the Jockey Club Cup, both over two and a quarter miles. A campaign that today may seem somewhat capricious for an Oaks winner – the *Cesarewitch*? – continued in spring 1936 with victory in the

The accordion player's monkey attracts admirers, 1935.

The start of the Royal Hunt Cup, 1936.

Ascot scenes in the 1930s.

2¼-mile Great Metropolitan Handicap at Epsom, followed up with the Ormonde Stakes at Chester.

On Gold Cup day Omaha started a firm market leader at 11–8 – though his supporters would have been made uneasy by his sweating profusely in the paddock, which he had not done before on a racecourse. Quashed traded at 3–1, with Valerius, winner of the Yorkshire Cup, at 9–1 and the other six runners (who included three French challengers) all very easy to back.

Quashed was ridden by Dick Perryman, and Omaha by Rufus Beasley, who had partnered the American colt in his two previous outings at Kempton Park.

The *Times* correspondent – anonymous, but almost certainly R. C. Lyle that day – prefaced his report of the race by describing it as 'one of the greatest races that I have ever seen, or can hope to see'. His report intimates why he felt that way:

The parade over, the field of nine went down to the start. There was no delay there before Captain Allison sent them off in a line. Passing the stands for the first time Chaudiere, a French filly, was in front, followed by Patriot King, who could not win an amateur riders' race recently at Lewes. Behind him came Buckleigh and Quashed. Going down the course after making the turn by the Paddock, Buckleigh went on in front, the field going a good gallop. At the end of a mile, or it may have been rather more, Buckleigh was still leading by two lengths from Chaudiere, with Patriot King third and Quashed fourth. Before the straight was reached Omaha and Quashed moved up, and soon after making the bend into the straight Quashed was in front. Omaha was close behind her. Two furlongs from the finish Quashed and Omaha had the race between them.

And now there took place a really epic encounter. P. Beasley and Omaha came repeatedly at Quashed, who was being beautifully ridden by Perryman. Every time he came at her she found a little more and beat him off. Omaha would not be beaten, and time after time he challenged the filly, but nothing would make her give way an inch, and she held on to win without being headed by a short head. As she got nearer and nearer to the winning-post, the cheering which had greeted her progress died down. After all, it seemed all the time that the great raking American colt would outstride her and that she would be beaten. She went past the winning-post in silence, for only the judge could say which of the two had won. I would not have been surprised if Mr Hancock had given the result as a dead-heat, but he is a fine judge, and few dead-heats come from him. He decided that

Omaha (far side) and Quashed fight out their epic duel in the 1936 Gold Cup.

Quashed had won by a short head and that the best of the French invaders had been beaten for second place by many lengths. When his decision was announced on the board there was more cheering and scurrying to the unsaddling enclosure to watch the great filly come back to be unsaddled …

I must admit that I have never been so thrilled with a race as I was with this Gold Cup. Never before have I seen a horse struggle on so gamely as did Quashed. Time after time she seemed to be beaten, and time after time she refused to give in.

Quashed was the first filly in the twentieth century to win the Gold Cup (the next to do so was Gladness in 1958), but even as her achievement was being acclaimed the Omaha camp started trying out excuses. If only Beasley had not dropped his whip inside the final furlong; if only William Woodward had not insisted that Omaha attack Quashed early in the straight, rather than (as the jockey wanted) being held up for one deadly burst close home. Much more sinister was the suggestion that Omaha had been 'got at' in the paddock by a 'Squirt Gang' – horse nobblers who would squirt burning acid at a favourite to ruin its chance – and certainly the colt's agitated demeanour before the race supported such a sensational idea. Thirteen years after that famous Gold Cup, Woodward – not noted for being a bad loser – wrote to Boyd-Rochfort from the USA:

I am confident that some underworld fellow sprayed Omaha with 'high-life'. They do this at a distance of three or four feet by using little so-called guns which look like a fountain pen. They use these things in holding up banks in this country.

Whatever the true circumstances, both Omaha and Quashed had been involved in a gargantuan battle,

Harrods – where you can buy a top hat for £2.

Ascot
1937

The Grey Topper	40 -
The Morning Coat	6½ Gns.
The Grey Waistcoat	30/-
The Cashmere Trousers	63/-
The White Shirt	15/6
The Linen Collars (dozen)	11/6
The Large Shape Tie	8/6
The White Linen Handkerchiefs (dozen)	21/-
The Silver Grey Gloves	16/6
The Umbrella (with Pigskin-covered handle)	55/-

The Man's Shop
HARRODS

Harrods Ltd   London SW1

and the race took its toll, as neither reached the same heights again. Omaha ran just once more, beaten a neck in the Princess of Wales's Stakes at Newmarket the month following Ascot, after behaving badly at the start. Quashed won the Jockey Club Cup for a second time later in 1936 from a single rival, and in 1937 tried for a repeat Gold Cup: she ran third behind Precipitation.

Jack Leach struck the right note about this fabled race: 'To see Quashed and Omaha battle out the finish of the Ascot Gold Cup took years off a man's life, though it was well worth it.'

The Right Honourable Gavin George, Baron Hamilton of Dalzell, KT, CVO, MC, was appointed His Majesty's Representative at Ascot in March 1934 to succeed Viscount Churchill, who had died early that year, and the responsibility for running the meeting was divided between Hamilton and Lord Granard, who was appointed to the new post of His Majesty's Comptroller at Ascot and put in charge of entrance to the Royal Enclosure. (The position of Comptroller was very short-lived, being discontinued in 1945.)

One of Hamilton's early tasks was overseeing the redevelopment of the Royal Stand, which commenced in 1935 and which involved a tricky decision. A design feature was to be the incorporation of masks on the keystones of the arches – but what should they depict? The sculptor Percy Bentham (a descendant of the philosopher Jeremy Bentham) was commissioned to undertake the work, and at first it was felt that the masks should represent the dominions of the British Empire: a Native Canadian for Canada, a Rajah for India, a Maori for New Zealand, a Bantu for South Africa and an Aborigine for Australia. But Sir Frederick Ponsonby reflected that he was uncertain 'that this treatment will please the visitors from overseas', and it was decided to opt for masks that would not be named as representing a particular dominion but would rather represent different types of people in the Empire: a bearded Anglo-Saxon, a Polynesian, a negro, a Sikh and a Native Canadian. George V and Queen Mary visited the course in April 1935 to inspect work in progress.

Amid the changes one man stayed resolutely in place, his shoelaces still gleaming and freshly ironed. Sir Gordon Carter had been Clerk of the Course since 1910, but rarely had he seen a sight at Ascot to match that which greeted him as he made his regular non-raceday round one morning in September 1936: Marlene Dietrich dressed in black silk pyjamas under a large fur coat. The fabled German siren was at the course with co-star Robert Donat to shoot a scene of Ascot races set in 1913 for the film *Knight Without Armour*, produced by Alexander Korda. Exactly the effect that the sight of Miss Dietrich had on Sir Gordon is not recorded, but the *Daily Sketch* correspondent made a guess:

> The only person I suspected of being slightly amused by this desecration of Royal Ascot was the aristocratic Sir Gordon Carter ... He met pyjamaed Marlene and walked with dignity to see the sound-film being made in the beautiful enclosure. He remembers the Ascot of 1913 well.

This interlude must have been a welcome distraction for Sir Gordon, for by that point in 1936 the monarchy was being rocked by its gravest crisis of the twentieth century.

George V had died on 20 January 1936 at the age of seventy, to be succeeded by his oldest son, who became Edward VIII. The new King was a keen follower of horse racing and had ridden point-to-point winners, but he never attended the Royal Meeting as reigning monarch. With the court still in mourning there was no Royal Procession and no royal attendance in 1936, and by the end of the year Edward had abdicated in order to fulfil his desire to marry Mrs Wallis Simpson, an action that propelled his younger brother to the throne as George VI. The new King and his Queen – the former Lady Elizabeth Bowes-Lyon – paid their first official visit to Ascot in 1937.

Around this time there was a good deal of debate about repositioning the course itself, primarily in order to provide more room in the enclosures and make the racing more visible, but also to make runners in races over the Straight Mile less susceptible to the caprice of the draw, and thus render that course fairer: the rails of the round course were not in line with the far rails of the Straight Mile, and in a straight race a horse drawn on the far side of the course, then coming to the junction of the two courses, had to swerve to the

The Prince of Wales with Mrs Wallis Simpson at Ascot in 1935.

right if he wished to race alongside the far rails, thereby going farther than the horse drawn on the stands side. 'This is wrong,' argued Hamilton: 'A race ought to be a test of speed and endurance, not a lottery.' So in 1936 the junction of the round course and the Straight Mile was improved with temporary fencing, and this alteration proved so successful that in 1937 permanent rails were installed. Previously horses in races on the straight course generally seemed to win under the stands, and an analysis of the results showed that this was true: jockeys drawn on the far side tried to pull their horses over to the stands side, which made the field bunch up at the finish. The effectiveness of the change was soon registered: Fairplay won the 1937 Royal Hunt Cup from a far-side draw of 31 in a field of 33, jockey Peter Maher riding him up the far side while all the other jockeys kept to the old habit of crossing to the stands side. Fairplay alone stayed on the far side, and with the new course layout the tactic worked.

The other objective, to make more room in the enclosures, was less easy to achieve. Hamilton argued for the proposal in his 1937 report to the King:

> So far as the Royal Enclosure is concerned greater comfort might be achieved by limiting the number of vouchers for admission, though this would cause widespread disappointment. The same result might be obtained in the other enclosures by raising the price of admission, which would be extremely unpopular. The only alternative and, I think, the right remedy is to increase the size of the enclosures. This could be done by pulling down the stands and re-building them further back from the course. Apart from the expense of this − which would be enormous − it is impossible because it involves the demolition of a large number of houses at the back of the 6/- enclosure … The only practicable remedy is to make a new straight course. I strongly recommend that this shall be done as soon as possible.

There were far weightier matters for a king to worry about, of course. The week before the 1939 Royal Meeting took place, hundreds of Polish Jews in Germany were repatriated to their homeland; the week after, the Nazis set about curbing the business activities of Czech Jews in Berlin. The Second World War was inexorably on its way, and this time there would be no debate

MADCAP MILLINERY AT THE 1939 ASCOT

The Striking, the Bizarre, and the Incomprehensible Viewed in Paddock and Enclosure

THIN MESH . . .

GREASED LIGHTNING . . .

SURREALIST . . .

VICTORIAN POSY . . .

BURGUNDIAN . . .

PORK PIE . . .

SUNKEN GARDEN . . .

FINE FEATHERS . . .

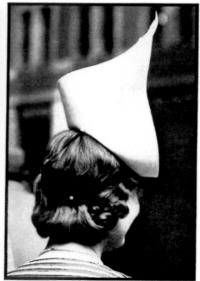

MAINSAIL . . .

about whether Ascot should take place. Confirmation that the next meeting would be cancelled came in February 1940, and in April it was made known that the Gold Cup and Wokingham Stakes would be run at Newmarket, where a skeleton programme of racing would be sustained. Then in June it was announced that all racing was cancelled without further notice, and the sport did not resume until Ripon in September 1940, with Newmarket following in October – without the Ascot races.

Ascot racecourse was commandeered by the army. The grandstand provided accommodation for gunners of the Royal Artillery, and when the King and Queen paid a visit in December 1940 they suggested that the Royal Stand be used for storage, with the other buildings in the Royal Enclosure providing accommodation for officers and men.

Bomb warning, June 1944

Racing resumed at the course on 15 May 1943 with an eight-race card that bore no relation to the usual fare of the Royal Meeting, and in all the course staged nine days' racing that year between May and October. A notable feat on Saturday 28 August 1943 was Tommy Carey's riding five consecutive winners, the last five of an eight-race programme, and the same month details of races at Ascot were first given out over a public-address system – though commentary in running was not to follow for nearly a decade. There were ten race days at Ascot in 1944 – some with marathon programmes of twelve races – and seven in 1945, beginning with a ten-race card on Easter Monday. These wartime fixtures were run under the aegis of the Jockey Club, not the Ascot Authority.

On Whit Monday, 21 May, 1945, less than two weeks after VE Day, Ascot staged its first post-war fixture – when among the enthusiastic crowd was the nineteen-year-old elder daughter of the King and Queen, Princess Elizabeth.

Opposite: 'Madcap millinery' pictured in *The Sphere*, 1939.

BROWN JACK

Unlike many of the world's greatest racecourses, Ascot does not yet have on permanent display a large statue of a famous horse. Newmarket has Eclipse and Brigadier Gerard (and Hyperion is outside the Jockey Club Rooms in the High Street); Epsom has Generous; Kempton Park has Desert Orchid; both Aintree and Ayr have Red Rum; Sandown Park has Special Cargo; Doncaster has Double Trigger. Cheltenham has scaled-down versions of Arkle, Golden Miller and Dawn Run. Outside Britain, Gladiateur is at Longchamp, Vintage Crop at The Curragh, Secretariat at Belmont Park. Each of these statues provides a monumental expression of how the spirit of famous horses permeates the atmosphere of the courses with which they were most closely associated.

Ascot's greatest horse, by contrast, is celebrated more quietly by a much smaller statue, no more than two feet high, an exquisite Alfred Munnings bronze cast in 1935 that spends most of its time locked away in a safe and is exhibited to public gaze just twice a year, first on the day of the Queen Alexandra Stakes, final race of the Royal Meeting, and for the second time to coincide with the two-mile handicap at the July Meeting that commemorates him: Brown Jack, the course's most beloved equine hero.

Brown Jack won at the Royal Meeting seven years in a row, taking the Ascot Stakes in 1928 and then the Queen Alexandra Stakes – at two and three quarter miles the longest Flat race in the calendar – for six consecutive years from 1929 to 1934. But behind that bare statistic lies an affection from the Ascot crowd which over the years grew into deep love. Brown Jack was not the most brilliant horse ever to race on the course, but he was indisputably the most popular.

Previous pages: Brown Jack.

Brown Jack was bred in Ireland. His sire Jackdaw had been runner-up in the Gold Vase in 1912 and – more to the point as far as family tradition is concerned – had won the race then named the Alexandra Plate the same year. In the summer of 1923 he covered – for the second time – a mare named Querquidella, and on 5 April 1924 she gave birth to a brown colt foal.

'As a yearling Brown Jack was very troublesome to handle,' remembered his breeder George Webb, 'especially he was hard to manage on the road when we were getting him ready for the sales.' But the colt was such a handsome individual that Webb took him to the Birr Show – where, much to his breeder's consternation, he finished last of four in the yearling class.

Brown Jack was entered for the Goff's yearling sale at Ballsbridge, Dublin, in August 1925, but was led out of the ring unsold. (One can only speculate on the feelings of those judges of horseflesh who had disregarded him as his later career unfolded ...) Later in the day Webb encountered at the sales Marcus Thompson, who was looking for a promising young horse. He was taken to have a look at Brown Jack, was very impressed with what he saw – 'we considered him a promising youngster and an exceptionally good mover with those peculiarly bowed forelegs which showed he could stand plenty of galloping' – and after £110 had changed hands Brown Jack was on his way to Kilmore House, near Cashel in County Tipperary. He was gelded and turned out in a field with a yearling donkey for a grazing companion.

Brown Jack returned to the show ring as a two-year-old, but again failed to win a prize, and Thompson's suggestion to the local butcher after the show that he purchase a half share in the horse for £50 so that 'we should sport our luck and put him on the Turf' was declined.

In late June 1926 the County Dublin trainer Charlie Rogers was driving round Tipperary looking for prospective steeplechasers to buy, and not far out of Cashel his car spluttered to a halt. He had run out of petrol. This was especially annoying as he had a runner in the first at Limerick Junction and was anxious not to be late. He made for the nearest house and asked the man who opened the door to him whether he could possibly drive him to Limerick Junction racecourse. Marcus Thompson readily agreed. 'On driving down his avenue,' recalled Rogers years later, 'I saw a horse grazing on the lawn with a donkey and asked what horse it was. Thompson replied that it was a two-year-old gelding by Jackdaw.'

Rogers was very keen on Jackdaw as a sire, and instantly decided that examining this horse was more important than rushing to the races. He liked what he saw, but not the price Thompson was asking. They agreed to differ and drove off to Limerick Junction.

That evening, after reflecting, Rogers telephoned Thompson to make a better offer. They agreed on £275, and early in July 1926 Brown Jack bade goodbye to his donkey to move to Rogers's Balfstown Stud at Mullhadart, County Dublin. Here life did not immediately become noticeably more strenuous for the gelding. In order that he should strengthen and mature he was turned out for six months in a field, where his companion was another two-year-old who would later be named Arctic Star, a horse Brown Jack would meet again in serious competition on the racecourse.

Early in 1927 came the time to start training Brown Jack, and the horse who as a yearling had proved difficult to handle had been made so fat and placid by ambling around his field with Arctic Star that initially it proved difficult to interest him in any pursuit other than leaning against his manger and enjoying a doze. But on 23 May 1927 he was stirred from his slumbers and taken to Proudstown Park, Navan, for his first race, the Meath Plate for three-year-olds over six furlongs: he started at 50–1 and lived up to those odds, finishing last.

The Alfred Munnings bronze of Brown Jack.

But connections noticed how he had been perked up by the racecourse experience, and further encouragement came from his second outing, at Phoenix Park, Dublin, in June. Still far from tuned up, he started a 20–1 outsider and finished unplaced, but there was clearly a stirring of much better things to come. Charlie Rogers recalled: 'He became a lion instead of a lamb.'

Meanwhile in England Sir Harold Wernher, who was one of the leading racehorse owners of the day, had asked his trainer Aubrey Hastings to spend £1,000 to buy him a horse to win a new race named the Champion Hurdle, which had been first run at Cheltenham earlier that year. Hastings was a man with a true feel for jumping horses – he had ridden and trained the 1906 Grand National winner Ascetic's Silver, and trained three other National winners. Shortly after receiving Sir Harold's commission he opened a letter from Charlie Rogers telling him of a very promising young horse who would be for sale at the right price, and went speedily across to Ireland. He took an instant liking to Brown Jack and made a deal on the spot: £750, plus an extra £50 should the gelding win a race. (In the event he won twenty-five.)

So in July 1927 Brown Jack came to Aubrey Hastings's stables at Wroughton, near Swindon in Wiltshire, to join one of the most powerful National Hunt trainers in the land, with a yard brimming with steeplechasing talent. In such exalted company, the still unprepossessing Brown Jack stood out like a sore thumb, and when the stable lads were asked which of them would like to look after the newcomer, the standard reaction was somewhere between horror and hilarity. Eventually a young lad named Alfie Garratt was persuaded to take on the task – and remained Brown Jack's closest companion to the very end of his racing career.

In his early days at Wroughton the gelding was struck down by a chill and high fever. His basic diet of oats was supplemented with hot beer, eggs and whisky, and the recipe clearly proved efficacious, as by September he was ready for his first race in the Wernher colours. He started a 10–1 chance in a field of nine three-year-olds for the Southampton Hurdle over one and a half miles at Bournemouth and finished third, nine lengths behind the winning favourite Betting Tax (a topical name, as Chancellor of the Exchequer Winston Churchill had introduced a betting tax the year before, a move so unpopular that bookmakers at Windsor racecourse went on strike).

Brown Jack's next outing came in the Juvenile Hurdle at Wolverhampton on 26 September: he started at 100–6 and made the winner's enclosure at his fourth attempt, winning by three lengths from the even-money favourite Soccer.

That first victory proved the start of a sequence of five: by the end of 1927 he had also won twelve-furlong hurdle races at Wincanton, Cardiff, Nottingham and Liverpool, and was building a reputation as one of the most promising youngsters around.

Then came a reverse. Soon after the Liverpool race Brown Jack had suffered a recurrence of the fever, and he was not fully fit when unplaced in a two-mile handicap hurdle at Newbury in February 1928, less than a month before the Champion Hurdle. But he picked up the winning thread at Leicester at the end of February, then ran second to Peace River at Lingfield Park six days before his Cheltenham date.

Brown Jack, ridden by his now regular jockey Bilby Rees, started 4–1 third favourite for the second ever running of the Champion Hurdle in March 1928, with Blaris, winner of the inaugural running a year earlier and partnered by the great hurdle rider George Duller, a warm order at 2–1. Between the last two hurdles Brown Jack showed a fine turn of foot to burn off most of his rivals, and on the run up the hill to the line he kept going strongly to win by a length and a half from Peace River, with Blaris six lengths further back in third.

Aubrey Hastings's decision to purchase Brown Jack to win the Champion Hurdle for Sir Harold Wernher had been vindicated, but all this was a very far cry from the glories of the Royal Meeting – and now, to span that gap, enter the man most closely associated with Brown Jack in racing's folk memory: Steve Donoghue.

While the familiar cry of 'Come on, Steve!' was still to be heard ringing around the stands of Britain's racecourses, it was apparent to most that the great jockey's career, if not yet approaching the finishing line, was at least turning into the home straight. He had last been champion jockey when he tied for the title with Charlie Elliott in 1923, and a major new talent was now flying high in the shape of Gordon Richards. But Donoghue was still a man of huge experience, and Hastings made a point of asking him to go to Cheltenham and watch Brown Jack in the Champion Hurdle: how would the horse shape up on the Flat? After the race he received Donoghue's opinion: 'Yes, he'll win on the Flat, and I'll ride him.'

That was the end of Brown Jack's hurdling career, and he did not make the transition to the level completely smoothly. His first outing on the Flat was in the Durham Plate over one and three quarter miles at Hurst Park in early May, and Donoghue, as good as his word, took the ride:

> He did not win the race; in fact, he barely tried to win it. It was a new game to him and he did not understand what it was all about. He kept cocking one ear and then the other; he gazed ahead in a puzzled way and I expected him to turn to me and ask, 'Hey, Steve, what sort of race is this? When are we coming to the jumps? Are you sure we're on the right course? I've never been in a race without jumps before.'
> The intelligent fellow was working it all out for himself!
> That one race taught me what a genuine, game animal he was.

Donoghue rode the gelding in his next race, over a mile and a half at Windsor in late May, and Brown Jack scored his first win on the Flat, following up under Michael Beary in the Queen's Plate over two miles at Kempton Park.

The Royal Meeting was not far off, and the Ascot Stakes, a two-mile handicap on the opening day, seemed an ideal opportunity. On form Brown Jack had every right to be at the year's most socially elevated meeting, but did he have the correct breeding? Steve Donoghue wrote:

> Jack and I talked it over and we felt that though some folk might think us more at home on the commoner racecourses, we would like to have a look at this Royal Ascot and see how we liked it.

So the four-year-old Brown Jack made his first appearance at Ascot on Tuesday 19 June 1928 – and by an extraordinary coincidence his co-favourite in a field of twenty-one was none other than Arctic Star, with whom as a two-year-old he had shared that lazy few months at Balfstown: the old friends started at 5–1.

Having latched on to the theme of the social distinctions of Ascot, Steve Donoghue was not about to let go when telling the story of Brown Jack's first Ascot race:

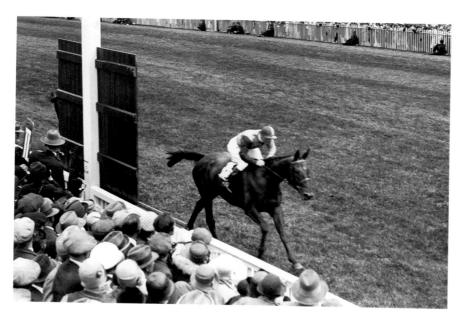

Brown Jack wins the Ascot Stakes in 1928.

We had done well enough in our prep schools, now we would have a look over the public school. As the old lad went down to the post for the Ascot Stakes over two miles, he felt the place suited him down to the ground.

We heard the shouts of the bookmakers, and when Jack heard them bawling, 'Five to one Brown Jack and Arctic Star ...' he did a little dance in his stride and I thought I heard him saying, 'How about that, Steve? They've made us favourites! Ah! Well, we'll give 'em a show.'

There were 21 of us at the starting-gate, and Jack seemed to get on all right. He behaved perfectly; took his place and waited for the gate to go up. We got off nicely, slipped along at our own pace – rather fast.

I could feel that the old fellow was anxious to make a good impression among the silk hats. He knew he was not quite out of the same drawer, but also he knew the sort of thing they liked. We won just as we liked, by three lengths.

For a moment I thought Jack intended to go round again. But he stopped eventually.

As we went back to weigh-in Jack was very pleased with himself and I could see that he liked Ascot and would like to come here again.

From that moment onwards Jack made Ascot his own gallop.

With that Ascot prize in the bag, it was decided to aim Brown Jack at another of the season's great staying handicaps, the Cesarewitch. Without a race between Ascot in June and Newmarket in October, he went off 5–1 favourite but finished unplaced behind his old grazing companion Arctic Star. In the fullness of time it would be acknowledged that Newmarket's staring expanses – the Cesarewitch, over two and a quarter miles, takes in just one turn – did not suit the horse, but after that first Cesarewitch defeat there was deep gloom in the Brown Jack camp, only to be dispelled when later in October he won the Hwfa Williams Handicap at Sandown Park.

Brown Jack's five-year-old campaign began over a mile and quarter at Nottingham in March 1929, when he was unconsidered in the betting and finished last behind a horse whose unrelated namesake would, decades later, wear his mantle as long-distance darling of the Ascot crowd: Trelawny. He was then beaten over a mile and a half at Derby before going to Manchester for the prestigious Manchester Cup over the same distance: he finished unplaced again.

Shortly after he had arrived back at Wroughton after that race Aubrey Hastings fell seriously ill, and within three days of the Manchester Cup he was dead: legend has it that his last words to his wife were, 'Brown Jack is a hell of a horse.' Charge of the horses at Wroughton passed to Hastings's assistant, Ivor Anthony.

Two days after Aubrey Hastings's funeral Brown Jack ran at Salisbury. It was well known that this was the latest of the gelding's warm-up races for an attempt at a second Ascot Stakes, and, partnered by Rufus Beasley, he started at 20–1 – only to make a mockery of that price by notching up his first win of the season, beating Coster Boy a short head.

On 18 June 1929 Brown Jack, reunited with Steve Donoghue, lined up for the Ascot Stakes, a 100–9 shot marginally preferred in the betting by 10–1 joint favourites Old Orkney and Clear Cash. It proved a great race, the closing stages of which are well described by R. C. Lyle (racing correspondent of *The Times*) in his wonderful book about Brown Jack published in 1934:

Quite early in the straight, the race underwent a change. Stamina began to tell, and two horses were seen to draw out in front of all the others. It was obviously going to be a duel between these two: they were soon lengths in front of the rest of the field. The two horses were Brown Jack and Old Orkney. And all the way up the Straight they fought out their terrific battle. At one moment it looked as if Brown Jack would repeat his victory of the year before. But at the lower Number Board [about two furlongs out] Old Orkney was slightly in front, and seemed to be going a little more easily than Brown Jack. Brown Jack and Donoghue were not done with: they came again and almost drew level with Old Orkney. Nearing the winning post they made a last desperate effort. But it just failed. Old Orkney won by a short head. The Consul was eight lengths away, third.

Brown Jack had already shown his connections that he was exceptionally tough, and as he seemed to show no ill effects of that struggle with Old Orkney it was decided to bring him out again for the Alexandra Stakes – by now run over two miles six furlongs 85 yards – on the Friday, the final day of the meeting. He started 2–1 favourite, with Arctic Star at 5–2. R. C. Lyle again:

Brown Jack allowed the French horse Ramon to make the running until just before the turn into the Straight. Then Brown Jack and Arctic Star moved up and took the lead. Donoghue did not press Brown Jack but allowed Arctic Star to run level with him. But about a quarter of a mile from the winning post Brown Jack, so it seemed, decided that whatever Donoghue might think the time had come for him to win: he drew right away from Arctic Star and won easily with his ears pricked, by four lengths. Chasselas, who was third, was ten lengths behind Arctic Star.

It was at the end of this race that I for the first time noticed Brown Jack dance his curious shuffle as he neared the winning post. I believe he had begun to develop the odd steps of that peculiar dance quite early in his career, but never before had it been so generally observed. He does it, so Donoghue and Beary say, just to amuse himself and show his delight at having won.

What better testimony could there be to the quality of the horse and the skill of his trainer than that he should turn out for a second long distance race so soon and win it with such ease and evident enjoyment? His two performances at Ascot showed that, like the majority of us, he loves to win, and, like the brave gentleman that he is, he is a good loser.

Just over a month later Brown Jack went to Hurst Park to run unplaced in a seven-furlong handicap (in which he carried 10 stone 7 pounds), a tuning-up exercise for his next major target, the Goodwood Cup, in which he started 5–4 on against familiar rivals Old Orkney and Arctic Star. After a furious struggle Brown Jack went down by a short head to Old Orkney, with Arctic Star beaten off in third. Brown Jack and Old Orkney renewed rivalry in the Prince Edward Handicap at Manchester, where they finished second and third respectively behind Medarlin, but Brown Jack took his revenge on the winner on his next outing, landing the Nottingham Handicap by a head from Saracen with Medarlin not in the frame. Next came a second bid for the Cesarewitch. Brown Jack started 15–2 favourite but could finish only third behind West Wicklow and Friendship, conceding twenty-two pounds to the winner and twenty-six to the second.

Eleven races were considered enough for 1929, and Brown Jack went off to his owner's stud at Thorpe Lubenham to while away a lazy winter.

In 1930 Ascot was again top of the agenda, and by the time he lined up for the Ascot Stakes on the opening day of the meeting he had again visited Derby and Salisbury, as expected running unplaced at long prices. The Ascot Stakes did not go at all to plan. Badly boxed in, Donoghue could never get him out for a proper run, and eased up near the finish – doubtless mindful of another date three days later – to allow Brown Jack to come home in his own time.

With Old Orkney and Arctic Star (neither of whom had run in the Ascot Stakes) back in the fray, the Alexandra Stakes looked a cracker, and the betting suggested a close race:

11–8 Brown Jack
7–2 Old Orkney
9–2 Arctic Star
8–1 bar

Favourite backers had little cause for concern. Brown Jack took the lead early in the straight and beat off the determined challenge of Old Orkney to win his second Alexandra – and register his third Ascot victory – by a length and a half.

He then won the Goodwood Cup at 9–4 on, a facile victory on the face of it but a significant race in the Brown Jack story, as for the first time he was accompanied to post by another Wroughton inmate in the shape of Mail Fist.

After an in-and-out career when trained by Cecil Boyd-Rochfort for Sir Harold Wernher's wife Lady Zia Wernher, Mail Fist was moved to Ivor Anthony's yard in the hope that he might be put over hurdles. But it soon became apparent that he had a higher calling as the ideal companion for Brown Jack – lead horse in his home gallops and pacemaker in his races. 'One was good before breakfast and bad in the afternoon,' said Anthony. 'The other was bad before breakfast and good in the afternoon.' Mail Fist was installed in the box next to Brown Jack's, and they became close companions.

Mail Fist fulfilled his pacemaking role admirably at the first time of asking in the 1930 Goodwood Cup, leading until Brown Jack was ready to take command – which he duly did, winning by a length from Jugo.

Without Mail Fist to help him along in the Ebor Handicap at York – his services were deemed unnecessary over a distance of a mile and three quarters – Brown Jack nevertheless ran a sterling race, finishing third after suffering interference in the straight. Next stop Doncaster. With Mail Fist back in the pacemaking role, Brown Jack defied 9 stone 11 pounds to win the Doncaster Cup by five lengths. Then a Nottingham warm-up before another crack at the Cesarewitch – and another failure, unplaced in a field of twenty-eight.

In the spring of 1931 Brown Jack was seven years old, but there was no sign of decline, and he embarked again on a campaign aimed at Ascot, with a very decent prize on the way there. After the usual warm-up runs – this time at Nottingham and Derby – he started at 100–8 for the Chester Cup. The hot favourite at 2–1 was Trimdon – who would go on to enjoy his own moments of Ascot glory by winning the Gold Cup later that season and in 1932 – but Brown Jack (ridden by Michael Beary as Donoghue was injured) was far too good for him, cruising to the front in Chester's short straight and winning with his ears pricked, in the process netting the largest single prize of his entire career: £2,580.

A month later Sir Harold Wernher hosted a dinner at the Savoy to mark the Chester Cup victory. The guests – who included Charlie Rogers – tucked into a seven-course gastronomic stayers' event, the centrepiece of which was *suprême de chapon Brown Jack*, served with *petits pois clamart* and *pommes olivettes*.

Brown Jack's fourth Ascot Stakes on the opening day of the 1931 Royal Meeting proved one of his most disappointing races. With Mail Fist being kept for later in the meeting, the pace was too slow and Brown Jack never showed with a chance behind the winner Noble Star. But the form of the Chester Cup was given a distinct boost when Trimdon won the Gold Cup on the third day, and Brown Jack started odds-on to land a third Alexandra – this year given the new name of the Queen Alexandra Stakes. Mail Fist led until the field started the climb out of Swinley Bottom, leaving Donoghue and Brown Jack to sit in behind the French challenger Delate until taking over close home and sauntering to an easy four-length victory from none other than Arctic Star – the last time the boyhood friends raced against each other.

Brown Jack had now won at the Royal Meeting four years in a row – clearly a stayer of the highest order as well as an Ascot specialist. So why did he not run in the Gold Cup? The answer is simple. Geldings were ineligible to compete in that race (on the grounds that the winner should be able to pass on his or her excellence to the next generation, which is not in a gelding's power). It was not until 1986 that this rule was relaxed, and Arcadian Heights in 1994 became the first gelding to land the main event of the Royal Meeting.

Brown Jack's public following had now reached the stage where his fans would send him food parcels, as R. C. Lyle mentioned when describing the horse's domestic routine at Wroughton:

When the morning grooming is complete Alfie [Garratt] will stay in Brown Jack's box and unwrap his snack of bread and cheese. And Brown Jack shares the meal. He nibbles the cheese with relish. His liking for cheese became known, and in later years presents of cheeses of every sort, large and small, rare and expensive, were sent to him at Wroughton by his many admirers. But most of them he would not touch. I have to confess that for a gentleman of his breeding and accomplishments his taste in cheese is singularly uneducated. He will eat only the cheapest American cheddar such as he is wont to share with Alfie in his box at Wroughton or in the motor box or railway box on his way to race meetings. Apples and carrots he is fond of too, and they have been showered on him from all parts of the country. His parcels vary from a single apple wrapped in brown paper, addressed to him and posted by a child admirer in a Lancashire factory town, to a large crate despatched across the Atlantic by a hard-working farmer in Canada.

The gelding's racecourse performances continued to match his fame: indeed, he seemed to be improving with age. After the 1931 Queen Alexandra he was beaten a neck in the Goodwood Cup by Salmon Leap (a very good horse who would win the Coronation Cup in 1932), with Gold Cup winner Trimdon four lengths away third. He then won the Ebor Handicap easily under 9 stone 5 pounds and was runner-up in the Doncaster Cup behind 1930 St Leger winner Singapore.

Business as usual in 1932: Lingfield Park (unplaced), Derby (unplaced), and the Chester Cup (unplaced under 9 stone 13 pounds); then Epsom (second, carrying 10 stone 2 pounds in a two-and-a-quarter-mile handicap). This time the Ascot programme was varied, with Brown Jack bypassing the Ascot Stakes in favour of the Gold Vase on the opening day. He finished unplaced, but his main target was three days later, and the run in the Vase put the finishing touches to his fitness.

Less than fit, though, was Steve Donoghue. A fall from a wayward horse named Banned on the first day of the meeting had damaged his wrist, and in addition there were rumours that Sir Harold was displeased with Donoghue's riding of Brown Jack in the Gold Vase and was minded to put up Michael Beary for the Queen Alexandra. Donoghue ranted ('I was, possibly, a bit unreasonable in some of the things I said to Sir Harold') and persuaded his doctor to strap up the damaged wrist, with the result that it was the usual partnership that landed the race for the fourth year in succession: Brown Jack took the lead before the turn into the straight and won easily. Characteristically, he started to pull himself up as he approached the winning post, and yet again won with his ears pricked.

The 1931 Oaks winner Brulette, two lengths runner-up in that race,

The Queen Alexandra Stakes in 1932 …

reversed the form in the Goodwood Cup, beating Brown Jack by four. Brown Jack then ran unplaced in the Ebor before winning the Prince Edward Handicap at Manchester and finishing third of six runners behind Foxhunter in the Doncaster Cup. The winner went on to win the Gold Cup in 1933.

Brown Jack ran in ten races as an eight-year-old in 1932, but with advancing years he could not be expected to go on for ever, and his 1933 programme was restricted to just five outings, beginning with the usual long-priced début in a handicap (20–1, unplaced at Sandown Park), then a one-length defeat of Foxearth at Epsom. The runner-up was owned by George V, who summoned Sir Harold Wernher and told him: 'Although everybody likes winning races, nobody could possibly object to being beaten by such a great horse as Brown Jack.'

Then Ascot – just the one race in 1933, after four consecutive years of dual appearances. The Queen Alexandra Stakes was now Brown Jack's private fiefdom, and there were only three other runners. Sigiri started at 7–1, Corn Belt at 10–1, and the ubiquitous Mail Fist at 50–1, while Brown Jack himself was a seemingly stone-cold certainty at 5–1 on.

Mail Fist led until fading out at his usual place in Swinley Bottom, where Brown Jack and Donoghue took the lead. With just over a furlong to go he seemed to be coasting, but this time he started to indulge too early his habit of pulling himself up, and to the horror of the crowd Joe Childs conjured a late surge from Corn Belt. As the upstart reached Brown Jack's quarters, Donoghue showed the old horse the whip – and the response was immediate. Brown Jack made his little shuffle and pulled away from the challenger to win by a length and a half.

It is commonplace to think of the 1930s as a commercially innocent age compared with the early part of the twenty-first century, and while nowadays Brown Jack would doubtless have his own website and an agent busily negotiating the best deals on product endorsement and merchandising rights,

... and 1933.

the original Brown Jack had to put up with the irritations of fame beyond being sent cheese too posh for his liking. R. C. Lyle reported that:

> Brown Jack's mail is as large as that of a popular film star. Bad poems and good wishes are showered upon him. He has been asked to grace charity bazaars with his presence and, I believe, to lend the lustre of his name to patent foods and medicines.

But for all the adulation, there were still races to be won. Even at the age of nine Brown Jack could hold his own at the highest level, and he followed up his fifth Queen Alexandra with his fifth consecutive appearance in the Goodwood Cup. Here he faced the Gold Cup winner Foxhunter, who started at 11–4 on; Brown Jack was an easy-to-back second favourite at 5–1, with the previous year's winner Brulette on 13–2. The other two runners were Sans Peine on 20–1 and Ximenes on 33–1, and it was these two outsiders who dominated an extraordinary race. Ximenes set up a lead of nearly a furlong, then Sans Peine caught him and led into the straight, with the other three well in arrears. Brown Jack set off after the leaders, caught Ximenes and went in pursuit of Sans Peine, but the lightly weighted three-year-old had too much left in the tank, and Brown Jack was beaten four lengths. None the less, his Goodwood Cup record was remarkable: one win and four seconds from five runs. There was one more race for Brown Jack in 1933 – unplaced at Manchester in September – and that autumn there was speculation about whether the great horse would be seen in public again.

To the delight of the racing world he was kept in training, with just one object in mind: to win the Queen Alexandra Stakes for the sixth year running. *En route* to Ascot he ran unplaced at Lingfield Park and Derby, and came third when second favourite for the Chester Cup.

In the build-up to Ascot that year the Queen Alexandra Stakes was the race that most exercised the public imagination, and there was even a sermon preached by a visiting vicar in Wroughton parish church on the theme of Brown Jack's being an example to us all – for the way he brightened people's lives, for his courage, his kindliness and always giving his best.

Brown Jack was taken to Ascot on the opening day of the meeting with the intention of running in either the Ascot Stakes or the Gold Vase, but the going was too firm and he did not take part. He was taken back to Wroughton.

Three days later, on the sunny but windy morning of Friday 22 June 1934, the newspaper billboards on the approach roads to Ascot declared 'BROWN JACK TODAY' – though it is inconceivable that any racegoer that day would have needed reminding. This was clearly going to be a very special racing occasion, and for once the early races on the final day were mere sideshows to the Queen Alexandra Stakes.

Brown Jack was now a ten-year-old. It was widely assumed – though it had not been formally announced – that this would be his last race, but the sentiment of the occasion had not prevented other owners and trainers trying to ruin the fairytale ending, and there were nine runners. This was no contest to bet on, but for those poor souls who simply could not resist taking a financial interest, Brown Jack was favourite at 6–4, with Gordon Richards's mount Loosestrife on 100–30, Harinero, winner of the Irish Derby in 1933, on 4–1, and the 1932 Cesarewitch winner Nitsichin on 13–2.

The story of one of the most famous races in Ascot's history is begun by R. C. Lyle:

'They're off!' It was 4.34 p.m. – the start was four minutes late. Mail Fist, as ever, jumped into the lead. He did his best, but there were other horses in the race who, aided and abetted by their riders, thought that it would not be fair that he should always have the honour of being pacemaker: and they also set off as fast as they could go, thinking that the old gentleman behind might crack up and cry 'enough' long before the winning post was reached. As the field came past the Stands for the first time, rather more than seven furlongs from the start, Benskin and Mail Fist were leading, followed by Solatium and Loosestrife. Brown Jack was running with Nitsichin several lengths behind the leaders. Quite early on the stretch of the course going down to the Swinley Bottom Loosestrife went on in front with a definite lead. Mail Fist had done his bit and retired gracefully. Solatium followed Loosestrife, and it seemed to some visitors just for a moment that Loosestrife might run away. On the far side of the course Brown Jack moved up, followed by the French horse, Dark Dew. Before the Straight was reached Loosestrife was in trouble and Brown Jack came on in front with

Solatium, the latter running a much better race than he had done in the race for the Ascot Stakes earlier in the week.

The bell rang and Brown Jack and Solatium entered the Straight well clear of any other runner. It was certain then that one of the two would win. Solatium, on the rails, hung on most gallantly to Brown Jack. Indeed, he hung on so long that the suspense to me became almost unbearable.

Steve Donoghue takes up the story:

We battled along side by side for the best part of a hundred yards, and I know people on the stands must have been thinking that old Jack had at last met his match, but he had not.

Solatium was dead game, but that 100 yards of Brown Jack at his best was too much for any horse, and slowly he fell back beaten.

What happened after that only proves what a great old character Jack was. It had always been his custom to slow down after he had beaten his opponents, knowing that they would not come again, and once or twice I had to work a bit to keep him going until the post was passed. Here he was racing in the last race of his career. I had lost my whip some distance before the end of the race. Now no horse that was ever foaled was gamer than Brown Jack. He would not flinch from a gruelling finish, as threatened us in the last stages of that race; in fact, he enjoyed that sort of a finish. But as soon as I dropped my whip – we had just got into the lead at the time – he seemed to know it and immediately he began to show signs of shortening his stride. I talked to him very firmly.

'Get on there, you old scamp,' I said to him. 'Get along there, you know damn well I have dropped my whip but I won't stand for any monkey tricks and you know it. Get along there.'

And as I spoke to him I kept touching his side with my hand. He knew me and he knew the occasion and he battled on splendidly, but as sure as my name is what it is, I am certain that the old rogue was laughing at me for having dropped my whip and I know that he enjoyed giving me that fright. Just as he had done every time before, he pricked his ears as he approached the post and did his comic little dance – he always did this when he won – as he passed it.

Never will I forget the roar of that crowd as long as I live. Ascot or no Ascot, they went mad. I have never seen so many hats flung in the air, and I have never heard such shrieks of joy in my life. All my six Derbys faded before the reception that was awaiting Jack and myself as we set out to return to weigh-in. I don't think I was ever so happy in my life as I was at that moment.

A great Ascot moment as Brown Jack wins the 1934 Queen Alexandra Stakes from Solatium.

Nor was R. C. Lyle:

I have never seen a sight anywhere, and especially never at Ascot, as I was privileged to see when Brown Jack went past the winning post. Eminently respectable old ladies in the Royal Enclosure gathered up their skirts and began, with such dignity as they could command in their excitement, to make the best of their way as quickly as they could towards the place where Brown Jack and Donoghue would return after the race. Hats were raised in the air in every enclosure and there were cheers from all parts of the course. Such a scene could be witnessed only in this country, and it has never in my time been witnessed here in such intensity. The unsaddling enclosure to which Brown Jack was returning for the sixth time after winning this race was surrounded many times deep. Crowds were waiting round the gateway leading from the course to the Enclosure. Police made a lane for the triumphant pair, Brown Jack and Donoghue. The trainer, Ivor Anthony, as shy and bashful as ever, had already gone into the unsaddling enclosure where he was standing stroking his chin and trying to look unconcerned: he had been too nervous to watch the race, and had sat alone under the trees in the Paddock until the great roar of cheering told him all was well.

And then at last Brown Jack came in. He looked to the right and to the left as he walked through the lane from the course to his own enclosure. His ears were pricked and he knew full well what was happening and what had happened. He was being patted on both sides from head to tail as he made his progress. 'Half his tail was pulled out,' Sir Harold Wernher told me afterwards. And then when he got to the gateway to his own enclosure he stood still. Donoghue tried to persuade him to go in, but he would not move. His ears were pricked and he was most certainly watching the people still pouring into the Paddock to see his return. He would not disappoint them. When he thought that all had arrived he walked in quietly and received the congratulations of his owner, his owner's wife, and his trainer. Donoghue, in some wonderful way, wormed his way through the people to the weighing room, and after that came the end.

Before Brown Jack and his companion Mail Fist (who had broken down in the race) were loaded into their horsebox for the return to Wroughton someone wrote the two magic words 'BROWN JACK' in white paint on the windscreen, and Alfie Garratt later reported that they sailed past every traffic jam, waved through by the police.

As had been widely anticipated, Brown Jack did not run again. He retired the winner of twenty-five of his sixty-five races, and his Ascot record reads: ran eleven times, won seven.

The name and spirit of Brown Jack has lived on – in the pub in Wroughton, named after him; in the local football team, the Brown Jacks; with every running of the Brown Jack Stakes and in the twice-yearly exposition of his statue; and, obliquely, in one of the best loved poems about horses in the English language. In January 1950 the poet Philip Larkin, bored by his job in the university library at Leicester, went to the cinema in search of some stimulation, and before the main feature saw a short documentary about Brown Jack and Mail Fist in retirement. He recalled the film in a television interview with Melvyn Bragg in 1981:

It was a film about, you know, 'Where is Brown Jack now?' Where Brown Jack was now was at grass, quite happy, moving about, no harness, no jockey, nobody shouting the odds, simply cropping the grass and having a gallop when he felt like it.

Well earned rest.

On walking home from the cinema Larkin could not get the film out of his mind, and the result was the poem 'At Grass', a wistful contemplation of the state of retired racehorses in a field – 'Do memories plague their ears like flies?' – and how they relax after the rigours of the racetrack.

Brown Jack lived out an honourable retirement at Thorpe Lubenham, where he died in 1948 at the age of twenty-four. His feat of winning at the Royal Meeting for seven years in a row is as secure as a sporting record can be, and his ghost surely sneaks out on to the home straight when nobody is watching, to perform a reprise of that funny little shuffle as it shimmies past the Ascot winning post.

AFTER THE WAR

There was no Royal Meeting in 1945, although many of the traditional Ascot races – some of which had been evacuated to Newmarket for the duration of hostilities – were held at the course for the first time since 1939. The Coventry Stakes and the Queen Mary Stakes were run at a one-day meeting in June, both won by horses owned by the Aga Khan: Khaled took the Coventry and Rivaz the Queen Mary.

The July fixture included the Royal Hunt Cup and the Gold Cup, in which Ocean Swell, winner of the substitute Derby at Newmarket the previous year, faced Tehran, whom he had narrowly beaten in the Derby and who had turned the tables when winning the St Leger. Tehran was noted for his battling qualities, so Jack Jarvis, trainer of Ocean Swell, instructed Eph Smith to bring the colt over towards the stands in the home straight in order not to lock horns with the odds-on favourite, and the plan worked triumphantly. Gordon Richards on Tehran admitted: 'I saw him too late. Tehran thought he had nothing to pull out the usual extra against. I tried to get over to Ocean Swell but Eph had now got first run on me, and I could not get near him.' (A similar tactic was used in a much more recent big race at Ascot, when Observatory beat the 'Iron Horse' Giant's Causeway in the Queen Elizabeth II Stakes in 2000.)

At the August 1945 meeting the Britannia Stakes (first run in 1928) and the Wokingham Stakes returned to the programme.

By the summer of 1946 life was gradually returning to at least a semblance of normality, and on Tuesday 18 June the Royal Meeting was revived. With the country still deep in the age of austerity – bread rationing had been

Post-war austerity reflected in Ascot fashion: a ball of wool and knitting needles commandeered to decorate a hat in 1946.

introduced three weeks earlier – this was no time for an ostentatious parade of fashion, and the dress code in the Royal Enclosure eschewed morning suits in favour of service dress or lounge suits, a ruling not to everybody's satisfaction. A tongue-in-cheek leader in *The Times* told of a reader who had complained to the newspaper that 'he only has a top hat and morning coat respectable'.

The royal party attended on all four days – though the Royal Procession took place only on the Tuesday and Thursday.

Understandably Ascot was nothing like it had been before the war, and a distinct note of regret was registered by a report for *The Times*:

Royal Ascot has been restored to the calendar of social events, but, like much else in our new peacetime, its grandeur is greatly diminished … Neither the Royal Enclosure nor the paddock had any startling note of fashion to catch the eye, nor was there any procession of elegantly dressed people to the Heath, across the course, because the Heath had none of its marquees for the sumptuous luncheons and teas of bygone days.

One particularly cheerless constable, whose job it was to see that people did not stand on the seats, pointed out that before the war people's manners were enough to prevent them doing so.

Nor could the food and drink be up to the previous standard: 'The refreshment pavilion and the lesser buffets … suffered severely from the prevailing austerity. Even so, there were strawberries and ice-cream for half-a-crown and champagne for sixty shillings a bottle, while on the course a peach could be bought from a tray for five shillings.' Even bearing in mind that one of the most popular wartime songs had been entitled 'When Can I Have A Banana Again?', five shillings (twenty-five pence) for a peach seemed a bit steep.

On the track, the first day of the first post-war Royal Meeting was

Previous pages: The Royal Procession, 1950.

dominated by the two-year-old Tudor Minstrel. Trained by Fred Darling, this exceptionally good-looking colt had attracted such a reputation before he ever set foot on a racecourse that he started at 5–2 on for his first race at Bath in April. He won easily, then followed up with an equally facile Salisbury victory at 10–1 on before facing five opponents at Ascot for the Coventry Stakes (then run over five furlongs rather than today's six). The betting market had him down as a certainty at 13–2 on, with second favourite Firemaster at 10–1, and the story of the race is briskly told in the shorthand of the official form book: '2nd to ½ way: tk ld: qckly wnt clr'. Tudor Minstrel – who would be back at Ascot the following year – was the first leg of an opening-day treble for Gordon Richards.

Wednesday of the 1946 meeting opened with a new race for two-year-old fillies over five furlongs named in honour of the King and Queen's elder daughter – the Princess Elizabeth Stakes (won by Neocracy, later dam of 1952 Derby and King George winner Tulyar) – and on the Thursday the Gold Cup saw French-trained horses fill the first three places: Caracalla II, owned by Monsieur Marcel Boussac, won from Chanteur II and Basileus. The following day M. Boussac won the Hardwicke Stakes with Priam II and the Queen Alexandra Stakes with Marsyas II, and the French domination of post-war staying races was well under way: Caracalla II was the first of four French horses to win the Gold Cup in the six runnings between 1946 and 1951. At the other end of the distance scale the King's Stand Stakes, final race of the meeting, was won by Vilmorin, a very good sprinter who by one of those quirks of Thoroughbred breeding became the paternal grandsire of a famous horse who excelled over extreme distances – triple Grand National winner Red Rum.

The first Royal Meeting since the war saw significant changes in Ascot personnel.

Sir Gordon Carter had died in 1941 and was succeeded as Clerk of the Course by Colonel Sir Arthur Erskine, who was himself succeeded in January 1946 by Major John Crocker Bulteel, whose father had owned the great steeplechaser Manifesto when he won the Grand National in 1899 (though not at the time of his 1897 victory): Manifesto spent his declining years in a field at Ascot. Crocker Bulteel (who was knighted in 1955) had worked as a handicapper, and had great experience as Clerk of the Course at Newbury, Chester, Haydock Park and Hurst Park.

No less significant for the immediate future of Ascot was the appointment in 1945 of Bernard Marmaduke Fitzalan-Howard, 16th Duke of Norfolk, to succeed Lord Hamilton of Dalzell as the King's Representative. Only thirty-six years old at the time of his appointment, the Duke had served briefly in the Royal Horse Guards, and was joint Parliamentary Secretary at the Ministry of Agriculture during the war. As Earl Marshal of England, a hereditary role which he took on in 1929, he had been responsible for organising state ceremonial occasions, and had been closely involved with the funeral of George V in 1936 and the coronation of George VI in 1937. (His later triumphs of organisation included the coronation of Elizabeth II in 1953, the state funeral of Sir Winston Churchill in 1965 and the investiture of the Prince of Wales in 1969.)

Crocker Bulteel and the Duke of Norfolk were such important figures in the history of Ascot racecourse that it is worth quoting the assessments of the pair in the *Biographical Encyclopaedia of British Flat Racing* by three of the sport's most distinguished historians, Roger Mortimer, Richard Onslow and Peter Willett. Of John Crocker Bulteel they wrote:

> The outstanding racing administrator of his day, Sir John realized the necessity of having the highest standard of facilities in all enclosures at a time when most men in his position were notoriously indifferent to such matters. He was determined to stage programmes that would attract the general public to Ascot and Hurst Park and was particularly anxious to help encourage the breeding of stayers by providing races over a distance of ground for late-maturing horses. In doing so he played a big part in reversing the trend towards the over-production of sprinters that allowed the French to dominate the long-distance races in Britain during the years immediately after the Second World War.

And of the Duke of Norfolk:

> From an early age he was accustomed to shoulder weighty responsibilities, some hereditary, others assumed from a highly developed sense of duty ... He always took immense pride in Ascot

and no detail of the organization there was too small to escape his attention. It was his ambition to make Ascot second to none among European racecourses and under his direction the course was thoroughly modernized.

One of the big issues facing Ascot as these two settled into their new posts was that of enlarging the fixture list at the course. With the exception of the years towards the end of the war, when unusual circumstances clearly applied, Ascot had staged only the one meeting each year for as long as anyone could remember. There had been occasional suggestions that the course should be used more – back in 1931 the *Sunday Graphic* had asked, 'Why not have two or three additional Ascots in a year, while at the same time maintaining the Ascot of June as the real thing?' – and the spirit of change following the war provided the right mood in which to effect such a move.

George VI had in 1942 given his approval to the idea of extra fixtures being looked into, and by 1944 the notion was taking hold that the course could sustain two-day meetings in July, September and October. The King and the Jockey Club gave the go-ahead, and in 1946 the Royal Meeting was followed by three additional fixtures at the course.

On Friday 19 July a six-race programme included the Eclipse Stakes, transferred from Sandown Park as that course was not yet ready to resume racing. Lord Derby's three-year-old colt Gulf Stream, who had been beaten a length by Airborne in the Derby, won the Eclipse – the most valuable race run at Ascot that year – by three lengths from Edward Tudor. Also run on that July Friday were the first Royal Lodge Stakes (then over five furlongs, nowadays one mile at the September meeting) and King George V Handicap (one and a half miles, added to the Royal Meeting in 1948). Saturday saw the first running of the Princess Margaret Stakes for two-year-old fillies over five furlongs, named in honour of the King and Queen's younger daughter. The same card brought Tudor Minstrel back to the course for a stroll in the National Breeders' Produce Stakes (like the Eclipse, transferred from Sandown Park), and staged the first running of the Gordon Carter Handicap over two miles (though a race bearing the same name had been run in May 1945 over the Straight Mile).

A two-day meeting followed in September, with Friday featuring the inaugural Brown Jack Stakes over the full distance of the Queen Alexandra Stakes. This reminder of the Ascot hero who even as 'his' race was being run was cropping grass placidly at Thorpe Lubenham was tinged with sadness, as his great comrade-in-arms Steve Donoghue had died in March 1945 at the age of sixty. That Friday also had the first Princess Royal Stakes, and Saturday's most valuable contest was the first running of the Diadem Stakes over six furlongs, won by that year's Wokingham winner The Bug. The two-day fixture in October included the Cornwallis Stakes for two-year-olds on the Friday, but much the most interesting event at this fixture was the King George VI Stakes over two miles on the Saturday. With a first prize of £5,432 10s, this was a seriously valuable race (at the 1946 Royal Meeting only the Gold Cup was worth more), and attracted a suitably distinguished field, notably Airborne. The Derby winner started 5–4 on favourite, but those damned French were set on plundering the best British staying races, and Souverain, trained by Henri Delavaud, won very easily, with Bright News five lengths adrift in second place and Airborne only third in what turned out to be his last race.

The presence of horses of the quality of Gulf Stream, Tudor Minstrel and Airborne at non-royal fixtures was highly encouraging, and the late 1940s continued to associate Ascot with sheer quality of racing.

Tudor Minstrel turned out again for the 1947 Royal Meeting. Since last running at Ascot he had won the Two Thousand Guineas by eight lengths but failed to stay in the Derby, finishing fourth behind Pearl Diver at 7–4 on and losing his unbeaten record. He faced just two rivals in the St James's Palace Stakes, last race on the opening day (a scheduling it was to endure until being moved up the running order in 1980), and saw them off as easily as his starting price of 100–6 on suggested he would, his winning margin of five lengths requiring no recourse to the new technology of the photo-finish camera, introduced that year.

Tudor Minstrel's trainer Fred Darling won five other races at the meeting to record an Ascot six-timer in his last year of training.

But as one great trainer prepared to exit the Ascot stage, another was making his entrance. Noel Murless, then based in Thirsk and destined to become one of the legends of his calling, sent out his first winner at the course with Oros in the Britannia Stakes.

A dead heat was called in the 1947 New Stakes when Lerins – a horse who would cause difficulties to unwary Turf historians by winning the Two Thousand Guineas the following year under the name My Babu – was caught on the line by Delirium, ridden by the irrepressible Charlie Smirke. Lerins's owner the Maharajah of Baroda, one of the big owners of that period, was so struck by Smirke's strength and determination in getting Delirium up on the line that he made him his retained jockey (and thus put him in for the Classic-winning ride on My Babu the following spring).

Unusual Ascot footwear in 1947.

At the same meeting Migoli won the King Edward VII Stakes *en route* to winning the Eclipse Stakes (beating Tudor Minstrel at Sandown Park) and Champion Stakes later in 1947 and landing the Prix de l'Arc de Triomphe in 1948, while Souverain returned to Ascot to win another Gold Cup for France.

Of the year's later meetings the most interesting came in September. Finnure, runner-up in the Brown Jack Stakes, had won the Irish Cesarewitch in 1946 and went on to become a top-class steeplechaser, winning the King George VI Chase in 1949 and finishing runner-up to Cottage Rake in the 1950 Cheltenham Gold Cup. And Tudor Minstrel won the Knight's Royal Stakes over one mile at 11–10, with The Bug, who at the Royal Meeting had added the Cork and Orrery Stakes to his earlier Ascot haul of 1946 Wokingham and Diadem, last of the five runners.

Abernant, a grey grandson of Mumtaz Mahal trained by Noel Murless, made his first Ascot appearance in the Chesham Stakes (then five furlongs) at the 1948 Royal Meeting. Ridden by Charlie Smirke, he made all the running to win impressively. By the time he returned a year later for the King's Stand Stakes he had been touched off by Nimbus in the Two Thousand Guineas over one mile and was now reverting to sprinting, at which he was to become one of the all-time greats. Abernant had a particular place in the affections of Gordon Richards, who became his regular rider:

> He was a kind horse, absolutely placid although he took a great interest in all that was going on around him. He would canter quietly down to the start, and then when he got to the other side of the gate he would give a great big sigh, prop himself lazily on three legs, and have a look round at everything and everybody … He was just like a big, faithful old dog.

In the 1949 King's Stand Stakes he started at 6–4 on and, in the words of the form book, 'mde all: impressive'. Later that year he won the July Cup at Newmarket, King George Stakes at Goodwood and Nunthorpe Stakes at York, and scored repeat wins in those three in 1950 – before which he was narrowly beaten by Tangle in the King's Stand Stakes.

That defeat notwithstanding, Abernant over five or six furlongs was a reasonably rock-solid bet, but one Gordon Richards-ridden Ascot runner in 1948 underlined that, truly, there is no such thing as a racing certainty. The September fixture was that year extended to three days – further reflection of the appeal of Ascot to owners and trainers as well as racegoers – and on the Thursday a two-year-old named Royal Forest was partnered by Richards in the Clarence House Stakes. Royal Forest was unbeaten in two outings, the latter of which was a head victory over Nimbus (who would win the Derby as well as the Two Thousand Guineas in 1949) in the Coventry Stakes at the Royal Meeting. Of his three opponents in the Clarence House Stakes, two were unraced and the other, Vineyard, had finished a well-beaten last on her only previous outing. Against such opposition Royal Forest was a stone-cold certainty, and the starting prices for the race had an appealing simplicity:

> 1–25 Royal Forest
> 33–1 others

Gordon Richards describes one of the lesser moments of his career:

> It was a six-furlong race, and I went confidently to the front a furlong from home. Then I had the biggest shock of my life. I felt him fading to nothing under me. The Duke of Norfolk's Burpham came up and ran me out of it. As with Glendower [a horse Richards had ridden when beaten at 20–1 on at Chepstow the previous year], I heard later of people who had laid the odds. They must have been insane.

Certainly they must – and it would have been little consolation for them that next time out Royal Forest won the Dewhurst Stakes at Newmarket, with Burpham back in fourth.

Ascot at this time was becoming more international. Irish horses had long

been competing at the course, the French were stepping up their bid for a monopoly of the staying races, and in 1948 Italy made its mark. At the 1948 July meeting the Queen Elizabeth Stakes over a mile and a half was won by Signor Federico Tesio's colt Tenerani, who was to sire Tesio's brilliant dual Prix de l'Arc de Triomphe winner Ribot (whose one race in England was at Ascot). Tenerani won the Queen Elizabeth Stakes by a short head from Black Tarquin, who would go on to win that year's St Leger.

Black Tarquin's great rival in later races was to be Alycidon, who in 1948 made two appearances at Ascot, finishing third in the King Edward VII Stakes at Royal Ascot (the first year that that name was formally used for the meeting) and in October – by which time he had been beaten by Black Tarquin in the St Leger and won the Jockey Club Stakes at Newmarket – winning the King George VI Stakes.

Alycidon, owned by Lord Derby and trained by Walter Earl, was unbeaten in 1949, when his greatest moment came in the Gold Cup. Black Tarquin had remained in training, and after winning his three build-up races went off 11–10 favourite at Ascot. The blinkered Alycidon, who for his preparation had won the Ormonde Stakes at Chester and then scored a twelve-length victory in the

Fabled BBC commentator Raymond Glendenning at Ascot in 1949.

Corporation Stakes at Doncaster, started at 5–4. The other five runners seemed to have little chance, but two of this quintet held the key to Alycidon's chance. For the 1949 Gold Cup seemed to be the classic clash between a relentless galloper – Alycidon – and a horse with a real turn of foot – Black Tarquin – and, as with Bustino in his famous clash with Grundy twenty-six years later, connections of the relentless galloper came up with the plan of running not one but two pacemakers: Stockbridge and Benny Lynch.

Doug Smith, who rode Alycidon, relates a famous Ascot occasion:

Stockbridge, ridden by Percy Evans, and Benny Lynch, ridden by Tommy Lowrey, played their parts to perfection. Stockbridge led up the straight and past the stands the first time round, with Benny Lynch a couple of lengths behind him and Alycidon next, so that Lord Derby's three horses were in single file at the head of the field of seven. When we had swung round the paddock turn and were beginning the descent into the Swinley Bottom I felt that Stockbridge was weakening and shouted to Tommy to go on on Benny Lynch. Tommy was quick to respond, and Benny Lynch was going great guns all the way through the Swinley Bottom, where I was still tracking him closely on Alycidon. So we continued on until we were three-quarters of a mile from the finish of the 2½ mile race, where I glanced over my shoulder to see Black Tarquin galloping ominously well within himself, and Edgar Britt looking very happy on his back. I shouted to Tommy to increase the pace, but Benny Lynch was already giving all he had, and I realised that it was time for Alycidon himself to take over. Accordingly, I gave Alycidon a slap down the shoulder and away he went, giving me a punch that nearly shot me onto his neck as he accelerated. We were in front as we began to meet the last five furlongs from home, and as we completed the turn Black Tarquin and Edgar Britt loomed up beside me. For a while we raced almost together, but then the great pounding stride of Alycidon began to tell. At first we edged ahead, and then opened up a clear lead length by length, until Alycidon passed the winning post 5 lengths in front of an absolutely exhausted Black Tarquin. So complete was the superiority of these two outstanding horses that Heron Bridge, who was third, finished a further ten lengths behind.

Alycidon had proved himself the great stayer we believed him to be, and had turned the tables on Black Tarquin in the most decisive fashion. Afterwards Edgar Britt told me that Black Tarquin was going so easily before I took up the running that he felt he could go on and win the race whenever he wanted. But when I gave Alycidon a backhander he saw the horse's quarters expand, giving an extraordinary impression of power as they drove him forward. In the end this remorseless power and devouring stride of Alycidon were more than the gallant Black Tarquin could match.

Alycidon went on to win the Goodwood Cup and the Doncaster Cup – thus securing the 'Stayers' Triple Crown'.

On 8 July 1949, less than a month after Alycidon's Gold Cup, a thirteen-year-old apprentice jockey named Lester Piggott rode against his seniors in

Alycidon and Doug Smith sail home in the 1949 Gold Cup.

The Royal Box in 1950 – open to the elements (**above**) and – **opposite** – closing the windows when the weather turns inclement.

the Brown Jack Stakes on a horse named Argine. Carrying 6 stone 3 pounds and starting at 20-1, Argine finished unplaced. In 1950 Piggott had his first ride at Royal Ascot – unplaced on Eastern Saga in the Ascot Stakes – and rode his first Ascot winners at the September meeting, scoring one on each of the three days: Tancred in the Buckingham Palace Stakes on Thursday 21 September followed up with Moorish Spangle in the Wild Boar Stakes on the Friday and Abraham's Star in the Swinley Forest Handicap on the Saturday. One of the great Ascot riding careers was under way.

The race following the Swinley Forest Handicap that Saturday brought victory in the Kensington Palace Stakes for Sir Winston Churchill's popular grey Colonist II. After twice running unplaced as a juvenile in his native France in 1948, Colonist had been bought as a three-year-old in 1949 by trainer Walter Nightingall for Sir Winston Churchill, in whose pink and chocolate colours he first ran in England in a maiden race at Salisbury that August. He won that race, won again at Windsor, and then went to Ascot in

September for the Ribblesdale Stakes (at the time open to colts), in which he cruised home by eight lengths.

Colonist II ran fourth to Supertello in the Gold Cup in 1950 (the year that for the first time the Royal Meeting was followed on the Saturday by a non-royal Ascot Heath meeting), and his Kensington Palace Stakes victory was the fourth in a sequence of six consecutive wins, which culminated in the Jockey Club Cup at Newmarket.

In June 1951, four months before his owner returned to Downing Street after six years in opposition, the five-year-old Colonist II was runner-up in the Gold Cup, three lengths behind the Etienne Pollet-trained colt Pan II.

Colonist II's one other run at Ascot in 1951 was in an event that opened a new chapter in the history of the course.

THE 'KING GEORGE' –
AND A NEW QUEEN

The nineteen runners in the King George VI and Queen Elizabeth Festival of Britain Stakes at Ascot on 21 July 1951 formed a classy field.

Winners of three of the four Classic races already run that year in England were in the line-up: Arctic Prince, who had won the Derby by six lengths; Ki Ming, Australian jockey Scobie Breasley's first Classic winner when landing the Two Thousand Guineas though unplaced when favourite for the Derby; and Belle Of All, who had won the One Thousand Guineas under Gordon Richards before following up in the Coronation Stakes at the Royal Meeting.

A six-strong French challenge was led by the four-year-old Tantième, who had run at Ascot as a three-year-old when taking the Queen Elizabeth Stakes at the 1950 July meeting, and the same year had won the Poule d'Essai des Poulains (French Two Thousand Guineas) and Prix de l'Arc de Triomphe (which he would win again later in 1951); he returned to Ascot fresh from winning the Coronation Cup at Epsom. The other main French hopes were Scratch II, who had narrowly beaten Tantième in the 1950 Prix du Jockey-Club (French Derby) and gone on to win the St Leger, and Aquino II, who would return to Ascot in 1952 to win the Gold Cup.

Supreme Court, ridden by Charlie Elliott, had been so backward as a yearling that he had not been entered for the Classics, and both Noel Murless and Marcus Marsh, two of the leading trainers of the day, had declined to have him in their yards. So his owner Mrs Vera Lilley sent the colt to the much humbler operation run by Evan Williams at Kingsclere, where he thrived to such a degree that he came to Ascot in July 1951 unbeaten as a three-year-old,

Toppers ready for Ascot action at Moss Bros, 1951.

having won the White Lodge Stakes at Hurst Park, the Chester Vase, and the King Edward VII Stakes (beating Derby runner-up Sybil's Nephew) at the Royal Meeting.

Three-year-old Zucchero had disgraced himself by being left at the start in the Derby but had made minor amends by winning three races since, and was ridden at Ascot (as he had been at Epsom) by the fifteen-year-old *Wunderkind* Lester Piggott. Then there was Colonist II, such a favourite with the Ascot crowd; Wilwyn, a tough three-year-old; and Dynamiter, who would take the Champion Stakes in 1951 and 1952.

The betting market suggested an open race:

100–30 Arctic Prince
7–2 Tantième
10–1 Scratch II
100–9 Supreme Court
100–8 Zucchero, Belle Of All
100–7 Colonist II
20–1 Dynamiter, Wilwyn, Aquino II
33–1 bar

What had attracted such a cast was not so much the setting and occasion – the royal racecourse in Festival of Britain year – as the prize money on offer. With the winning owner netting £25,322 10s, this was the richest purse ever run for in Britain, over a quarter as much again as that year's first prize in the Derby: £19,386 5s.

The 'King George', as the race is affectionately known throughout racing, is now not only the jewel in Ascot's racing crown but an event whose roll of honour excels that of any other in the Flat calendar in Britain over the last fifty years, and a major race on the international stage. So it comes as a surprise to discover that the race was initially intended as a one-off event.

The Festival of Britain, which ran from May to September 1951 and was centred on the South Bank in London (where its lasting monument is the Royal Festival Hall), was intended to provide a showcase for British achievement and rejuvenation after the Second World War, a century after the Great Exhibition of 1851. Racing was invited to play its part when in 1950

Previous pages: Aggressor (Jimmy Lindley) holds off the grey Petite Etoile (Lester Piggott) to win a controversial King George VI and Queen Elizabeth Stakes, 1960.

Lord Ismay, chairman of the Festival, approached the Jockey Club about staging a major race to mark the event. The Jockey Club Minute Book records that the Stewards considered that 'Ascot would be a better place at which to have it than Newmarket' and that the race should be 'racing's contribution to the Festival arrangements'. The Club agreed to contribute £5,000 towards the prize fund.

At Ascot, both the Duke of Norfolk and John Crocker Bulteel were highly enthusiastic, and the Duke put the idea to George VI, who expressed himself 'very keen that every form of sport and other activity would do its best to make the Festival a success'. Furthermore, the King indicated that he felt the race should be run at Ascot's July meeting, where it would not clash with other big races. Naturally such a race needed a huge prize, and this was achieved by combining the money allotted to the Queen Elizabeth Stakes, first run in 1948 over a mile and a half at the July meeting, with that of the two-mile King George VI Stakes at the October fixture (which was then discontinued and replaced by the Cumberland Lodge Stakes). In addition, the King would contribute a piece of plate to the winning owner.

But the idea did not meet with universal approval. At the AGM of the Thoroughbred Breeders' Association in 1950, Lord Derby read out the presidential speech of Lord Rosebery, who was unable to attend in person, in which he expressed his dislike of 'these mammoth races', and when the Jockey Club discussed prospects for the race in October 1950, Lord Derby suggested that it would be detrimental to English racing if there were suddenly a race whose value far exceeded the Derby's. He also suggested that it was not the right moment to put on an exceptionally valuable race for the first time since much of the prize money might end up in France – at which he was shouted down for being 'defeatist'.

Even those who had opposed the original idea must have been impressed with the turnout for the King George VI and Queen Elizabeth Festival of Britain Stakes, and the huge crowd that poured into Ascot was rewarded with an exciting race. The early pace was fierce, with Mossborough, Belle Of All and Tantième cutting out the running until Wilwyn was pushed up to join them at Swinley Bottom, while Charlie Elliott and Lester Piggott bided their time. In the home straight Tantième still led, but with a quarter of a mile to go hung left towards the stands, allowing Arctic Prince, Supreme Court and Zucchero through the gap. Arctic Prince faltered, leaving Elliott and Piggott to fight out a furious finish, with Supreme Court staying on just the better to win by three-quarters of a length, beating the course record for the distance.

Supreme Court never ran again, but the race was considered a massive success, and fears that it might be plundered by the French had been proved groundless. As the *Daily Telegraph* proudly proclaimed:

> When the Festival race was first projected last year, there were some who said it would be foolish to run it over a mile and a half, for it would be at the mercy of the French. Fortunately, such faint-hearted counsel did not prevail.

Although the race had originally been conceived as a one-off, there was now an understandable reaction that it should become a permanent fixture. While some feared that a prize of this order would overshadow the Classics and thus undermine the whole shape of the racing year in Britain, the less reactionary could see only benefits. The race would attract an international field, and would form a valuable opportunity for the Classic generation of three-year-olds to race against their elders over the Derby distance of a mile and a half at a time of year when horses could be expected to be in prime condition. Ample evidence that such a race would work had been provided by the quality of the 1951 field, and indeed by its size (which has never been exceeded in later runnings).

Trainer George Colling wrote that the race should continue in order to encourage owners to keep horses in training as four-year-olds: 'I have seen several that have improved a great deal from three to four years. Owners therefore should be encouraged – even by commercial temptation if you like – to keep their good horses in training as four-year-olds.' For leading journalist and amateur rider John Hislop, the 1951 race 'was an outstanding success in every way and should be repeated provided a stake in the £20,000 region can be put up'. In the Duke of Norfolk and John Crocker Bulteel, Ascot itself had men with the vision and determination to make the King George a regular feature, and it was decided to include the King George VI and Queen Elizabeth Stakes at the July meeting in 1952.

But the King who gave his name to the race never saw a running of it.

George VI had long been suffering from pulmonary disease, and although he was able to perform the opening ceremony at the Festival of Britain in early May 1951, his health was deteriorating and Princess Elizabeth stood in for him at Trooping the Colour on 7 June. The King missed Royal Ascot later that month – the Queen and Princesses led the Royal Procession – and his condition, now diagnosed as pneumonitis, ruled out his attendance at the July meeting.

In September 1951 the King underwent an operation to have his left lung removed. He was recovering at the time of the Ascot October meeting in 1951, when the Saturday programme included the first Ascot races to be televised live. (In 1952, the Ascot Authority made an agreement with BBC Television for three years at an initial facilities fee of £1,000 per annum, reserving to itself the rights for any footage to be 'rediffused' by cinemas. The fee was doubled in 1953, and in 1954 was increased to £2,300 for twelve days' racing. In 1953 BBC Sound made an agreement for broadcasting seven races for 350 guineas, and in 1954 proposed a three-year agreement for £500 per year for all the racing days.) That first television transmission was brought forward half an hour so that the King, convalescing at Windsor, could see his horse Good Shot win the Tankerville Nursery.

George VI died on 6 February 1952, and the second Elizabethan age began.

The new Queen's father had been a keen supporter of the Turf – his best horse was the great filly Sun Chariot, who won the One Thousand Guineas, Oaks and St Leger (all run at Newmarket on account of the war) in 1942 – and she had already shown a marked enthusiasm for and knowledge of racing. On her marriage to Prince Philip in 1947 she had been given as a wedding present by the Aga Khan a filly foal whom she named Astrakhan, and when two years later it was time for Astrakhan to race, the then Princess registered her first racing colours: scarlet, purple hooped sleeves, black cap. Trained at Arundel by William Smyth, Astrakhan provided the Princess with her first runner at Ascot when a highly respectable runner-up to hot favourite The Golden Road in the Sandwich Stakes on 7 October 1949, and with her first winner when taking the Merry Maidens Stakes at Hurst Park in April 1950. (Astrakhan also furnishes early evidence of the Queen's aptitude in naming

Princess Margaret in the Royal Procession in 1952. Throughout the 1950s the younger daughter of George VI and Queen Elizabeth was as much a fashion icon at the meeting as the Princess of Wales in the 1980s.

her horses: the filly was by Turkhan out of Astra.) At this time the Princess also shared ownership with her mother of the very good steeplechaser Monaveen.

On her accession to the throne the Queen inherited the royal colours, and the colours that she had herself registered were next seen on a winning jockey when her daughter the Princess Royal won a steeplechase at Worcester on Cnoc-na-Cuille in September 1987.

Queen Elizabeth II attended her first Royal Ascot as sovereign in 1952, and had a runner in the Queen Anne Stakes, the opening race run in memory of the founder of the meeting. In *Cope's Royal Cavalcade of the Turf*, published to commemorate the Coronation in 1953, bookmaker Alfred Cope described the royal presence in 1952:

Until the time of Queen Elizabeth II there had been a certain studied formality about the movements of the Royal Family at the Royal meeting, but on this occasion racegoers were astonished to see an absorbed young woman leaning casually on the paddock rails while watching the saddling of the horses.

They rubbed their eyes, looked again – it was the Queen. So strange it was to see her mingling freely with her people that as she left the rails and walked back to the Royal Enclosure she went unrecognised by many.

Her three-year-old, Choir Boy, was engaged in the Queen Anne Stakes on the opening day – an event which, truly, it would have been appropriate for Her Majesty to win – but Choir Boy was almost out of sight at the finish and, as he came labouring past the stands, many people heard a cascade of laughter. Shocked at this reception of a Royal loser they looked about to discover the offender – and saw Her Majesty, her face crinkled with amusement at the forlorn spectacle!

She was a Queen – when official duty called, none could compare with her for self-possession and quiet dignity – but she was a woman too, and saw no reason why the regal mask should not lift for a moment to reveal the fact.

There was a historic result in the Wokingham Stakes on the final day of the 1952 meeting, though few watching the victory of Walter

Nightingall-trained Malka's Boy would have guessed at its significance. On the other hand, you did not have to be much of a judge of jockeyship to suspect that sixteen-year-old Lester Piggott, riding his first Royal Ascot winner on Malka's Boy, was not riding his last. (In the event Lester's final winner at the Royal Meeting came forty-one years later, when he won the 1993 Cork and Orrery Stakes on College Chapel.)

The Queen was also present on 19 July 1952 for the second running of the race named in honour of her parents. This time worth £23,302 10s to the winning owner, a little less than the inaugural race, the King George again attracted an excellent field – in terms both of quality and quantity. There were fifteen runners, headed in the betting by that year's Derby winner Tulyar, owned by the Aga Khan and ridden by Charlie Smirke.

Tulyar had been a promising but by no means exceptional two-year-old, and it was only at three that he started to give any hint of becoming a Classic horse. He won the Henry VIII Stakes at Hurst Park, the Ormonde Stakes at Chester and the Lingfield Derby Trial before becoming the subject of a major gamble in the Derby. Backed down from 100–8 the day before the race to a starting price of 11–2, he won by three-quarters of a length from Gay Time (who deposited Lester Piggott on the turf just beyond the line), occasioning Charlie Smirke's famous quip: 'What did I Tulyar?'

After Epsom, Tulyar won the Eclipse Stakes at Sandown Park and was then aimed at Ascot. As a three-year-old, he was set to carry 8 stone 4 pounds in the King George, and this posed a problem for Smirke, who was not used to riding so light. If he could not do the weight, he was told, Gordon Richards would ride Tulyar at Ascot. Never one to overdo the camaraderie of the weighing room – a trained boxer, he was only too ready to stick one on a colleague – Smirke was determined that Richards should not get the ride, and spent most of the week before the race in the Turkish baths in Jermyn Street, sweating off ten pounds. This was enough to satisfy the Aga Khan and Tulyar's trainer Marcus Marsh, but not enough to get down to Tulyar's allotted weight: Smirke still rode at two pounds overweight.

Tulyar started a seemingly generous favourite at 3–1. Second favourite at 7–1 was Zucchero, a reformed character as a four-year-old who had won the Princess of Wales's Stakes at Newmarket. But this time Piggott was on 15–2 third market choice Gay Time, on whom he had finished runner-up to Tulyar in the Derby. The King George had clearly caught the imagination of the French, who sent over no fewer than seven challengers (notably Alec Head-trained Coronation Cup winner Nuccio, who later in 1952 would win the Arc), and there was a German challenger in the shape of Niederlander.

After Mat de Cocagne, one of the French-trained runners, had caused a delay by terrorising his opponents at the start, then landing a kick on Zucchero, the race was off five minutes late. A quarter of a mile out Gay Time led, with Tulyar and Worden II close behind, but once Charlie Smirke pushed the Derby winner into the lead with a furlong to go the race was as good as over. Piggott on Gay Time made a determined challenge but Smirke had plenty up his sleeve, and although the winning distance was only a neck there was no doubting Tulyar's superiority. Thus the Aga Khan's colt started a distinguished line of Derby winners who have gone on to land the King George in the same season, a line which (at the time of writing) stretches to Galileo in 2001 and in between takes in Pinza, Nijinsky, Mill Reef, Grundy, The Minstrel, Troy, Shergar, Reference Point, Nashwan, Generous and Lammtarra. (Royal Palace and Teenoso won the Ascot race the year after Epsom triumph.) Tulyar's victory took his career earnings to £60,597, a new record for a British-trained horse – and, amazingly, beat the previous record of £57,455 set by Gold Cup winner Isinglass way back in 1895. Tulyar's final race brought victory in the St Leger, and he retired the winner of eight races worth £76,417.

Choir Boy, whose dismal effort in the 1952 Queen Anne Stakes had so tickled the Queen, made significant amends when providing her with her first Royal Ascot winner in the 1953 Royal Hunt Cup, run just two weeks after she had been crowned in Westminster Abbey (the ceremony organised with characteristic precision by the Duke of Norfolk). The icing on the cake would have been a royal victory in the Derby four days after the coronation, and the Queen had a serious contender for the premier Classic in Aureole, a chesnut son of Hyperion trained (as were most of the Queen's horses at this time) by Captain Cecil Boyd-Rochfort. The colt had won the Lingfield

Tulyar and Charlie Smirke return to the winner's enclosure after the 1952 King George VI and Queen Elizabeth Stakes.

Derby Trial and was well fancied to provide a fairytale Derby result, but in the event finished runner-up to Pinza. Nevertheless, the result of the 1953 Derby was hugely popular, as Pinza was ridden by Gordon Richards, landing the Derby at his twenty-eighth attempt.

Pinza and Aureole (who after the Derby ran a disappointing third in the Eclipse Stakes) were among the thirteen runners for the third running of the King George VI and Queen Elizabeth Stakes in July 1953, when their opponents included Zucchero, in the race for the third year running; Two Thousand Guineas and St James's Palace Stakes winner Nearula; two representatives of Italy in Alberigo and his pacemaker Telemaco; Wilwyn, who had run in the 1951 race and had since won the inaugural Washington DC International; and five runners from France, including two who had taken part the year before, Worden II (third to Tulyar) and Nuccio.

Again there was pre-race drama. As the horses were leaving the paddock the French colt Pharel kicked Aureole in the ribs, the royal colt reared, and jockey Harry Carr crashed to the ground. After a few anxious moments it became clear that neither horse nor rider was hurt. The pre-race parade continued with the field intact, and the race proved a fairly straightforward proposition for Pinza, who cruised into the lead at the two-furlong marker and sauntered home as Aureole made an unavailing attempt to get on terms. At the line Pinza was three lengths clear. Like Supreme Court after his 1951 victory, Pinza did not run again.

Aureole's own moment of King George glory was to come. A year later Pinza had long since retired to stud and the royal colt was going from strength to strength. Although his trainer Cecil Boyd-Rochfort insisted that 'there is no vice in him whatsoever', Aureole had a reputation as something of a wayward character, and he became a patient of Dr Charles Brook, a London neurologist who among other results managed to dissuade this impulsive colt from bolting his food. In his biography of Boyd-Rochfort, Bill Curling described how Brook 'would go into Aureole's box, and would put his left hand on Aureole's withers and his right on his girth, and resting his head on the colt's shoulder, would stand quietly alone with him for perhaps twenty minutes whilst Aureole continued to eat his hay, surprisingly making no fuss'.

Though beaten in the 1953 St Leger, Aureole had ended that season on a winning note at Ascot in the Cumberland Lodge Stakes, a race in which

Harry Carr, who could not do the weight, was replaced by Eph Smith – and to Carr's disappointment Smith kept the ride for Aureole's future races.

Aureole opened his four-year-old campaign in 1954 with defeat by Irish Derby winner Chamier in the Coronation Stakes at Sandown Park and wins in the Victor Wild Stakes at Kempton Park and the Coronation Cup at Epsom. He then won the Hardwicke Stakes on the final day of Royal Ascot – the Queen's second winner that day, after Landau had won the opening Rous Memorial Stakes, giving Gordon Richards what proved to be his last Ascot winner. In a desperately close finish to the Hardwicke Stakes, Aureole beat the French colt Janitor by a short head. (On the morning of the Hardwicke Stakes the Queen had arrived early to inspect the course with Crocker Bulteel. After doing so she mounted her mare Betsy and rode down the course with two attendants. This enthusiasm for early-morning rides around Ascot racecourse soon spread to other members of the Royal Family and became an informal tradition during the formality of Ascot week.)

Janitor was among Aureole's sixteen rivals for the 1954 King George, along with fellow French colts Vamos (trained by François Mathet and ridden by Roger Poincelet) and Savoyard. But the royal colt's main rival appeared to be the Italian three-year-old Botticelli, who had won the Italian Two Thousand Guineas, the Italian Derby, the Gran Premio d'Italia and the Gran Premio di Milano, while others who attracted support in the betting were Aureole's stable companion Premonition (who had beaten him into third when winning the 1953 St Leger), Chamier (who had beaten him at Sandown), and Arabian Night and Darius (respectively second and third to Never Say Die in that year's Derby). Among the 33–1 outsiders was Souepi, who had won the Gold Cup in 1953.

The story of the race is told in Timeform's *Racehorses of 1954*:

> The prevailing conditions, heavy going and almost continuous rain, were such as to make a mockery of form and judgment. On top of this Aureole was a bit full of himself in the preliminaries. He put Smith on the grass on the way to the post, and played up a little once he did get down to the start. Not surprisingly when the tapes went up he was one of the last to leave the gate; but Smith, realising the foolishness of lying too far out of his ground in these conditions, steadily threaded

The Queen, Queen Mother and Princess Margaret with trainer Captain Cecil Boyd-Rochfort greeting Aureole after the colt's victory in the 1954 King George.

Aureole through the field, so that he was up with the leaders entering Swinley Bottom. Chatsworth was first into the straight with Aureole hard on his heels, and soon he moved into the lead. There were still three furlongs to go, however, and at this point Vamos emerged from the pack in the wake of the royal colt; steadily the French horse came on, and with a furlong to go he had almost reached Aureole's quarters. Once again Smith asked Aureole for a great effort and, without flinching for an instant, the colt held Vamos decisively over the last 150 yards to win by three-quarters of a length.

Darius was third, Souepi fourth.

Aureole did not race again, but was retired to embark upon a stud career that proved remarkably successful. Among his many top-notch offspring were St Paddy, winner of the Derby and St Leger in 1960, other St Leger winners in Aurelius (who has a race at Ascot named after him) and Provoke, and Vienna (sire of the 1968 Arc winner Vaguely Noble, who himself won as Ascot as a two-year-old in 1967).

For the Queen to have owned such a horse so early in her reign was remarkable, and although she has enjoyed many famous moments since –

Ronald Searle's view of Royal Ascot in the *News Chronicle Saturday Sketchbook*, 1954.

notably with Classic winners Carrozza (1957 Oaks), Pall Mall (1958 Two Thousand Guineas), 1974 One Thousand Guineas and Prix de Diane heroine Highclere, and 1977 Oaks and St Leger winner Dunfermline – it is fair to say that Aureole represents a golden period in the fortunes of the royal colours, and the chesnut's 1954 King George victory was indisputably one of the great Ascot moments. Aureole did not retire from stud duties until 1974, and he died in 1975 at the good age of twenty-five.

The name of Lester Piggott is conspicuous by its absence from the list of jockeys who rode in Aureole's King George, and the reason for the omission takes us back exactly a month before the royal victory to one of the most controversial races in all Ascot history: the King Edward VII Stakes on the third day of the Royal Meeting, 17 June 1954.

Two weeks before Royal Ascot, eighteen-year-old Lester Piggott had ridden the first of his nine Derby winners on Never Say Die, and he was reunited with the colt at Ascot. Arabian Night, second at Epsom, was now favoured by the weights and was made favourite to reverse the Derby form: he started at 13–8, with Never Say Die on 7–4; third favourite at 5–1 was Rashleigh, ridden by Gordon Richards. Early in the straight came an argy-bargy which provoked so much argument and caused so many ripples that, in the absence in those days of camera patrols and given the difficulty of seeing what happened from the one grainy film of the race, it is worth considering the accounts written by Richards and Piggott in their respective autobiographies.

First, Gordon Richards:

Coming into the straight, Blue Prince and Dragon Fly were making the running, with [Bill] Rickaby on Garter third, [Tommy] Gosling on Arabian Night fourth, and I was fifth. Dragon Fly dropped out, and Rickaby and I began to move up to the leader. All of a sudden, Lester Piggott on Never Say Die started to make a move. I was on the outside, and so I do not know whether Never Say Die was hanging or not. Lester claimed he was. At any rate, Never Say Die charged into Garter, and Garter hit my quarters and practically turned me round. Then Never Say Die charged Garter again, and Garter turned me broadside on. I suspect that it did look, from the Stand, as if my horse was doing the damage: but if another horse hits yours in the rump, it will throw you into him, and that is what happened.

Rashleigh recovered marvellously, and he and Tarjoman – being ridden by that splendid French jockey Poincelet – went on to challenge Arabian Night who had taken up the running with Blue Prince. Arabian Night dived twice, first of all putting Blue Prince on to Tarjoman, and then Tarjoman on to me. But Rashleigh would not be beaten whatever happened to him, and we went on to win.

Of course it was a most unsatisfactory race, and the Stewards objected to me. But immediately they had heard the evidence, they withdrew their objection.

They did, however, stand Lester Piggott down.

Whether the incident was preceded by Lester's customary suggestion (so it is reported) to Richards at such moments – 'Move over, Grandad!' – is not known. Lester's own account, written four decades after the event, is characteristically laconic:

Everything went normally until soon after we had made the turn into the short home straight. Gordon on Rashleigh was on the outside, with Garter (Bill Rickaby) and Dragon Fly (Doug Smith) on his inner. Never Say Die was just behind this trio, full of running. Then a gap opened up between Dragon Fly on the inside and Garter, one off the rail, which looked inviting, so I pushed Never Say Die up to go through it. At that moment Gordon started to bring Rashleigh in towards the inner, causing Garter to be sandwiched and bumped from each side by both Rashleigh and Never Say Die. For a few seconds there was a fair amount of scrimmaging, then we sorted ourselves out and ran straight for the post – where Rashleigh won by a length from Tarjoman and Blue Prince II (neither of whom had been involved in the incident), with Never Say Die fourth.

I was hauled before the course stewards, informed that I had caused the rumpus by trying to force my way through when there was no gap, and suspended for the rest of the day. Worse, I was told I had to see the Stewards of the Jockey Club at the course the following day, which did not augur well. And worse still, when I learned that I would be appearing before the Duke of Norfolk I knew I'd be for the high jump, even though my record that season had to date been reasonably good, with only one earlier suspension. The Duke ruled Ascot with a rod of iron and following my earlier scrapes with the racing powers that be was hardly my greatest fan. The interview with the Stewards of the Jockey Club that Friday dealt me a severe blow: I was not to be allowed to set foot on any racecourse for the next six months ...

The official Jockey Club statement announced that the Stewards had 'taken notice of his dangerous and erratic riding both this season and in previous seasons, and that in spite of continuous warnings, he continued to show complete disregard for the Rules of Racing and for the safety of other jockeys'.

In those early years of his extraordinary career Lester Piggott had a reputation for a win-at-all-costs attitude which his disciplinary record at the time did little to dispel: the sentence following the King Edward VII Stakes, swingeing as it might have appeared, was his ninth suspension (most of them for rough riding) since 1950. But when ruminating about this notorious Ascot occasion, Piggott makes a pertinent point:

It has to be remembered that all this happened not long after the end of the war, when race-riding on the Flat was dominated by a generation of older jockeys – Gordon, Charlie Smirke, Charlie Elliott, Doug and Eph Smith, Edgar Britt and Bill Rickaby among them – who had had their own way on the track for a good while and possibly resented the arrival of a new generation of young jockeys. Because of the war that young generation of riders was tiny in comparison with the established riders: the usual process of integrating a group of young performers, which happens in any sport, had been disrupted by the hostilities.

Piggott's sentence was commuted, and − ironically − one of his first winners on his return to the saddle in the autumn was on the Duke of Norfolk's colt Wordsworth in the Sandwich Stakes at the Ascot October meeting.

The mid 1950s saw significant advances in racecourse technology, the most beneficial of which (at least from the racegoers' point of view) was the introduction of race commentaries. Live commentary had been introduced to British racing at Goodwood in 1952 and the same year limited experiments were carried out at Ascot, where in 1953 the Jockey Club gave permission for commentaries to be broadcast into all enclosures. Crocker Bulteel reported that 'only one or two per cent of people' did not approve of this facility.

There were also changes in the shape of the racecourse itself.

Down in Swinley Bottom the running surface was realigned to produce one long sweeping bend instead of the half bend, then short straight, then another bend, which tended to interrupt the stride pattern of galloping horses. Both the paddock bend and the home turn were also improved. To make more room in the enclosures, and to provide a better view from the stands, the new Straight Mile, which had long been planned to replace the 'old' Straight Mile (not to be confused with the Old − that is, round − Mile) measuring a little short of a true mile, was finally opened for use in 1955. It is situated to the north of the road, whereas the old Straight Mile − which is still easily identifiable from the stands, to the right of the new − was immediately to the south. The new version (complete with new Golden Gates) is precisely one mile long (from starting stalls to winning post) and rises by sixty-nine feet from start to finish.

During the weeks before the 1955 Royal Meeting, Britain was in the grip of a rail strike, and after a great deal of discussion the Royal Meeting was postponed until July − when, since the Court was not in residence at Windsor, there was no Royal Procession. (The scheduled Ascot Heath meeting that June was transferred to Newbury.) All went to plan on the first two days of the

The racing form as fashion accessory, 1955.

meeting. Wednesday was Gold Cup day that year, and Botticelli won easily by three lengths from Blue Prince II to make up for his disappointment in the 1954 King George. Two races later the great three-year-old filly Meld, who had won the One Thousand Guineas and the Oaks, justified odds of 9–4 on when strolling home in the Coronation Stakes. (She went on to win the St Leger and thus secure the 'Fillies' Triple Crown'.)

On the Thursday three races had been run when yet again the weather gatecrashed the party. The *Daily Herald* reported:

> Lightning hit Royal Ascot this afternoon. As it cut a swathe through the crowd on the Heath side a woman fell dying. Forty-nine others lay injured among the 100 or more knocked flat or hurled into the air.
>
> For a few minutes there was chaos. Stunned men and women, screaming children, staggered and ran round in circles. Then three very calm, efficient policemen took charge.
>
> When the last of the injured had been taken away a twisted and charred umbrella remained. It is believed to have been carried by the woman who died on her way to Windsor hospital.

The woman was Mrs Barbara Batt, pregnant with her first child. When news of her death reached the course, racing was abandoned for the day, and it was then learned that there had been a second fatality: Leonard Tingle, an evangelist from Sheffield. Through the Duke of Norfolk a message was relayed: 'The Queen is shocked to hear the news of the incident at Ascot and wishes me to send her sympathy to those who may be bereaved.'

On the other hand, there was good news in 1955 – at least for some Ascot regulars – when the prohibition of divorcées from the Royal Enclosure was lifted, which meant that any old person could apply for a voucher: anyone, that is, except undischarged bankrupts, defaulters in betting, and those who had served a prison sentence. The issuing of vouchers remained at the discretion of Her Majesty's Representative, and new applicants usually had to be sponsored by someone who had been granted vouchers during recent years and whose name was therefore 'on the list'. (The Ascot Authority still had at its disposal the so-called 'stop list' of people known to the racing authorities as 'undesirables' or who had been convicted of doping, and the divorce rule still applied within the Royal Household Stand and in the extended Queen's Lawn – but even this restriction was dropped in 1963.)

Social change was rampant, and the Royal Enclosure was now occupied by a much broader range than ever before. Another sign of the times – and another instance of innovation and vision at Ascot – came in 1955 after the Duke of Norfolk had grown tired of the constant stream of announcements about lost children. Sir Billy Butlin advised him that a playground was the answer, and sure enough a facility soon opened for children under two, thought to have been the first ever crèche on a British racecourse. There were sandpits, swings and roundabouts, skipping ropes and balls, and parents who found such attractions more alluring than the sport out on the racecourse were allowed to stay there with the children. Furthermore, a section of the Silver Ring enclosure was cordoned off for children of eight years and under.

The rescheduling of the 1955 Royal Meeting meant that the fifth running of the King George VI and Queen Elizabeth Stakes was held on the very day after the Royal Meeting closed. (With the last two races on the Thursday cancelled on account of the storm, the Bessborough Stakes was transferred to the Friday and the Rous Memorial Stakes to the Saturday.) Derby winner Phil Drake started 11–8 on favourite for the King George, but could finish only sixth behind Vimy, ridden by Roger Poincelet and trained by Alec Head, who beat Acropolis a head to become the first French-trained winner of the race. Vimy, like Supreme Court, Pinza and Aureole before him, never ran again after the King George.

Roger Poincelet and Alec Head were back at Ascot later in the year to take the first running of what instantly became – and has remained – one of the racing highlights of the Ascot year: the Queen Elizabeth II Stakes over the Old Mile, first run on 24 September 1955. With added prize money of £5,000, this was a valuable addition to the Ascot programme which the *Daily Telegraph* described as 'bait for foreign entries'. Certainly the result of the inaugural running, when Hafiz II took the prize across the Channel, bore out such a suggestion. Hafiz II returned to England the following month to win the Champion Stakes at Newmarket. But the first Queen Elizabeth II Stakes proved a catastrophe for the Queen in whose honour it was named. Her colt Sierra Nevada broke a fetlock when trying to mount a challenge in the home straight and had to be put down.

Sir John Crocker Bulteel, one of the founding fathers of the Ascot we know today, died suddenly of a heart attack at his home in February 1956. He had lived to see his vision for putting the course on the international stage with the King George VI and Queen Elizabeth Stakes become reality, but he died before that race lured to England, for the one and only time, one of the all-time superstars.

Ribot, the greatest Italian horse ever to race in England, was already a living equine legend by the time he lined up at Ascot on 21 July 1956. A son of the 1948 Queen Elizabeth Stakes winner Tenerani bred by Federico Tesio, Ribot had first drawn breath not in Italy but at the National Stud's yard at West Grinstead in Sussex. He was so small as a foal that he was nicknamed 'Il Piccolo' – the little one – but it soon became clear that there was nothing small about the engine inside his diminutive frame, and he went into training with Ugo Penco with great expectations. Tesio died at the age of eighty-five in May 1954 before his finest horse saw a racecourse, but by the end of that year Ribot was unbeaten in three outings. As a three-year-old he continued to carry all before him in Italy, but that country had nothing which could get near him, so he made an ambitious trip to Paris for the 1955 Prix de l'Arc de Triomphe. Starting at 9–1 and ridden by his

A royal victory in the 1956 Royal Hunt Cup: Harry Carr pushes the Queen's colt Alexander home. (Alexander did not win as easily as it appears from this photograph: the second, third and fourth are on the other side of the course, and Alexander won by only half a length.)

regular jockey, the veteran Enrico Camici, he won by three lengths, then returned to Italy to take the Gran Premio del Jockey Club at Milan by fifteen.

With a record of nine wins in nine races, Ribot was kept in training as a four-year-old, a repeat Arc the main target. First, however, connections wanted to go for a big race in England, and although for a while there was a chance that he might run in the Gold Cup, the still infant King George already had sufficient pulling power to draw Ribot to Ascot in July. He came there unbeaten in four races in 1956 – three minor events and the Gran Premio di Milano – giving him a career record of thirteen out of thirteen, and it was no surprise that he scared off most serious opposition. Ribot started at 5–2 on in a field of nine (smallest yet in six runnings of the race), with no other runner at odds of under 10–1. The Queen's High Veldt, who had won the Two Thousand Guineas Trial at Kempton and the Thirsk Classic Trial before disappointing in the St James's Palace Stakes, was a 100–7 chance.

The weather was foul, but a large crowd turned out for their first chance to see the Italian phenomenon. Timeform's *Racehorses of 1956* provides a thorough description of the great horse's day at Ascot:

> The King George VI and Queen Elizabeth Stakes was destined to be the hardest race of Ribot's career. It is not altogether easy to see why this should have been so, but it is worth remembering that he was racing in conditions which were completely unfamiliar to him. The going was very sticky, and Ribot, who had hitherto been unaffected by the state of the ground, was plainly ill at ease on it. In the paddock he was by no means outstanding, but it was immediately apparent that he was tough, powerful, extremely muscular and well built. While nobody would have called him a handsome horse, he was a long way from being a plain one. After he was saddled, he introduced a touch of comedy by declining at first to file between the ranks of spectators who lined the way to the parade ring, but once Daemon, who had been through it all before and knew the ropes, showed him the way, he did not hesitate to follow. Completely nonchalant in the parade, Ribot moved particularly impressively in the canter down to the post.
>
> The start was delayed while Todrai relieved himself of his jockey, and went to have a look round the course on his own. Though he

covered something like two miles before he was captured, he was never out of a steady canter, and no doubt suffered less than the innocents kept waiting for him at the post.

When the field finally jumped off, Todrai lost a little ground, as he deserved to, but Chantelsey lost more, and Patras was left many lengths behind the rest. High Veldt was the first to strike the front, but was soon steadied, and Daemon took up the running. Todrai and Ribot moved up to join him, and consternation was general when it was observed that Camici was having to push the latter along for all he was worth. Out of Swinley Bottom Todrai went into the lead from Daemon, with Ribot third, and High Veldt and Chantelsey were handily placed.

It was not long, however, before Daemon dropped out, leaving Todrai and Ribot in the lead together. Camici was still riding Ribot hard, but very little seemed to be forthcoming, and he could not shake off Todrai, who was sticking to him grimly. They were still together as they came into the straight, closely followed by Chantelsey, High Veldt, Roistar and Cash And Courage, and at this point it might have been anticipated that Ribot would go right ahead, and win with the flamboyant brilliance that his performances abroad had entitled one to expect.

But nothing of the kind happened. Todrai ran a little wide entering the straight, leaving High Veldt, who had been close behind him on the rails, a clear run on the inside, and Carr lost no time in seizing the opportunity. Battle in earnest now began between Ribot and High Veldt, and enthusiasm mounted to a crescendo when it was seen that there was a possibility of a royal victory. Once Ribot reached better going in the last two furlongs, any such hopes evaporated. Lengthening his stride, he quickly wore down High Veldt, and as soon as he was in top gear, showed his true mettle by sprinting clear to pass the post an easy winner by five lengths, a margin which would have been doubled with a little further to go.

Ribot returned to Italy to win the Premio del Piazzale by fifteen lengths, then

Ribot (Enrico Camici) storms home to win the 1956 King George by five lengths.

wound up his career by slamming a strong international field to land a second Arc by six lengths in sensational style. He retired the winner of every one of his sixteen races.

At the time of Ribot's appearance, Ascot did not have a permanent Clerk of the Course. Crocker Bulteel's sudden death had led to the temporary appointment for the 1956 meetings of Major J. D. Watts, Clerk of the Course at Epsom, and only in August was it announced that the Queen had approved the appointment of Major General David Dawnay as Secretary to the Ascot Authority and Clerk of the Course. Dawnay had been an officer with the 10th Hussars and Commandant for the Royal Military Academy, Sandhurst, before becoming the Commanding Officer of the 56th London Armoured Division of the Territorial Army. He was a keen polo player, had ridden in point-to-points, and trained a few of his own horses for National Hunt races, winning the Grand Military Hunters' Chase at Sandown Park in March 1956 with Flying Rosette, ridden by his son Hugh.

Major General Dawnay was not long in his job before he was attracting controversy. Throughout the week before his first Royal Meeting in 1957, the warm and sultry atmosphere was rapidly drying out the ground, but Dawnay

The first of Lester Piggott's eleven Gold Cup victories: Zarathustra comes home clear of Cambremer and Tissot in 1957.

declined to water the course as he was convinced that thunder was on the way, and torrential rain pouring onto watered ground would produce a quagmire. In the event the weather did not break and the ground became firmer and firmer. On the Tuesday and Wednesday the going was officially described as 'Hard', on the Thursday and Friday (and for the Heath meeting on the Saturday) as 'V. Hard'. Many trainers, alarmed at the concrete-like going, withdrew their horses, and a measure of the level of defection is that the Wokingham Stakes, which traditionally attracts large fields, had just eight runners that year (compared with twenty-eight in 1956 and twenty-two in 1958). Of those who did run that week, mention must be made of Almeria, who won the Ribblesdale Stakes for the Queen; of Lord Howard de Walden's Amerigo, who won the Coventry Stakes in a canter by eight lengths in a new record time for six furlongs (itself an indication of the state of the ground); of the easy Jersey Stakes winner Quorum, who would achieve lasting fame as sire of Red Rum; of The Tuscar, who gave Sir Gordon Richards his first Royal Ascot winner as a trainer; of Chevastrid, who won the St James's Palace Stakes partnered by Jimmy Eddery, whose son Pat would later make a huge impact on the course; and of Zarathustra, first of Lester Piggott's eleven Gold Cup winners when beating off the foreign challenge of Cambremer from France and Tissot from Italy.

The following month Piggott could have been anticipating another good pay-day when Sir Victor Sassoon's Crepello, brilliant winner of the 1957 Two Thousand Guineas and Derby, was due to take on older horses for the first time in the King George. But Ascot was yet again hit by thunderstorms and a steady downpour on the morning of the race made the going heavy. Trainer Noel Murless, who had been reluctant to run Crepello in the race anyway as he wanted to prepare this delicate colt quietly for the St Leger (and thus the Triple Crown), was insistent that the horse could not be risked in such conditions and he was withdrawn shortly before the race – unleashing a barrage of press criticism on an unrepentant Murless and leaving Montaval to become one of the less glamorous King George winners and complete a clean sweep for the French challenge: with Montaval, Al Mabsoot, Tribord and Saint Raphael, French raiders filled the first four places.

June 1958 saw Major Dick Hern train his first Royal Ascot winner when None Nicer won the Ribblesdale Stakes for his patron Major Lionel Holliday. But that fixture is best remembered for the Gold Cup victory of Gladness, the first mare to win the race since Quashed beat Omaha back in 1936. Owned by John McShain (head of the American construction company which had built the Pentagon) and trained in Ireland by Vincent O'Brien, at that time scaling down his training of jumpers to concentrate on the Flat, Gladness had already run at Ascot, winning the Sunninghill Park Stakes in September 1957. In the Gold Cup – in which she was ridden by Lester Piggott – she started joint favourite with Scot II, who the previous month had beaten her a length in the Prix du Cadran (French equivalent of the Gold Cup) at Longchamp. She tracked the leaders until taking up the running on the home turn and stayed on strongly to repel the persistent challenge of Hornbeam. Gladness went on from Ascot to win the Goodwood Cup, then carried 9 stone 7 pounds to a six-length victory in the Ebor Handicap.

The name of Gladness is often bracketed with that of her even more

Poster for the 1964 film *My Fair Lady* showing the Ascot scene, famous for its fashion designs by Cecil Beaton. With lyrics by Alan Jay Lerner and music by Frederick Loewe, *My Fair Lady* was first staged in New York in March 1956, with the Ascot scene introduced by the 'Ascot Gavotte' – 'Every duke and earl and peer is here / Every one who should be here is here / What a smashing, positively dashing spectacle / The Ascot opening day.'

illustrious stable companion Ballymoss, also owned by John McShain. Ballymoss had become the first Irish-trained winner of the St Leger in 1957 after finishing runner-up at 33–1 to Crepello in the Derby, and his other victories as a three-year-old included the Irish Derby. As a four-year-old in 1958 he won the Coronation Cup in June and the Eclipse Stakes. A week after the Eclipse came the King George, and McShain and O'Brien had in Gladness and Ballymoss two horses capable of winning that race. The choice, according to O'Brien, was simple: 'Ballymoss to run if it was firm; Gladness if it was soft. It was firm, so I ran Ballymoss.'

The only serious rival to Ballymoss appeared to be Hard Ridden, who had won that year's Derby partnered by fifty-one-year-old Charlie Smirke, and these two dominated the market, Ballymoss going off 7–4 favourite, with Hard Ridden 2–1 and the third choice, the Queen's filly Almeria, out at 9–1. Ridden (as in all his races at four) by Scobie Breasley, Ballymoss dashed into the lead early in the straight and easily withstood the challenge of Almeria to win by three lengths. (Third, three-quarters of a length behind Almeria, was another of the Queen's horses, Doutelle, who had also run third to Gladness in the Gold Cup. A tough and consistent colt who won the Granville Stakes at Ascot as a two-year-old and the Cumberland Lodge Stakes at three, Doutelle was one of his owner's most popular horses.)

Ballymoss then went on to win the Prix de l'Arc de Triomphe and secure his position as the best Irish-trained horse of the 1950s.

Any owner with a colt like Ballymoss and a mare like Gladness would want to mate them, and John McShain duly did so. Their daughter Merry Mate won the Irish Oaks in 1966, while their son Bally Joy won three races and was third in the 1965 Hardwicke Stakes at Royal Ascot.

The Royal Ascot going had been officially described as 'Firm' for all four days of the 1958 meeting. In 1959 on all four days it was 'Hard', but the meeting still produced some notable results. The Queen Mother, whose colours – blue, buff stripes, blue sleeves, black cap, gold tassel – were a familiar sight at jumping tracks but seen less often on the Flat, won the Queen Alexandra Stakes with Bali H'ai III, trained by Cecil Boyd-Rochfort, and the Queen won the St James's Palace Stakes with Above Suspicion. Fulke Walwyn, better known as a jumping trainer, won the Windsor Castle Stakes with Monamolin. Cantelo won the Ribblesdale Stakes, and later in the season would land the St Leger. The outstanding sprinter Right Boy won at the Royal Meeting for the third year in a row, taking the Cork and Orrery Stakes under Lester Piggott to add to victories in the same race in 1958 and the King's Stand Stakes in 1957. Martial won the Coventry Stakes for Irish trainer Paddy Prendergast, and went on to win the 1960 Two Thousand Guineas, a double that no horse has achieved since.

But the race that really caught the public imagination at the 1959 Royal Meeting was the Gold Cup battle between Alcide and Wallaby II. Alcide, owned by Sir Humphrey de Trafford and trained by Cecil Boyd-

Cecil Beaton sketch for the Ascot scene in *My Fair Lady*.

Rochfort, had been hotly fancied for the 1958 Derby but not long before the race was found in his box with a broken rib: it was widely assumed that he had been 'got at' to rule him out of the premier Classic. In due course he recovered well enough to win the Great Voltigeur Stakes at York and the St Leger. Kept in training at four, Alcide opened his campaign by running second in the Jockey Club Cup (beaten a short head by Vacarme), then won the Victor Wild Stakes at Kempton Park and the Winston Churchill Stakes at Hurst Park. He seemed well on course for the Gold Cup, but two setbacks in training – first with a jarred joint, then when the injured leg began to fill after he had resumed serious work – affected his preparation, and on the day there were plenty of pundits who expected the French challenger Wallaby II, who on his most recent outing had been beaten a head in the Prix du Cadran, to exploit the chink in Alcide's fitness. The betting went 11–10 Alcide, 9–4 Wallaby II, 11–2 the Yorkshire Cup winner Cutter, 10–1 bar.

The race boiled down to a furious final-furlong battle between Freddie Palmer on Wallaby II and Harry Carr on Alcide, which Carr described:

> In the last hundred yards Alcide's head was at one moment in front, and the next it was Wallaby II's and so we alternated until the line where the camera recorded Wallaby II's nose had touched it first. The camera is a hard and at times a cruel task-mistress. When the heads of two fine horses are bobbing up and down in the final stages of a great and valuable race such as the Ascot Gold Cup, with no more than a few inches between them, it records with a clinical accuracy and detachment the winner and the loser at the point of crossing the line. A stride short of it I may have been in front on Alcide, and a stride after it Wallaby II might have been a fraction ahead, but at the all-important moment it gave its verdict to the French stayer.

Alcide and Wallaby II met again in the King George the following month. This time Alcide's fine-tuning had gone without any problem, and it was expected that he would turn the tables. He went off 2–1 favourite, with Gladness on 9–2 and Wallaby II a 5–1 chance, while next in the betting came two three-year-olds who had shone at the Royal Meeting: Ribblesdale Stakes winner Cantelo on 6–1 and the Queen's King Edward VII Stakes winner Pindari (a superbly bred colt by Pinza out of George VI's triple Classic winner Sun Chariot) on 8–1. Kept in the rear until three furlongs out, Alcide moved up on the outside as Gladness took the lead approaching the furlong pole, then swept past her to go clear, winning by two lengths. Balbo, one of the French challengers, was third and Cantelo fourth; Wallaby II, who never got into the race and clearly needed a longer distance, came last.

Yet again the King George proved the winner's final race: Alcide was retired to stud.

Of all the horses who ran at Ascot in 1959, none has more sombre associations than Priddy Fair. On Saturday 26 September this three-year-old filly was being taken to the start of the Red Deer Handicap by jockey Manny Mercer, elder brother of Joe (who had ridden a double that day, including Rosalba in the Queen Elizabeth II Stakes). Manny Mercer was one of the most admired and popular riders of the day. He had won two Classics earlier in the 1950s, and the inaugural running of the Washington DC International on Wilwyn in 1952, and in 1958 had enjoyed his best ever season, riding 125 winners in Britain, which put him in third place in the jockeys' championship behind Doug Smith and Scobie Breasley.

As Priddy Fair cantered back past the stands towards the mile-and-a-half starting gate, she slipped and fell, throwing her jockey against the rails. In struggling to her feet she seemed to kick Mercer in the head. Racegoers rushed to his assistance, but he was dead by the time they reached him. Although the Red Deer Stakes went ahead, the final race of the day was abandoned.

Of the twenty-four races run at Royal Ascot in 1960 (the year that the Gold Vase reverted to its old name of Queen's Vase), half were won by favourites, six of whom started odds-on – including Venture VII, beaten a head by Martial in the Two Thousand Guineas, who beat his sole opponent in the St James's Palace Stakes at 33–1 on, not exactly a working man's price. The final three races of the Royal Meeting all had favourites who went off at 15–8 on, and two of the three lost. First, 1959 Derby winner Parthia was turned over by Aggressor in the Hardwicke Stakes. Then Jim Joel's great

Manny Mercer winning the 1953 Queen Anne Stakes on Argur. Jimmy Lindley is second on the grey King's Mistake.

The road to Ascot, 1959.

stayer Predominate obliged for those who had laid the odds in the Queen Alexandra Stakes, sauntering home by six lengths. Finally the exceptionally fast colt Sing Sing was beaten in the King's Stand Stakes, last race on the last day.

There was a distinct whiff of something untoward about this race, as Sing Sing's jockey Doug Smith explained:

> Sing Sing, the brilliant speed he had shown as a two-year-old [he was now three] unimpaired, looked a natural for the race, and the weight of public money caused him to start at long odds on. It followed that any evilly disposed person who could procure the defeat of Sing Sing could put himself in a position to win a fortune. He jumped off well, but some way from the finish, though he was disputing the lead, I felt that he was not his usual brilliant self. In the end, for the first time since his initial race at Newmarket the previous year, I had to pull my whip through and hit him. It was then that I became sure that something was seriously the matter with him; for, instead of thrusting his head forward and battling for the lead as he always had done in the past, he sank it on to his chest and seemed to be distressed. It was a close finish, but Sound Track mastered a lifeless Sing Sing in the last hundred yards and beat him a neck.
>
> I have little doubt that Sing Sing was got at before the King's Stand Stakes, but the perpetrators of the crime rather underestimated the dose needed to stop him, with the result that it was an extremely close call.

Poor Sing Sing was got at again before the July Cup and withdrawn from that race, leaving Tin Whistle (who had won the Cork and Orrery Stakes at Royal Ascot) to walk over.

But for all the unproven suspicions about the King's Stand Stakes, there is no doubt that the most controversial race run at Ascot in 1960 was the King George VI and Queen Elizabeth Stakes on 16 July.

Petite Etoile, most brilliant filly of her age and talked of in the same breath as Pretty Polly nearly sixty years earlier, seemed to be, in the American betting parlance, a shoo-in. Her distinctive iron-grey colouring recalled some of the big names – and big Ascot names at that – in her pedigree: The Tetrarch was her great-great-great-great-grandsire, Mumtaz Mahal her great-great-great-granddam; her sire Petition had won the New Stakes as a two-year-old in 1946. At three Petite Etoile had won the One Thousand Guineas, the Oaks, the Yorkshire Oaks, the Sussex Stakes and the Champion Stakes. There was much rejoicing when it was announced that she would stay in training with Noel Murless as a four-year-old, and she opened her campaign in 1960 with an easy win at Kempton Park. She then scored a cheeky victory in the Coronation Cup at Epsom (a victory overshadowed by the death of her owner Prince Aly Khan in a car crash near Paris not long before the race), and seemed a certainty for the King George.

At Ascot she faced seven opponents, but nothing that seemed likely to interrupt her stately progress. Among them were Parthia and Aggressor, who had beaten Parthia in the Hardwicke Stakes. The five-year-old Aggressor was trained by 'Towser' Gosden (father of current trainer John) and owned by Sir Harold Wernher, for whom Ascot still echoed with memories of his great servant Brown Jack. Aggressor would never reach that fellow's level of popularity, but he was a consistent and genuine horse who as a four-year-old had won five races, including the Chesterfield Cup at Goodwood and the Cumberland Lodge Stakes at the Ascot September meeting, and had landed the John Porter Stakes at Newbury before winning the Hardwicke – very good form, but hardly in the same league as Petite Etoile's.

Lester Piggott had passed over Petite Etoile for another Murless runner, Collyria, in the 1959 One Thousand Guineas, and after the grey had won that race in the hands of Doug Smith, Piggott would not make the same mistake again. He was duly on board at Ascot.

Petite Etoile started at 5–2 on for the tenth running of the King George (the same price as Ribot four years earlier) with Parthia on 7–1, while bracketed on 100–8 were Aggressor and Paddy Prendergast-trained Kythnos (who had won the Irish Two Thousand Guineas and finished third to St Paddy in the Derby).

Lester Piggott relates one of his most infamous defeats:

If on paper it seemed a simple enough task, I had my doubts. The ground was a little soft that day, and the Ascot mile and a half can prove a good deal more searching than the distance at Epsom: I had reservations about whether Petite Etoile really got twelve furlongs. Furthermore, the filly had been coughing, and as a consequence had to forgo her planned appearance in the Princess of Wales's Stakes at the Newmarket July Meeting.

Planning to ride Petite Etoile in the usual way in the King George, I kept her well back until the turn into the straight, where I made my move up the inside. But the way was blocked, and in switching to challenge on the outer the filly was bumped by Kythnos. Once she'd righted herself we set off in pursuit of the leader Aggressor, ridden by Jimmy Lindley, and perhaps for the first time in her life she really had to dig deep. She responded gamely, but my fears about her lack of stamina proved right, and she just couldn't peg back Aggressor, being beaten half a length.

Piggott, never one to unburden his soul after an unexpected reverse, told the press after the race that 'I think they cut the grass the wrong way', which turned out to be not such a daft excuse as it sounds. Before that meeting, half the Straight Mile had been mown from east to west and the other half west to east. Lester brought Petite Etoile up a part of the track in the straight where the grass was leaning towards the filly – that is, had been cut west to east – while Aggressor on the rail was on an area where the grass was going away from him. Taking Piggott's comment to heart, since that day Ascot has mown all the grass in the same direction – from east to west up the Straight Mile and then clockwise round the round course.

The phrase 'the way was blocked' in Piggott's typically sparse account of a sensational race recalls the version of events revealed by Scobie Breasley, rider of the unconsidered Sunny Court, in his own autobiography. On King George day, Breasley was still bristling from an incident earlier in the season when Piggott had cut him up during a race, and decided that the time had come to settle the score and 'hit him where it would hurt most – in the pocket'. Breasley wrote:

My mount, the Irish colt Sunny Court, had no real chance of winning but I decided to do my level best to stop Lester collecting the big prize. I didn't intend to break the rules but I was determined to give Lester a hard time and so square the books. It worked a treat.

By the time Lester had shaken me off and got out of the pocket on the rails Jimmy Lindley and Aggressor had the race won ... I was only sixth but came back grinning like a Cheshire cat. Everyone thought that Lester had ridden a bad race and Jimmy Lindley probably thinks to this day that he and Aggressor stole the King George, but that's the real story of how the wonder-filly was beaten ...

Petite Etoile would live to fight another day – and to win at Ascot – but Aggressor did not race again.

At least punters reeling from the defeat of Petite Etoile had a stone-cold certainty in the last race that day, although even those dedicated to the benefits of lumping on in the 'Getting Out Stakes' might have baulked at taking the odds about the favourite in a perfectly symmetrical book for the Sunninghill Park Stakes:

1–50 High Perch
50–1 Red Influence

After High Perch had duly obliged by twelve lengths to give Jimmy Lindley a treble on perhaps the most memorable afternoon of his riding life, the Ascot crowd started to make their way to the exits or repair to the bars to discuss the momentous events of the day.

They would not see another race on the royal heath for nearly a year.

CHANGING FACES

On the opening day of Royal Ascot 1961 the racecourse had a very different face from the year before. The old grandstand had gone, and with it that varied skyline between the Royal Enclosure and the Silver Ring. In its place stood the massive, towering Queen Elizabeth II Stand.

Evocative as it was of an earlier age, the old grandstand, which had stood since 1839, had long been a source of concern to the Ascot Authority. Even with the new and much more viewer-friendly alignment of the Straight Mile, the stand was awkward and uncomfortable for racegoers. Worse, there had been suggestions that it was unsafe, and towards the end of the 1950s it became apparent that a major development was required. In July 1958 a deal was agreed with the building firm Wimpey, who had worked for Ascot before and were now signed up to design and build a new grandstand.

Timing was an issue. The Royal Meeting could hardly be transferred to another course, nor could the King George, so a schedule was agreed whereby the old would be demolished and the new erected within the space of forty-four weeks, from immediately after the 1960 July meeting until the opening of Royal Ascot in 1961. Up-to-date prefabricated building technology helped make such a timetable possible, and although the weather interfered – autumn and winter were the wettest on record – an army of builders, some 550 workers at the peak of the operation, kept construction on schedule. No attempt was made to continue a racing programme on the course: the September 1960 meeting was transferred to Newbury (where Sovereign Path won the Queen Elizabeth II Stakes) and the October meeting to Kempton Park.

The Queen Elizabeth II Stand, which had been built at a cost of around £1 million, first opened its gates to racegoers on 13 June 1961, opening day of the

The Queen Elizabeth II Stand – as pictured in the brochure advertising its arrival in 1961.

Previous pages: Arkle (Pat Taaffe) leading on the first circuit before going on to win the SGB Chase, 14 December 1966 – the last victory of his career.

Royal Meeting, and was received with widespread approval. The *Sporting Life* hailed 'the most impressive structure on any English racecourse'. *The Times* declared it 'hard to fault' and praised the Duke of Norfolk and Major-General Dawnay for their efforts, while the *Daily Telegraph* paid tribute to Wimpey – 'to finish so great an enterprise on time was a truly magnificent feat of engineering' – and rhapsodised about the stand's 'long, clean lines', predicting that it would 'do credit to the Royal meeting'.

In 1961 the Queen Elizabeth II Stand represented a state-of-the-art racecourse facility. Nearly two hundred yards long, it boasted a cantilever design which did away with pillars that obstructed the view. Escalators – the first installed on a British racecourse – served the rear entrance, and the *Sporting Life* advised racegoers to have 'a ceremonial ride' even if they had no need to, just for the experience.

The coming of the brave new world of corporate hospitality was anticipated in the provision of 280 private boxes, each with its own dining room, stretching in three upper tiers along the length of the stand. Ten electric hoists, connected with the kitchens in the basement, brought food for distribution to serveries at each dining room level. Below the boxes were 1,650 tip-up stall seats, which were numbered and could be reserved for a daily charge, and below those seats a terrace of steps which sloped down to the lawn and could hold 8,000 spectators. The stand itself could accommodate 13,000 people. Ground level provided a hundred Tote windows and a new bar, together with direct access to the existing restaurant above the main Tote overlooking the lawns behind the stand. (The private boxes also had access to a further thirty-two Tote windows.) A pleasing touch was that the old clock, which had been housed in a tower above the old grandstand since 1896 and had long been a much-loved Ascot landmark, was carefully preserved and set into a new tower above the stand.

Naturally enough, the new stand did not please everyone, and viewing remained a problem for some. David Hedges wrote in the *Sporting Life* that 'the angle of the stand is all wrong. When will racecourse planners realise that grandstands must be set at an angle to the course if everyone is to have a fair view?' Peter O'Sullevan's two-pronged objection, that the stand 'was set at an absurdly inadequate angle for viewing the straight, and incorporated no top-level area for the general public', found ready support from the actor Robert Morley, who concluded a long and dyspeptically anti-Ascot letter to O'Sullevan:

> At the cost of a million pounds all that the public is provided with are a few concrete steps rather narrower than before. Profits from Ascot are used not to improve facilities, which are now worse for the Silver Ring and the Iron Stand, but to make bigger profits in the years to come. Gone are the days when at the Heath meetings the boxes were free. Ours not to reason why, and certainly not to be told on these occasions there is no room at the top. But the horses are still there, Lester Piggott is still there, and I hope very much that you and I will still be there if we don't get ourselves deported to Ally Pally as counter-revolutionaries.

On the other hand, the angle was no problem to the sports editor of the local paper the *Windsor, Slough & Eton Express*, who went along on the opening day and was well pleased by the result of his systematic testing:

> For the first time in more than 30 years' racing at Royal Ascot, I saw the start and finish of all the races in complete comfort on Tuesday from the new Queen Elizabeth II Stand. For each race I chose a different vantage point in the mammoth building and no matter if I was seated on one of the luxury tip-up stalls, halfway up the terrace,

Her Majesty the Queen on Surprise about to go on to the racecourse for her morning ride, 1961.

or in a private box I had an uninterrupted view of the horses. So once and for all the old complaint that people in the grand stand on a busy day saw the jockeys only when they actually passed the enclosure, no longer applies.

Not only was there a new face to Ascot at the Royal Meeting in June 1961, there was also a new face to the whole sport of horse racing. The month before, on 1 May, betting shops had at last become legal. Until then a punter had had to have a credit account or go to the racecourse in order to bet on a horse race – and now you could merrily bet in your friendly High Street turf accountant's shop rather than go to the expense and effort of attending the meeting. Racecourses waited nervously to see the effect on attendances.

Royal Ascot, however, was unlikely to be much buffeted by such winds of change, and the early 1960s upheld the tradition of quality.

Star turn in 1961 was Petite Etoile, who started at 15–2 on for the Rous Memorial Stakes, opening race on the Friday, and cruised to an effortless victory. The same day the 1960 Derby and St Leger winner St Paddy provided another odds-on Lester Piggott winner, landing the Hardwicke Stakes in a canter from Sir Winston Churchill's Vienna. All in all it was a good meeting for Piggott, as he rode seven winners over the four days, including Pandofell, who won the Gold Cup easily at 100–7 with the hotly fancied French raider Puissant Chef (5–4 on) unplaced.

Having missed the entire meeting in 1962 – he was suspended over a 'not trying' incident at Lincoln earlier in the year – Piggott won his fourth Gold Cup in 1963 on the gigantic chestnut colt Twilight Alley, a horse with very delicate legs: his victory was hailed as one of the greatest training feats of his handler, the legendary Noel Murless.

But for all the undoubted merits of Petite Etoile, Twilight Alley and all those other classy performers, there is no doubt that *the* Ascot horse of this period was Trelawny.

A son of Black Tarquin, whose race against Alycidon in the 1949 Gold Cup was still reasonably fresh in the memory, Trelawny was bred by Sir John Astor. After one outing as a two-year-old when trained by Jack Colling he was gelded and, although he won three minor races as a three-year-old in 1959, was sent to the Newmarket December Sales, where he was bought by Mrs Leonard Carver. (Mrs Carver had a tenuous, if dramatic, connection with the Royal Family: it was her horse ESB who won the 1956 Grand National after the Queen Mother's Devon Loch had slithered to a sensational halt on the run-in when a certain winner.) Trained for the Flat by Syd Mercer, though it was expected that he would in due course pursue a hurdling campaign with Fred Rimell, Trelawny won the Chester Cup as a four-year-old in 1960 and seemed to be shaping into a very good staying handicapper. The same year he made his first appearance at Royal Ascot in the Ascot Stakes: ridden by Lester

Twilight Alley (Lester Piggott) beating Misti IV to win the 1963 Gold Cup.

Trelawny (Scobie Breasley) coasts home in the 1962 Ascot Stakes.

Piggott, he finished third behind a former stable companion at Colling's named Shatter. But then he broke a cannon bone in the Goodwood Stakes. It was recommended that he be put down, but Mercer refused to take this advice. The gelding's life was spared, and he was taken home to recuperate. Mercer retired at the end of the 1960 season and the newly restored Trelawny returned to Jack Colling.

In 1961 he was unplaced in the Ascot Stakes but returned to the course at the July meeting to win the Brown Jack Stakes (then run over two and three-quarter miles, the same distance as the Queen Alexandra Stakes) by ten lengths from Shatter. Later that year he went to Fred Rimell to embark upon a jumping campaign, and was placed in all four of his hurdle races in the 1961–2 season (including running second in a division of the Gloucestershire Hurdle at Cheltenham, now the Supreme Novices' Hurdle).

For the 1962 Flat season the six-year-old joined trainer George Todd at the famous yard of Manton, near Marlborough in Wiltshire, and now the Ascot legend started to be built. On the Tuesday of the Royal Meeting he teamed up with Scobie Breasley in the Ascot Stakes, which he won so cosily under 9 stone 8 pounds – 'ridiculous ease', *The Times* called it – that it was decided to bring him out again for the Queen Alexandra Stakes on the Friday. He duly won again, thereby landing the double of the two races in the same year which – while not unprecedented – had eluded his famous predecessor Brown Jack, and the feat did not go unnoticed. Tom Nickalls wrote in the *Sporting Life:* 'The racing this week may have been the poorest in quality we have seen at Royal Ascot, but the meeting will always be remembered for the great performance put up by that wonderful old hero Trelawny.'

By 1963 Trelawny was seven years old, an elder statesman of the sport. He started his campaign when running unplaced in a small race at Newbury, then ran in the Chester Cup for the fourth year running. His record in that historic race read: first in 1960, beaten a short head by Hoy in 1961, third in 1962 – but this time he failed to reach the frame, finishing fifth.

At Royal Ascot, however, Trelawny was in his element, and he went to post for his fourth successive Ascot Stakes joint second favourite at 9–1, despite carrying the crushing burden of ten stone. After sitting just behind the leaders entering the straight he took the lead a furlong out and ran on stoutly to win by three-quarters of a length from his stable companion Sea Leopard – and despite a Stewards' objection to the first three for interference, the result stood.

All thoughts turned now to the race three days later. Would Trelawny go for the double double? After some hesitation – 'I do not want to break his heart and take on fresh horses on Friday,' said Todd – it was confirmed that he would make his historic bid. The news was greeted with enthusiasm, but few who watched Breasley and Trelawny set off on the long canter down to the start of the Queen Alexandra Stakes were under any illusion. This would be no lap of honour, for among Trelawny's seven opponents was the four-year-old Grey Of Falloden, who had won the Queen's Prize at Kempton Park before finishing a close-up third under 9 stone 3 pounds in the Chester Cup. Grey Of Falloden was a very good staying handicapper indeed – the following year he won the Cesarewitch under 9 stone 6 pounds – and was well fancied to spoil Trelawny's day.

Timeform's *Racehorses of 1963* conveyed the feeling of another great Ascot occasion:

At approximately five o'clock on a Friday afternoon in June a burst of cheering, the like of which had not been heard since Brown Jack retired from the racing scene in 1934, broke out over the Ascot racecourse. Trelawny, having made most of the running in the Queen Alexandra Stakes, held a decisive lead over Grey Of Falloden passing the two-furlong pole, and he looked assured of victory. With every stride the roar increased in volume, and when he passed the post three lengths ahead of his rival, hats were flung into the air, and spectators made a concerted rush to the unsaddling enclosure to greet this great stayer.

The first horse ever to land the Ascot Stakes–Queen Alexandra Stakes double twice (a feat attributed by the *Daily Telegraph* to 'Trelawny's own great heart and bottomless stamina'), Trelawny seemed to be going from strength to strength. His next race was the Goodwood Cup, for which he started odds on and which he won very easily after making all the running. Raise You Ten, who the following year would win the Goodwood Cup and the Doncaster Cup was runner-up, and Balto, who had won the 1962 Gold Cup (a race for which Trelawny, as a gelding, was not eligible) finished last of the four runners. Now *The Times* called Trelawny 'unconquerable'.

The racing public always gives its heart to a good and reliable stayer who is around year after year, and by now Trelawny was the most popular Flat horse in training. His reappearance in 1964 was eagerly awaited, and an encouraging fourth behind Fighting Ship, Gaul and Grey Of Falloden in the Henry II Stakes at Sandown Park suggested that Trelawny could again make Ascot a very special occasion.

But the Royal Enclosure that willed the old horse on as he made his way to the start of the 1964 Ascot Stakes was very different from the one past which he had galloped when winning the 1963 Queen Alexandra. The spanking new Queen Elizabeth II Stand had accentuated the age of its neighbours the Iron Stand, Jockey Club Stand and Royal Enclosure stand, and in July 1963 the Duke of Norfolk unveiled plans for their replacement with a huge new stand that would abut and would complement the new grandstand. Again the builders were Wimpey – whose senior in-house architect Eric Collins designed both the Queen Elizabeth II Stand and the new Royal Enclosure – and again the work was commenced immediately after the July meeting and completed by the next Royal Ascot, at a cost of around £1,250,000. (Again the September meeting went to Newbury and the October to Kempton Park. The May 1964 meeting was also moved to Newbury, which thus, perversely, hosted the first Ascot running of the Victoria Cup, transferred to the royal course from the now defunct Hurst Park.)

As with the Queen Elizabeth II Stand, the new Royal Enclosure – which almost doubled the area of the previous enclosure and was designed to accommodate around 7,500 people (as opposed to about half that figure previously) – was warmly received. The *Sporting Life* called it 'a great step forward and a model of stand design', and *Horse and Hound* declared that 'Ascot is now what it should be – the mark for all courses to aim at'.

It was not only the racing public who benefited. The new weighing room, giving out on to the unsaddling enclosure at the west end of the stand, included a sweat box for the jockeys – the first on an English racecourse. Not that Ron Hutchinson, riding Trelawny on the opening day of the 1964 meeting as Scobie Breasley had been claimed by his retaining stable of Gordon Richards to ride Utrillo, had any need of the new facility: Trelawny was carrying the hefty burden of ten stone, despite which he started 9–2 favourite. To the great disappointment of the crowd, he was hampered when trying to mount his challenge and failed to catch Delmere (to whom he was conceding forty pounds) by two lengths.

The Queen Alexandra Stakes was still to come on the Friday.

No other horses wanted to take on Trelawny, and it became apparent that he would be walking over. But even that was snatched from him, as Ascot yet again fell foul of the weather. The rain started to fall not long after racing had finished on the Wednesday. It continued all through the night, and through Thursday morning. It was announced that the Royal Procession had been cancelled. ('All I really care about is the procession,' one lady racegoer was overheard saying, 'but I'm glad they've cancelled it. The Queen is subject to colds.') It was announced that the time of the first race was being put back. It was announced that racing was abandoned for the day, and that a ten-race programme would be run on the Friday – including Trelawny's Queen Alexandra Stakes. But come the Friday the ground was still unraceable, so it was announced that there would be twelve races (including Trelawny's) on the Saturday. Racing on Saturday proved impossible also, and Trelawny's third Queen Alexandra Stakes was not to be.

Losing two days of the Royal Meeting would have been bad in any year, but to lose them the year the new Royal Enclosure stand was being used for the first time was wretched, and a great deal of sympathy was expressed – none in form more tangible than the lady who sent the Ascot Authority a £1 postal order as she was so distressed by the course's bad luck. The Duke of Norfolk responded by inviting her to a day's racing.

Trelawny did run again at Ascot. On Friday 17 July 1964 the course staged its first ever evening meeting as a prelude to the following day's King George (which looked to be as much a walkover for Derby winner Santa

Ascot mini-skirts, 1966.

Claus as Trelawny's Queen Alexandra would have been), and Trelawny turned out for the Brown Jack Stakes. But the ground by now was baked hard (so hard that Todd would have withdrawn the horse had he been able to find his owner), and though a large crowd turned out to will him on, Trelawny found ten stone and the concession of thirty-nine pounds to his three-years-younger half-brother Gurkha too much. He went down heroically, Scobie Breasley easing him up close home when the cause was lost. It transpired that Trelawny had split a pastern, and for a while his future looked in doubt, but he made a good recovery, then shrugged off a virus, and in 1965 was back yet again for the Queen Alexandra. Sadly he seemed a shadow of his former self, finishing last behind old rival Grey Of Falloden. He then ran in the Goodwood Cup (fourth behind the Queen's good stayer Apprentice).

That was by no means the end of him, however, for alongside his recent Flat campaigns he had resumed hurdling with Fred Rimell. His biggest moment came when winning the Spa Hurdle – now the Stayers' Hurdle – on the same afternoon that Arkle won his third Cheltenham Gold Cup in March 1966: 'led 2 out: canter', says the form book, so there was clearly plenty of life left in the old boy.

There was even talk of sending him steeplechasing, as Terry Biddlecombe (who described winning the Spa Hurdle on him as 'something truly beautiful') relates:

> As Trelawny had displayed such brilliance over hurdles, Mrs Carver was keen to find out whether he would be as good over fences. Although Fred agreed over the telephone to give him a school, I could tell that he was not happy about the suggestion, and neither was I. We both thought so much of Trelawny that we did not want anything to happen to him.
>
> We said nothing to each other beforehand. Fred went in the Land Rover to the park where the schooling fences were and I took

Trelawny to meet him there. Nobody else was present. I turned Trelawny in, let him have a look at the first fence, turned him back and then away he went. He was foot perfect – like a Gold Cup horse – magic.

'How was that?' Fred asked as I pulled up.

'Great.'

'Do you want to jump him again?'

'No – I didn't particularly want to jump him anyway.'

To my relief Fred agreed with me.

'Neither did I,' he said.

We went back to breakfast and Fred telephoned Mrs Carver.

'The old horse tried to stop at the jump – diabolical. It's no use, he'll break his bloody neck and that would be rather sad, don't you think?'

... Trelawny finished his racing career honourably, as he deserved to do, and then retired to end his days with his owner.

His last outing on the Flat was in May 1966, when he finished unplaced in the Chester Cup. In all Trelawny won eleven races on the Flat (including five at Ascot) and three over hurdles. In his retirement he briefly followed hounds with the Cottesmore, but he died within two years of going out of training.

Meanwhile the King George VI and Queen Elizabeth Stakes had been continuing to consolidate its position as a major international race, a natural target for the top middle-distance three-year-olds graduating to all-aged races after running in the summer Classics, and for Classic horses from previous generations kept in training. Seven of the first ten runnings had included a Derby winner, either as a three-year-old or a four-year-old, and that fraction was increased in 1961 with the presence of St Paddy, winner in 1960 of the Derby and St Leger for owner Sir Victor Sassoon and trainer Noel Murless. With St Paddy and the French three-year-old Right Royal V, winner that year of two French Classics in the Poule d'Essai des Poulains and the Prix du Jockey-Club, the 1961 renewal was a King George high in class. But it was distinctly low on quantity, as there were only two other runners: Rockavon, who had won the 1961 Two Thousand Guineas at 66–1, a result many regarded as a freak, and the good four-year-old Apostle. The betting told the story. St Paddy, who the previous month had won the Hardwicke Stakes at the Royal Meeting and gone on to break the course record when winning the Eclipse Stakes, started 5–4 on favourite; Right Royal V, clearly a high-class colt with no obvious form line to suggest he was as good as St Paddy, was 6–4; the other pair were out at 20–1. Lester Piggott on St Paddy made the running at a less than breakneck pace, and tried to kick clear of his main rival early in the straight. Right Royal V, however, proved difficult to shake off, and responded to the hard riding of jockey Roger Poincelet to catch the favourite inside the final furlong and go on to score a three-length victory.

The French won the King George again in 1962, when Match III – beaten by Right Royal V in both the Prix Lupin and Prix du Jockey-Club the previous year – made all the running under Yves Saint-Martin to beat 1961 St Leger winner Aurelius by three-quarters of a length. In 1963 it was the turn of the Irish again when Paddy Prendergast-trained three-year-old Ragusa, who had won the Irish Derby and the Eclipse Stakes since finishing third to Relko in the Derby, won easily from Miralgo (though he would not have run in the race at all had the stable's first choice, the superlative Oaks winner Noblesse, not injured a hock a week before her intended appearance at Ascot). The King George favourite, the massive Twilight Alley, who had won that year's Gold Cup, split a pastern going into the home turn and had to be pulled up by Piggott. Ragusa went on to underline his class with a six-length victory in the St Leger.

If Ragusa was one of the best King George winners, his successor was widely regarded as the worst – and the 1964 renewal possibly the most unsatisfactory running in the race's history. Santa Claus, trained in Ireland by Mick Rogers, started favourite at 13–2 on (to this day the shortest priced runner in the history of the race) on the strength of victories in the Derby and the Irish Derby, and unsurprisingly he scared off most of the opposition. Only three dared take on the favourite, and none of them seemed to pose much threat. Royal Avenue, the only English-trained runner in the race, was a good but far from top-class horse, while the rest of the field consisted of the French pair Nasram II – good enough when in the lead but liable to down tools when challenged – and the mare Prima Donna II. Scobie Breasley had won the Derby on Santa Claus, but winning the premier Classic was not a good enough credential for him to keep the ride in the colt's subsequent races – a decision that understandably rankled with the great Australian. In the Irish Derby the colt had been ridden by Bill Burke, and the Irishman kept the ride at Ascot. Scobie Breasley, though, still played his part in the outcome of the race, when taking a phone call from another Australian rider:

> My old mate Bill Pyers rang to say Ernie Fellows was thinking of bringing a four-year-old named Nasram II over from Chantilly for the King George VI and Queen Elizabeth Stakes and as I'd ridden Santa Claus he wanted to know if they had a chance. Well, on the face of it, they didn't have a prayer but I told Bill that Santa Claus could be turned over if the going was firm and if they stretched him by setting a real gallop. It proved good advice.

It did indeed. Santa Claus seemed uneasy on the firm ground even when cantering to the start, while Nasram II looked perfectly comfortable. As soon as the tapes rose, Pyers pushed Nasram II into the lead, and coming out of Swinley Bottom the colt was all of eight lengths clear of his nearest pursuer. Burke on Santa Claus was confident that the class of the Derby winner would be sufficient to reel in the leader whenever he liked, but Nasram II kept up his relentless gallop into the straight, and with Santa Claus unwilling to let himself stride out on the ground kept going to win by two lengths. Royal Avenue was third and Prima Donna II last.

The firm ground and the way the race was run had clearly been against Santa Claus, while a more novel excuse aired in one quarter was that he had shown a coltish reluctance to go past the mare Prima Donna II. Whatever the reason for the greatest big-race upset at Ascot since Pretty Polly gave best to Bachelor's Button, when the winner and runner-up met again in the Prix de l'Arc de Triomphe at Longchamp in October, Santa Claus (now ridden by Jimmy Lindley) finished runner-up to Prince Royal II and Nasram was well in the rear.

In autumn 1953 Peter O'Sullevan, young commentator for the BBC and an avidly followed racing correspondent, had written in his 'Off The Record' column in the *Daily Express*:

'Steeplechasing at Ascot', one of the racing scenes depicted on a set of Swiss-made napkins on sale in England, causes much amusement among the cognoscenti. But let's hope it's prophetic. What a course could be built on the inside!

O'Sullevan – with characteristic modesty attributing his own foresight to a napkin – was not the only one intrigued by the idea that a racecourse of the quality of Ascot could sustain a programme of top-class National Hunt racing, thereby making use of the course through the winter rather than have it lie fallow from October until the spring. The fact that there was generous room for a separate hurdles track and a separate steeplechase track inside the existing course meant that wear and tear on the Flat course was not an issue.

The driving force behind this radical development at Ascot was not the Duke of Norfolk – often quoted as having said there would be jump racing on the course 'over my dead body' – but David Dawnay, and the scheme was first discussed formally after he had produced a very rough sketch of a possible jumps course at a meeting of the Trustees in March 1960. An approach was made to the National Hunt Committee – the separate authority which controlled jump racing – and the go-ahead was given for further investigations into its feasibility. The announcement of a definite go-ahead came in October 1962, and work on the new surfaces commenced.

Hurst Park racecourse, snugly positioned in a bend in the Thames near Hampton Court, closed down that autumn, its last fixture taking place on 10 October 1962. Twenty acres of its turf were carefully dug up and transported to Ascot to provide the surface for the new jumps course. Work progressed at about a furlong a day, with strips being dug up at Hurst Park, ferried the short distance to Ascot in a shuttle of lorries, and relaid the same day. By September 1963 Dawnay was able to report to the Trustees that the surface was knitting together well, and in December that year a group including Colonel Upton, Secretary of the National Hunt Committee, leading trainers Peter Cazalet and Fulke Walwyn and the great jump jockey Fred Winter (who would retire from the saddle in 1964 to embark on a wonderfully successful training career himself), met at Ascot to ponder the positions of fences, hurdles and starting gates. Once their deliberations had been converted

An early hurdle race at Ascot
– at the second flight in the
Eager Handicap Hurdle,
February 1966.

into recommendations, design of the final shape of the course was undertaken by Brigadier A. D. M. Teacher, National Hunt inspector of courses.

The ten fences on the steeplechase course incorporated recent safety features such as yellow groundlines – the colour showed up in all weather conditions and gave horses whose view was obscured by the rest of field a better chance of assessing the fence in a split-second glance – and it was anticipated that the two new courses, hurdles and steeplechases, each around one mile five furlongs in circumference, would meet the approval of the National Hunt fraternity.

The proof of the pudding came on Friday 30 April 1965, when the runners for the first National Hunt race were led into the new parade ring in front of the grandstand – specially constructed for the new code at Ascot. That day a hurdle race and a steeplechase opened a programme completed by five Flat races (including the White Rose Stakes won by I Say, who a few weeks later would finish third to Sea Bird II in the Derby). Sir Giles, trained by Fulke Walwyn and ridden by Willie Robinson, won the Inaugural Hurdle over two miles from Palycidon (ridden by Michael Scudamore, whose son Peter would ride his 1,678th and final winner on the course twenty-eight years later) and Riversdale (ridden by Terry Biddlecombe). Forty minutes later the first ever steeplechase at Ascot was won by Another Scot, ridden by Tim Norman, from Grand Amiral, ridden by a young amateur named Brough Scott. (Fifth in that race was Anglo, on whom Tim Norman would win the Grand National the following year.)

Press consensus was that the new jumping track was a great success, and the *Daily Telegraph* relayed the jockeys' opinion that the fences, 'though beautifully built, looked big, stiff and altogether formidable'. The *Sunday Times* found a 'Flat racing swell' who described jump racing at Ascot as 'like going to the Ritz and ordering fish and chips'.

As well as taking the Hurst Park turf for its new jumping tracks, Ascot took over that course's National Hunt fixtures, and in its first full season of jump racing staged thirteen days containing hurdles and chases in six meetings.

The three-day meeting early in October 1965 (when on each day the programme was shared with the Flat) promptly proclaimed that the quality which characterised Flat racing at Ascot would apply to National Hunt. The Frogmore Chase on the Thursday was won by the brilliant two-miler Dunkirk from Mill House, while the Datchet Hurdle on the Saturday went to Anselmo, trained by Lester Piggott's father Keith for pop idol Billy Fury: the colt had run fourth behind Santa Claus in the 1964 Derby. Towards the end of October a two-day meeting mixed Flat and jumps, and then in November the National Hunt fraternity had the place to itself with a meeting over two days, the Friday of which marked a small but important landmark for Ascot: the course's first commercially sponsored race. The Kirk and Kirk Handicap Chase, sponsored by the building company and worth £1,716 to the winner, was won by Rupununi after the favourite Rondetto had fallen. The same day another little piece of history was made when the Bingley Novices' Hurdle went to Ken Cundell-trained Aurelius, whom we last met in much more exalted company, finishing second to Match III in the 1962 King George VI and Queen Elizabeth Stakes when trained by Noel Murless.

Aurelius, who had proved infertile on going to stud and had been put back in training, had also won the King Edward VII Stakes and the Hardwicke Stakes, and so became the first Royal Ascot winner to win at the course under National Hunt Rules. (In February 1968 Aurelius won the Grange Chase at Ascot, thus posting the remarkable record of having won at the course on the Flat, over hurdles and over fences. He is remembered in the Aurelius Hurdle, run at the November meeting.)

On the Saturday of the November 1965 meeting Black and White Whisky sponsored the two main races, and a prize of £4,115 for the two-mile

Black and White Gold Cup was enough to attract one of the brightest stars in the jumping firmament, Flyingbolt. The great big white-faced chesnut, reportedly inclined to eat you as soon as look at you but a brilliant performer over both hurdles and fences, started 15–8 on and hardly broke sweat to win by fifteen lengths.

But the biggest draw in National Hunt racing at the time was Flyingbolt's fabled stable companion in Tom Dreaper's yard near Dublin, and when on Wednesday 14 December 1966 the name Arkle appeared on the Ascot racecard, jumping at the course had well and truly arrived.

Arkle was then at the height of his incomparable powers. He had won twenty-one of his twenty-four steeplechases, including the Cheltenham Gold Cup in 1964 and 1965 (beating Mill House on both occasions) and for a third time earlier in 1966. He had won the Hennessy Gold Cup twice, the Whitbread Gold Cup, the King George VI Chase, the Irish Grand National and many other big races. Wildly popular (he had even been celebrated in song by Dominic Behan), he was, both to jumping fans and to millions well beyond the sport, an equine god. True, his crown had slipped a tiny bit in his last race before Ascot, when he was beaten half a length in the Hennessy Gold Cup at Newbury by Stalbridge Colonist, but Stalbridge Colonist was a top-class horse and Arkle, having his first run of the 1966–7 season, had been conceding him thirty-five pounds. Arkle had come second, but had hardly been defeated.

In the three-mile SGB Handicap Chase at Ascot (sponsored by the scaffolding company Scaffolding Great Britain), Arkle faced four opponents, and naturally gave lumps of weight to them all. He carried 12 stone 7 pounds, Master Mascus 10 stone 3 pounds, and the other three – including Vultrix, who had won the inaugural running of the race a year earlier under 12 stone 1 pound – ten stone, but it was no contest. The form-book entry for Arkle's running reads: 'mde all: v easily'. Tom Nickalls in the *Sporting Life*, under the headline 'ARKLE PUTS HIS CROWN STRAIGHT!', was more forthcoming:

Mighty Arkle has decisively readjusted his crown, knocked slightly awry by Stalbridge Colonist at Newbury. So many of racing's greatest heroes have won on the Royal Heath and it was most fitting that this prince of steeplechasers should add his name to the roll of honour at Ascot yesterday.

In doing so he put up one of the great weight-carrying performances in the SGB Handicap Chase, though he caused slight misgivings among his legion of fans by appearing in the paddock in rather a sweat. But he soon cooled off and went out on to the course his usual imperturbable self.

He was over the first fence in front and was never actually headed, though Big George was with him down to the water. A little later Sunny Bright and Vultrix almost jumped up to him at the second open ditch.

The champion was fairly showing off – sailing high over his fences, and he must have given Pat Taaffe the most glorious ride.

Arkle won unextended by fifteen lengths from Sunny Bright, and Nickalls played down a moment of anxiety in the unsaddling enclosure afterwards:

> The very slight over-reach that he showed on his near fore when he was unsaddled is unlikely to have the slightest ill effect on him.
>
> It was really no more than a tiny nick, the sort of thing that can happen to any horse jumping as extravagantly as Arkle had done.
>
> I was interested to notice that, for once, Arkle's mane had not been plaited for this race, though whether there was any significance about this I cannot guess.

Trainer's wife Betty Dreaper explained: 'Plaiting his mane now makes him sweat up a little. And that wastes his nervous energy.'

The SGB Chase at Ascot proved to be Arkle's last victory. In his next race, the King George VI Chase at Kempton Park on 27 December 1966, he fractured a pedal bone in his off-fore hoof and never ran again. (There was subsequent speculation that the foot problem had its origins in the Ascot race, as jockey Pat Taaffe had reported after the SGB Chase that Arkle had jumped to the left over the last three fences.)

It seems entirely right that the name of Arkle, greatest of all steeplechasers, should have graced the Ascot turf.

Meanwhile the standard of sport on the Flat continued at a high level.

After the disastrous deluge of 1964, it was business as usual at the 1965 Royal Meeting. Lester Piggott rode eight winners over the four days, among them the Royal Hunt Cup on Casabianca (described in his jockey's autobiography as 'still fat and lazy') and the Gold Cup on Fighting Charlie, a son of Tenerani who won the Gold Cup again in 1966, when he was ridden by Greville Starkey as Piggott, given a choice of rides, for once chose wrongly. That second victory was a triumph for the veterinary profession – Fighting Charlie had very dodgy legs and was a doubtful runner until shortly before the race – and for jockeyship, as Starkey had held the horse together after he appeared to break down early in the straight and had gone on to win by eight lengths.

Anxious connections examine the mighty Arkle after his victory in the SGB Chase, December 1966. He was found to have suffered an over-reach (a cut caused by a hind shoe catching the heel of a foreleg).

And after the embarrassment of Santa Claus being turned over in the 1964 King George, order was restored to the July showpiece in 1965 when the Paddy Prendergast-trained three-year-old Meadow Court, who had won the Irish Derby after finishing runner-up to the phenomenal Sea Bird II in the Derby, started 6–5 favourite in a field of twelve and won as a 6–5 favourite should, giving Lester Piggott the first of his seven wins in the race. (Meadow Court was co-owned by Bing Crosby, who after the colt had won the Irish Derby had entertained the massed stands at The Curragh to an impromptu rendition of 'When Irish Eyes Are Smiling'.)

But Ascot lost one of its most loved characters in 1965 with the death of Ras Prince Monolulu, the flamboyant tipster who had been a colourful part of the big race meetings since the 1920s. (He reportedly once tried to sell the Duke of Windsor one of his Sixpenny Specials.) Dressed in ostrich-feather headdress, garishly decorated jacket and baggy trousers and touting an umbrella or shooting stick, he gathered racegoers around him with his famous cry, 'I gotta horse!', and once he had a large enough audience would dispense – for suitable payment – his tips, all the while keeping up his stream of doggerel:

> God made the bees,
> The bees made the honey.
> The public back the favourites,
> And the bookies take the money.

Nobody took seriously his claim to be 'Prince Monolulu from sunny Honolulu', and his real name was in fact the rather less exotic Peter McKay – born, it was said, in Abyssinia in 1885. With Prince Monolulu, nothing was as it seemed, but with his death a brightly coloured piece of the Ascot mosaic was removed.

On Friday 24 September 1965 Ascot staged the first of the charity meetings which were to become a highly popular feature of the Flat calendar at the course. Part of the profits and all of the car-park takings went to the St John Ambulance Brigade – at Ascot, as at so many other sporting venues around the country, true unsung heroes and heroines. Two years later the September Friday in 1967, organised by the Duke of Devonshire to benefit cancer research, consisted of races sponsored by a variety of companies, and with prize money of £34,000 was the most richly endowed sponsored meeting yet held in Britain.

The same year saw the first use of starting stalls at Ascot. Introduced to Britain at Newmarket in 1965, this now familiar piece of racing technology was deployed at the Royal Meeting to start the Queen Anne Stakes on 20 June 1967 (not long after they had first been used to start the Derby). At that 1967 meeting they were not used for races of over a mile, but proved invaluable in providing an even start for sprints such as the King's Stand Stakes, closing event of the meeting.

Long established as one of the big five-furlong races of the year, the King's Stand Stakes had been won by most of the great sprinters. Among the ten runners in the first stalls-started King's Stand in 1967 was the three-year-old Be Friendly, ridden by Scobie Breasley and owned by Peter O'Sullevan, who earlier that rain-soaked afternoon had been calling the horses for BBC Television:

> The BBC transmission was ended, so I was free to agonize over the race in silence. The watery paddock felt great underfoot. 'Himself', flaunting the muscle bulk that is the hallmark of the explosive sprinter, looked wet and wonderful. I went back up to the commentary box, which is suspended from the roof above the fifth floor level (the floor had to be lowered after construction, to enable cameramen and commentators to stand up), to watch the action alone through the tripod-mounted long-range binoculars.

Prince Charles arrives in the Royal Procession, 1968.

> Falcon, owned by US millionaire Charlie Engelhard, ridden by Lester Piggott, had been backed down from 100–30 to 2–1 favourite; Be Friendly from 4–1 to 3–1; Yours from 6–1 to 5–1 ... Two out, Scobie had Lester well in his sights, but Falcon was still running on strongly and Yours improving.
>
> Peter Bromley was in the next box, covering the race for radio. I heard him shout, 'And now Be Friendly is putting in a tremendous challenge.' He sure was, too. In a matter of strides he had taken Falcon just outside the furlong pole. Now Yours was the danger. I found myself darting anxious glances from the action to the winning line and back. But it was proprietor's funk. As Scobie said afterwards,

'Nothing could come and get him once he'd hit the front the way he was galloping.' Even so Yours, officially beaten half a length, with Falcon one and a half lengths away third, ran a fine race from the worst draw, three wide of the winner.

Peter leaned out and gave me a thumbs-up (and later his signed colour chart of the race) as I was running from the box to get down to the unsaddling enclosure.

Another innovation introduced around this time and now a familiar part of the racing scene was the Tote Jackpot, first operated on the opening day of Royal Ascot 1966. The idea was simple, if far from easy. Punters had to predict the winners of all six races on the card, and stake in units of five shillings (twenty-five pence). All the money invested went into a pool, the Tote raked off its percentage, and what remained in the pool was shared out among the winners. If the pool was not scooped one day, it would be carried over and added to the next day's, but it had to be won by the end of the meeting (and on the final day could be won with fewer than six winners) – which in the case of Ascot in 1966 brought in the Heath fixture on the Saturday. Sure enough, all four days of the Royal Meeting went by without the Jackpot being won, and Mrs Eileen Garnett, a widow from Ipswich, netted £63,114. 5s by finding the first five winners on the Saturday.

There was a limit to how Ascot, steeped as it was in tradition, could be expected to swing during the Swinging Sixties, but the dress code for the Royal Enclosure started to come under scrutiny. The policy remained that ladies should wear day dress with hats and gentlemen morning dress or service dress. Then in 1968 the Ascot Authority experimented with permitting men to wear lounge suits on the Friday – but only about half a dozen took advantage of the dressing-down concession, and it was dropped the following year.

Female fashion presented far more tricky problems, and in 1967 the Duke of Norfolk imposed a formal ban on trouser suits in the Royal Enclosure. In 1968 a nineteen-year-old heiress named Jayne Harries, and a year later Maria Subiza, wife of an Argentinian diplomat, both wrote footnotes in Ascot history by being turned away from the Royal Enclosure for wearing such outrageous garb. These exclusions brought public derision, and in 1970 the policy was changed. Trouser suits were now acceptable. The following year the

Enclosure was under attack from an even more insidious fashion of the time – hot pants. The *Daily Mail* reported:

> There is now a hot-bed of confusion on whether women wearing hot-pants will be allowed into the Royal Enclosure at Ascot races. On Monday an Ascot racecourse official ruled them OK. But yesterday the Duke of Norfolk issued a statement declaring shorts out.

A lady named Denise Lee got round Norfolk's decree by wearing a cutaway skirt over clearly visible orange pants. But other excesses, such as the bare midriff, remained well beyond the pale.

This was the age of the miniskirt. The fashion model Jean Shrimpton famously scandalised Australian society when appearing at the Melbourne Cup in November 1965 wearing a dress whose hemline was all of two and a half inches above her knee, and Ascot hemlines were likewise rising – a trend

The legendary Gertrude Shilling in full cry in 1969. Throughout the 1960s – and well beyond – Mrs Shilling's outrageous headgear was as much a part of the Ascot scene as Lester Piggott. Her creations included a five-foot-tall giraffe, a piano keyboard, a dartboard on which the three darts had scored 180, an apple skewered by an arrow, a snooker cue and set of balls, and a hamper with strawberries and champagne glasses. She died in 1999.

Ascot wine list and menu, 1966.

wryly noted by Peter O'Sullevan when he observed that in 1967 'the mini-skirt fashion seemed to be exploited by those least suited to exposure'. But the miniskirt did not seem to exercise the Duke of Norfolk to the degree that trouser suits and hot pants had done.

In any case, the Duke had more portentous matters on his mind as the 1960s came to an end. While there were faint signs that the Jockey Club was slowly adopting a more modern outlook – for example, the victory of Precipice Wood in the King George V Stakes in 1969 was the first Royal Ascot winner officially credited to a lady trainer, Rosemary Lomax – racing politics was still enmeshed in deep-rooted and reactionary attitudes. The war of words between traditionalists and reformers came to a head in an extraordinary fashion at the Ascot jumping meeting on 20 December 1969, when the Duke of Norfolk commandeered the public address system in the unsaddling enclosure to deliver a broadside at George Wigg, chairman of the Betting Levy Board (set up in 1961 to collect the levy from bookmakers). The details of this long-running feud between two very different leviathans of the Turf at that time are too tedious to rehearse, but Wigg had upset the Duke when in a television interview a few days earlier he had, according to *The Times*, compared the Jockey Club with 'a well kept veteran motor car, interesting for use on the occasional drive if you have infinite time and patience and willingness to judge the article by its original quality and value', while at the same time acknowledging that the Stewards of the Jockey Club were doing a good job. The Duke of Norfolk's response, delivered to a mostly baffled Ascot crowd on the Saturday before Christmas, was short on Yuletide spirit:

> Lord Wigg, in his own wisdom, entered the realms of a platform which, if I may say so with respect, was badly chosen. He referred to the Stewards of the Jockey Club being superb. He referred to the rest of the Jockey Club as being a veteran car. I have been a member of the Jockey Club for thirty-six years, and I served as a Steward for fifteen. Therefore I suppose that in the eyes of Lord Wigg I have been superb for fifteen years, and now I belong to that car.

Wigg was at Ascot that day and reacted with fury – not least because the Levy Board had paid for the very public address system on which he was being attacked – and one eyewitness related how 'an irate Lord Wigg hopped from one foot to another in an audience which, if the ovation at the end was anything to go by, was behind the Duke almost to a man'. In a radio interview the following day, Wigg complained that the Duke of Norfolk 'acted as if he owned Ascot … He and the Jockey Club believe that my function is the plebeian task of collecting the money. Theirs is the aristocratic task of spending it.'

The row was defused by a conciliatory statement by Sir Randle Feilden, Senior Steward of the Jockey Club, and though the bad feeling continued to simmer, it would never boil over again at Ascot.

The King George VI and Queen Elizabeth Stakes continued to attract the top horses in Europe and further afield, but in the latter half of the 1960s the home defence held the upper hand, principally through Noel Murless, who won the race three years in a row.

In 1966 Aunt Edith won the Yorkshire Cup, suffered a surprise defeat in the Hardwicke Stakes at the Royal Meeting and then beat subsequent St Leger winner Sodium by half a length to give Lester Piggott his second King George. (An interesting runner in this race was Hill Rise, now trained in England by

Not quite Gertrude Shilling, but a brave attempt at ludicrous headgear in 1969.

Princess Anne – now the Princess Royal – arrives in the Royal Procession with the Duke of Beaufort, 1969.

Noel Murless after a career in the USA which included being runner-up to Northern Dancer in the 1964 Kentucky Derby. Hill Rise had won the Rous Memorial Stakes at Royal Ascot before finishing fourth to Aunt Edith, and would return to Ascot in September to win the Queen Elizabeth II Stakes.)

The 1967 King George boasted an exceptionally strong field which included the winners of four versions of the Derby – Nelcius (1966 French), Appiani II (1966 Italian), Sodium (1966 Irish) and Ribocco (1967 Irish) – plus the 1966 Arc winner Bon Mot III. But none of these proved in the same class as the late-developing four-year-old Busted, who came to Ascot off a brilliant victory over Great Nephew in the Eclipse. Ribocco started favourite at 5–2, Busted second favourite at 4–1. Nelcius was pulled up in Swinley Bottom, his rider believing him (wrongly) to have broken down, and this manoeuvre hampered Ribocco, who lost several lengths. Meanwhile George Moore moved Busted into a challenging position behind the leader Salvo early in the straight, and after a brief tussle went clear to win by three lengths, with Ribocco finishing fast to take third. It was Busted's last race in England: after winning the Prix Foy at Longchamp he was retired to stud, where he sired top-class – and like him late-developing – horses such as Bustino and Mtoto.

In 1968 Royal Palace, who ran in the 'black, scarlet cap' of Jim Joel, became Murless's third King George winner in a row, and the first Derby winner to land the big Ascot race in the year following Epsom triumph. Ascot was already familiar terrain to Royal Palace. As a two-year-old he had finished sixth in the Coventry Stakes and won the Royal Lodge Stakes there, and after a brilliant three-year-old career had brought him the Two Thousand Guineas and the Derby (he missed the St Leger through injury), he started his four-year-old campaign by winning the Coronation Cup, then returned to Ascot at the Royal Meeting in 1968 to beat solitary opponent Djehad in a canter to take the Prince of Wales's Stakes. (Not having been run since 1939, that race was revived in 1968 in honour of Prince Charles, who was invested as Prince of Wales the following year.) After Royal Ascot, Royal Palace had beaten Taj Dewan and 1968 Derby winner Sir Ivor in a famous finish for the Eclipse Stakes, and he started a hot favourite for the King George at 7–4 on, with only Ribero (conqueror of Sir Ivor in the Irish Derby) at all fancied to beat him; the other five runners, two of whom were from Italy, seemed to have little hope.

After Ribero – like so many sons of Ribot a horse with a mind of his own

The gallant Royal Palace (Sandy Barclay) holds off Felicio II (Roger Poincelet) in the 1968 King George.

– had unshipped Lester Piggott and delayed the start, the race seemed to be plain sailing for Royal Palace. Taking the lead a furlong out, he cruised towards the winning post – then began to falter. He had torn ligaments in his near foreleg, his rhythm was gone, and French raiders Felicio II and Topyo were closing fast. But Sandy Barclay on Royal Palace kept his head and nursed the horse home with just half a length to spare – a heroic effort that marked the end of a great career.

We leave the 1960s with a mare who ran five times at Ascot during a career that spanned four years and made her one of the most popular racehorses of her era: Park Top.

Bought by trainer Bernard van Cutsem as a yearling for just 500 guineas and subsequently sold on to his great friend the Duke of Devonshire, Park Top did not run until she was a three-year-old, when she won minor races at Windsor and Newbury before taking on the cream of her age and sex in the Ribblesdale Stakes at Royal Ascot in 1967. Starting second favourite, she won 'smoothly' (the form book's description) from St Pauli Girl. She then won the Brighton Cup before finishing unplaced in the Prix Vermeille.

In 1968 she continued to show herself a high-class performer, winning the Brighton Cup again and the Prix d'Hedouville at Longchamp and finishing second to Chicago in the Cumberland Lodge Stakes at the Ascot September meeting.

But it was 1969 which put Park Top among the greatest staying fillies of the century. She won the Prix de la Seine at Longchamp, the Coronation Cup (by three-quarters of a length from Mount Athos under a typical cheeky Piggott ride), and the Hardwicke Stakes at the Royal Meeting. Geoff Lewis, who won the Hardwicke on her, kept the ride for the Eclipse Stakes, where she was runner-up to Wolver Hollow (ridden by Lester Piggott) after twice getting boxed in up the straight. Lewis, whose handling of the mare won him no riding awards, later admitted that as he pulled Park Top up that day he prayed for the earth to open up and swallow him.

It occasioned little surprise that Piggott was back in the saddle for the King George, for which Park Top started 9–4 joint favourite with Felicio II, runner-up to Royal Palace the year before.

Unusually, the race lost its 'clash of the generations' dimension as for the first time in its history there were no three-year-olds in the field. Nine runners went to post (including the King George's first Japanese-trained runner Speed Symboli), and it is only proper that the race be described in the words of Park Top's devoted owner the Duke of Devonshire, in his great book *A Romance of the Turf*:

The day of the race was hot and sunny. Superstitious as always, I did not want to wear the same brown hat as I had donned for the Eclipse. I could not very well wear the top hat that had witnessed the mare's Coronation Cup triumph. In the end I settled for a straw hat and hoped for the best …

The sun was shining on Lester's straw silks as it had shone on them on the day of the Ribblesdale more than two years before. I could only hope and pray history would repeat itself.

Debo [the Duchess of Devonshire] and I stationed ourselves at the top and back of the stand next to a doorway so that we could escape quickly after the race. Quickly, to avoid having to put a good face on defeat in front of friends and even more quickly if the miracle happened and Maureen [Foley, Park Top's stable lass] would lead her into the winner's enclosure.

Park Top was the last to enter the stalls and a few seconds later they were on their way. As expected Greville Starkey took Coolroy to the front setting a strong gallop down the hill to Swinley Bottom. He was followed by Speed Symboli and Timmy My Boy with Hogarth close behind, then Chicago and Soyeux. Felicio was last but one with only Park Top behind him. The order remained virtually unchanged as they passed the mile post and swung right-handed up the hill. Bill Pyers on Felicio knew his horse had to come from behind while Lester was equally determined to ride a waiting race on Park Top.

From the start until the turn into the straight the two horses remained at the rear of the field, alternating between last and last but one. At the head of affairs, Coolroy continued in front, admirably fulfilling his role of pacemaker. With about half a mile to go, Felicio repassed Park Top and although the angle of Lester's behind still gave cause for confidence, I was getting anxious. The mare had all of ten lengths to make up on the leaders and it is usually essential to be well placed at the turn into the straight where there are only three furlongs left to run. Indeed, as they swung right-handed for the last time Park Top was still last and I momentarily lost faith, turning to Debo muttering 'Not today'.

As I spoke the words, a transformation came over the race. The bell rang and the nine runners were in the straight. Coolroy was still just in front but Speed Symboli quickly drew level and then passed him. Timmy My Boy on the outside of the Japanese colt was almost upsides the leaders with Hogarth just behind, and followed by Crozier and Chicago. Soyeux ran a little wide coming into the straight carrying Pyers on Felicio with him just as the latter was starting his run on the outside of the field. Piggott also made a forward move on the turn but kept the mare on the inside. With just over two furlongs to go Speed Symboli was in front with Coolroy weakening rapidly on the rails. Crozier took over with about a furlong and a half left to run, while both Felicio and Hogarth had every chance if they were good enough. Meanwhile Piggott found an opening between Coolroy on the rails and Speed Symboli. He was through it and past Crozier in a few strides and with more than a furlong left to run the race was to all intents and purposes over … As soon as Piggott asked her to go she just swept the opposition aside in a matter of moments. Crozier, probably running the best race

of his long and honourable career, ran on gamely and finished second, beaten one and a half lengths, with Hogarth a neck further away. Then came Felicio another three lengths back ...

The Duke and Duchess rushed down to the unsaddling enclosure:

We got there before Bernard, and when he arrived, apparently unmoved, I did not risk speaking for fear of tears. Instead I contented myself with throwing an arm around his shoulder. It was a moment of supreme happiness ...

Then came an invitation to Debo and myself to receive the Cup from Her Majesty in the Royal Box. It would have been better if I had had a greater sense of reality since my only response to the Queen as she handed me the trophy was to exclaim 'Goodness Ma'am – it's heavy', which indeed it was. Her Majesty replied with just a hint of asperity 'Of course it is – it's real' ... Her Majesty's next action was to send her Representative for a bottle of champagne. My mind went back to the other triumphant day when the mare had won the Ribblesdale, and the rueful look Bernard Norfolk had given to the accumulated empty champagne bottles surrounding Bernard, myself and our friends. Now he returned in next to no time with a full bottle, and the seal of one of the great days of my life was set by the Queen and Queen Mother drinking a toast to Park Top.

Opposite: Park Top and Lester Piggott saunter home to win the 1969 King George from Crozier (quartered cap) and Hogarth.

A DIAMOND DECADE

David Dawnay retired as Clerk of the Course after the final Flat meeting of the season in October 1969 and was succeeded by Captain Nicholas Beaumont, who had a suitably horsey background. He had learnt to ride at the age of three, had spent some time running the Household Cavalry musical ride, and as an adjutant in the cavalry rode winners as an amateur. Invaluably for his new role, he had long experience at Ascot, having begun work at the course in 1964 as assistant to Dawnay, with special responsibility for the development of National Hunt racing. His first Royal Ascot on the staff had been the rain-ravaged 1964 meeting. 'Beaumont,' the Duke of Norfolk had told him, 'you commence your duties in a baptism of fire.'

When taking over as Clerk of the Course, Beaumont had firmly placed maintaining the standard of racing at the top of his list of priorities, and on that front the first decade of his time in office could hardly have been bettered, with a stream of famous horses and epic races making the 1970s a golden period for Ascot – or, perhaps more appropriately, a Diamond Decade.

First into the spotlight steps the imperious form of Nijinsky.

Charles Engelhard's famous colt ran only once at Ascot, but the royal course was the perfect setting for an equine aristocrat, and by the time he strode into the parade ring before the 1970 King George VI and Queen Elizabeth Stakes, Nijinsky was already a legend. A son of Northern Dancer, he had been bought as a yearling in Canada by Engelhard for $84,000 and sent to Ireland to be trained by the even more legendary Vincent O'Brien.

Nijinsky won all five of his races as a two-year-old – four in Ireland, followed by the Dewhurst Stakes at Newmarket – then as a three-year-old had beaten Deep Run at The Curragh in April 1970 before sauntering home under Lester Piggott in the Two Thousand Guineas and the Derby, both of which were won with the minimum of fuss.

Then the Irish Derby – no problem. Next, Ascot.

The twentieth running of the King George produced, for the first time in the race's history, a clash between two winners of the Derby. Four-year-old Blakeney had won at Epsom in 1969 but despite having finished runner-up to Precipice Wood in the Gold Cup the month before the King George was not considered in the same league as Nijinsky, as their respective starting prices indicated: 85–40 on Nijinsky, 100–7 Blakeney. The four other runners were Caliban (who had won the Coronation Cup the month before), Karabas (winner of the Washington DC International under Piggott in 1969), Hogarth (winner of the Italian Derby in 1968 and third to Park Top in the 1969 King George) and Crepellana (winner of the Prix de Diane – French Oaks – in 1969).

The race itself saw Nijinsky at his mighty prime, as Lester Piggott described in his autobiography:

> That day Nijinsky was at his absolute peak, and victory was never in doubt. He took up the running a furlong out while still on the bridle and was going so easily in the closing stages that I eased him down, which allowed Blakeney to close up a little. But it only took a gentle push at Nijinsky for a stride or two to put the issue beyond doubt. He was never better than he was that day.

Despite having been laid low with a bout of American ringworm, Nijinsky then won the St Leger – thus becoming the first winner of the Triple Crown since 1935 – before losing his unbeaten record with a controversial defeat in the Prix de l'Arc de Triomphe (beaten a head by Sassafras) and finishing his career with another defeat, second to Lorenzaccio in the Champion Stakes. Those last two were sad occasions, but to recall Nijinsky at his superlative best you remember Ascot. Lester Piggott summed up that performance: 'I have never been more impressed with a horse.'

The day that Nijinsky won the King George in July 1970, the Ascot grass probably still bore the scorch marks from the most scintillating performance of the Royal Meeting the previous month, when a two-year-old had observers scrabbling for new superlatives after an eight-length victory in the Coventry Stakes. His name was Mill Reef.

Bred by his owner Paul Mellon, trained by Ian Balding and ridden in all his races by Geoff Lewis, Mill Reef was one of those horses with whom, for most people, it was simply love at first sight. John Oaksey, whose devotion to the horse was distilled into one of the finest racing books of recent memory, *The Story of Mill Reef,* describes the colt at Ascot for the Coventry Stakes:

Mill Reef started at 11–4 on. That's hardly a working man's price with betting tax to pay but the five runners had not been in the Ascot paddock long before a steady stream of determined looking punters was to be seen marching across the Royal Enclosure

Vincent O'Brien leads in Nijinsky and Lester Piggott after their victory in the 1970 King George.

towards Tattersalls' rails as though a free issue of diamonds had just been announced.

They looked like people who had seen a marvel – and they had. For no lover of horses, or indeed of beauty in any form, will easily forget his first sight of Mill Reef at Ascot. With the possible exception of the 1971 Eclipse I do not believe he ever again came quite so near to physical perfection.

Though always superbly balanced and with quality etched in every line, he often tended afterwards to run up light behind the saddle in hard training. But at Ascot his middle piece was so deep and his quarters so round that no lack of scope was apparent. Under the gleaming mahogany coat the muscles of his forearms and second thighs rippled like sleepy snakes and as he danced light-footed around the tree-lined paddock, long ears cocked to the unfamiliar sights and sounds, the blend of explosive power with easy natural grace was unforgettable.

Only one of the other four runners, the Crepello colt Cromwell, had previous winning form and he was quite unable to make the Coventry Stakes anything but a triumphal progress. Clear at halfway, Mill Reef drew relentlessly further and further ahead and passed the post pulling so hard that Geoff Lewis could not contrive to stop him for fully another quarter of a mile.

Between the Coventry Stakes and his next appearance at Ascot in the 1971 King George, Mill Reef was beaten a short head at Maisons-Laffitte by My Swallow; won the Gimcrack Stakes by ten lengths; won the Imperial Stakes at Kempton Park; won the Dewhurst Stakes by four lengths; started his three-year-old campaign by winning the Greenham Stakes at Newbury; was beaten by Brigadier Gerard in the Two Thousand Guineas; won the Derby easily from Linden Tree; and beat the French colt Caro in the Eclipse Stakes.

Mill Reef was a brilliant horse, but – as had twice been demonstrated – he could be beaten, and nine lined up against him at Ascot. The betting – 13–8 on Mill Reef – suggested that their chances were forlorn, though Irish Ball, fourth in the Derby before winning the Irish Derby, seemed to have the best chance of exploiting any chink in Mill Reef's armour, while Politico (ridden by Lester Piggott) had some high-class form to his name and Ortis had won the Italian Derby in 1970.

The race turned out to be another exhibition round for Mill Reef, who sailed effortlessly into third place on the home turn, and then, in John Oaksey's words, 'Ortis, who had just taken over from Politico, was tossed aside like a leaf in an autumn gale'. Mill Reef won by six lengths, at the time a record distance for the race. (Generous in 1990 won by seven.)

As with Nijinsky, the winning jockey considered the 1971 King George the greatest performance in his partner's career. 'Daylight was second at Ascot,' said Geoff Lewis. 'If I'd given him one slap the judge would have left his box before the others got there.' And Lester Piggott's more minimalist tribute to Mill Reef that day is worth recording: 'He just keeps going.'

Yet Mill Reef's career had not even peaked. After Ascot he beat Pistol Packer by three lengths to win the Arc, and at four in 1972 won the Prix Ganay by ten lengths before scoring narrowly in the Coronation Cup. While being prepared for a return match against Brigadier Gerard, one of only two horses ever to have beaten him, he fractured a foreleg on the gallops and was retired to pursue a highly successful stud career.

Mill Reef after winning the 1971 King George.

Brigadier Gerard himself is the third of the immortals who graced the Ascot turf in the first three years of the 1970s, and he ran at the course more times than Nijinsky and Mill Reef put together.

Unbeaten in four races at two, Brigadier Gerard came to Ascot for the St James's Palace Stakes at the 1971 Royal Meeting fresh from beating Mill Reef and My Swallow in a famous renewal of the Two Thousand Guineas. Having disgraced himself in the pre-parade ring by neighing at the royal carriage horses being prepared for their return to Windsor, he started 11–4 on favourite. The rain was pouring down – conditions that Brigadier Gerard grew to dislike intensely – and the going was becoming treacherous. As Joe Mercer on Brigadier Gerard started his run in the straight in pursuit of Lester Piggott on Sparkler, the colt hit a patch of false ground and lost his rhythm so badly that his owner and breeder John Hislop was convinced his first defeat was imminent:

> Joe Mercer is a magnificent jockey at any time, but in times of stress he is superb and in the St James's Palace Stakes he excelled himself. Keeping the Brigadier perfectly balanced, which was no mean task in such going, he encouraged him with hands, heels and the swing of his whip; he gave him a tap, and when the horse responded did not touch him again, knowing that he was doing his utmost and would only resent further pressure.
>
> Never have I seen a horse battle harder to win; he simply would not accept defeat and with every stride crept nearer and nearer to Sparkler. He got to his quarters about a hundred yards from home, when Lester looked round; till then he must have thought he was coasting home, having taken an earlier glance back and seen the Brigadier's plight. Suddenly he realised that the Brigadier was on him and he gave Sparkler everything he knew in a desperate endeavour to hang on to his lead. But, inexorably, the Brigadier gained on him, drew level twenty-five yards from home and in the last few strides got his head in front. Ten yards past the post he was half a length to the good.

Brigadier Gerard had won by a head.

In the autumn of 1971, having in the meantime won the Sussex Stakes at Goodwood and the Goodwood Mile to take his career record to eight wins from eight races, he was back at Ascot for the Queen Elizabeth II Stakes, in which he faced just two opponents. Starting at 11–2 on, he won by eight lengths from the French-trained colt Dictus. He wound up his three-year-old season by beating Rarity a short head in foul conditions in the Champion Stakes to bring his score to ten out of ten, and the news that he would stay in training at four – as would Mill Reef – was enthusiastically received.

After winning first time out in 1972 at Sandown Park, it was back to Ascot for the Brigadier – this time for the Prince of Wales's Stakes on the opening day of the Royal Meeting. Joe Mercer, who rode the colt in all his races, explains what happened:

Each one of his eighteen races remains clearly etched in my mind, but the greatest race he ran for me was in the Prince of Wales's Stakes at Royal Ascot in June 1972. On the Sunday before the meeting I'd been due to fly to ride in Brussels, travelling in a light plane from Newbury. Shortly after take-off the plane hit overhead cables and crashed: tragically the pilot was killed but I was thrown clear, and though my injuries were not severe I was fairly shaken by the incident. Not so shaken, though, that I could bear the thought of not partnering the Brigadier at the Royal meeting. I insisted I was fit enough to ride, but John Hislop wanted proof, and had Jimmy Lindley on standby just in case I could not convince him. The morning of the race I took a handful of painkillers to alleviate the ache from my cracked ribs before riding work, where they made me push a horse five furlongs up the gallop. I came through all right and John Hislop agreed to let me ride, and I'm convinced that the Brigadier knew I wasn't right that day. It's as if he said to me before the race: 'Just sit tight, I'll get you through.' He looked after me – didn't pull, and absolutely sluiced in, beating subsequent Irish Derby winner Steel Pulse by five lengths. I managed to get off him in the winner's enclosure but didn't ride again that afternoon – nor for another week.

The following month Brigadier Gerard won the Eclipse Stakes – not impressively, but again the conditions were foul – then returned to Ascot for his fourth race at the course, and his greatest challenge yet in the King George. In his book *The Brigadier*, John Hislop explained:

Though Mill Reef was not to be in the field [he had suffered a setback in training], the opposition included some of the best middle-distance horses in Europe, whose riders were certain to ensure that the race was run from start to finish, in order to test the Brigadier's stamina to the utmost. This was the crucial point of the venture since the Brigadier would be racing for the first time over a mile and a half, a distance beyond the expectation suggested by his pedigree.

A top-class field turned out to test the Brigadier, lured by the prestige of the race, but also by the prize money – at £60,202 to the winning owner nearly twice the amount that had gone to Mill Reef's owner Paul Mellon in 1971. This increase had been made possible by the King George being sponsored for the first time in 1972, by the diamond company De Beers Consolidated Mines, who put up £44,000 towards the prize fund. Sponsorship at Ascot – especially of a race that bore a royal title – was naturally a sensitive issue, and the Queen's permission was needed before the 1972 King George could become the first Flat race at Ascot to be sponsored, other than races on the charity day. Whereas nowadays the traditional name of a race is often sacrificed if it proves inconvenient to the sponsor, the initial sponsorship of the King George was so discreet that the title of the race did not change at all for the first three runnings with De Beers' support.

The principal French challenger to Brigadier Gerard was the three-year-old Riverman, winner of the Poule d'Essai des Poulains. Gay Lussac, ridden by Lester Piggott, represented Italy and had won his last seven races (including the Italian Derby). Steel Pulse, beaten by Brigadier Gerard at Royal Ascot, had since won the Irish Derby and seemed at the top of his form. Then there was Parnell, ridden by Willie Carson (at that point well on the way to his first jockeys' championship) and trained at Newmarket by Bernard van Cutsem (who had won the race three years earlier with Park Top). Parnell had won the Irish St Leger in 1971 and the Prix Jean Prat at Longchamp earlier in 1972 and was exactly the sort of horse to test Brigadier Gerard's stamina to the limit, though he started at 28–1 whereas Brigadier Gerard was a warm 13–8 on favourite.

The race revolved around whether Brigadier Gerard would last home, and as Parnell led at the final turn, all seemed under control – at least to John Hislop:

> After turning into the straight, the Brigadier had two lengths to make up and set about it with his wonted determination. It took him a furlong to catch and master Parnell, who showed no sign of stopping but had not the speed to cope with the Brigadier's challenge.
>
> As the Brigadier gained the lead, the cheering of the vast crowd grew in volume and intensity to a roar such as can seldom have been heard over Ascot Heath. Having struck the front he veered towards the rails, probably wishing to race along them as he liked to do. At the same time, Parnell hung towards the centre of the course. Once in

command, the Brigadier was never in danger of being caught and passed the post with a length and a half to spare.

Never in danger of being caught, maybe, but there was real danger in the immediate announcement of a Stewards' Enquiry. Brigadier Gerard had indeed come across Parnell, but the enquiry at first seemed a mere formality before confirming him the winner. But as time dragged on and no result of the enquiry was announced, connections started to get anxious – then, after thirteen minutes of building tension, a huge sigh of relief broke over Ascot (or at least most of it) with the news that the placings remained unaltered. Brigadier Gerard had won fifteen out of fifteen.

But he was not to match Ribot's career record of sixteen out of sixteen, being beaten three lengths by 1972 Derby winner Roberto in the inaugural Benson and Hedges Gold Cup at York in August.

So – as with Arkle a few years before – a famous crown needed straightening when Brigadier Gerard came to Ascot for the fifth and final time to face three opponents in the Queen Elizabeth II Stakes on 23 September 1972. Sparkler, so narrowly beaten in the previous year's St James's Palace Stakes, was the only conceivable danger – the other two runners were

Brigadier Gerard and Joe Mercer being led in after winning the Queen Elizabeth II Stakes for the second year running in 1972.

the appropriately named Redundant and Brigadier Gerard's pacemaker Almagest – and the Brigadier turned in a mighty display. John Hislop again:

> As usual, the Brigadier took about three strides to reach his full momentum. As he attained it, he was coming into the last furlong and from there he left Sparkler standing, opening up an ever-increasing gap till, at the post, he was six lengths clear. It was a staggering performance, the seal being set on it when the discovery was made that he had beaten the record by over a second, and he received a deserved ovation. The Brigadier had re-established himself with a vengeance, running one of the finest races of his career.

Brigadier Gerard ran one more race, beating Riverman in the Champion Stakes, before retiring to stud, the winner of seventeen of his eighteen starts. A truly great horse – and a truly great Ascot horse – he shares with his rival and contemporary Mill Reef the distinction of giving his name to an Ascot bar. Appropriately, the two bars face each other.

Parnell was back for another crack at the King George in 1973, on a July afternoon that saw the first ever ladies' race at Ascot. The Cullinan Diamond Stakes, sponsored by De Beers, followed the big race and was won by Caroline Blackwell on Hurdy Gurdy, beating twenty-eight rivals.

The 1973 King George boasted a very high-class field, including a filly whose name would have meant little to most British racing fans eight days before the race, but would soon be lodged in the select pantheon of all-time favourites: Dahlia.

Owned and bred by the silver magnate Nelson Bunker Hunt and trained in France by Maurice Zilber, Dahlia had exploded onto the big-race scene just a week before the 1973 King George when she displayed an extraordinary turn of foot to win the Irish Oaks at The Curragh, beating the Oaks winner Mysterious. That was quite something, but surely not enough to bear repetition seven days later against the likes of Roberto and Rheingold, first and second in a pulsating finish to the 1972 Derby. Since then Roberto had beaten Brigadier Gerard, and in June 1973 had won the Coronation Cup, while Rheingold's four-year-old career had already brought victory in the John Porter Stakes at Newbury, the Prix Ganay, the Hardwicke Stakes and the Grand Prix de Saint-Cloud.

Hurdy Gurdy and Caroline Blackwell return after winning the first ladies' race at Ascot, the Cullinan Diamond Stakes on 28 July 1973.

Rheingold was favourite at 13–8, with Roberto 3–1, then came a long gap in the betting market to Dahlia and Parnell on 10–1, and good horses like Scottish Rifle (winner of that year's Eclipse Stakes, run at Kempton Park), Weaver's Hall (fresh from landing the Irish Derby) and 1972 Prix du Jockey-Club winner Hard To Beat all at longer odds.

Whichever way you looked at it, this was an extremely high-class field, but Dahlia – ridden by Bill Pyers, who had tasted King George glory nine years earlier on the shock winner Nasram II – slaughtered them, producing a scarcely believable burst of acceleration halfway up the straight to shoot clear of her rivals. Rheingold kept on to claim second place, six lengths adrift – so Dahlia had equalled the record winning distance set by Mill Reef two years earlier.

It was an extraordinary performance by the first three-year-old filly to win the King George, but Dahlia's wondrous career was just beginning. Later that year she won the Washington DC International, then in 1974 took the Grand Prix de Saint-Cloud *en route* to another stab at the King George, and for the 1974 renewal she was partnered by Lester Piggott. It was widely hoped that victory on Dahlia would bring Piggott the 3,000th winner of his career, since by the end of the Friday programme (which had seen a promising two-year-old named Grundy make his racecourse début) he had ridden 2,998, and he was likely to win the second race on Saturday's card, the Princess Margaret Stakes, on Roussalka. But Lester, being Lester, produced a variation on the expected, winning the opening race on Olympic Casino and reaching 3,000 on Roussalka.

Dahlia's great rival Allez France had been aimed at the King George but in the event did not run, so the vanguard of the opposition at Ascot appeared to be three formidable three-year-olds in the form of Snow Knight, who had won the Derby at 50–1, Highclere, the filly who had won the One Thousand Guineas and Prix de Diane for the Queen, and French raider Dankaro, runner-up in the Prix du Jockey-Club. Piggott and Dahlia were both at their

Above: Bill Pyers displaying the ring he received from sponsors De Beers after winning the 1973 King George on Dahlia.
Below: Dahlia herself in the winner's enclosure in 1974.

sublime best that day, the filly cruising into the lead inside the final furlong as the horses around her toiled away and winning without coming off the bit by two and a half lengths from Highclere.

Dahlia thus became the first horse to win the King George twice. But even that was not nearly enough for a filly described by her jockey Lester Piggott as 'tough as old boots'.

She would be back.

With horses like Nijinsky, Mill Reef, Brigadier Gerard and Dahlia hogging the column inches, you could be forgiven for thinking that the King George dominated racing at Ascot in the early 1970s. But there was still plenty newsworthy about the Royal Meeting.

In 1970 Gold Cup day was postponed until the Saturday (and the planned Saturday card cancelled), since Thursday 18 June was general election day, and the matter of turfing Harold Wilson out of 10 Downing Street – albeit temporarily – and installing Edward Heath's grand piano took precedence over the great triviality of Royal Ascot. The Queen's colt Magna Carta won the Ascot Stakes on the Tuesday under a Labour government, but the Conservatives were settling in by the time Precipice Wood won the Gold Cup, beating Blakeney (the first Derby winner since Ocean Swell in 1945 to run in the Ascot marathon) half a length to become the first Gold Cup winner trained by a lady (Rosemary Lomax). At the same meeting a young trainer named Henry Cecil sent out his first Royal Ascot winner – Parthenon in the Queen Alexandra Stakes on the Friday.

The following year another now familiar trainer scored his first success at the Royal Meeting when John Dunlop won the 1971 Prince of Wales' Stakes with Arthur.

But the first two Royal Ascots of the 1970s are most remembered for arguably the most unfortunate horse in the whole history of racing at the course: Rock Roi.

Her Majesty the Queen in the winner's enclosure after Magna Carta's victory in the 1970 Ascot Stakes.

Owned by Colonel Roger Hue-Williams and trained by Peter Walwyn (who had taken over the horse on the retirement of his first trainer Sir Gordon Richards), Rock Roi had run fifth to Nijinsky in the 1970 St Leger, and the following year developed into a top-class stayer, winning the Paradise Stakes at the Ascot April meeting, finishing second in the Prix du Cadran at Longchamp, then returning to Ascot to start favourite for the Gold Cup. Ridden by Duncan Keith, Rock Roi won easily by four lengths from Random Shot.

In his book *Handy All the Way,* Peter Walwyn relates how a couple of weeks later he was at Salisbury races when the Jockey Club inspector Bob Anderson came up and asked for a quiet word.

> It was very hot, and the stewards had announced that those in the members' enclosure could take off their coats and ties. I have never taken them off at the races since. The inspector told me that Rock Roi had tested positive with an illegal substance in the samples taken after the Gold Cup.

Rock Roi had been undergoing a course of the medicament Butazoladin to counter arthritis, and Walwyn, confident that it had been administered correctly, launched a robust defence at the Jockey Club enquiry at the end of August. After a five-hour hearing the Jockey Club decided that they had no choice but to disqualify Rock Roi. Walwyn was exonerated from any malpractice, but a race he had dearly wanted to win had been cruelly taken from him.

The following year Rock Roi started at 11–4 on to make amends in the Gold Cup. Walwyn relates:

Another outing for the Ascot umbrellas.

> Our only concern was the ground, which was worryingly firm. The thoroughly reliable Butomus gave Rock Roi a lead, making the running for about a mile and three-quarters until Rock Roi took it up and went for home. However, inside the final furlong Erimo Hawk, ridden by a young Pat Eddery, challenged and hit the front. Rock Roi fought back and regained the lead to win by a head, but leant left on to Erimo Hawk in the process. Inevitably there was an immediate stewards' enquiry and inevitably we were disqualified – for

The Duke of Norfolk greets Ron Hutchinson and Ragstone after their victory in the 1974 Gold Cup.

the second year running, which must be a record. It was a bit shattering, because the Ascot Gold Cup is one of the finest old-fashioned races in the country …

'A bit shattering' after twice passing the Gold Cup winning post in front and twice being disqualified must count as one of the great understatements of Ascot history, and Peter Walwyn never trained a Gold Cup winner.

Another remarkable – and remarkably unsatisfactory – Royal Ascot outcome occurred in the opening Queen Anne Stakes in 1974, which will forever stand as a salutary lesson for losing punters inclined to rip up their tickets in exasperation before the result is officially declared. After a rough race a blanket finish saw Confusion – in the circumstances an uncannily well named horse – first past the post, a head in front of Gloss, with Royal Prerogative a further three-quarters of a length further back in third. A Stewards' Enquiry was hastily called, with the result that all three were disqualified for interference, and the race went to fourth-past-the-post Brook.

A much happier result at the same meeting came in the Gold Cup, when Ragstone dug deep to repel the late challenge of Proverb to win the most prestigious prize of the meeting for the man who had done so much for Ascot – the Duke of Norfolk.

By then the Duke had retired from the position of Her Majesty's Representative, succeeded at the end of 1972 by the Marquess of Abergavenny, who had been a Trustee of the Ascot Authority since 1952. From 1973 the New Stakes at the Royal Meeting was renamed the Norfolk Stakes in the Duke's honour.

The Duke of Norfolk died in February 1975 at the age of sixty-six, and among a welter of tributes received this, in the House of Lords, from his old adversary Lord Wigg:

> We quarrelled, and we quarrelled publicly. He believed he was right – I am quite sure I was. But it is that which makes me say what I want to say. Here was a man of great honesty of purpose, who saw his duty and did it to the best of his ability. He never dissembled, and to such men much may be forgiven.

At least the Duke was not alive to witness a march of stable lads up the course before the opening race of the Royal Meeting in 1975, at the height of the bitter pay dispute which the previous month had brought chaotic scenes to the Guineas meeting at Newmarket as lads tried to stage a sit-down in front of the starting stalls, and affronted members leapt over the rails with the view to giving them a good thrashing. Mercifully, Royal Ascot did not see anything on that scale. The protesting lads picketed the meeting, and a petition was presented to the Marquess of Abergavenny stating their grievances. Fears that brewery firms would decline to cross the picket lines were alleviated by news that the caterers had already laid in enough supplies to keep the crowd well lubricated in the event of a blockade, and the worst sufferers in the dispute (apart from the lads themselves) were television viewers. BBC outside-broadcast staff would not cross picket lines and there was no coverage all week. Leading bookmaking firm Ladbrokes estimated that the lack of television exposure reduced off-course betting on Royal Ascot 1975 by 20 per cent.

Ascot fashion moves with the times. In 1971, these three employees of a computer company used computer keyboard keys to create their outfits.

Lester Piggott rode eight winners at Royal Ascot in 1975, equalling his total ten years earlier and securing the first Ritz Club Trophy (now London Clubs Trophy) for leading rider at the meeting. This award, the idea of Peter O'Sullevan, involved a hefty donation from the sponsors to a charity of the winning jockey's choice. Four of Piggott's winners in 1975 were for Vincent O'Brien, who in all won six races from seven runners. But Piggott's most significant winner that week was sent out not by O'Brien but by the almost equally revered French trainer François Boutin – the four-year-old Sagaro, who was steered home by Lester to win the Gold Cup easily from Mistigri (subsequently disqualified for interference), Le Bavard and Kambalda. Sagaro would be back for more.

Jump racing at Ascot went from strength to strength in the 1970s, with a host of the big names following in the hoofprints of Arkle. The two-mile chase in November won by Flyingbolt in 1965 had become the Buchanan Whisky Gold Cup by the end of the 1970s, and had been won by some of the biggest names of all – Pendil in 1972, Bula in 1973, Night Nurse in 1979 – while the other pre-Christmas highlight was the SGB Chase. Spanish Steps won this in 1971, and twice in the decade the race went to a horse who would go on to land steeplechasing's most prestigious prize, the Cheltenham Gold Cup: Glencaraig Lady in 1970 and Midnight Court in 1977.

The December meeting had another high-class race in the Long Walk Hurdle over three and a quarter miles. Lanzarote, 1974 Champion Hurdler, won in 1975 ridden by John Francome, while John Cherry, a great staying handicapper on the Flat as well as a fine hurdler, won in both 1977 and 1978.

At the February meeting, the Reynoldstown Novices' Chase produced a clutch of top-notch winners – Killiney in 1973, subsequent triple Irish National winner Brown Lad in 1975, Lanzarote in 1977 (his last race before being killed in the Cheltenham Gold Cup), and Little Owl in 1980 (he won the Gold Cup the following year).

(For the record, it should be pointed out that Red Rum, far and away the most famous steeplechaser of the 1970s, never ran at Ascot.)

But steeplechasing is a dangerous business, and alongside the triumphs there have also been tragedies – none more painful than the death of the brilliant Fred Winter-trained novice chaser Killiney in April 1973. Winter and his stable jockey Richard Pitman had enjoyed a wretched spring that year. Pendil had been caught on the line and beaten a short head by The Dikler in the Gold Cup. Crisp had had the Grand National snatched away by Red Rum after putting up an astounding front-running performance. But in Killiney, unbeaten in nine chases, they had a novice of unlimited potential. He came to Ascot for the Heinz Chase on 7 April 1973 (seven days after Crisp's Grand National defeat) fresh from winning the Totalisator Champion Novices' Chase (now the Royal & SunAlliance Chase) at Cheltenham, and started at 9-4 on against three opponents. Richard Pitman tells the story in his book *Good Horses Make Good Jockeys*:

Thrills and spills – Barnard catapults Johnny Haine from the saddle in the Black and White Hurdle, November 1971. (Horse and jockey were unhurt.)

> Not wishing to give him a hard race, I restrained him more than usual, allowing him to be upsides in front rather than twenty lengths clear at halfway.
>
> We turned away from the packed stands to start on the final circuit, skipping over a plain fence to approach the downhill open ditch where Killiney was right for one of his enormous jumps. As he started to rise I went with him but then he changed his mind and tried to put a short stride in before the fence. His speed and size did not allow this to happen and he 'put down' right into the open ditch itself. I was catapulted out of the saddle for some way before landing on my head, suffering severe concussion and dislocating a shoulder. I dimly remember my old pal Killiney standing still while I was carried to the ambulance. It was the last time I ever saw him. He had broken his shoulder, and had to be destroyed.

If that was one of the grimmest moments in the history of jump racing at Ascot, 18 February 1976 delivered one of the happiest, when Sunyboy, ridden

by Bill Smith, won the Fernbank Hurdle to give the Queen Mother her 300th
winner under National Hunt Rules.

In 1975 the De Beers sponsorship of the King George was for the first time
acknowledged – very discreetly – in the title of the race, and it was the King
George VI and Queen Elizabeth Diamond Stakes that attracted eleven
runners to Ascot on 26 July that year. While there was disappointment that
the great French mare Allez France would again be missing, the field none the
less represented the clash of the very best of different generations that
epitomised the whole point of the King George, and vindicated the vision of
John Crocker Bulteel two and a half decades earlier.

To take the runners in the order of their starting prices:

Grundy, owned by Dr Carlo Vittadini (whose daughter Franca won the
ladies' race, opening race on the card, on Hard Day) and trained by Peter
Walwyn, was a worthy favourite at 5–4 on. This bright chesnut colt with the
jagged blaze down his face was the horse of the moment, having won the Irish
Two Thousand Guineas, the Derby by five lengths from Nobiliary, and the
Irish Derby easily from King Pellinore. On all the evidence, he was an
exceptional three-year-old.

Similarly, on all the evidence Bustino, a 4–1 chance owned by Lady
Beaverbrook and trained by Dick Hern, was an exceptional four-year-old.
A late developer – as a son of the 1967 King George winner Busted could be
expected to be – Bustino had won the St Leger in 1974, and already in 1975
had lowered the course record for one and a half miles at Epsom when beating
Ashmore in the Coronation Cup. As a four-year-old he had to carry 9 stone
7 pounds, a stone more than Grundy.

Dahlia was back. Since the 1974 King George she had added to her haul
the Benson and Hedges Gold Cup at York and two major races in North
America, and although she had failed to be placed in her four races before the
1975 King George, word was that she was coming back to her best. Her
starting price was 6–1.

On 13–1 came the German-trained Star Appeal, who earlier that July had
won the Eclipse Stakes at Sandown Park at 20–1. Then on 18–1 the French-
trained Ashmore, narrowly beaten by Bustino in the Coronation Cup;

Outer Circle (Joe Mercer, near side) beats Nagwa (Willie Carson) to win the Princess Margaret Stakes in July 1975 – the race before the King George.

on 20–1 another French raider, On My Way, winner in 1974 of the Prix du Prince d'Orange; at 33–1 were bracketed Dibidale, a four-year-old filly desperately unlucky not to have won the 1974 Oaks after her saddle had slipped, then winner of the Irish Oaks and the Yorkshire Oaks, and the three-year-old Libra's Rib, second in the King Edward VII Stakes and then winner of the Princess of Wales's Stakes at Newmarket; on 66–1, the seven-year-old Card King, who that season had won the Prix d'Harcourt and run second to Allez France in the Prix Ganay.

The other two runners, Highest and Kinglet, were both priced at 500–1. They had no chance of winning whatsoever, but these two no-hopers held the key to how the race would be run. For Highest and Kinglet were both trained by Dick Hern and both ran in the colours of Lady Beaverbrook, and were both in the race to stretch the young Grundy's stamina to the absolute limit. Bustino's usual pacemaker Riboson – a good enough horse in his own right to have run third when Bustino won the 1974 St Leger – was sidelined through injury.

For a description of a race that launched a thousand breathless chronicles, here is Grundy's jockey, Pat Eddery:

It was no surprise that the Bustino team should seek to capitalise on their horse's strength, but the pace which those two set from the start was staggering. I'd expected a good mile-and-a-half clip early on. Instead we hammered down from the start to Swinley Bottom like six-furlong sprinters – it was amazing! Highest led us for the first half mile or so, with Kinglet second and Bustino third. I was in fourth, with Star Appeal upsides. At Swinley Bottom, Star Appeal went by me as Highest gave up the ghost and the stayer Kinglet took up the running, while I stayed tracking Joe Mercer on Bustino. Kinglet led for most of the long stretch out of Swinley Bottom until Bustino took it up approaching the home straight. With Grundy already off the bridle, I desperately tried to keep him in my sights, thinking: I'd better get after him. But I just couldn't go with him: he was gone – three or four lengths up – and kept on finding more, and it was well into the straight before I thought I'd reach him. Halfway up the straight I started to come alongside him, a furlong out I thought: I've got you! I just headed him and felt that we'd go on for a hard-fought but decisive victory, then – shit! – those green and brown colours appeared on the inside again. That tough old bugger was fighting back!

Grundy was not a big horse – Bustino was a size larger – but was endowed with tremendous guts and honesty, and now his bravery saw him home. He just kept going and hung on through the final half furlong as Bustino finally cracked. We got there by half a length, with Dahlia five lengths back in third.

Four or five strides after the line Grundy wobbled to a halt. He was an amazingly tough racehorse but that race bottomed him, and he was so tired that I thought for a moment I'd have to get off him to enable him to walk into the unsaddling enclosure. In the event he managed it all right, but he was completely drained.

Not to short-change an epic duel, which instantly was branded 'The Race of the Century', this is how it was seen by the other jockey, Joe Mercer:

Highest, ridden by Frankie Durr, set off at a tremendous lick, but Bustino, far from dropping in behind, was running away until I got him covered up. After four furlongs Highest came to the end of his tether and Eric Eldin on Kinglet – a lovely little horse and a very good performer in his own right – took it up. By the time we got round Swinley Bottom, with about seven furlongs to go, Bustino was third or fourth, still running away. I would have loved Kinglet to have led me right into the home turn but he could not keep up the pace. With about half a mile to go – and rapidly approaching the final bend – I was breathing down Kinglet's neck, and had no option but to take it up.

I was not at the time aware of where Grundy was – all I knew was that he was somewhere behind me! – and as far as I could tell from those around me I was the only one still on the bridle, so I kicked on into the bend and straightened up for the winning post. Bustino was a horse who would always keep on finding, finding, finding, and he responded with the courage that was his greatest quality. He hammered up the straight, and it was not until around the furlong marker that I became aware of the chesnut head with the crooked white blaze coming up the stands side. Grundy! The battle was on.

Grundy got to me but he couldn't get past, and we knuckled down to the tussle I'd been expecting. I hit my fellow one smack. His tongue came out and he faltered as he changed his legs, but he kept on battling. It took a long time for Grundy to get to Bustino's head, but gradually the younger horse got the upper hand and started to go clear. Then for a moment Bustino started to get back: I knew in my heart of hearts that he would not make it, and his one final effort petered out as Grundy went clear to win by half a length.

Bustino pulled up and walked back towards the unsaddling enclosure. He was shattered – though not quite as shattered as the winner, who stood stock still for a while before mustering the strength to walk back. A great, great race, even though we'd lost.

Grundy had lowered the course record for the distance by 2.36 seconds, and even as the two heroes came back to unsaddle some form-book anoraks started to ask whether a whole stone was too much for a four-year-old to concede to a three-year-old in late July. (The concession was reduced to thirteen pounds the following year, and further shaved to twelve pounds in 1990.) For most people, though, such arcane matters could wait. This was a moment to salute two brave horses who had fought head to head all the way up the Ascot straight and produced perhaps the greatest race ever seen at the course.

The press was as euphoric as the crowd. Len Thomas in the *Sporting Life* invoked the spirit of an earlier struggle, calling the 1975 King George VI and Queen Elizabeth Diamond Stakes 'the most fantastic race I have seen on Ascot's Royal Heath since the titanic struggle between Quashed and the American horse Omaha in the 1936 Gold Cup'. Peter Willett in the *Sporting Chronicle* called it 'one of the greatest races in living memory' amid 'scenes of enthusiasm that I have seldom seen equalled on any racecourse' before elaborating:

I am sure that this race will go down in Turf history as one of the really great races, to be compared with such epic struggles of the past as that between Ormonde and Minting in the Hardwicke Stakes over the same course and distance in 1887 and that between Ard Patrick and Sceptre in the 1903 Eclipse Stakes. The memory of this wonderful finish will be etched on my mind indelibly until my dying day.

Brough Scott in the *Sunday Times* hailed it as 'the hardest, most implacable, most moving flat race that I have ever seen'. Hugh McIlvanney in the *Observer* declared that 'only those with iced water for blood could remain aloof from the excitement that flooded through the stands at Ascot … The roars that welcomed Grundy home might have been for an England football team with the World Cup in their hands, and there was not an undeserved decibel. Some of the coolest citizens in the game were leaping around like schoolboys, exulting over what they had seen.' In *The Times* two days after the race, Michael Phillips was 'confident that I speak for most of those present at Ascot when I say that Saturday's race was the most thrilling that I have ever witnessed'. John Oaksey in *Horse and Hound* wrote with characteristic passion that 'I never expect to meet a single man or woman who could honestly deny that here, for a moment, two horses and two men came as near to perfection as any of the great ones around whom the history of the Turf is built … The play's the thing and here, from overture to curtain, the play caught all who saw it by the throat, leaving us full of wonder, gratitude and pride.'

Although Bustino never ran again, and Grundy only once (a dispirited fourth behind the indefatigable Dahlia in the Benson and Hedges Gold Cup at York the following month), no one suggested that the word 'Diamond' newly grafted onto the race's title was not completely appropriate, and the race continued to sparkle.

The 1976 King George seemed dominated by French-trained three-year-olds. The filly Pawneese, owned by art dealer Daniel Wildenstein and trained in France by Angel Penna, had been a brilliant winner of the Oaks and then its French equivalent the Prix de Diane (the first horse to achieve that double since 1864). Youth, like Dahlia owned by Nelson Bunker Hunt and trained by Maurice Zilber, had won the Prix du Jockey-Club and three other races as a

An exhausted Grundy returns to unsaddle.

three-year-old. Malacate had beaten Derby winner Empery in the Irish Derby. The home defence was led by the grey Bruni, winner of the 1975 St Leger, and Orange Bay (owned like Grundy by Dr Carlo Vittadini), who had beaten Bruni in the Hardwicke Stakes at the Royal Meeting the previous month.

Youth started favourite at 15–8, but it was 9–4 chance Pawneese who won the day, making all the running and keeping going stoutly up the straight to withstand the challenge of Lester Piggott on Bruni by a length, with Orange Bay a short head away third.

The following year Orange Bay, starting at 20-1 and again ridden by Pat Eddery, improved a place into second and so nearly went one better than that, going down to Derby and Irish Derby winner The Minstrel by a short head after a desperate last-furlong battle. (Vincent O'Brien-trained The Minstrel had won earlier in the season at Ascot, taking the Two Thousand Guineas Trial on 2 April 1977 – a day when the eyes of most of the racing world were on Red Rum winning his third Grand National. The Two Thousand Guineas Trial was run over the now discontinued distance of the last seven furlongs of the Old Mile, and had been successfully used as a Classic preliminary in 1968 by another Vincent O'Brien hero, Sir Ivor. The same programme featured a One Thousand Guineas Trial, and on the day that The Minstrel won his stable companion Cloonlara disgraced herself by planting at the start – a flag start, as the stalls were unusable on account of the heavy going – and taking no part in the race.) The King George proved to be The Minstrel's last race. With the export of bloodstock under threat following an outbreak of contagious equine metritis, he was sent across the Atlantic to embark on a career at stud.

In 1978 the Queen must have been hopeful of landing for the second time the race named after her parents when her great filly Dunfermline, winner of the Oaks and the St Leger in 1977, lined up for the King George against such high-quality opposition as Acamas (winner of that year's Prix du Jockey-Club), the Prix Ganay winner Trillion (who would later become the dam of Triptych), Hawaiian Sound (beaten a head by Shirley Heights in the Derby),

Exdirectory (beaten a head by Shirley Heights in the Irish Derby), Montcontour (winner of the Hardwicke Stakes the previous month), the Irish-trained Orchestra (winner of the John Porter Stakes at Newbury) and the New Zealand horse Balmerino (runner-up to Alleged in the 1977 Prix de l'Arc de Triomphe). There was also the three-year-old Ile de Bourbon, who after a quiet time as a two-year-old had really flourished at three, winning the King Edward VII Stakes at the 1978 Royal Meeting under twenty-two-year-old John Reid.

Sea Boat was in the pacemaking role for Dunfermline, but the filly was never going well enough to suggest she would emulate her owner's first King George winner Aureole, and early in the straight Ile de Bourbon came storming through to win by a length and half from Acamas, with Hawaiian Sound third.

Such form made Ile de Bourbon appear home and hosed for the St Leger and he started odds-on favourite at Doncaster – but finished unplaced behind Julio Mariner.

In 1979 Troy, who a few weeks earlier had won the 200th Derby by seven lengths and followed up in the Irish Derby, started at 5–2 on for the King George, and despite skidding on the firm ground at the home turn won without undue fuss from the French challenger Gay Mecene. (Troy then won the Benson and Hedges Gold Cup and finished third to Three Troikas in the Arc.)

But for all those great King George winners, perhaps the most notable Ascot horse of the 1970s was Sagaro. Having followed up his 1975 Gold Cup victory with a repeat in 1976, easily beating Crash Course and Sea Anchor, he came to the Royal Meeting in 1977 as a six-year-old in search of an unprecedented Gold Cup treble. He faced formidable opposition, including Bruni (who had been exported to California and then returned after disappointing in the USA) and the four-year-old Buckskin, who had recently beaten Sagaro in the

Willie Carson and Troy come back after winning the 1979 King George.

Prix du Cadran at Longchamp. Timeform's *Racehorses of 1977* described a great Ascot occasion:

> Most thought that Buckskin would confirm his superiority over Sagaro in the Gold Cup, and he started favourite at Royal Ascot. The confrontation between Sagaro, Buckskin and the repatriated St Leger winner Bruni excited public interest in the Gold Cup as rarely in recent seasons. The Ascot executive must consider themselves fortunate to have attracted such a magnificent field for a first prize of £17,837. The Prix du Cadran third Citoyen, the Yorkshire Cup winner Bright Finish and the Paradise Stakes winner Centrocon [later the dam of 1983 King George winner Time Charter] made up the field of six. The story of the race is easily told. Piggott, riding Sagaro for the first time since the 1976 Gold Cup, was content to wait as first Citoyen and then Buckskin dictated a strong pace. Turning into the short final straight Buckskin was still in command but both Sagaro and Bruni were right behind him, travelling easily, and poised to strike. Bruni was soon in trouble, and Buckskin and Sagaro left him and the others struggling. Approaching the last furlong Piggott calmly tacked to the outside, set Sagaro going with the minimum of fuss and it was all over in no time. Buckskin had no answer to Sagaro's splendid turn of finishing speed and Sagaro beat him, without coming off the bit, by five lengths.

The only triple Gold Cup winner is commemorated in the Sagaro Stakes, run at the May meeting (and, in 1985, the only Flat race in which Desert Orchid ever ran). Lester Piggott, who rode Sagaro to his three Gold Cup victories, described him as 'a magnificent stayer, as good as any I rode, and his turn of foot was, for a long-distance performer, phenomenal'.

The human face of Ascot was changing. Noel Murless trained his fifty-sixth and final winner at the Royal Meeting when Jumping Hill won the Royal Hunt Cup in 1976, while in 1977 Etienne Gerard's victory in the Jersey Stakes put the name Michael Stoute on the Royal Meeting scoresheet for the first time. Many of Stoute's future winners would be ridden by the fresh-faced seventeen-year-old whose own first Royal Ascot victory came on Mon's Beau in the 1979 Ascot Stakes: Walter Swinburn.

Sir Noel Murless, who trained
56 Royal Ascot winners
between 1947 and 1976.

And there were plenty of signs of the times. When Greenland Park won the Queen Mary Stakes in 1978 and Abeer the same race in 1979, both winners represented developments in the nature of racehorse ownership as now seen in the Royal Ascot winner's enclosure. Greenland Park, who ran in the colours of the Hertfordshire building company of the same name, became the first company-owned horse to win at Royal Ascot, while Abeer was the first winner at the meeting for Khalid Abdullah, a Saudi prince and one of the major league of Arab owners who would come to dominate the sport in the 1980s and 1990s. Early Ascot winners had mostly been owned by the aristocracy, but by the end of the twentieth century the common man would get a look in, with syndicates and racing clubs becoming very popular ways of giving a piece of the action to those not inclined or not able to invest millions.

Some aspects of Ascot, however, steadfastly remained the same, and among them was the tradition of the Royal Meeting providing an opportunity for pupils at a distinguished local school to spend a surreptitious day at the races. Back in 1838 Queen Victoria had written in her diary that 'The Eton boys are now not allowed to go to Ascot', but plenty managed to get there. In the 1860s Lord William Beresford slipped away for a day's racing and on his return received a thrashing, while the future trainer George Lambton was at Eton in the 1870s:

> One Summer half I got into trouble for going to Ascot Races. It was the custom in those days to run over during Ascot week in the afternoons and hope for a lift back on a coach. And on this occasion, nearly a hundred boys, myself among the number, were caught on the way home and reported to the Head Master. He gave us a Georgic to write out, and we had to put in a hundred lines every day at his house.

A far more elaborate scheme was worked out by the 5th Earl of Rosslyn, who in 1883 teamed up with two Eton friends to hire a hansom with windows painted white so that no one could see inside. Dressed as negro minstrels – complete with painted faces and instruments – they went round the racecourse playing and collecting money, even taking two shillings off one of their Eton masters without their disguise being uncovered. Another nineteenth-century truant was Ralph Nevill, who reported that it was fairly easy for absconding

Eton boys to get a lift to the races with Old Etonians who had themselves nipped off during their own schooldays – and Nevill also revealed the telling fact that while skipping school for Windsor races was leniently regarded by the Eton authorities, Ascot was a much graver matter.

That this tradition lasted to the present day is attested by Charlie Brooks, former racehorse trainer and a figure who has graced many a lunch party in No. 1 Car Park. Brooks was at Eton in the 1970s, and wrote in his autobiography *Crossing the Line*:

> A friend of mine sneaked off to Royal Ascot and had the misfortune to walk straight into his housemaster. Getting caught at Ascot was a sackable offence for the boy, but he had the presence of mind to hold out his hand and say, 'Hello, sir, you must be my twin brother Robert's housemaster. I've heard so much about you' – and then scarper.
>
> That evening, as the housemaster went round the house, he sought out Robert.
>
> 'I met your twin brother at Royal Ascot today.'
>
> 'Oh really, sir? How was he?'
>
> 'Shut up, Robert – but if you should be speaking to him, do say that I never want to meet him there again.'

THE LATE
TWENTIETH CENTURY

It was the stayers who took centre stage in the early 1980s, when the Gold Cup day crowd was privileged to witness two of Ascot's very finest: Le Moss and Ardross.

Unpalatable as it was, the truth could not be avoided that the Gold Cup's prestige had long been fighting a rearguard action against a trend in the bloodstock industry. The increasing influence of American bloodlines throughout the 1970s had put much greater emphasis on speed than on stamina, and, as trainer Peter Walwyn lamented, victory for a horse in the Gold Cup over 'its exceptionally long distance of two and half miles is the kiss of death for a prospective stallion'.

In racing (as opposed to breeding) terms, this did not mean that there was no place at the top table for the stayers, but their moments in the limelight were limited. The European Pattern system, first implemented in the early 1970s to impose necessary planning on the nature and timing of Europe's biggest races, dictated that only one British race over more than two miles would be considered worthy of Group One status: the Gold Cup. While it was gratifying for Royal Ascot's big race to have that official stamp of approval, the Gold Cup none the less seemed in some quarters to be becoming an anachronism. Calls for its distance to be reduced – which culminated in pressure from the Jockey Club for the race to be run over two miles, with the suggestion that its Group One ranking might be in jeopardy without such a change – were stoutly resisted by Ascot, a course with a long and honourable tradition of staging top-class staying races.

In this context, the stud career of Sagaro is salutary. A great racehorse over long distances, he made little appeal to breeders. After his record-breaking

third Gold Cup victory in 1977 he was sold to the Horserace Betting Levy
Board for £175,000, to stand as a stallion at the National Stud in Newmarket.
By contrast, that year's Derby winner The Minstrel went to stud in the USA
at a valuation of $9 million. To have your mare covered by Sagaro in 1978
would have cost you £700, with another £700 payable when a live foal was
born, a total of £1,400. To have your mare bred to The Minstrel in 1978 would
have cost you $50,000.

The racegoing public, on the other hand, loved the good stayers. These
horses were around for year after year, they showed that racing is not only
about speed and precocity but also about endurance and staying power, and
the showdowns between the top performers produced wonderful races – none
more wonderful than the 1980 Gold Cup duel between Le Moss and Ardross.

Le Moss, trained by Henry Cecil, already had one Gold Cup under his
belt, having beaten the great stayer Buckskin in 1979.

Buckskin had himself written a footnote in Gold Cup history in 1978.
A horse with notoriously problematic feet, he failed to stretch out on the
ground and was well beaten behind Shangamuzo. Owner Daniel Wildenstein,
incensed by what he considered an injudicious ride by Pat Eddery, declared to
Buckskin's trainer Peter Walwyn that he did not want Eddery to ride his
horses again – to which Walwyn, a man for whom loyalty is second nature,
replied that if Wildenstein refused to have the stable jockey ride his horses, he
could remove them. The Wildenstein horses were duly moved from Walwyn
to Henry Cecil.

Under Cecil's charge, Buckskin defied his chronic foot problems by
winning the Doncaster Cup and Jockey Club Cup late in the 1978 season, and
it was announced that he would stay in training as a six-year-old in 1979 with
one objective – to win the Gold Cup. He tuned up by winning the Henry II
Stakes at Sandown Park by fifteen lengths. Henry Cecil takes up the tale:

> What followed at Ascot makes me feel like Judas Iscariot. Out of
> sentiment Joe Mercer [Cecil's stable jockey] had chosen to ride
> Buckskin in preference to Le Moss, and in the short straight they
> looked all over the winners. But Buckskin began to tire, and changed
> his legs. Lester Piggott had been pushing Le Moss along in the rear
> of the field, and eventually got a run out of him that brought him

upsides Buckskin. It was now obvious that, despite Buckskin's efforts to fight off his stablemate, his poor legs would not match his mental enthusiasm. Seven lengths was Le Moss's winning margin, and although I saddled the first two it remains the saddest moment of my training career. Buckskin finished a leg-weary horse. I hardly dared look him in the eye, for had his legs not needed all that cotton wool and bandaging he was a horse who could have won a King George and an Arc de Triomphe.

However sad the 1979 Gold Cup was for Buckskin, for Le Moss the race was a great victory, and he went on to land the Goodwood Cup and Doncaster Cup.

Meanwhile Ardross, trained in Ireland by Kevin Prendergast and owned by his father, the legendary trainer Paddy Prendergast, had been slowly maturing into a serious rival for the stayers' crown. Unraced at two and the winner of one race at three, he came to Ascot in June 1980 as a four-year-old with two earlier races that season behind him. Le Moss, ridden by Joe Mercer, was making his seasonal début, but still started favourite at 3–1, with Ardross (ridden by Christy Roche) fifth choice at 6–1. Timeform's *Racehorses of 1980* provides a graphic description of the race:

It is rare for a horse to make all the running over so long a distance as two and half miles or more, but the tactics had been employed in the [1979] Goodwood Cup and the prospect held no fears for Le Moss's connections. Mercer set out to ensure that no horse would win the Gold Cup unless he stayed two and a half miles thoroughly at racing pace. They went a good clip from the start and, except for a few strides when Croque Monsieur showed in front about seven furlongs from home, Le Moss was never headed. The field was strung out a long way from home but Mercer took no chances and began to drive Le Moss along for all he was worth when there was still three quarters of a mile to be covered. Rounding the home turn, Vincent, Arapahos and Ardross were still in close touch but as soon as the field straightened out it became clear that Ardross was going to be the biggest danger. Ardross got on terms with Le Moss just inside the two-furlong marker and from that point the pair battled it out magnificently to the line.

Le Moss (Joe Mercer) wins his second Gold Cup, 1980.

Many horses would have capitulated to the sustained challenge of Ardross. But not Le Moss. The more Ardross tried to pass, the more Le Moss seemed to be spurred on and at the winning post there was three quarters of a length between the pair; the third horse Vincent, who was six lengths behind Ardross, was the only one to finish within ten lengths of the first two. Le Moss's performance was one of the most stirring seen on a racecourse in many a year; it was an unforgettable display of endurance and courage. Ardross too came out of the race with enormous credit; seldom have we seen two horses galloping so resolutely at the end of a truly-run Cup race.

But that was by no means the end of the rivalry between these two horses. They next met in the Goodwood Cup, when after another duel Le Moss won by a neck, and for a third time in the Doncaster Cup, when Le Moss again prevailed by a neck – thus winning the 'Stayers' Triple Crown' for the second year running.

By the time of the 1981 Gold Cup, Le Moss had been retired to stud and Ardross had been sold to Charles St George and moved to Henry Cecil's Newmarket yard Warren Place. On his first outing for his new stable he won the Yorkshire Cup, then faced three opponents at Ascot, coasting home under Lester Piggott to win by a cheeky length from the filly Shoot A Line. He then won the Goodwood Cup and the Geoffrey Freer Stakes at Newbury before finishing fifth to Gold River in the Prix de l'Arc de Triomphe, and wound up his season by winning the Prix Royal-Oak at Longchamp.

The 1982 Gold Cup was Ardross's fourth outing of the season, and he went into the race unbeaten, having won the Jockey Club Stakes, the Yorkshire Cup and the Henry II Stakes at Sandown Park. Ridden at Ascot by his regular jockey Lester Piggott, he toyed with the opposition, cantering home by three lengths from Tipperary Fixer and in the process breaking the course record. Next time out he was only third behind Height Of Fashion (later dam of Nashwan) in the Princess of Wales's Stakes at Newmarket, then won the Geoffrey Freer Stakes and the Doncaster Cup before going across to Longchamp for the Prix de l'Arc de Triomphe. The last Gold Cup winner to win the Arc had been Levmoss in 1969, and Ardross so nearly emulated him, being beaten a head by Akiyda after a whirlwind finish. He did not run again, but his career and his manner of racing earned this tribute from Lester Piggott:

> One characteristic above all stuck out with Ardross: his determination. More than any horse I've ridden, I could feel Ardross trying: come the moment for his maximum effort, he would lower himself towards the ground, put his head down, and stretch out as if his life depended on it. No jockey could ask more of a horse.

Henry Cecil, who by 2001 had trained 69 Royal Ascot winners, in the Royal Procession in 1999.

The 1982 Gold Cup marks an appropriate moment to pay tribute to Piggott himself, for Ardross was his eleventh – and, as it turned out, last – victory in the race, Zarathustra in 1957 being followed by Gladness (1958), Pandofell (1961), Twilight Alley (1963), Fighting Charlie (1965), Sagaro (1975, 1976, 1977), Le Moss (1979) and Ardross (1981, 1982).

For all the quality of the stayers at this period, the big one-mile races for three-year-olds at the Royal Meeting continued to be natural targets for the Classic generation, and no race in the early 1980s attracted more controversy than the St James's Palace Stakes in 1981. To-Agori-Mou, trained by Guy Harwood and ridden by Greville Starkey, had won the Two Thousand Guineas at Newmarket, then went down by a neck in the Irish Two Thousand to Kings Lake (ridden by Pat Eddery) after a rough race. The Stewards at The Curragh disqualified Kings Lake and awarded the race to To-Agori-Mou, but Kings Lake's owner Robert Sangster and trainer Vincent O'Brien got that decision reversed on appeal to the Irish Turf Club, making Kings Lake the winner after all.

In some quarters it was felt that the Turf Club had reinstated Kings Lake on grounds other than the strict interpretation of the rules, and there was still rancour in the air when the two colts met again on the opening day of Royal Ascot. This time the verdict of a neck went in favour of To-Agori-Mou, and just past the winning post Starkey stood up in his stirrups and, in Eddery's words, 'raised his fingers in what may have been a victory sign to the crowd or could have been something more unpleasant directed at me'. The Ascot Stewards considered it the latter and called Starkey in to have a word with him about what is and is not an acceptable gesture at the Royal Meeting. The next time the two colts met, in the Sussex Stakes at Goodwood, Kings Lake beat To-Agori-Mou by a head, and no untoward gestures were observed.

A less sour running of a big race on the Round Mile was the memorable Queen Elizabeth II Stakes at the September meeting in 1980, when Known Fact, winner of that year's Two Thousand Guineas on the disqualification of Nureyev, became locked in a grinding struggle with Kris. In 1979 Kris had won the St James's Palace Stakes and Queen Elizabeth II Stakes in a string of victories that pronounced him one of the best milers of the modern age. He came to Ascot beaten only once (by Tap On Wood in the 1979 Two Thousand Guineas) in fifteen races, and started 2–1 on favourite, with Known Fact 3–1.

Opposite: Ardross and Lester Piggott led in by Christine St George, wife of owner Charles St George, after winning the 1981 Gold Cup.

Ridden by Joe Mercer, Kris poached a two-length lead on the home turn, but Willie Carson on Known Fact launched a fierce challenge inside the last two furlongs, and after a ding-dong struggle won by a neck. Neither horse ran again.

The Marquess of Abergavenny stood down as Her Majesty's Representative in September 1982, lauded for how Ascot had flourished during his decade in office. He was succeeded as a Trustee by Malcolm Kimmins and as Her Majesty's Representative by Colonel Piers Bengough, who had been a Trustee since 1972. Bengough was a notable amateur rider, winning the Grand Military Gold Cup at Sandown Park four times – three of these on his good horse Charles Dickens, who when ridden by Andy Turnell ran third in the 1974 Grand National behind Red Rum and L'Escargot.

Bengough's first Royal Meeting was in 1983, when trainer Martin Pipe sent out his first Royal Ascot winner (Right Regent in the Ascot Stakes) and the Gold Cup was won by Little Wolf, ridden by Willie Carson and trained by Dick Hern for the Queen's racing manager Lord Porchester (later Lord Carnarvon). But the highlight of that meeting was the remarkable double achieved by the five-year-old Irish mare Stanerra. Owned and trained by Frank Dunne and ridden in both races by Brian Rouse, she won the Prince of Wales's Stakes conclusively from Sabre Dance on the Tuesday, then followed up by producing an outstanding turn of foot to win the Hardwicke Stakes from Electric, breaking Grundy's course record. Later in 1983 she gave even greater testament to her class and toughness by winning the Japan Cup.

In terms of jockeys, Ascot in the 1980s saw a succession of comings and goings. Steve Cauthen, who had set American racing alight by winning the US Triple Crown on Affirmed as a teenager in 1978 and moved to England the following year, registered his first Royal Ascot winner in 1982 on Kind Of Hush in the Prince of Wales's Stakes, first of his four winners at that year's meeting. In 1984 another famous American jockey appeared at Royal Ascot: Bill Shoemaker, who for many years held the world record of races won as a jockey, took the Bessborough Stakes on Sikorsky. Gay Kelleway became the first lady jockey to ride a Royal Ascot winner when landing the 1987 Queen Alexandra Stakes on Sprowston Boy (trained by her father Paul Kelleway).

But the biggest landmark for a Royal Ascot jockey – at least, that was what it was considered at the time – came with the victory of Never So Bold in the 1985 King's Stand Stakes.

Early that year Peter O'Sullevan – long a past master of the art of quiet investigative journalism, and (more to the point) a close intimate of the man in question – had revealed in a *Daily Express* exclusive that Lester Piggott would retire at the end of the 1985 season. The 'Long Fellow' himself, under contract to the *Daily Star*, went through the motions of denial by getting that newspaper to declare that 'The *Daily Star* columnist has not yet made up his mind when he will retire.' This lukewarm rebuttal was tantamount to confirming the O'Sullevan scoop, and throughout the 1985 Flat season there was an air of 'catch him while you can' about Piggott's appearances at the big meetings. So when he steered Never So Bold, his last ride on the last day of the Royal Meeting, into the winner's enclosure after beating Primo Dominie three lengths in the King's Stand to complete a double that day (he had won the Hardwicke on Jupiter Island), Piggott's adoring public assumed that they were witnessing the curtain call of a very special part of the history of Ascot. Little did they (or he) know …

The following year Piggott was back in that winner's enclosure, not as a jockey but as a trainer. In his very first season as master of Eve Lodge, Newmarket, he sent out Cutting Blade to win the Coventry Stakes in a finish of two short heads: 'The first three were so close as they passed the post', Piggott wrote later, 'that I genuinely did not know whether we'd won or not, but Sheikh Mohammed, in whose box I was watching the race, had no doubts: "You've won – come on, you've got to lead him in!" He was right.'

Sheikh Mohammed bin Rashid al Maktoum, second youngest of the four brothers from Dubai whose influence on racing around the world has been so immense, first saw his colours (maroon, white sleeves, maroon cap, white star) carried to victory at Royal Ascot in 1983 when High Hawk, trained by John Dunlop, won the Ribblesdale Stakes – and for good measure the Sheikh notched a Royal Meeting double that year when Defecting Dancer, trained by Henry Cecil, won the Windsor Castle Stakes. But the first Maktoum brother to own a Royal Ascot winner was Maktoum al Maktoum, then Crown Prince and now ruler of Dubai, whose Widaad won the Queen Mary Stakes in 1982.

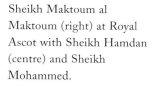

Sheikh Maktoum al Maktoum (right) at Royal Ascot with Sheikh Hamdan (centre) and Sheikh Mohammed.

Throughout the 1980s the King George VI and Queen Elizabeth Diamond Stakes maintained the standards it had enjoyed in the glittering 1970s.

Ela-Mana-Mou, third behind Troy in 1979 when trained by Guy Harwood, beat Mrs Penny in 1980, by which time he was trained by Dick Hern, and the following year's race provided the one and only Ascot appearance of a great horse whose name is known well beyond the confines of the sport: Shergar. Owned by the Aga Khan, Shergar lined up for the 1981 King George as indisputably the season's top Classic horse. He had won four races already that year, including the Derby by a record-breaking ten lengths and the Irish Derby in a canter, and was widely held to be the best middle-distance three-year-old since Mill Reef a decade earlier. Shergar lured a huge crowd to Ascot and rewarded them with an authoritative performance. Tongue lolling out in characteristic manner, he scampered to the line to win by four lengths from Madam Gay and give Walter Swinburn his only King George. It proved to be Shergar's last victory. He was beaten into fourth in the St Leger and was retired to his owner's Ballymany Stud in County Kildare – from where he was abducted by the IRA on the evening of 8 February 1983 and never seen again.

Kalaglow added the King George to Eclipse Stakes victory in 1982 when beating Assert by a neck, and in 1983 the previous year's Oaks winner Time Charter beat Diamond Shoal and Sun Princess (who had herself won the Oaks the previous month by twelve lengths and would win the St Leger).

Shergar (Walter Swinburn) scampers home to win the 1981 King George.

Time Charter and Sun Princess were in the field again in 1984, but this time could finish only fourth and fifth as Teenoso emulated Royal Palace in 1968 by winning the King George in the year following victory in the Derby. In beating a high-quality field – Sadler's Wells (winner of the Eclipse Stakes earlier that month and now the most influential sire in the world) was second, with Tolomeo (winner the following month of the Arlington Million in Chicago) third – Teenoso gave Lester Piggott his seventh (and last) King George victory.

The 1985 King George field oozed quality. Sheikh Mohammed's filly Oh So Sharp had won the One Thousand Guineas and the Oaks and started at 5–4 on. Law Society, trained by Vincent O'Brien, had won the Irish Derby and was a 3–1 chance. Rainbow Quest, who had won the Coronation Cup, was 12–1, along with the Australian six-year-old Strawberry Road and Lady Beaverbrook's three-year-old Petoski, trained by Dick Hern and winner of the Princess of Wales's Stakes at Newmarket. In a blanket finish Petoski, ridden with typical energy by Willie Carson, beat Oh So Sharp a neck, with Rainbow Quest three-quarters of a length further away third. The quality of the race was underlined when later in the season Oh So Sharp won the St Leger (and thus the 'Fillies' Triple Crown') and Rainbow Quest the Prix de l'Arc de Triomphe (albeit on the disqualification of first-past-the-post Sagace).

The 1985 King George: Willie Carson on Petoski (no. 13) comes through to head Oh So Sharp (Steve Cauthen, no. 15) and Rainbow Quest (Pat Eddery, no. 6).

Sadly, Petoski himself achieved little after the 1985 King George to enhance his own reputation, though he did return to Ascot in July 1986 to play a bit part in the drama of that year's King George. The star turns were now the three-year-olds Dancing Brave (owned by Khalid Abdullah) and Shahrastani (owned by Shergar's owner the Aga Khan), and they had a score to settle. Dancing Brave had been a brilliant winner of the Two Thousand Guineas that year, but in a highly contentious Derby his jockey Greville Starkey had seemed to lie too far out of his ground, leaving the horse too much to do and failing to catch Walter Swinburn and Shahrastani by half a length. Arguments raged about whether Dancing Brave had been poorly ridden or just plain unlucky at Epsom, but the fact remained that Shahrastani had won the Derby, and Dancing Brave had not.

After Epsom, Shahrastani won the Irish Derby by eight lengths to prove himself a top-class colt, while Greville Starkey and Dancing Brave made some amends by winning the Eclipse Stakes. Only a rematch between the Derby first and second would decide which horse had the better claim to be considered the season's top three-year-old.

Dancing Brave – on whom an injured Greville Starkey had been replaced by Pat Eddery – had a legion of admirers, but there was a question mark over his stamina and, besides, Shahrastani's display at The Curragh when landing the Irish Derby had been brilliant. It was the Aga Khan's colt who went off favourite at Ascot, when the betting market reflected the nature of what appeared to be a two-horse race:

11–10 Shahrastani
6–4 Dancing Brave
14–1 Shardari, Petoski
25–1 Triptych
100-1 bar

Boldden and Vouchsafe, two 1,000–1 shots in the race as pacemakers for Petoski (the Hern camp adopting similar tactics to those that had so nearly paid off with Bustino), had a ten-length lead round Swinley Bottom, but by the turn into the home straight Shahrastani and his stable companion Shardari were setting sail for home and trying to draw the sting out of

Dancing Brave. Pat Eddery's mount was full of running, as the jockey related:

> We cruised into the straight and I felt he could go and win exactly when I chose to, so I asked him to quicken, and quicken he did, in dramatic fashion. He shot to the front and it seemed to me inevitable that he would go on and win by ten lengths. Instead he did absolutely nothing in front and we only managed to beat Shardari a length after I had given my horse a smack.

Dancing Brave – who in fact had won by three-quarters of a length – went on to win the Prix de l'Arc de Triomphe and is generally regarded as the best middle-distance horse of the 1980s, while third-placed Triptych returned to Ascot for the 1987 King George and was again third – this time to Reference Point, who became the first Derby winner to win the King George in the same year since Shergar in 1981.

The 1988 King George first saw Maktoum colours successful in Ascot's midsummer showpiece – not those of the three most prominent brothers Maktoum al Maktoum, Hamdan al Maktoum or Sheikh Mohammed, but the 'yellow, black epaulets' of the youngest brother Sheikh Ahmed. His handsome white-faced Mtoto, by then a five-year-old and dual winner of the Eclipse Stakes, defied the soft going he was supposed to dislike and ran on in determined fashion to beat Unfuwain and Italian challenger Tony Bin. Two Thousand Guineas winner Doyoun was sixth, Derby runner-up Glacial Storm eighth, and 1986 St Leger winner Moon Madness last of ten. Tony Bin reversed the form in the Prix de l'Arc de Triomphe the following October, just getting the better of the fast-finishing Mtoto.

Following in the hoofprints of Shergar, Teenoso, Shahrastani and Reference Point, the final

Above: Dancing Brave (Pat Eddery) wins the 1986 King George from Shardari, with Triptych third and Shahrastani back in fourth.

Below: Mtoto (Michael Roberts) beats Unfuwain (Willie Carson) in the 1988 King George.

Derby winner of the 1980s to run in the King George was Hamdan Al Maktoum's mighty colt Nashwan. Having won both his races as a two-year-old (the second the Red Oaks Autumn Stakes at the October meeting at Ascot), Nashwan proved an exceptional three-year-old in 1989, landing the Two Thousand Guineas, then the Derby by five lengths and the Eclipse Stakes by the same margin. This huge chestnut had captured the imagination of the racing public, and he went off at 9–2 on against six opponents in the King George. Those opponents included that season's Coronation Cup winner Sheriff's Star (who started at 10–1) and subsequent Arc winner Carroll House (33–1), but on paper the only danger to Nashwan – and that a 6–1 chance – was Cacoethes, who had shrugged off the indignity of originally being named Our Friend Elvis to become a very good three-year-old, finishing third to Nashwan in the Derby and then winning the King Edward VII Stakes at Royal Ascot. Nashwan duly won, but not in the princely manner expected. Never a horse to display instant acceleration, he was gradually stoked up by Willie Carson to mount a challenge to the front-running Top Class, and reached the front early in the straight. He looked likely to go clear, but Greville Starkey on Cacoethes came alongside, and for the final furlong and a half they battled it out, first Nashwan, then Cacoethes, then Nashwan again holding a slight advantage. Nashwan's gigantic stride was just enough to keep Cacoethes at bay, and at the post he was a neck in front.

Like several other King George winners – including, in the 1980s alone, Ela-Mana-Mou, Shergar, Kalaglow and Petoski – Nashwan did not win another race. After his surprise defeat by Golden Pheasant in the Prix Niel at Longchamp plans to run him in the Arc were dropped, and a proposed farewell in the Champion Stakes was abandoned a few days before the race. Nashwan was probably at his glorious best in the 1989 Derby, but the King George roll of honour is none the less illuminated by his inclusion.

Nashwan was not the only benefit that Sheikh Hamdan Al Maktoum brought to Ascot in 1989. The first race on the charity day in September was the Shadwell Estates Private Stakes, sponsored by the Sheikh's breeding operation and bringing together two teams of riders – not all in the first flush of youth – from the rival television racing coverage of the BBC (Jimmy Lindley, Richard Pitman and Bill Smith) and Channel Four (Brough Scott, John Francome and Lord Oaksey). Jimmy Lindley on Wabil won by a short head from Bill Smith on Polemos, and for many years after the celebrity riders' race was a highly popular feature of the charity day. The 1992 running wrote two minor footnotes in Ascot history: Brough Scott rode his first winner for twenty-one years, and at the age of sixty-two Lord Oaksey decided that it was time to call a halt to to his exploits in the saddle: 'As we turned into the straight I looked up and the winning post appeared to be about four miles away. I realised then it was time to hang up my riding boots.'

Having concluded his racing career with a defeat in France, Nashwan did not even have the distinction of being officially rated the best three-year-old of 1989. That honour went to Sheikh Mohammed's Prix du Jockey-Club and Irish Derby winner Old Vic, who was kept in training as a four-year-old in 1990 and come July was fancied to add the King George to his already impressive list of victories. Favourite that year was another Sheikh Mohammed-owned colt In The Wings, who had won the Grand Prix de Saint-Cloud. It was a sign of the times that three of the eleven-strong King George field belonged to the Sheikh, 15–2 chance Belmez, winner of the Chester Vase and then third to Salsabil in the Irish Derby, making up the trio. Cacoethes was back for another go, while Assatis had started at 50–1 when winning the Hardwicke Stakes at the Royal Meeting (with Old Vic third on his seasonal début). It was the three-year-old Belmez who headed a Sheikh Mohammed one-two to beat Old Vic a neck and give jockey Michael Kinane his first (though not his last) King George. Belmez won the Great Voltigeur Stakes at York next time out (beating Snurge a head), then finished fifth behind Saumarez in the Arc.

Models Jerry Hall and Marie Helvin at Royal Ascot in 1982.

Horses and races are all very well, but what about the other important aspects of Ascot, royalty and fashion?

The two came together in spectacular manner on the opening Royal day in June 1981 with the appearance in the Royal Procession of Lady Diana Spencer, who was to marry the Prince of Wales the following month. Shrugging off a potentially treasonable incident when a gateman tried to stop her entering the Royal Enclosure as she was not displaying her badge – 'She just looked startled, then somebody said it was Lady Diana, and she gave me a wonderful smile and walked on,' reported the red-faced custodian – she proceeded to excite Ascot royal-watchers almost beyond containment.

Princess Anne coming in after winning the 1987 Dresden Diamond Stakes on Ten No Trumps, trained by Michael Stoute. She thus became the first member of the Royal Family to ride a winner at Ascot.

For the next few years the Princess of Wales in effect dictated the fashion agenda at the Royal Meeting, even if she occasionally wrong-footed her sartorial disciples. In 1986 the *Daily Telegraph* reported of the Tuesday:

> Spurred on by the Princess of Wales's recent appearances, clad head to toe in polka dots, everyone predicted a spotty Ascot opening day. They weren't wrong ... But predictably, after such a rush of spotty outfits, the Princess of Wales eschewed spots altogether. She picked instead the coolest of cream silks for a suit and perfectly toning Spanish hat.

The fashion contribution of the Queen's next daughter-in-law was less obviously successful. In 1985 the *Daily Telegraph* reported that 'Prince Andrew strode laughing to the Royal Box at Ascot yesterday with Sarah Ferguson', and the following year the Queen entertained Mrs Susan Barrantes, mother of the then engaged Miss Ferguson, to tea in the Royal Box the month before the royal wedding was due to take place on 23 July. Before long the Duchess of York (as Sarah Ferguson became) was bracketed with the Princess of Wales as a fashion leader, as the *Bracknell and Ascot Times* noted in 1988:

> Princess Di and the Duchess of York delighted followers of fashion with their outfits through the week. Particularly eye-catching was the Princess of Wales' grey mock morning suit worn on Ladies' Day – mirroring the traditional male dress of the week.

The Thursday – Gold Cup day – has been known as Ladies' Day since the first half of the nineteenth century. A poem written in 1823 described the Thursday as 'Ladies' Day ... when the women, like angels, looked sweetly divine', and in 1827 Pierce Egan versified:

'Twas a day on which fashion and beauty were cited,
And the King and his subjects seemed highly delighted:
Many thousands assembled to witness the scene,
Half of whom might well rival the Cyprian Queen,
Bedecked in gay tints of each varying glow,
Which imparted the splendour of Iris's bow.

By the early 1990s Ladies' Day tended to be reported in more prosaic terms, and with a recession taking hold even the grandest Royal Ascot visitor did not necessarily feel disposed to fork out for a brand new outfit. The *Daily Telegraph* wrote in 1991:

> Ascot Opening Day on Tuesday was dominated by black and white, with the Princess of Wales leading the monochromatic field in a tailored, double-breasted Yves Saint-Laurent-style white suit stamped with black buttons ... The Princess's suit was not new: she wore it previously when she played the piano for orphans at the House of Children in Prague Castle.

At the centre of Ascot fashion was still the hat. Standards of outrageousness had been set in the 1960s by 'The Ascot Mascot' Mrs Gertrude Shilling, whose creations became more outlandish as the years wore on, and whose topical choice – a football pitch when the meeting coincided with the World Cup, for instance – invariably provided an Ascot news story. The Ascot tradition of outlandish headgear was lampooned in 1976 by the appearance of Australian actor Barry Humphries in his Dame Edna Everage persona, wearing on his/her head a four-foot-wide hat featuring a huge model of the Sydney Opera House. Dame Edna told the world's press that it was her first visit to Ascot, and confessed: 'I didn't know it was a racing event until the other day. I always thought it was an exhibition of gas water heaters.'

The Princess of Wales's enthusiasm for wearing hats stopped short of her wearing a football pitch on her head, but it did wonders for the millinery business in the 1980s, and Ascot became more than ever the shop window for the hat trade. In 1983 the *Bracknell and Ascot Times* related how 'The mad

Racy headgear, 1991.

Queen Elizabeth the Queen
Mother arriving with the
Princess of Wales in 1986 ...

hatters were out in force, and out to out-do each other with creations ranging
from elegant to eccentric', and in 1988 the same newspaper reported:

> But of course Ladies' Day is really about hats ... Those who wanted
> to conform wore plain hats with a band or flower. There were
> surprisingly few box hats. But most ladies did not want to conform.
> Huge rims, bunches of flowers, ribbons and lace were cunningly
> balanced precariously on top of heads. Some measured almost three
> feet in diameter, whilst others went for height. On occasion, the
> designs were so alternative the only clue they were in fact hats was
> that they were on top of heads.

Being on the top of the head was a mandatory requirement for an Ascot hat.
The dress stipulation for the Royal Enclosure did not legislate about the
acceptability of a hat constructed from the wearer's own hair (as had been seen
in 1983) or a model of the Eiffel Tower (1997), and the more high-profile the
head, the more high-profile the hat: in 1995 one observer of the BBC
television coverage meanly referred to 'a dead crow which appeared to have
fallen on Clare Balding's head'. All that the dress code demanded was that the
hat cover the crown of the head.

... and with the Queen, defying the elements in 1997.

The same code gave men the straightforward options of morning dress (either black or grey), service dress or national dress, and with fewer occasions demanding morning dress it was becoming increasingly unusual for a male visitor to the Royal Enclosure to have morning dress of his own. Hiring was the sensible option, though for some traditionalists this smacked of a lowering of standards. The racing journalist Roger Mortimer wrote in the *Sunday Times* in 1981 that 'Sartorially and socially the meeting may have slipped a little ... The many men who hire their suits for the occasion are about as likely to obtain a good fit as a new recruit with his uniform.' But Moss Bros, for so long a company associated with the indignity of having to hire your own morning dress, knew which way the wind was blowing and in 1988 set up a dedicated Ascot Room in its main store in Covent Garden, from where it hired out some 6,000 morning suits for the Royal Meeting, clothing roughly half the male population of the Enclosure.

But of course Royal Ascot is much more than simply the Royal Enclosure, and in the late 1990s a reporter from *The Times* sampled the infield:

> Between the last fence and the winning post on the steeplechase course, in the midfield area known as the Heath, the atmosphere yesterday was that of a country point-to-point or a 1950s street party ... There is no cut glass, either in the accents or among the

The Queen Mother at Ascot in her motorised buggy: its livery echoed her racing colours of blue and buff.

picnics, which are more Safeways than Fortnums. Babies, not a feature of the Royal Enclosure, doze in buggies and men show their chests and tattoos in a manner that would send even the friendliest bowler hats across the way into apoplexy … At the catering huts alongside the portable toilets, the sandwiches were toasted, the ketchup plentiful, the coffee instant, the ambience compelling.

The Royal Meeting maintained its reputation for sustained quality over four days. It still managed to grab the headlines for reasons other than *haute couture*, and the 1988 Gold Cup provided a talking point which lingered for months after the last picnic basket at the Royal Meeting had been packed away into the boot of the Bentley.

There were fourteen runners. Tony Clark on El Conquistador set a blistering pace and was still in the lead coming round the final turn, but he started to weaken rapidly, and as the rest of the runners closed on him there was a bout of scrimmaging which pushed Clark out of the saddle and under the running rail. Horse and jockey were unharmed, and Royal Gait – ridden by Cash Asmussen and trained in France by John Fellowes – powered on to score a five-length victory from Sadeem, with third-placed Sergeyevich another fifteen lengths adrift. A Stewards' Enquiry was called, and after twenty-five minutes of deliberation – during which they had viewed the offending incident from every available angle – it was announced that Royal Gait was disqualified and placed last, and the race awarded to the well-beaten Sadeem. Asmussen was declared guilty of careless riding. It appeared from the patrol film that Royal Gait had bumped El Conquistador while starting his winning run, and by strict interpretation of the rules then prevailing he had to be disqualified, even though his action had not affected the finishing order – El Conquistador being clearly beaten at the moment of the incident.

The racing press fulminated – 'There will never be a luckier big-race winner', declared the *Daily Telegraph* – and the case went to an appeal at the Jockey Club, but the Ascot Stewards' decision was upheld. The controversial Rule 153, which dictated that disqualification of a horse was automatic if its rider was deemed guilty of an offence, was derided by Timeform as 'an affront to anyone with a sense of justice and fairness', but, rage as it would, the controversy could not affect the result, and the official winner of the 1988 Gold Cup was Sadeem. He won again in 1989, by the much more straightforward system of running faster than his rivals and passing the winning post first, while Royal Gait, a horse with a particularly resonant position in the profile of late twentieth-century Ascot, was sold to Sheikh Mohammed and, then trained by James Fanshawe, got his name onto a major roll of honour by winning the 1992 Champion Hurdle.

But Royal Gait was not the only major talking point on Gold Cup day 1988. The other was: what on earth had happened to Ile de Chypre?

A furlong from home in the King George V Handicap, last race of the day, Greville Starkey must have been feeling satisfied with his afternoon's work. His mount Sadeem had been awarded the Gold Cup on the disqualification of Royal Gait, and now he was well clear of his rivals on Ile de Chypre and about to score a Royal Ascot double. Suddenly, without any warning, Ile de Chypre swerved violently to the left, leaving Starkey no chance of staying on board. As the jockey hit the turf and Ile de Chypre careered away

Persian Heights (Pat Eddery) winning the St James's Palace Stakes in 1988.

Shadeed (Walter Swinburn) winning the 1985 Queen Elizabeth II Stakes from the blinkered Teleprompter (winner of the race the previous year) and Zaizafon (right).

towards the stands, Thethingaboutitis and Tony Culhane were gifted a Royal Ascot victory. Starkey was shaken but not badly injured.

No one knew what had caused Ile de Chypre to behave in such a way, but late the following year the story took a very curious turn. During the trial at Southwark Crown Court of three men on cocaine-related offences, Jonathan Goldberg QC, representing the defendant James Laming, stood up and told the jury:

> The story you are about to hear is one of the most remarkable ever presented in Crown Court ... James Laming did enter into a serious criminal conspiracy with René Black [another of the defendants] but it had nothing whatsoever to do with cocaine but a conspiracy to undermine the entire system of racecourse betting ... by using a device which is a technologically brilliant stun gun.

Goldberg then showed the jury a leather binocular case, from which he produced what appeared to be an ordinary pair of binoculars, before continuing:

> It would attract no suspicion; but take off the lens cap and you see … the lenses have been removed and replaced by two high-powered ceramic transducers. These are basically a pair of loudspeakers of a very high power indeed … This is an ultrasonic gun, and when the trigger under the binoculars is pressed, the device shoots at a passing racehorse, at a distance of up to fifty feet, a loud ultrasonic noise inaudible to humans. The device subjects the horse to a sudden and terrifying noise, the equivalent in suddenness of a loud firework exploding in its ears, and the actual noise would be equivalent in human terms to a hideous, ear-piercing shriek.

Mr Laming, Goldberg pointed out for the benefit of any juror not quite following, had invented 'the perfect way of nobbling racehorses', but Laming was arrested on the cocaine charge before the operation could be put into practice.

Laming's story did not convince the jurors, and he received a fourteen-year prison sentence after being found guilty on the drugs charge, while in racing circles his claim that his brother had been pointing such a device at Ile de Chypre at Ascot was largely taken with a pinch of salt. But the Jockey Club undertook tests, Starkey himself was convinced enough to carry out his own experiments with his teenage daughters' ponies, and the electronics company GEC developed an ultrasonic interference detector, to be carried by each horse in a race, which could detect the whereabouts of the stun-gunner. Eventually the story fizzled out, with Laming's claim being given little credence.

But a binocularised stun gun emitting a 23-kilohertz noise wave seemed way down the scale of improbability compared with the sight that greeted Ascot racegoers on 1 May 1991 – Lester Piggott walking out to ride Nicholas in the Insulpak Victoria Cup.

The blossoming training career which in its very first season had delivered a Royal Ascot winner was brought to a juddering halt by a three-year prison sentence for tax fraud in October 1987. Piggott was released on parole in

October 1988, and seemed to be living a quiet life in Newmarket, punctuated by the occasional ride in a charity race, until in October 1990 he stunned the world of sport by making a comeback to the saddle a few weeks short of his fifty-fifth birthday.

Never So Bold in the 1985 King's Stand Stakes had not been his final Royal Ascot ride after all, and each of the first three Royal Meetings of his revived riding career brought a victory: Saddlers' Hall in the King Edward VII Stakes in 1991, Niche (owned by Lord Carnarvon, the Queen's racing manager) in the Norfolk Stakes in 1992, and College Chapel in the Cork and Orrery Stakes in 1993 – Piggott's 114th and final Royal Ascot winner. College Chapel was trained by Piggott's long-time comrade-in-arms Vincent O'Brien, which guaranteed a poignant return to the winner's enclosure. The famously unmovable Piggott related:

> It was an emotional moment after the race when Vincent was persuaded to lead in the horse himself, to a glorious reception from the Ladies' Day crowd. Royal Ascot has always been my favourite race meeting, but I've rarely enjoyed it as much as I did that day.

College Chapel was Vincent O'Brien's twenty-fifth and last winner at the Royal Meeting, thirty-seven years after Adare had got him off the mark in the Jersey Stakes in 1956.

A rather more unlikely ride for Lester Piggott during his Second Coming was in the Queen Alexandra Stakes in 1991, when he partnered Norton's Coin, 100–1 winner of the Cheltenham Gold Cup the previous year. They finished unplaced.

Nor was Piggott finished with the King George. In 1991 he rode Saddlers' Hall to finish sixth of nine runners behind the runaway seven-length winner Generous, who became the eleventh Derby winner to score the Epsom–Ascot double in the same year (and like five of those – Nijinsky, Grundy, The Minstrel, Troy and Shergar – Generous had also won the Irish Derby). Like so many previous King George winners, Generous did not win again after Ascot, finishing unplaced behind Suave Dancer in the Arc and then being retired to stud.

That trend of the King George providing a horse's final victory continued

Opposite: Vincent O'Brien leads in College Chapel and Lester Piggott after their victory in the 1993 Cork and Orrery Stakes – a final Royal Ascot winner for both jockey and trainer.

in 1992 with the Irish-trained St Jovite (who started at 5–4 on at Ascot after a staggering twelve-length defeat of Derby winner Dr Devious in the Irish Derby) and then with two horses who won in Sheikh Mohammed's colours, Opera House in 1993 and King's Theatre in 1994. (Both 1993 and 1994 saw the Derby winner beaten: Commander In Chief was third to Opera House, while Erhaab ran unplaced behind King's Theatre.) The 1994 race was marred by Ezzoud tipping Walter Swinburn out of the saddle as he left the stalls and then continuing to make a nuisance of himself by running loose with the other runners during the race.

Changes in Ascot personnel in the mid 1990s were followed by a sea-change in the demeanour of the course.

The Ascot Minute Book records how at a Trustees' meeting on 13 April 1994 'Sir Piers Bengough warmly welcomed Brigadier Douglas Erskine-Crum and Mr Nicholas Cheyne to their first Ascot Authority Meeting and was delighted that they were joining the team.' Later that year, in October 1994, Nick Cheyne formally took over as Clerk of the Course from the retiring Nicholas Beaumont. Less retiring (in another sense of the word) was Beaumont's wife Ginny, famed in Royal Ascot history for conducting the band in the bandstand during the much-loved singsong at the end of each day's

Double Trigger (Jason Weaver) goes clear of his rivals to win the 1995 Gold Cup. The hugely popular Mark Johnston-trained chesnut ran in the race four years in a row: he was runner-up to Classic Cliche in 1996 and to Kayf Tara in 1998, and unplaced behind Celeric in 1997.

racing. She would be sorely missed. At thirty-three, Nick Cheyne was the youngest Ascot Clerk of the Course in the twentieth century, and came to the post after a highly successful tenure at Sandown Park.

Brigadier Douglas Erskine-Crum became the course's first Racecourse Director, in recognition that the traditional role of Clerk of the Course was becoming too diverse for one individual to handle. In short, Cheyne would handle the racing side of the equation, Erskine-Crum the business. (Erskine-Crum's job title changed to Chief Executive in 1998.)

The appointment of a Brigadier Erskine-Crum to a central place in the running of Ascot did not immediately suggest the dawning of a radical new age in the course's history, but the sneers were soon drowned out by waves of applause for a completely new mood at Ascot. For years 'ordinary' racegoers at the course had felt like the poor old maiden aunts you feel you have to invite for Christmas, even though you'd rather not: their presence was tolerated but they were hardly made to feel welcome, and they'd better behave in the proper way, or else. Under Erskine-Crum and Cheyne that attitude changed, and it changed rapidly. The Festival of British Racing in September 1994 was branded 'The Best of British Racing', and the event won a positive review from Julian Muscat in *The Times*:

Nicholas Beaumont, Clerk of the Course from 1968 until 1994, in his office at Ascot.

> The undeniable impression from this year's Festival of Racing is that Ascot, in casting off the shackles of tradition, has recast itself for enjoyment by the general public ... Here was this jewel of a racecourse ... driving away the patronage which it craved. But there was never much wrong with the place. It just needed fine tuning.

The acid test would be the 1995 Royal Meeting, and this too won approval from *The Times*. Richard Evans wrote:

> For all its success, Royal Ascot has been in danger in recent times of losing its charm because of fussy formality and unnecessary

Douglas Erskine-Crum, Chief Executive.

The Trustees of the Ascot Authority in 1990. *From left to right:* Malcolm Kimmins, who became a Trustee in 1985 and retired in 2002; Colonel Sir Piers Bengough, Trustee 1973–82 and Her Majesty's Representative 1982–97; and the Marquess of Hartington, Trustee 1982–97 and Her Majesty's Representative since 1997.

intransigence. In the 1990s, people do not take kindly to having their belongings searched after paying good money to attend a sports event; they do not expect to be subjected to endless notices telling them 'By Order' what they must not do. Above all, they expect to enjoy themselves. Faltering crowd figures at Ascot told their own story …

The delicate task facing the new duo was to modernise Ascot without impinging in any way on the quality of racing or the tradition and ceremony which combine to underpin the royal meeting.

In a matter of months they have managed to fine-tune Royal Ascot by putting customers first and concentrating on basics …

At long last, Ascot is going out of its way to make customers feel welcome and wanted. Tradition and custom have not been sacrificed in the process and an air of relaxed formality has returned to the royal meeting.

However welcoming the course wanted to be, a line had to be drawn somewhere, and that year the rotund television personality Mr Blobby and his consort Mrs Blobby turned up suitably attired – he in morning suit, she wearing the required hat – and tried to gain entrance to the Royal Enclosure. They were turned away. At the same meeting a group of gay rights activists calling themselves 'The Alternative Queens' staged a demonstration which resulted in one of their number – Mr Madam Molesta – being arrested for obstruction.

Two years on, and the new Racecourse Director was still enjoying rave reviews. *The Times* reported that each day of Royal Ascot 1997 saw record crowds, adding:

This is an incredible success story especially given the sorry state of Ascot only a few years ago. Hidebound by officialdom and voted the worst course by owners, it has been transformed in three years –

largely due to the efforts of Douglas Erskine-Crum ... His philosophy can be summed up in two words: customer care. The response has been dramatic and Ascot is now the model for other racecourses to follow.

In November 1997 Sir Piers Bengough retired, to be replaced as Her Majesty's Representative by the Marquess of Hartington. 'Stoker' Hartington already had a close connection with the course. He had been a Trustee of the Ascot Authority since 1982, his father the Duke of Devonshire had owned the great mare Park Top – winner of the King George in 1969 – and he himself had seen his own colours carried at the Royal Meeting for the first time in 1996 when his filly Shemozzle had finished third in the Ribblesdale Stakes. More to the point, Hartington had already proved himself a racing administrator of singular vision. As Senior Steward of the Jockey Club between 1989 and 1994 he had developed a blueprint for the reform of how the sport was run which led to the founding of the British Horseracing Board in 1993.

Meanwhile in the late 1990s Ascot's management team had been considerably strengthened by the appointments of John Woodrow as Finance Director, Danny Homan and subsequently William Derby as Commercial and Marketing Director, Danny Demolder as Events Director and John Holdstock as Buildings Director.

As Ascot approached the twenty-first century, the course was in good hands.

All the fun of the fair
at the Ascot Festival.

Desert Orchid (Simon Sherwood) and Panto Prince (Brendan Powell) head to head at the last fence in the Victor Chandler Chase, January 1989 …

Desert Orchid ran in fifteen races at Ascot – nine steeplechases, five hurdles, and once on the Flat (unplaced behind Longboat in the 1985 Sagaro Stakes). Of these fifteen he won eight – from the Haig Whisky Novices' Hurdle Qualifier on 29 October 1983 (the very first of his thirty-four victories) to the Victor Chandler Chase in January 1989.

In early 1989 the grey was at his peak, having won a second King George VI Chase at Kempton Park on Boxing Day less than three weeks earlier, and the Victor Chandler (over two miles, a mile shorter than the Kempton race) produced one of the most famous finishes of his illustrious career.

For much of the way Desert Orchid vied for the lead with Panto Prince, to whom he was conceding twenty-two pounds, and at the turn into the home straight the pair were joined by Long Engagement. Then Panto Prince forged ahead, with Desert Orchid trying to cling on. At the second last Panto Prince seemed to be increasing his lead, but then the Ascot crowd, the January chill warmed out of them by as thrombotic a steeplechase as they would ever see at the course, gave out a full-throated roar to encourage their hero. Cue Desert Orchid's owner Richard Burridge, in his book *The Grey Horse*:

... and Dessie (ridden by Richard Dunwoody) being led back by Janice Coyle after finishing fourth behind Blitzkrieg in the 1991 Victor Chandler Chase.

Des is level with Panto Prince as they take the last and land running. The roar grows. But again Panto Prince goes a length and a half up. The roar dies, then starts to build again, as again Des fights back. Panto Prince is on the rail, but Des is going for him, closing the gap, leaning on him, as Simon flashes his stick. Every stride he's gaining, but only by inches.

'Desert Orchid's fighting back though. Dessie's fighting back like a tiger!' yells Peter O'Sullevan, his reserve cracking under the strain, as Simon throws everything he's got at his horse. The line is only yards away now, Panto Prince is still ahead and not stopping. Simon puts down his stick as Des drifts towards Panto Prince, both horses are flat out, Des giving his rival twenty-two-pounds, but still he's closing the gap, inch by inch; he's still fighting back. The crowd is going berserk, the black head of Panto Prince is stretching for the line, with Des going for him, leaning on him, as they come to the line ...

'It's a photo!' shouts Peter O'Sullevan above the crowd, then a moment later, 'Dessie's won it; he's won it. Desert Orchid has won it by a fraction I would say!'

The screams of the crowd segue into applause, and some people say they think it's one of the best races they've ever seen at Ascot ...

Peter Scudamore in the winner's enclosure with Arden on 18 November 1989 after becoming the most successful jump jockey to date ...

Desert Orchid beat Panto Prince by a head, and two months later got the better of Yahoo in the Cheltenham Gold Cup to seal his place as one of the most popular racehorses of all time.

On 18 November 1989, Ascot's winner's enclosure was focused on another of jump racing's greats, jockey Peter Scudamore. By winning the

Kennel Gate Novices' Hurdle on Lord Howard de Walden's Arden, Scudamore was riding his 1,139th winner in Britain, thereby breaking John Francome's record as the most successful jockey in the history of jump racing. And three and a half years later, on 7 April 1993, Ascot was the venue for another Peter Scudamore landmark – his 1,678th and final winner, Sweet Duke, who won the Alpine Meadow Handicap Hurdle.

… and in the same location after the winning the final race of his riding career on Sweet Duke, 7 April 1993.

In 1987 the three-day September meeting was reorganised, with the Saturday providing an exceptionally well endowed programme featuring several top races – among them the Queen Elizabeth II Stakes, Royal Lodge Stakes, Diadem Stakes and Fillies' Mile. (The last-named, over the Old Mile for two-year-old fillies, was first run as the Green Shield Stakes in 1973 (won by the Queen's Escorial), and soon became a significant pointer to the next year's Classics, with winners including such top-class performers as Oh So Sharp (1984) and Bosra Sham (1995).)

The Festival of British Racing – as the Saturday was now named – put on offer over £400,000 in prize money, along with plenty of entertainments and sideshows. The Queen Elizabeth II Stakes, run as a Group One race for the first time that year, attracted two of the finest fillies in training, Miesque and Sonic Lady, but both were beaten by another brilliant filly in the shape of Coronation Stakes winner Milligram.

Refinements to the programme continued to be made over the years – notably with the arrival of Ascot's first Sunday race meeting on 25 September 1995. That year the fixture which had been run from Thursday to Saturday in 1994 was compressed into two days, Saturday and Sunday. The Festival of British Racing has remained Saturday and Sunday ever since (though the Saturday was rained off in 1999, the Queen Elizabeth II Stakes and the Fillies' Mile being added to the Sunday card) and is now even more firmly established as one of the high points of the Flat calendar.

The Festival Saturday in 1990 saw nineteen-year-old Frankie Dettori, fresh-faced son of thirteen times Italian champion jockey Gianfranco Dettori, ride his first Group One winner in Britain when Markofdistinction won the Queen Elizabeth II Stakes. He rode his second Group One winner when Shamshir won the very next race, the Fillies' Mile.

Born in Milan in December 1970, Lanfranco Dettori had ridden his first winner in England at Goodwood in June 1987 and his first Royal Ascot winner on Markofdistinction in the Queen Anne Stakes in 1990. Throughout the 1990s he made a major mark on the Royal Meeting with such horses as Drum Taps, on whom he won the Gold Cup in 1992 and 1993, and the flying mare Lochsong (King's Stand Stakes 1994). Frankie Dettori was rapidly becoming a riding star but he knew his place, and after winning the 1995 Ribblesdale Stakes on the Queen's filly Phantom Gold he sought the sovereign's permission before planting a kiss on the horse's muzzle. According to Phantom Gold's trainer Lord Huntingdon, 'Princess Anne was standing nearby and she observed drily, "I hope the kissing will stop at the horse!"'

Frankie Dettori and Lochsong after their victory in the 1994 King's Stand Stakes.

Frankie Dettori's first King George win came the following month, in July 1995. The chesnut colt Lammtarra had been ridden by Walter Swinburn when winning the Derby on his seasonal début, but, for reasons never made public, Dettori was asked to take over the ride at Ascot. Swinburn did, however, unstintingly offer guidance to the man who replaced him, as Dettori recalled in the book *The Race of My Life*:

[Walter] was very good about it, not only wishing me good luck but giving me some crucial advice about Lammtarra: the one thing to remember is that when you dig, you'll find; don't give up on him – keep digging, and you'll keep finding …

Lammtarra was favourite for the race, but was challenged in the betting market by Carnegie and by Pentire, who had gone through the season unbeaten: he had not been thought good enough to enter in the Derby, but then had won the Classic Trial at Sandown Park, the Predominate Stakes at Goodwood, the Dee Stakes at Chester, and the King Edward VII Stakes at Royal Ascot. The other four runners were the Irish Derby winner Winged Love, Broadway Flyer, Strategic Choice and old Environment Friend.

Lammtarra was very well behaved in the parade before the race and I got a good lead down to the start, but once there he started to fool about. It was a very hot day and I'd wanted him to cool down under the trees by the mile and a half start, but he began to monkey around and refused to keep still. One of the stalls handlers came to help, but Lammtarra continued to try to take me for a joyride, until eventually we managed to get him into the stalls. That is what he was like – completely genuine in a race but too keen to lark around beforehand.

He jumped off well and settled down as Broadway Flyer made the early pace with Strategic Choice. Environment Friend was in front of me, Winged Love and Carnegie on my inner, Pentire behind. I was not keeping an eye on any other runner in particular – if anything I thought the Arc winner Carnegie more of a danger than Pentire – and my main concern was keeping my colt going easily. So we slotted in behind, went a good pace early on and then eased up a little.

Ascot's short straight means that it is dangerous to try to make up too much ground from the home turn, and unless you have a horse with an explosive turn of foot you have to build up your run coming up the stretch from Swinley Bottom. Lammtarra in the Derby appeared to have a tremendous turn of foot, but in reality that was a combination of the horse finding his stride and the leaders rapidly coming to the end of their tether. At Ascot I couldn't expect him to accelerate instantly, so I had to get him to speed up gradually – to get a little nearer, then a little nearer still. When I asked him to take closer order he at first responded as I'd thought he might, running green and taking a little bit of time to get the message. But get the message he gradually did, and started going forward. I had to niggle him along, but he wasn't losing any ground.

We were approaching the turn when one of the French runners

gave Environment Friend a bump, and he in turn nudged us: Lammtarra stumbled, but that seemed to wake him up. Once in the straight I was working hard on him, though I was worried that something with a turn of foot would collar him inside the final furlong. He was running on, running on, and everything else seemed to be coming off the bridle – when all of a sudden here came Michael Hills on Pentire ...

So I was on the inner, pushing Lammtarra for all I was worth, Pentire was outside us and looking as if he had the race at his mercy. But Michael was not going clear, and I thought: Once you come off the bridle, I've got you! When Pentire went a neck up I thought he had me cooked, and then I remembered Walter's words: dig deep, and he'll find. I dug deep, gave him a few back-handers, and felt his huge engine working harder and harder. Lammtarra just refused to give in, and as Pentire ran out of petrol forged his way back into the lead to win by a neck.

Lammtarra, who followed the select quartet Ribot, Ballymoss, Mill Reef and Dancing Brave in going on from Ascot to win the Prix de l'Arc de Triomphe the same season, was the first of three King George winners for Dettori within the space of five runnings.

By the time of his second, in 1998, Frankie Dettori was as much an Ascot legend as Brown Jack.

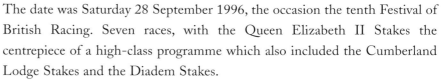

MAGNIFICENT SEVEN

The date was Saturday 28 September 1996, the occasion the tenth Festival of British Racing. Seven races, with the Queen Elizabeth II Stakes the centrepiece of a high-class programme which also included the Cumberland Lodge Stakes and the Diadem Stakes.

Frankie Dettori, the reigning champion jockey, looked set for a good day, with fancied mounts in several races. A four-timer, or at least a treble, was a distinct possibility, and the legion of betting shop punters who like to follow one jockey (usually the scenic route to penury) filled out their betting slips with a more acute sense of expectation than usual. The first four races – the Cumberland Lodge Stakes, Racal Diadem Stakes, Queen Elizabeth II Stakes and Tote Festival Handicap – were all due to be broadcast live on BBC television, and a popular bet was to combine Dettori's rides in these four in a Yankee, consisting of six doubles, four trebles, and one accumulator (in which winnings from the first race go on to the selection in the second race, and if that wins on to the third, and if *that* wins on to the fourth).

Other, even more adventurous Dettoriphiles noted that their hero had good chances in the fifth and sixth races and spread their selections into yet more Byzantine combination bets (such as a Super Yankee combining five horses in twenty-six bets, or a Heinz combining six horses in fifty-seven bets). Really reckless souls, boldly pushing aside the widely held opinion that Dettori's last ride of the day – Fujiyama Crest in the 5.35 – was probably his least likely winner and forecast to start at 12–1, laboriously filled out the form for the Super Heinz, combining seven horses in 120 bets. The attraction of such wagers for the small-time punter is that they offer the prospect – usually

Previous pages: Seven out of seven: Frankie Dettori and Fujiyama Crest win the Gordon Carter Handicap on 28 September 1996.

remote – of a very big return for a fairly small outlay in the event of all the selections coming up.

But most racegoers making their way to Ascot that Saturday would have been more buoyed up by the prospect of a thrilling race for the Queen Elizabeth II Stakes than by the niceties of how to fill out your slip for a Super Heinz. Long established as one of the top one-mile races, and recently as the mile championship of Europe, the Queen Elizabeth II Stakes had in 1996 the look of an exceptional renewal. The winners of the first two Classics back in May were both in the field – Mark Of Esteem, narrow winner of the Two Thousand Guineas, and the white-faced chesnut filly Bosra Sham, winner of the One Thousand Guineas when still feeling the effects of a foot problem and not seen out since. But the likely favourite was the Aga Khan's colt Ashkalani, who had won the French equivalent of the Two Thousand Guineas, the Poule d'Essai des Poulains, and more recently the prestigious Prix du Moulin. Then there was Bijou d'Inde, narrowly beaten by Mark Of Esteem when third in the Two Thousand Guineas and then winner of the St James's Palace Stakes at the Royal Meeting (beating Ashkalani). The seven-strong field would be completed by three other top-notch horses in Soviet Line, Charnwood Forest and First Island.

That was a contest to savour, but first there were two other races to be decided.

The 2.00 was the Cumberland Lodge Stakes. Frankie Dettori rode the three-year-old Wall Street, owned by Godolphin, the racing operation set up by the Maktoum brothers (principally Sheikh Mohammed) in 1994 which had taken European racing by storm as it developed the idea of wintering horses in

Number one: Wall Street beats Salmon Ladder in the Cumberland Lodge Stakes.

Dubai, then returning them to Godolphin's Newmarket base to be primed for the big races. Wall Street was hardly in the same league as Godolphin's biggest star that afternoon, Mark Of Esteem in the Queen Elizabeth II Stakes, but he was a promising colt with useful form and he went off 2–1 favourite, with Royal Court 11–4 and Salmon Ladder third choice at 4–1.

Wall Street led all the way to win by half a length from Salmon Ladder, and Dettori's fans had at the very least got off to a good start.

Next came the Racal Diadem Stakes over six furlongs, the race commemorating the great sprinting mare who had won the Rous Memorial Stakes and King's Stand Stakes in both 1919 and 1920. Here Dettori rode another Godolphin colt, Diffident, but unlike Wall Street he seemed an unlikely winner. Lucayan Prince was hot favourite at 15–8, while Diffident, who had won in Abu Dhabi back in February but had been comprehensively beaten in two races since then, was 12–1. In a furious finish, Dettori got Diffident home a short head in

Number two: Diffident just gets home from Lucayan Prince in the Diadem Stakes.

front of Lucayan Prince, with Leap For Joy another short head back in third. Those punters with their Yankees, Super Yankees, Heinzes and Super Heinzes now had one double up, and would have something, however small, to collect at the end of the afternoon.

Then came the highlight of the day, the Queen Elizabeth II Stakes. Mark Of Esteem had won the Celebration Mile at Goodwood five weeks earlier and was joint second favourite at 100–30, along with Bosra Sham, with only 9–4 chance Ashkalani preferred in the betting. Mark Of Esteem put up a brilliant performance. 'I couldn't believe it when I came to the furlong pole,' reported his jockey. 'It was as good a mile field as I'd ridden in and yet Mark Of Esteem was still on the bridle. When I asked him the response was electric.' Mark Of Esteem won by

Number three: Mark Of Esteem accelerates past Bosra Sham in the Queen Elizabeth II Stakes.

a length and a quarter from Bosra Sham, and Frankie had a treble. (So did Godolphin and trainer Saeed bin Suroor.)

Most competitive race of the afternoon seemed on paper to be the Tote Festival Handicap, with twenty-six runners over seven furlongs. Dettori's ride Decorated Hero had top weight, a crushing 9 stone 13 pounds, but as the large field came towards the two-furlong marker the 7–1 second favourite could be seen making significant progress. Hitting the front with a furlong to go, Decorated Hero made a nonsense of his huge weight and only had to be ridden out to win by three and a half lengths. Frankie's four-timer was

Number four: Decorated Hero wins the Tote Festival Handicap.

Number five: Fatefully gets the better of Abeyr in the Rosemary Rated Stakes.

achieved, and the Frankie Yankee on the four scheduled BBC races had come up trumps. (The BBC production team itself then showed remarkable prescience by keeping the lines open to enable the fifth race to be broadcast live – just in case.)

Dettori was back in the royal blue Godolphin silks to ride 7–4 favourite Fatefully in the fifth, the Rosemary Rated Stakes. 'The worry for me here was whether the split would come when I needed it,' he said later. 'It wasn't very wide when I went for it, but when it's your day the gaps come and this one did.' Fatefully won by a neck from Abeyr.

Five out of five (and four out of five for Godolphin). The BBC decided to hang around and show the sixth race live.

Plenty of jockeys had ridden five winners in a day, but in the twentieth century only two in Britain had managed six out of six – Gordon Richards at Chepstow in 1933 (and he rode the first five the following day) and Alec Russell at Bogside in 1957 – and after Fatefully had won there was already a strong feeling around the course that something very unusual was taking place.

The sixth race was the Blue Seal Stakes over six furlongs for two-year-old fillies, and Dettori's mount here already had an Ascot association, for Lochangel was a half-sister to the wonderful Lochsong, on whom Dettori had won the King's Stand Stakes two years earlier. Lochangel, trained like Lochsong by Ian Balding, started 5–4 joint favourite for the Blue Seal with Henry Cecil-trained Corsini in a field of five, and again the man of the moment gives a succinct account of the race:

Ian Balding told me to sit in behind. But she jumped off in front and I thought, 'To hell with it', and let her bowl. She relaxed and quickened up well when I asked her.

Lochangel kept going all the way to the line to beat Corsini by three-quarters of a length.

Number six: Lochangel in the
winner's enclosure after the
Blue Seal Stakes.

Six out of six. No disrespect to Chepstow or Bogside, but Dettori's feat
had already outstripped the six-timers of Gordon Richards and Alec Russell,
which were each achieved on an 'ordinary' day's racing. Dettori's six had come
on one of the biggest days of the season.

Those who had backed the Italian to ride four, five or six winners were
now sitting very pretty indeed, but the first six winners had meant that a vast
amount of money was now riding on his ride in the last race, Fujiyama Crest.
The on-course betting market reflects not so much the true chance of each
horse in a race as the bookmakers' attitude towards their liabilities should that

horse win, and while on the morning of 28 September 1996 Fujiyama Crest was widely available at 12–1 (despite the fact that he had won the same race the year before), there was no way that the Michael Stoute-trained gelding could now start at such odds. On course and off, there was a bandwagon effect, a rush to be involved in an historic racing occasion by backing Frankie's seventh ride, and such was the Niagara of money on to Fujiyama Crest that he started 2–1 favourite.

BBC television had switched to an old episode of *Dad's Army* by the time the runners for the two-mile Gordon Carter Handicap went into the stalls at 5.35 p.m., but for the twenty thousand-strong crowd at Ascot and for listeners to *Sports Report* on Radio Five Live, the excitement was coming to the boil. (A few racegoers of dubious temperament actually left after the sixth and before the seventh race in order to miss the worst of the traffic.)

Fujiyama Crest, sporting a visor, had more than the hand of history on his shoulder as he was loaded into the stalls. He also had the considerable burden of 9 stone 10 pounds and was conceding at least seven pounds to all his seventeen rivals. Despite that, Dettori pushed the horse into the lead after a couple of furlongs. Fujiyama Crest was still in the lead rounding the home turn, as Pat Eddery started to stoke the well fancied Northern Fleet up to challenge. Halfway up the straight Dettori was still in front, but for how long?

> I could feel Fujiyama getting tired – the weight was beginning to tell. I could see this horse appearing, and I could hear him – Pat at his very best, going all out, really going for it. I was just praying to God – please, winning post, please come. Old Fujiyama was so tired and just managed to get there on the line. I just punched the air and I was that exhausted I nearly fell off.

Fujiyama Crest had won by a neck.

The scenes that followed in the winner's enclosure produced a very special moment in the history of Ascot. Thousands rushed to greet Dettori, who rewarded them with a trademark flying dismount from Fujiyama Crest. The next half hour was a blur of champagne, sprayed Formula One-style over the crowd packed around the enclosure, speeches, autographs (even one of the Ascot Stewards asked for his racecard to be signed), interviews – and the knowledge that Ascot had yet again delivered an extraordinary sporting moment. No jockey had ever before won every event on a seven-race card, and it was no exaggeration to rank this feat alongside Jim Laker's nineteen wickets against the Australians, Roger Bannister's first sub-four-minute mile, Bob Beamon's long jump in Mexico City, the Obolensky try or any other of the landmarks of world sporting history.

'The Magnificent Seven' – what other name could be given to such a feat? – put racing on the front pages and made Frankie Dettori an instant celebrity well beyond the parochial world of the Turf. On the Monday after, a leader in *The Times* declared: 'To win seven races in an afternoon turns men into gods.' On the Thursday, Dettori joined other sporting luminaries at a reception hosted by Prime Minister John Major at 10 Downing Street. On the Friday John Prescott, gearing up the Labour opposition in advance of the following spring's general election, told the party conference that 'The only Tory worth backing to win at the moment is Frankie Dettori.' Racing's new superstar presented *Top of the Pops* on television, and was made odds-on favourite to take that year's Sports Personality of the Year Award, which had never been won by a jockey (and in the event went in 1996 to Formula One driver Damon Hill, with Frankie third).

Much was made of the betting dimension of Dettori's feat. The cumulative odds about the seven winners came to 25,095–1, and the Magnificent Seven was said to have cost the bookmakers £30 million. Stories abounded of small punters whose lives were transformed by huge winnings – such as Darren Yates of Morecambe, who incurred the wrath of his wife by having a 50 pence Super Heinz and a £1 each-way win accumulator on all seven Dettori rides, an outlay of £67.58 including tax. Mrs Yates was less wrathful when a few days later he received a cheque – presented by Dettori himself – for £550,823.54. Spare a thought, though, for Pat Epton, a cleaner from Lincolnshire and Frankie fan, who had a 50p single on each of his seven rides that afternoon but felt an additional 50p accumulator on the seven would be going a bit far. She made a profit of £14.66. Had she had the 50p accumulator as well she would, at the starting prices, have won an additional £12,047.50.

But for the purists the mind-boggling winnings were beside the point. The Magnificent Seven had provided a masterclass in the skills of jockeyship. Wall Street and Fujiyama Crest had been ridden from the front with exquisite

Opposite: Lord Hartington
and Frankie Dettori – in the
Fujiyama Crest colours –
at the unveiling of David
Roper-Curzon's bronze,
29 September 2001.

judgement of pace; Mark Of Esteem had been set alight at precisely the right moment to go clear of his rivals; Lochangel had made the running despite her trainer's instructions, as that was what Dettori had instinctively known was required as the race unravelled; Decorated Hero had been steered through a big field to get to the front at the right time; Diffident had been driven out just enough to repel his rapidly closing rivals; Fatefully had been slotted through a small but crucial gap to hit the front exactly when it mattered.

The afterglow from an unforgettable day in the history of British horse racing lingered long, and around Ascot racecourse there are reminders of Dettori's astounding feat. The number cloths from the seven winners, each signed by the man himself, are displayed in a glass case in the administrative building, and on 29 September 2001, five years and a day after the event, a bronze statue by sculptor David Roper-Curzon of Dettori in flying dismount mode was unveiled by the entrance to the Members' Enclosure as a permanent memorial.

Nor has Ascot forgotten the horses who made that day happen. At the end of his racing career Decorated Hero was given to the British Racing School in Newmarket, where he will play his part in the education of future Frankie Dettoris, and his box there is sponsored by Ascot.

Frankie Dettori has his own living memorial in a paddock beside his Newmarket home. Fujiyama Crest was sold out of Michael Stoute's stable to go hurdling with Nicky Henderson, and in May 1998 scored his first win since 28 September 1996 when landing a hurdle at Stratford, partnered by Richard Dunwoody. He later reverted to the Flat and, then in the care of trainer Roger Curtis, ran his last race at Nottingham in July 2000. Later that year Derek Heeney, who had looked after Fujiyama Crest at Michael Stoute's and had maintained an interest in the horse, was at Sandown Park races when a familiar Italian accent called across to him: 'How's the old horse?' Before Fujiyama Crest knew it he had been bought from Roger Curtis and moved to Newmarket, with plans that he should become a hack for Frankie's wife Catherine. 'This horse made me famous', said Dettori, 'so giving him a home for the rest of his life is the least I can do.'

THE TURN OF THE MILLENNIUM

As the new millennium arrived, Ascot was going from strength to strength.

Attendances were increasing in a very satisfactory manner, from an average of around 23,500 per racing day on the Flat in 1994 to just over 27,700 in 2000, while over the same period the average jumping crowd went from just some 7,300 to around 10,400. (Naturally the Royal Meeting attracts crowds well above average, with around 70,000 on Gold Cup day and around 60,000 on the other three.)

There were twenty-five days' racing scheduled for 2000, compared with twenty-three in 1990 (and, to maintain the historical perspective, twelve in 1950 and just four in 1900).

Prize money was high. On the Flat, Ascot offered more than any other British racecourse in 2000, with a little over £6 million to be won. Indeed, outside Japan and Hong Kong, Ascot had the highest average prize money per race in the world. Over jumps, Ascot's total prize money was second only to Cheltenham's.

Most important of all – and hardly surprising in the light of the prize money on offer – the standard of racing remained at a very elevated level.

Take the King George VI and Queen Elizabeth Diamond Stakes. The late 1990s and early 2000s represented a golden age for what was already a race of the highest class. Pentire, so narrowly edged out by Lammtarra in 1995, received ample consolation when beating Classic Cliche and Derby winner Shaamit in 1996 (and the fact that Classic Cliche, winner of the 1995 St Leger, came to the King George after winning the Gold Cup proclaimed the wellbeing of the Royal Meeting's showpiece).

Previous pages: The parade ring, 2001.

The 1997 King George brought together a truly jewel-encrusted field. French challenger Helissio had won the 1996 Prix de l'Arc de Triomphe in brilliant style, and came to Ascot unbeaten in three earlier outings that season, including the Prix Ganay and Grand Prix de Saint-Cloud. Five-year-old Pilsudski, trained by Michael Stoute, had finished runner-up to Helissio in the Arc and had then won the Breeders' Cup Turf at Woodbine. In the early part of 1997 he had come third to Helissio in the Prix Ganay and second in the Hardwicke Stakes, but he then beat Derby winner Benny The Dip and the great filly Bosra Sham in the Eclipse Stakes and was clearly in top form at the right time. Also trained by Michael Stoute was another five-year-old, Sheikh Mohammed's evergreen Singspiel, who had won the Canadian International and the Japan Cup in 1996 and the Dubai World Cup – the world's richest race – and the Coronation Cup (by five lengths) earlier in 1997. A third five-year-old was Swain, who had been trained in France by André Fabre when winning five races in a row at three and the Coronation Cup and the Prix Foy at four. He was then transferred to the Godolphin team, but as the main Godolphin jockey Frankie Dettori had opted to ride Singspiel at Ascot, it was John Reid who donned the royal blue silks to partner Swain.

Torrential rain changed the going from good to firm on the Friday to soft on the Saturday – with part of the course under water on the morning of the race there was momentary doubt about whether the King George would take place at all – which probably played to Swain's advantage, though punters were reluctant to look beyond the big three. Helissio started 11–10 favourite, with Singspiel 4–1 and Pilsudski 6–1. But it was 16–1 chance Swain who put the others in their place, taking on the leader Helissio early in the straight and keeping going with tremendous resolution to repel the persistent challenge of Pilsudski and win by a length. Helissio was third, and Singspiel fourth.

Swain, ridden by Frankie Dettori, wins the 1998 King George – only the second dual winner in the history of the race.

Swain landed the King George again in 1998, ridden this time by Dettori. When beating Derby winner High-Rise a length, with Royal Anthem (who had won the King Edward VII Stakes at Royal

Ascot) third, Swain made two significant entries in the King George record book. He was only the second dual winner (after Dahlia in 1973 and 1974), and at six he was the oldest horse to win the race.

Fourth behind Swain in 1998 was the big grey four-year-old Daylami, who returned in 1999 and gave Godolphin its third King George in a row (and trainer Saeed bin Suroor his fourth in five runnings, following Lammtarra in 1995 and Swain in 1997 and 1998). Daylami had won the Tattersalls Gold Cup at The Curragh, the Eclipse Stakes and the Man O' War Stakes at Belmont Park as a four-year-old, and at five came to Ascot off a solid victory in the Coronation Cup. In the King George he produced a sharp turn of foot to stride clear of another Godolphin runner Nedawi (winner of the 1998 St Leger) by five lengths, with Derby winner Oath unplaced, to give Frankie Dettori his third win in the race. 'I had goosepimples down my back', enthused the Italian after the race. 'I could not believe that a horse in a tough King George like today could produce a turn of foot like that.'

The 1999 King George was included in the inaugural Emirates World Series, which linked eleven of the biggest races around the globe to produce world rankings for horse, jockey, owner and trainer, who scored points for placings in each event. Daylami, who after Ascot won the Irish Champion Stakes and Breeders' Cup Turf, was the winning horse of the World Series in 1999.

Celeric and Pat Eddery win the 1997 Gold Cup.

Meanwhile the Royal Meeting maintained its traditional level of excellence, and the Gold Cup remained the highlight. In 1997 Pat Eddery produced one of the greatest Ascot rides in living memory to produce the five-year-old Celeric at exactly the right moment to beat the previous year's winner Classic Cliche. On a filthy Gold Cup day the ground was subjected to a steady downpour, and although the going was officially declared 'good', Eddery knew that he had to preserve his mount's stamina. To make his jockey's task even more difficult, Celeric had a reputation for idling once he hit the front, so after bringing him up the outside early in the straight Eddery switched to the inner rail, going well but still not yet ready to pounce. Classic Cliche looked

Opposite: The paddock bend in the Ascot Stakes, 1998.

The 1999 Hardwicke Stakes – Fruits Of Love (right) beats Royal Anthem.

all over the winner inside the last furlong, then Eddery eased off the brakes and pushed Celeric into the lead with about fifty yards to go to win by three-quarters of a length – an object lesson in coolness under the pressure of a big race. (Celeric was only the second gelding to win the Gold Cup, after Arcadian Heights in 1994 had first flown the flag for the emasculated.)

In 1998 Frankie Dettori was top jockey at the Royal Meeting with seven winners, and later nominated that as his biggest achievement of the year: 'Going to Ascot is like going home for me.' His septet was headed by Godolphin horse Kayf Tara in the Gold Cup, which with sixteen runners generated such interest with the punting public that the race was, at least with Ladbrokes, the biggest betting event of the meeting, surpassing the Royal Hunt Cup and the Wokingham Stakes. Kayf Tara, a high-class colt who later that year won the Irish St Leger, beat 1995 Gold Cup hero Double Trigger (who started at 25–1) by a neck.

Kayf Tara was back in 1999, when seventeen runners made up the largest field in the long history of the Gold Cup – evidence of what Timeform called 'the rude health of Flat racing's greatest staying race'. This time he could finish only third behind the Aga Khan's Enzeli, trained in Ireland by John Oxx and ridden by Johnny Murtagh, but there was plenty left for Kayf Tara that year, and later in 1999 he won the Goodwood Cup, the Prix Kergorlay, and the Irish St Leger for a second time.

In 2000 Kayf Tara became the first horse since Anticipation in 1819 to regain the Gold Cup. Frankie Dettori had been badly injured when the light plane taking him from Newmarket to Goodwood races earlier that month had crashed on take-off, and it was Michael Kinane who produced Kayf Tara late to hold off the dogged challenge of Far Cry by a head – and then survive a Stewards' Enquiry into two possible cases of interference. Kayf Tara did not run again, but his Timeform rating of 130 in 1999 and 2000 made him the highest rated Gold Cup winner since Ardross on 134 in 1982.

Other Ascot landmarks in the late 1990s included the retirement of BBC television

Sir Peter O'Sullevan at Ascot with trainer Jimmy FitzGerald, one of the few trainers to have won Ascot races both at the Royal Meeting (Kayudee in the 1984 Ascot Stakes) and over jumps.

commentator Peter O'Sullevan in 1997 and the founding of the Royal Ascot Racing Club in 1998.

Sir Peter O'Sullevan – knighted in 1997 – had enjoyed a long association with the course. In 1944 he applied for a job with the Press Association, and as a test was asked to write a piece looking at prospects for the next Ascot meeting on 7 October. Three of his four selections won (the other broke down), including the 20–1 outsider Grand Opera, and he duly embarked on one of the great careers of racing journalism. His writing in the *Daily Express* enriched his readers both literally and figuratively, but it was as a television commentator that he became known as 'The Voice of Racing', his distinctive tones – described by journalist Russell Davies as a 'hectic drawl' – providing the soundtrack to so many indelible Ascot memories. He first commentated on the Royal Meeting in 1953, and for the next forty-four years was, for viewers at home, almost as much a part of Ascot week as the Royal Procession. In the *Sporting Life* in June 1996, John Sexton wrote:

> There are some things that are instinctively right. One of them is Royal Ascot with Peter O'Sullevan commentating for the BBC. Say what you like, it is a match made in heaven … The O'Sullevan voice and the BBC's generally deferential approach to this Great British event are so perfect and so much a part of the scene that you feel sorry for those who have never known it.

Ascot also has special associations for O'Sullevan as an owner. His great sprinter Be Friendly won the King's Stand Stakes in 1967 – 'Winning a race at Royal Ascot had seemed a totally unattainable dream,' he wrote – and in December 2001 his hurdler Never, trained in France by François Doumen, won the Gerrard Novices' Hurdle (formerly the Kennel Gate Novices' Hurdle) to give him the fiftieth winner in his colours.

The Royal Ascot Racing Club was set up in 1998 as a top-of-the-range racing club but, uniquely, with its own viewing stand and lounges with first-class catering behind. Membership also gave an interest in six horses in training whose careers were managed by Harry Herbert, son of the Queen's racing manager Lord Carnarvon. In 1999 Brancaster was second in the Craven Stakes and fourth in the Two Thousand Guineas, while the same year Siege was runner-up in the Britannia Handicap at Royal Ascot and in the John Smith's Cup at York. In August 2000 the club's two-year-old colt Bannister won the Gimcrack Stakes at York. (Lord Carnarvon himself, who died suddenly in September 2001, enjoyed much success at Royal Ascot, where his wins included – in addition to Little Wolf's 1983 Gold Cup – the St James's Palace

The Aga Khan (left) and trainer Sir Michael Stoute debrief jockey Kieren Fallon after the victory of Kalanisi in the Queen Anne Stakes in June 2000.

Stakes with Tamerlane back in 1955 and the Queen Mary Stakes in 1992 with the 'Pocket Rocket' Lyric Fantasy.)

In 1999 the Bessborough Stakes, the one-and-a-half-mile handicap for three-year-olds at the Royal Meeting, was renamed the Duke of Edinburgh Stakes. The race formerly known as the Duke of Edinburgh Stakes, a six-furlong event for two-year-olds at the October meeting which in 1972 had been won by the future dual Champion Hurdler Sea Pigeon, was dropped when the October meeting was reduced from two days to one in 1999. Fittingly, the first winner of the new incarnation of the Duke of Edinburgh Stakes was the Queen's colt Blueprint, ridden by the top American jockey Gary Stevens, then riding for Sir Michael Stoute. (The trainer had been knighted in 1998 for his services to tourism in his native Barbados.)

Blueprint was the Queen's seventeenth winner at Royal Ascot as sovereign, the latest in a line stretching back to Choir Boy in the 1953 Royal Hunt Cup forty-six years earlier and including such equine luminaries as Landau (Rous Memorial Stake 1954), Aureole (Hardwicke Stakes 1954), Pall Mall (New Stakes 1957), Almeria (Ribblesdale Stakes 1957), Above Suspicion (St James's Palace Stakes 1959) and Hopeful Venture (Hardwicke Stakes 1968).

The year 2000 marked the start of a new millennium and brought to Royal Ascot for the Prince of Wales's Stakes the appropriately named

Jockeys entering the parade ring for the Ribblesdale Stakes at Royal Ascot, 1999.

Godolphin colt who most experts agree was one of the finest racehorses ever seen at the royal course: Dubai Millennium. Originally called Yaazer, the colt had been renamed by Sheikh Mohammed once it became apparent – before he ever raced – that this was a horse way out of the ordinary, one fit to be aimed at the Dubai World Cup (which like Godolphin had been the Sheikh's brainchild) in millennium year.

Dubai Millennium won his only race as a two-year-old at Yarmouth, and at three in 1999 lost just once (in the Derby) in six races: his victories included a six-length demolition of Almushtarak in the Queen Elizabeth II Stakes. He was then trained for the Dubai World Cup at Nad Al Sheba in March 2000, where, ridden by Frankie Dettori, he turned in an astonishing performance, leading all the way and keeping going with such power that some of the best middle-distance horses in the world could get nowhere near him. He won by six lengths from the American horse Behrens, leading Sir Michael Stoute to observe, 'On Dubai World Cup night I thought he was the best horse I'd ever seen' – which coming from the trainer of Shergar is a major compliment.

The Prince of Wales's Stakes at Royal Ascot was upgraded to Group One for the first time in 2000 and switched from the Tuesday to the Wednesday (thereby allowing each day of the Royal Meeting to have a Group One race: St James's Palace Stakes on Tuesday, Prince of Wales's Stakes on Wednesday, Gold Cup on Thursday and Coronation Stakes on Friday). With Frankie Dettori still recovering from his plane crash, the American jockey Jerry Bailey was brought over to ride Dubai Millennium, who despite his outstanding form did not go off favourite. That position went to the brilliant French miler Sendawar, who started at 6–5, with Dubai Millennium marginally longer at 5–4 in a field of six.

Frankie Dettori and Sheikh Mohammed briefed Bailey before the race, suggesting that he simply let the horse have his head, and the result was as spectacular an individual performance as Ascot had seen for many a year. Once warmed up towards the end of the first furlong, Dubai Millennium galloped his rivals into the ground. Coming out of Swinley Bottom he had a lead of about three lengths over Sendawar, and by the entrance to the straight the margin had increased to four lengths, with the others already strung out behind like a row of washing. With the huge crowd yelling him home, Dubai Millennium simply powered on and on up the straight, and at the line had an eight-length margin over Sendawar. It was stupendous, just the sort of performance that brings out the rhapsodic best in Alastair Down in the *Racing Post*:

> Here, poured into two indelible minutes, was what this game can soar to – a once-in-a-lifetime vantage point from which you can look back down the years on the hundreds of thousands of thoroughbreds who have walked the earth and say with certainty that this horse has his place in a tiny handful of the most remarkable.

Quite a claim, but within six weeks there was another horse whose Ascot performance demanded he be included in that tiny handful.

Montjeu, who ran in the colours of Michael Tabor and was trained in France by John Hammond, was an established equine superstar when he came to Ascot for the 2000 King George VI and Queen Elizabeth Diamond Stakes, for which the prize fund was now increased to £750,000. In 1999 Montjeu had won the Prix du Jockey-Club, the Irish Derby and the Prix de l'Arc de Triomphe, and had opened his 2000 campaign by winning the Tattersalls Gold Cup at The Curragh and then the Grand Prix de Saint-Cloud.

King George day 2000 was already very special by the time Montjeu went into the stalls for the fiftieth running of this famous race. To mark that half century, and her own imminent 100th birthday six days later, the Queen Mother took part in a special royal procession with the Queen, to the delight of a record King George crowd of 36,604. Her carriage halted in front of the grandstand, where Pony Club members dressed in the colours carried by the forty-nine previous winners of the big race lined up to pay their respects. Lord Hartington then called for three cheers for Her Majesty before leading the crowd in a full-throated rendition of 'Happy Birthday to You'. It

Dubai Millennium receives the appreciation of trainer Saeed bin Suroor and sidelined Frankie Dettori after the colt's astonishing victory in the 2000 Prince of Wales's Stakes.

Stewards scrutinising the
action at Royal Ascot, 1998.

was an unusual – but wildly popular – Ascot moment, and it expressed not only the nation's affection for the Queen Mother, but also her special place in the history of Ascot. We have already seen how the course had been the venue for her 300th winner over jumps when Sunyboy landed the Fernbank Hurdle in February 1976. Her 400th came when Nearco Bay won a handicap chase at Uttoxeter in May 1994, and in October that year Ascot hosted a special lunch party – complete with her trainers and many of her horses – to celebrate this landmark. On Wednesday 3 April 2002, at the first Ascot fixture following her death on 30 March at the age of 101, Lord Hartington led a minute's silence in her memory.

Many of the huge crowd on King George day 2000 would have been content just to watch Montjeu in action, but those who felt compelled to back him at 3–1 on never had the slightest cause for concern. Michael Kinane kept the colt covered up until early in the straight, where he let out half an inch of rein and sat still as Montjeu cruised past his rivals, still on the bridle and contemptuous of Fantastic Light's efforts to stay with him. The winning margin was a length and a quarter, but Montjeu had never been out of a canter, and the manner of his victory invited comparisons with the similarly nonchalant King George stroll of Nijinsky thirty years earlier.

Now the racing world was in a fever of excitement over the prospect of a showdown between Montjeu and Dubai Millennium. Sheikh Mohammed proposed a match between the two over ten furlongs – with Ascot one of three possible venues, along with York and Newmarket – but scarcely was the ink dry on the edition of the *Racing Post* bearing this wondrous news than it was reported from Newmarket that the Godolphin colt had broken a hind leg in training and would not race again, though he had been saved for a career at stud. The match was off, but worse was to follow. In April 2001 Dubai Millennium contracted the equine disease grass sickness, and this great horse died on 29 April of that year. Ascot racegoers had been privileged to see him at his very peak.

Montjeu won his Arc prep, but then could run only fourth behind Sinndar in the big race itself. He nearly salvaged his reputation when beaten half a length by Kalanisi in the Champion Stakes, then ran unplaced in the Breeders' Cup Turf at Churchill Downs before retiring to the Coolmore Stud in Ireland. Despite those disappointments late in his career, he was a superb horse the day he won the King George.

The other great Ascot performer in 2000 was Giant's Causeway, who ran twice at the course. Nicknamed the 'Iron Horse' in tribute to his battling quality, he won the St James's Palace Stakes by a head from Valentino, the first leg in his extraordinary run of five Group One victories in a row. After Royal Ascot he won the Eclipse Stakes by a head from Kalanisi, the Sussex Stakes by three quarters of a length from Dansili, the International

The pre-racing picnic in the car park is a long-standing Ascot tradition.

Stakes by a head from Kalanisi (again!) and the Irish Champion Stakes by half a length from Greek Dance. The prospect of his landing a record six consecutive Group Ones in a season in the Queen Elizabeth II Stakes set the Ascot crowd buzzing, but after yet another sterling effort he went down by half a length to Observatory, who had been taken wide up the straight by jockey Kevin Darley to avoid getting into the sort of head-to-head that Giant's Causeway relished. Giant's Causeway was then beaten a neck by Tiznow in the Breeders' Cup Classic – a battling end to a battling career.

In August 2000 Ascot played host for the first time to the Shergar Cup, a contest between two teams representing Europe (captained by former England football manager Kevin Keegan) and the Rest of the World (captained by Les Benton, Chairman of the Dubai World Cup). This unusual event, brainchild of Peter Savill, chairman of the British Horseracing Board, had attracted scepticism when first staged at Goodwood in 1999, but the switch to Ascot gave it a considerable boost. Total prize money of £400,000 –

including two races with a £100,000 purse each – attracted a high standard of runners, and energetic sponsorship by the bookmaking company Blue Square generated such a level of advance interest that nearly 19,000 turned up for an unorthodox afternoon's sport.

The European team (whose horses were ridden by Frankie Dettori, Johnny Murtagh, Michael Kinane, Kevin Darley and Pat Eddery) beat the Rest of the World (Greg Hall, Damien Oliver, Mirco Demuro, Basil Marcus and Jumaat Saimee) easily by the points system in use, but the result was less important than the reaction of crowd, participants and press, which was almost uniformly positive. The late Graham Rock wrote in the *Observer* that 'in the sunshine at Ascot this unique event blossomed, and while some fine tuning will bring a closer finish, the event is destined to succeed.' In *The Times* Alan Lee wrote:

> Racing has a suspicious, reactionary community that instinctively resists change. Predictably the Shergar Cup initiative was belittled and beleaguered last week and derided by the hidebound. How delicious, then, that the event should triumph over such scepticism on Saturday, drawing a crowd that even exceeded Ascot's ambitions, producing a series of thrilling finishes and, most pertinently, confirming the untapped potential in promoting jockeys as the evangelists of racing among the young.

Graham Rock's hope for a closer finish was fulfilled in the 2001 Blue Square Shergar Cup. This time the contest was between jockeys rather than owners, and the Rest of the World team of David Flores, Norihiro Yokoyama, Craig Williams, Gerald Mosse and Frankie Dettori (captained by former Australian fast bowler Jeff Thomson) snatched the event from the Britain and Ireland squad of Mick Kinane, Johnny Murtagh, Pat Eddery, Kieren Fallon and Richard Hughes (captained by footballer-turned-actor Vinnie Jones) by 125 points to 115. The competition seemed to be going the way of Britain and Ireland until Flores, Yokoyama and Williams filled the first three places in the very last race.

No one pretended that the Shergar Cup would ever rival the Gold Cup or King George in the Ascot calendar, but it is an event that has generated a large amount of interest in racing – especially for a young audience – and looks set to stay.

A far less satisfactory day's racing came on Saturday 7 October 2000. Heavy rain had threatened the programme, but after an inspection of the course an hour before the scheduled first race the Stewards gave the go-ahead. That first race went to Sheikh Hamdan al Maktoum's two-year-old Nayef, a half brother to Nashwan who had won on his début at Newbury. At Ascot he sluiced through the heavy going and, in the words of the form book, 'went clear when given the office in the style of a Classic horse in the making'. As the runners for the second race, the Cornwallis Stakes due off at 2.00, were gathering at the start, the public address system gave out the urgent announcement that the stands had to be cleared. A bomb threat had been made at 1.50 to the switchboard at Charing Cross Hospital in London, using an authenticated codeword and stating that a device would explode in the Ascot grandstand at 2.11. The stands were evacuated – though the horses down at the five-furlong start could not return to the racecourse stables until the all-clear was given – and the decision made to abandon racing for the day so that a proper search could be made. No device was found.

Nayef did not, in the event, win a Classic, though he developed into a top-notch horse, returning to Ascot in September 2001 to win the Cumberland Lodge Stakes before going on to land the Champion Stakes at Newmarket.

The 2001 Royal Meeting produced one of the great Gold Cup finishes of recent memory, and so nearly a victory in the race at the fifth attempt for the popular stayer Persian Punch. This huge chestnut, trained by Desert Orchid's trainer David Elsworth, had compiled a remarkable record in the biggest staying races, with the notable exception of the biggest staying race of all. For some reason the Gold Cup at Ascot had consistently brought disappointment, and he had not even gone close, finishing twelfth in 1997, sixth in 1998, twelfth again in 1999 and sixth again in 2000. Victory at last at the age of eight would have raised the Ascot roof, and for much of the race it seemed possible. Starting at 10–1, Persian Punch adopted his usual front-running role for most of the early part of the race, and with five furlongs to go Richard Quinn seized the initiative by kicking for home and going six lengths clear.

The Frankie Dettori flying dismount – here deployed after winning the 2001 Prince of Wales's Stakes on Fantastic Light.

But by the entrance to the straight Royal Rebel and Marienbard were breathing down his neck. The three were line abreast for a few strides, then Marienbard faded and Royal Rebel – owned by Peter Savill – forged half a length ahead. Persian Punch was not finished with, however, and fought back like a lion throughout the final furlong as his thousands of supporters in the stands worked themselves into hysterics. The winning post came just in time for Royal Rebel, who held on to win by a head. Gamely as the winner had fought, it was one of those races when most of the crowd wished the verdict had gone the other way.

If that was the race of the 2001 Royal Meeting, the individual performance of the week came when the Godolphin five-year-old Fantastic Light – winner of the Emirates World Series in 2000 after landing the Hong Kong Cup at Sha Tin – took the second running of the Prince of Wales's Stakes as a Group One event. Beating Kalanisi, Hightori and Observatory with a searing turn of foot was top-class form, and made Fantastic Light a leading candidate for the King George the following month.

Here he met the hero of the moment in Galileo, who had won the Derby and the Irish Derby in devastating fashion – the *Racing Post* had headlined its front-page Derby report 'PERFECTION' – and seemed on the brink of true greatness. A son of Sadler's Wells out of the 1993 Arc winner Urban Sea, Galileo ran in the dark blue colours of Mrs Susan Magnier but was in effect a flag-bearer for the huge racing and bloodstock operation based at the Coolmore Stud in County Tipperary, which had been developed in the mid 1970s by Robert Sangster, Vincent O'Brien and John Magnier (Vincent O'Brien's son-in-law) and was now fronted by Magnier and Michael Tabor. Galileo, like all the Coolmore horses, was trained by

Aidan O'Brien, who had moved into the famous training centre at Ballydoyle when Vincent O'Brien (no relation) retired.

Galileo versus Fantastic Light was Coolmore versus Godolphin – a battle of the Titans that drew a record Diamond Day crowd of 38,410 to Ascot and was broadcast live in the USA as part of the ESPN Sports Network's coverage of the Emirates World Series races: an estimated 23 million homes tuned in for the race.

A little local difficulty in Ireland over a suspension that would have prevented Michael Kinane riding Galileo was sorted out with an injunction in the High Court in Dublin, and twelve runners faced the starter for what, according to the betting, was a lap of honour, or at the very best a two-horse race. Galileo was 2–1 on and Fantastic Light 7–2, with the third horse in the market, Prix du Jockey-Club winner Anabaa Blue, way out at 18–1.

There were distinct shades of Grundy and Bustino about this race. For one thing, it was a clash of generations – the three-year-old Derby and Irish Derby winner against the best older horse around – but the comparison did not end there. For a few heart-pounding strides in the straight, as first Galileo and then Fantastic Light emerged from the pack and the pair went eyeball to eyeball, a repeat of the 1975 epic seemed to be taking place – only for Fantastic Light to reach the limit of his stamina and falter, allowing Galileo, getting stuck into a real battle for the first time in his racing career, to dig deep, forge clear and win by two lengths, leaving Fantastic Light to finish King George runner-up for the second year running. The *Racing Post* front page the following day summed up a memorable race in just three letters: 'WOW!'

Sheikh Mohammed conceded that 'We were beaten by a better horse,' adding wistfully that 'Fantastic Light is a very good horse – but he is not Dubai Millennium', while Clerk of the Course Nick Cheyne declared, without much fear of contradiction, that 'Anyone who saw the race will remember it for a very long time. It was without a doubt the best King George that I have seen since I have been working here.'

Galileo and Fantastic Light met again in the Irish Champion Stakes at Leopardstown over a mile and quarter early in September, and over the shorter distance Fantastic Light took his revenge, winning by a head after a wonderful duel up the straight. He went on to win the Breeders' Cup Turf at

The bell rung to instruct jockeys to mount in the parade ring. The other bell familiar to modern Ascot racegoers is rung when the runners are coming into the straight – a tradition which stretches back to the time when spectators were allowed on the course and needed to be cleared away before the horses bore down on them.

Galileo (Michael Kinane) starts to pull clear of Fantastic Light (Frankie Dettori) in the 2001 King George VI and Queen Elizabeth Diamond Stakes.

Belmont Park, while on the same day Galileo could finish only sixth in the Breeders' Cup Classic, his first race on dirt.

The victory of Galileo, who followed Swain, Daylami and Montjeu as a King George winner of the highest class, is an appropriate moment to consider the objective evidence for the quality of the race – and indeed of Ascot's Flat racing in general.

A measure of a racehorse's merit is provided by the annual International Classifications, rankings agreed by a panel of handicappers from the major racing countries around the globe. Each of the leading horses in different categories is given a rating based on the number of pounds it would carry in a hypothetical international handicap, and by this measure the King George is demonstrably the highest-class race run in Britain during the Flat season – and often the top race in the world. The runners in the 1997 renewal which brought together Helissio, Singspiel, Pilsudski and Swain averaged an International Classification ranking at the end of that year of 130.25, making it the highest-class race ever assessed by that measure. Of the twelve highest-rated Flat races in Britain over the three years 1999 to 2001, no fewer than five are run at Ascot – King George, Prince of Wales's Stakes, Queen Elizabeth II Stakes, Coronation Stakes and St James's Palace Stakes. If you take the average ranking of the top five races at each of the world's major racecourses, Ascot comes top of the table, ahead of Longchamp and Belmont Park.

In 2001 it was not only King George day that saw new attendance records. At the Royal Meeting, Ladies' Day brought 72,589 people through the gates, the largest recorded crowd in the history of racing at Ascot. Friday marked a new high for the fourth day of the meeting – 60,852. Overall attendance for the four days was 233,808, the second biggest total ever. (Of that number, just thirty-four were arrested for minor offences, proving the effectiveness of Ascot's policing and security arrangements.)

Tote turnover at Royal Ascot marked a new high in 2001 with around £7 million wagered (compare that with the £227,711 back in 1931), and the betting market at the meeting maintained its position as one of the biggest

The Royal Ascot betting ring, 2001.

events in the punter's calendar, with some monstrous wagers being struck. Wednesday produced the week's biggest result when Mozart was backed down from 9–2 in the morning to 7–4 at the off before winning the Jersey Stakes, a result estimated to have relieved bookmakers around the country of £2 million, of which some £300,000 was removed from the Ascot betting ring itself – including one single bet of £50,000 to £25,000. The following day Johannesburg won the Norfolk Stakes in the same Michael Tabor colours to take another £200,000 from the on-course bookies. It is a mark of the strength of the Royal Ascot betting market that, despite such reverses, most bookmakers declared that they had enjoyed a reasonably good week!

Sodexho, the company that looks after most of the catering at the course, reported a large increase in turnover at the meeting, confirming the description of Royal Ascot as 'Europe's biggest lunch party'. Racegoers during the Royal Meeting in 2001 consumed:

2.7 tonnes of beef
2.9 tonnes of fresh salmon
2.4 tonnes of smoked salmon
6,000 lobsters
4.5 tonnes of strawberries
550 gallons of cream

Fancy a drink with your lunch? Thirsty racegoers got through:

120,000 bottles of champagne
75,000 bottles of wine
12,000 bottles of Pimms
14,000 pints of beer

The world's largest mobile pub – the Black Bull Inn – is brought to the Silver Ring at the Royal Meeting to ease the strain on the course's 106 bars, many of

which are named after the great racehorses to have run at the course over the decades, such as Mill Reef and Brigadier Gerard in the Members' Enclosure; The Minstrel and Troy in the paddock area; royal heroes Aureole, Persimmon, Doutelle and Pall Mall in the grandstand; Busted, Alcide, Arkle, Tulyar, Pinza, Botticelli, Ragusa, Alycidon, Park Top and Ballymoss in the Silver Ring. Staffing all these catering outlets is an army of some 4,500 people who make up a large proportion of the 6,000 employed during the Royal Meeting. (The permanent staff at Ascot number about seventy.)

But Ascot is about much more than just the Royal Meeting, and the programme during the rest of the year has been constantly ringing the changes to give racegoers maximum enjoyment. In keeping with its tradition of ancillary activities over the centuries, modern Ascot goes out of its way to provide entertainment beyond the racetrack itself. For example, the Hong Kong day on the Sunday of King George weekend 2001 – which featured the Hong Kong Stakes, richest five-furlong handicap in Europe – was promoted as 'an exotic day for the whole family to enjoy' and included displays of traditional Chinese arts, including dragon and lion dancing and acrobatics. There was a Hong Kong Village, which featured demonstrations of ancient Oriental crafts, from calligraphy to fortune-telling and noodle-making, and the Hong Kong Jockey Club offered special 'Fortune Windmills' to the first 9,000 people through the gate.

In the same vein, the Festival of British Racing in 2001 – sponsored by the new betting exchange company Betdaq – had dodgems, a carousel, inflated run-around and helter-skelter among many other attractions for those to whom the effect of the draw over six furlongs is of limited interest.

Yet these days it is not enough for a racecourse to think of itself just as a racecourse, and Ascot has become much more aware than it was a generation ago of the necessity for catering for non-racing activities. By the turn of the new millennium the course facilities were in use some 300 days a year for purposes other than horse racing – conferences, social functions, exhibitions and trade fairs. The Ascot Jazz Festival on the course in July 1998 had familiar names like Cleo Laine and Jools Holland on stage, while in the same month Lesley Garrett and Gloria Gaynor also appeared in other concerts at the course.

In April 1998 Lord Hartington revealed that major changes were being contemplated at Ascot, and since then the plans have gradually taken shape – to the point where a specific scheme was due to be unveiled after Royal Ascot in 2002, with a proposed completion date of 2007 (though the building schedule would, as before, be worked around the retention of the Royal Meeting at the course).

The existing stands are to be replaced and the course realigned accordingly, and with such extensive redevelopment in mind Ascot has scoured the globe for ideas and inspiration. Special care has been taken to consult those closely involved, such as the local community and racegoers, and including a total of forty-six different groups of people who have been and continue to be consulted about their own particular requirements.

This redevelopment has been driven by Ascot's commitment to enhancing its already pre-eminent position in world racing, and one major aim is to attract more runners at the course from other racing spheres – to achieve what Douglas Erskine-Crum calls 'our intercontinental ambitions'. There have already been moves in this direction. The first Japanese-trained runner at Royal Ascot was Agnes World in the 2000 King's Stand Stakes (though the first Japanese runner in the King George was Speed Symboli back in 1969), Hong Kong-trained Indigenous ran unplaced in the 1999 King George, and the occasional challenger from the USA has crossed the Atlantic in recent years.

As racing grows increasingly intercontinental, Ascot is bent on holding a position in the front rank of world racecourses, and in order to do so it must provide an even, consistent racing surface. To achieve this, the course has had to address a longstanding problem. It is a peculiarity of Ascot that one of the world's greatest racecourses has no fewer than six crossings: clockwise from the grandstand, they are the crossing from No. 1 Car Park to the inside of the track; the Kennel Gate crossing (on the run down to Swinley Bottom); the crossing at Swinley Bottom itself; Holloway's Crossing (between the fourth and third last steeplechase fences); the golf course crossing; and the Winkfield Road, which intersects the Straight Mile just short of the junction with the round course. If Ascot is to provide a world-class racing terrain it must minimise the effects of these crossings. Major steps have already been taken, and more plans are afoot.

The Movable Turf Crossing (MTC) at Kennel Gate, which allows for a complete section of racetrack to be removed to reveal the road beneath, was used for the first time at the jumps meeting in November 2000, following trials in which top jockey Mick Fitzgerald had ridden horses across the mobile piece of ground and declared himself 'very impressed': crucially, the crossing was indistinguishable from the rest of the track.

The eventual aim is to eradicate all the crossings on the racecourse, either by an MTC or an underpass – the latter the likely solution at the Winkfield Road crossing. At present the course is restricted by the 1948 Ascot Race Course Act to shutting the road half an hour before the start of racing, and the only covering that can be applied under such circumstances is the laying down of sixty-two mats, each three feet wide by sixty-two feet long, bedded together with Polytrack (the synthetic material used on the all-weather circuit at Lingfield Park) and then covered in grass cuttings.

Any tunnel built under the Winkfield Road will be part of a fresh realignment of the course in order to make room for the proposed redevelopment of the stands. After the consideration of various possibilities, the likelihood is that the Straight Mile will be repositioned so that the one-mile start remains in the same place, but the rest of the course pivots to the north, relocating the round Flat course and the jumping course at the winning post about forty metres north of where they are at present. Such a move would retain the essential nature of Ascot as a racecourse – for example, the rise from the Golden Gate to the finish, and a similar gradient from Swinley Bottom – which is so much a part of its excellence.

Removal of the crossings and deployment of the latest developments in turf technology should make the Ascot track a world-class racing surface – a course comfortable with its long history and royal tradition yet constantly closing on that ambition to be, beyond argument, one of the five best racecourses in the world.

The Movable Turf Crossing at Kennel Gate.

Tony McCoy on Wahiba Sands leads Jim Culloty on subsequent Cheltenham Gold Cup winner Best Mate at the final fence of the First National Gold Cup in November 2001 – McCoy's 157th winner of a season in which his 289 smashed Gordon Richards's record of 269, set on the Flat in 1947.

Such an aspiration is not realised by reliving the glories of the past, and for all the great horses and remarkable characters woven into the tapestry of Ascot history, the present pre-eminent position of the racecourse is the result of the transformation of Ascot as a business over the last decade. The course's pre-tax profit has increased from less than £1 million in 1991 to nearly £11 million in 2001, and a measure of the success of the current management team is that over the five-year period from 1997 to 2001 turnover at the course increased by 81 per cent and pre-tax profit by 83 per cent.

Those inclined to grumble that talk of turnover and pre-tax profit is a far cry from Omaha and Quashed should remember that only by achieving such

results can Ascot afford the present level of prize money and the exciting plans for the future. Without business success, the redevelopment scheme would be no more than a pipe-dream, and the course would be struggling to maintain its position on the national stage, never mind aspiring to be one of the world's leading courses.

In order to maintain this momentum, in the autumn of 2001 Ascot successfully applied to the High Court to update its business structure through incorporation, allowing for much greater scope in raising funds for investment than was possible before. Lord Hartington declared:

> In keeping with the original intention of the 1913 Act, Ascot's priority is the success, welfare and prosperity of Ascot Racecourse. A key part of this is the redevelopment and modernisation of Ascot to ensure it maintains its position as a world-class racecourse. The ability to update our business structure, through incorporation, is an important milestone in this next era for Ascot.

Incorporation did not mean any loosening of the bond between Ascot and the sovereign. The Crown Estate owns the racecourse, which is leased to the Ascot Authority until 2045, and the three Trustees – in 2002 Lord Hartington, Johnny Weatherby (Chairman of Weatherbys) and businessman and Jockey Club member Mark Davies – are responsible for running the Ascot Authority, which operates under the ultimate control and direction of the Queen. Ascot started life in 1711 as a royal racecourse, and will remain so.

A significant moment in the history of the Royal Meeting came with the announcement that the 2002 fixture would be expanded to five days – Tuesday to Saturday – to celebrate the Queen's Golden Jubilee, with the Cork and Orrery Stakes being renamed the Golden Jubilee Stakes and upgraded to Group One, thereby having a Group One event on each of the five days. Prize money of over £3 million would be on offer at the meeting, which would be a one-off, Royal Ascot reverting to the traditional four days in 2003.

In this move, as in so much else, the present Ascot management has shown itself comfortable with history and tradition yet alive to the need to

respond to a changing world with flexibility and innovation. The afterglow of the Royal Meeting in 2001 saw Laura Thompson write in the *Racing Post:*

> For most people, the meeting is a delight, a place that they yearn to inhabit, a golden time suspended from real life for which they plan (dress/hat/shoes/matching bag/hire car/six for the price of five vintage champagne/organic guacamole/awning) with the attention to detail given by Napoleon to the Battle of Austerlitz.
>
> Royal Ascot racegoers might not always quite know what to do with themselves when they actually get on the course. But, boy, do they want to be there. For Ascot has learned how to perform an immaculate two-step: it has moved into the present while never, for a moment, forgetting that what it offers is an image of the past.
>
> This is demonstrably the most successful way in which to market the sport to the world outside. People who are not remotely interested in racing are nonetheless fascinated by the idea of it, by an image of it which Royal Ascot magically embodies. One dresses up, one swans around all day among top hats and bright colours, one has picnics, one cheers when Frankie Dettori does his wretched leap, one reverts cosily to the class system of a century ago. These are all things that, given half a chance, the British love to do, and that racing – being a world unto itself – allows.

Modern ambitions will not displace the course's sense of the past, and the current management is committed to maintaining that balance between tradition and innovation which makes Ascot a unique sporting venue – and Royal Ascot a unique social occasion.

It is a safe bet that one Ascot tradition will not change – that the Queen Anne Stakes will continue to be run in memory of the monarch who founded the course nearly three centuries ago. As the starting stalls slam open and the horses thunder up the Straight Mile, who's to say that they won't be joined by a ghostly carriage driven by a prodigiously fat spectre – 'a mighty hunter like Nimrod' frenetically urging her horse on?

APPENDICES

ROYAL MEETING

THE QUEEN ANNE STAKES (Group 2)

Distance: 1 mile (Straight Mile)
For 3-year-olds and upwards

First run in 1840 as The Trial Stakes.
Renamed The Queen Anne Stakes in 1930.

YEAR	WINNER	SIRE	OWNER	TRAINER	JOCKEY	SECOND	THIRD	RUNNERS	SP
1946	Royal Charger	Nearco	Sir John Jarvis	J Jarvis	E Smith	Langton Abbot	Dagworthy	5	5–6
1947	Woodruffe	Bois Roussel	J A Dewar	F Darling	C Richards	Swiss Flower	Solina	8	7–1
1948	Solina	Fair Copy	Mme P Thomas-Moret	P Moret	J Doyasbere	Panair	Fast Soap	14	10–1
1949	Pambidian	Fairford	C R Harper	W Nightingall	G Richards	High Endeavour	Bel Amour II	10	7–4
1950	Garrick	Wyndham	Duchess of Norfolk	W Smyth	T Burns	Princess Trudy	Donore	10	20–1
1951	Neron	Nearco	HH Begum Aga Khan	H Wragg	D Greening	Ki Ming	Selector II	11	100–6
1952	Southborne	Mustang	A L Hawkings	P J Prendergast	G Richards	Miss Winston	Pareo	12	7–1
1953	Argur	Djebel	Marcel Boussac	J Glynn	E Mercer	King's Mistake	Tip the Bottle	11	7–4
1954	Upadee	Fairfax	T McCairns	B Gallivan	T Burns	Big Berry	L'Ange du Lude	11	100–6
1955	Golden Planet	Solonaway	P Bartholomew	F N Winter	D Smith	Tip the Bottle	Chamier	6	7–1
1956	Kandy Sauce	Hard Sauce	Sir Victor Sassoon	N Murless	D Smith	Venus Slipper	Olean II	11	10–1
1957	Baron's Folly	Blue Peter	H Leggat	P Beasley	E Britt	Fairy Stone	Westmarsh	10	100–7
1958	Teynham	Wilwyn	R C Boucher	G Colling	D Morris	Tharp	Quorum	8	15–2
1959	Lucky Guy	Pink Flower	Joseph McGrath	S McGrath	J Sime	Rexequus	Glyndebourne	9	100–8
1960	Blast	Djebe	R N Richmond-Watson	A Budgett	W Snaith	Givenaway	Fagus	12	100–7
1961	Amber Light	Borealis	E R Hill	F N Winter	D Smith	Lucky Guy	Abat Jour	10	9–1
1962	Nereus	Neron	P N Robinson	K Cundell	P Robinson	Le Prince	Persian Wonder	11	8–1
1963	Welsh Rake	Abernant	J Philipps	J Jarvis	R Hutchinson	Agreement	My Myosotis	12	8–1
1964	Princelone	Princely Gift	A J Allen	W Nightingall	R Maddock	Piccadilly	Crepone	8	100–8
1965	Showdown	Infatuation	D Prenn	F N Winter	D Smith	Pally	Noble Record	9	5–4
1966	Tesco Boy	Princely Gift	J E Cohen	S Ingham	R Hutchinson	Orabella II	Great Nephew	10	8–1
1967	Good Match	Match III	G Dudley	J Tree	D East	Arenaria	Town Life	13	6–1
1968	Virginia Gentleman	Crocket	James F Lewis	D Smith	A Barclay	Frankincense	Starry Halo	10	9–2
1969	Town Crier	Sovereign Path	Evelyn de Rothschild	P Walwyn	D Keith	Jimmy Reppin	Grey Portal	8	11–2
1970	Welsh Pageant	Tudor Melody	H J Joel	N Murless	A Barclay	Fred Babu	Corrieghoil	6	30–100
1971	Roi Soleil	Skymaster	Mrs D Riley-Smith	C Bartholomew	J Lindley	Mon Plaisir	Gold Rod	7	11–4
1972	Sparkler	Hard Tack	Mrs M Mehl-Mulhens	F Armstrong	L Piggott	Calshot Light	Rocket	8	9–4
1973	Sun Prince	Princely Gift	Sir Michael Sobell	Major W R Hern	J Mercer	Sparkler	Parachuting	4	3–1
1974	Brook	Birdbrook	Dr C Vittadini	M Bennetti	B Taylor	My Friend Paul	Coup de Feu	11	12–1
1975	Imperial March	Forli	Walter F Mullady	M V O'Brien	G Dettori	Deerslayer	Boldboy	11	2–1
1976	Ardoon	Track Spare	F Feeney	G Pritchard-Gordon	B Taylor	Record Token	Boldboy	9	11–2
1977	Jellaby	Pals Passage	Essa Alkhalifa	H R Price	B Taylor	Lord Helpus	Free State	8	9–4
1978	Radetzky	Huntercombe	C Elliot	C Brittain	E Hide	Ovac	Gwent	9	25–1
1979	Baptism	Northfields	J H Whitney	J Tree	L Piggott	Pearlescent	Boitron	9	6–1
1980	Blue Refrain	Majority Blue	Mrs L Wood	C Benstead	B Rouse	New Berry	Foveros	11	8–1
1981	Belmont Bay	Auction Ring	D Wildenstein	H Cecil	L Piggott	Last Fandango	Slenderhagen	10	4–1
1982	Mr Fluorocarbon	Morston	J McAllister	H Cecil	L Piggott	Noalcoholic	Spanish Pool	10	3–1
1983	Valiyar	Red God	Garo Vanian	H Cecil	Pat Eddery	Montekin	Noalcoholic	10	10–1
1984	Trojan Fen	Troy	S S Niarchos	H Cecil	L Piggott	Welsh Idol	Cormorant Wood	6	9–4
1985	Rousillon	Riverman	K Abdullah	G Harwood	G Starkey	Celestial Bounty	King Of Clubs	8	11–4
1986	Pennine Walk	Persian Bold	Mrs Maria I Niarchos	J Tree	Pat Eddery	Efisio	Teleprompter	9	5–2
1987	Then Again	Jaazeiro	R J Shannon	L Cumani	R Cochrane	Water Cay	Sonic Lady	6	4–5
1988	Waajib	Try My Best	Hamdan Al Maktoum	A Stewart	M Roberts	Soviet Star	Then Again	5	5–2
1989	Warning	Known Fact	K Abdullah	G Harwood	Pat Eddery	Reprimand	Sweet Chesne	7	2–5
1990	Markofdistinction	Known Fact	Gerald Leigh	L Cumani	L Dettori	Mirror Black	Distant Relative	9	7–1
1991	Sikeston	Lear Fan	Luciano Gaucci	C Brittain	M Roberts	Rami	Fair Average	11	9–1
1992	Lahib	Riverman	Hamdan Al Maktoum	J Dunlop	W Carson	Second Set	Sikeston	9	100–30
1993	Alflora	Niniski	Circlechart Ltd	C Brittain	M Kinane	Inner City	Hazaam	9	20–1
1994	Barathea	Sadler's Wells	Sheikh Mohammed	L Cumani	M Kinane	Emperor Jones	Gabr	10	3–1
1995	Nicolotte	Night Shift	Mollers Racing	G Wragg	M Hills	Nijo	Soviet Line	7	16–1
1996	Charnwood Forest	Warning	Godolphin	S bin Suroor	M Kinane	Restructure	Mistle Cat	9	10–11
1997	Allied Forces	Miswaki	Godolphin	S bin Suroor	L Dettori	Centre Stalls	Ali-Royal	11	10–1
1998	Intikhab	Red Ransom	Godolphin	S bin Suroor	L Dettori	Among Men	Poteen	9	9–4
1999	Cape Cross	Green Desert	Godolphin	S bin Suroor	G Stevens	Docksider	Almushtarak	8	7–1
2000	Kalanisi	Doyoun	HH Aga Khan	Sir Michael Stoute	K Fallon	Dansili	Swallow Flight	11	11–2
2001	Medicean	Machiavellian	Cheveley Park Stud Ltd	Sir Michael Stoute	K Fallon	Swallow Flight	Arkadian Hero	10	11–2

THE KING'S STAND STAKES (Group 2)

Distance: 5 furlongs
For 3-year-olds and upwards

First run in 1860 over the 2-year-old course of about 6 furlongs.
Distance reduced to 5 furlongs in 1907.

YEAR	WINNER	SIRE	OWNER	TRAINER	JOCKEY	SECOND	THIRD	RUNNERS	SP
1946	Vilmorin	Gold Bridge	John Read	J Lawson	C Richards	Golden Cloud	Royal Charger	7	10–1
1947	Greek Justice	Fair Trial	J A Dewar	F Darling	G Richards	Julius	Port Blanc	10	100–30
1948	Squander Bug	Gold Bridge	Mrs E P Moss	M Collins	W Rickaby	Careless Nora	Port Blanc	15	33–1
1949	Abernant	Owen Tudor	Major R Macdonald-Buchanan	N Murless	G Richards	Cul de Sac	Robert Barker	7	4–6
1950	Tangle	Mustang	Lady Baron	W Payne	E Smith	Abernant	Skylarking II	3	3–1
1951	Stephen Paul	Panorama	J Olding	H Persse	N Sellwood	Hard Sauce	Make Tracks	12	7–2
1952	Easter Bride	Emir d'Iran	W J Rimell	T R Rimell	E Fordyce	Set Fair	Todman	6	7–1
1953	Fairy Flax	Pensive	R S Clarke	J Lawson	A Breasley	La Ronde	Spaghetti	13	20–1
1954	Golden Lion	Golden Cloud	W T Barrett	C Mitchell	B Swift	Urshalim	Four Of Spades	11	10–1
1955	Pappa Fourway	Pappageno II	Mrs E Goldson	W Dutton	W H Carr	Democratic	Ginger Quill	5	4–7
1956	Palariva	Palestine	H H Aga Khan	A Head	R Poincelet	Vigo	Edmundo	14	6–1
1957	Right Boy	Impeccable	G A Gilbert	W Dutton	L Piggott	Edmundo	Nanavati	8	4–1
1958	Drum Beat	Fair Trial	J S Gerber	W A O'Gorman	A Breasley	Texana	Abelia	5	2–1
1959	Chris	Vilmorin	H F Hartley	W Nevett	J Sime	Welsh Abbot	Krakenwake	8	9–4
1960	Sound Track	Whistler	Lady Hemphill	A S O'Brien	A Breasley	Sing Sing	Monet	8	8–1
1961	Silver Tor	Grey Sovereign	Stanhope Joel	R Fetherstonhaugh	G Lewis	Floribunda	Tin Whistle	8	7–4
1962	Cassarate	Abernant	Countess Margit Batthyany	M V O'Brien	N Sellwood	La Tendresse	Silver Tor	7	5–1
1963	Majority Rule	Democratic	J Muldoon	W A O'Gorman	L Piggott	Matatina	My Goodness Me	9	100–8
1964	*race abandoned*								
1965	Goldhill	Le Dieu d'Or	R G Johnson	M H Easterby	J Etherington	Spaniards Mount	Golden Apollo	11	10–1
1966	Roughlyn	Ballylinan	J D Pickering	W D Francis	G Cadwaladr	Zahedan	Washington	10	20–1
1967	Be Friendly	Skymaster	P J O'Sullevan	C Mitchell	A Breasley	Yours	Heavenly Sound	10	3–1
1968	D'Urberville	Klairon	J H Whitney	J Tree	J Mercer	So Blessed	Porto Bello	12	4–1
1969	Song	Sing Sing	Bryan P Jenks	D Candy	J Mercer	Excessive	Be Friendly	8	Evens
1970	Amber Rama	Jaipur	Arpad Plesch	F Mathet	Y Saint-Martin	Huntercombe	Balidar	11	4–1
1971	Swing Easy	Delta Judge	J H Whitney	J Tree	L Piggott	Mummy's Pet	Calahorra	9	7–1
1972	Sweet Revenge	Compensation	Mrs B Attenborough	T Corbett	G Lewis	Abergwaun	Montgomery	7	7–2
1973	Abergwaun	Bounteous	C A B St George	M V O'Brien	L Piggott	Marble Arch	Rapid River	7	7–4
1974	Bay Express	Polyfoto	P Cooper	P Nelson	B Taylor	Bitty Girl	Noble Mark	10	9–4
1975	Flirting Around	Round Table	Mrs A Hausmann	R Carver	Y Saint-Martin	Hot Spark	Auction Ring	12	9–2
1976	Lochnager	Dumbarnie	C Spence	W Easterby	E Hide	Realty	Hittite Glory	13	6–4
1977	Godswalk	Dancer's Image	R E Sangster	M V O'Brien	L Piggott	Girl Friend	Haveroid	11	4–6
1978	Solinus	Comedy Star	D Schwartz	M V O'Brien	L Piggott	Oscilight	Music Maestro	8	4–6
1979	Double Form	Habitat	Baroness H H Thyssen	R F Johnson Houghton	J Reid	Ahonoora	Golden Thatch	13	12–1
1980	African Song	African Sky	G Kaye	P Kelleway	Pat Eddery	Runnett	Abdu	14	10–1
1981	Marwell	Habitat	E Loder	M Stoute	W R Swinburn	Standaan	Runnett	12	5–4
1982	Fearless Lad	Import	G Soulsby	D Peacock	E Hide	Chellaston Park	Blue Singh	14	10–1
1983	Sayf El Arab	Drone	M Dabaghi	W A O'Gorman	M Thomas	Soba	On Stage	16	33–1
1984	Habibti	Habitat	M A Mutawa	J Dunlop	W Carson	Anitas Prince	Sayf El Arab	11	4–5
1985	Never So Bold	Bold Lad	E D Kessly	R W Armstrong	L Piggott	Primo Dominie	Committed	15	4–1
1986	Last Tycoon	Try My Best	R C Strauss	R Collet	C Asmussen	Double Schwartz	Gwydion	14	9–2
1987	Bluebird	Storm Bird	R E Sangster	M V O'Brien	C Asmussen	Perion	Orient	12	7–2
1988	Chilibang	Formidable	Mrs H J Heinz	J Dunlop	W Carson	Governor General	Ever Sharp	8	16–1
1989	Indian Ridge	Ahonoora	Mrs Anne Coughlan	D Elsworth	S Cauthen	Tigani	Gallic League	15	9–4
1990	Dayjur	Danzig	Hamdan Al Maktoum	Major W R Hern	W Carson	Ron's Victory	Lugana Beach	15	11–2
1991	Elbio	Precocious	Brian Brackpool	P J Makin	S Cauthen	Irish Shoal	Archway	10	13–8
1992	Sheikh Albadou	Green Desert	Hilal Salem	A A Scott	W R Swinburn	Mr Brooks	Elbio	10	7–2
1993	Elbio	Precocious	Brian Brackpool	P J Makin	W R Swinburn	Wolfhound	Paris House	8	12–1
1994	Lochsong	Song	J C Smith	I Balding	L Dettori	Blyton Lad	West Man	8	3–10
1995	Piccolo	Warning	John White and Partners	M Channon	R Hughes	Struggler	Mind Games	10	20–1
1996	Pivotal	Polar Falcon	Cheveley Park Stud	Sir Mark Prescott	G Duffield	Mind Games	Almaty	17	13–2
1997	Don't Worry Me	Dancing Dissident	M J F Gribomont	G Henrot	O Peslier	Titus Livius	Hever Golf Rose	18	33–1
1998	Bolshoi	Royal Academy	Mrs David Brown	J Berry	C Lowther	Lochangel	Lord Kintyre	19	10–1
1999	Mitcham	Hamas	T G Mills	TG Mills	T Quinn	Flanders	Sainte Marine	17	20–1
2000	Nuclear Debate	Geiger Counter	J R Chester	JE Hammond	G Mosse	Agnes World	Bertolini	23	16–1
2001	Cassandra Go	Indian Ridge	Trevor C Stewart	G Wragg	M Roberts	Misty Eyed	Funny Valentine	22	8–1

THE ST JAMES'S PALACE STAKES (Group 1)

Distance: 1 mile (Old Mile)
For 3-year-old colts

The inaugural race was run in 1833 and named in 1834. From its inception to 1998 the race was open to 3-year-old colts and fillies.

YEAR	WINNER	SIRE	OWNER	TRAINER	JOCKEY	SECOND	THIRD	RUNNERS	SP
1946	Khaled	Hyperion	HH Aga Khan	Frank Butters	G Richards	Aldis Lamp	Radiotherapy	5	2–1
1947	Tudor Minstrel	Owen Tudor	J A Dewar	F Darling	G Richards	Tite Street	Welsh Honey	3	6–100
1948	Black Tarquin	Rhodes Scholar	William Woodward	Capt C Boyd-Rochfort	E Britt	The Cobbler	Djerid	5	5–1
1949	Faux Tirage	Big Game	J A Dewar	N Murless	G Richards	Bobo	Prince Royal	8	11–10
1950	Palestine	Fair Trial	HH Aga Khan	M Marsh	C Smirke	Rising Flame	The Golden Road	4	4–7
1951	Turco II	Fighting Fox	William Woodward	Capt C Boyd-Rochfort	W H Carr	Kameran	Titian	10	7–1
1952	King's Bench	Court Martial	A J Tompsett	M Feakes	G Richards	Argur	Bob Major	7	3–1
1953	Nearula	Nasrullah	W Humble	Capt C Elsey	E Britt	Victory Roll	Masai King	6	4–6
1954	Darius	Dante	Sir Percy Loraine	H Wragg	E Mercer	Umberto	Narrator	7	Evens
1955	Tamerlane	Persian Gulf	Lord Porchester	N Bertie	A Breasley	Blue Blazes	Our Babu	5	8–11
1956	Pirate King	Prince Chevalier	Major L B Holliday	H Cottrill	D Smith	Buisson Ardent	Ratification	6	6–1
1957	Chevastrid	Prince Chevalier	Joseph McGrath	S McGrath	J Eddery	Tempest	Pipe of Peace	5	8–1
1958	Major Portion	Court Martial	H J Joel	T Leader	E Smith	Guersillus	Bald Eagle	5	Evens
1959	Above Suspicion	Court Martial	HM The Queen	Capt C Boyd-Rochfort	W H Carr	Carnoustie	Piping Rock	5	9–4
1960	Venture VII	Relic	Exors of Prince Aly Khan	A Head	G Moore	Riverdare		2	1–33
1961	Tudor Treasure	King Of The Tudors	Lord Derby	J Watts	D Smith	Eagle	Test Case	9	11–4
1962	Court Sentence	Court Martial	H J Joel	T Leader	E Smith	Sovereign Lord	Cyrus	8	100–8
1963	Crocket	King Of The Tudors	D G Van Clief	G Brooke	D Smith	Follow Suit	Ionian	10	9–2
1964	Roan Rocket	Buisson Ardent	T F C Frost	G Todd	L Piggott	Acer	New South Wales	8	5–4
1965	Silly Season	Tom Fool	Paul Mellon	I Balding	G Lewis	Kirsch Flambee	Sovereign Edition	12	5–1
1966	Track Spare	Sound Track	R E Mason	R Mason	J Lindley	Watergate	Double U Jay	7	100–9
1967	Reform	Pall Mall	Michael Sobell	G Richards	A Breasley	Chinwag	Bold Lad	5	4–6
1968	Petingo	Petition	Capt M Lemos	F Armstrong	L Piggott	Atopolis	Berber	3	10–11
1969	Right Tack	Hard Tack	J R Brown	J Sutcliffe jnr	G Lewis	Habitat	Murrayfield	4	4–6
1970	Saintly Song	Aureole	Stanhope Joel	N Murless	A Barclay	Gold Rod	Pithiviers	6	11–10
1971	Brigadier Gerard	Queen's Hussar	Mrs J Hislop	Major W R Hern	J Mercer	Sparkler	Good Bond	4	4–11
1972	Sun Prince	Princely Gift	Sir Michael Sobell	Major W R Hern	J Lindley	Home Guard	Grey Mirage	5	7–4
1973	Thatch	Forli	J Mulcahy	M V O'Brien	L Piggott	Owen Dudley		2	Evens
1974	Averof	Sing Sing	Capt M Lemos	C Brittain	B Taylor	Cellini	Hard Fighter	7	7–4
1975	Bolkonski	Balidar	C d'Alessio	H Cecil	G Dettori	Royal Manacle	Nurabad	8	4–5
1976	Radetzky	Huntercombe	C Elliot	C Brittain	Pat Eddery	Earth Spirit	Patris	8	16–1
1977	Don	Yellow God	E Ryan	W Elsey	E Hide	Marinsky	Tachypous	7	11–2
1978	Jaazeiro	Sham	R E Sangster	M V O'Brien	L Piggott	Persian Bold	Formidable	8	5–2
1979	Kris	Sharpen Up	Lord Howard de Walden	H Cecil	J Mercer	Young Generation	Alert	5	11–10
1980	Posse	Forli	Ogden Mills Phipps	J Dunlop	Pat Eddery	Final Straw	Last Fandango	8	11–2
1981	To-Agori-Mou	Tudor Music	Mrs A Muinos	G Harwood	G Starkey	Kings Lake	Bel Bolide	8	2–1
1982	Dara Monarch	Realm	Mrs L Browne	L Browne	M Kinane	Tender King	Ivano	9	7–2
1983	Horage	Tumble Wind	A Rachid	M McCormack	S Cauthen	Tolomeo	Dunbeath	7	18–1
1984	Chief Singer	Ballad Rock	J C Smith	R Sheather	R Cochrane	Keen	Kalim	8	85–40
1985	Bairn	Northern Baby	Sheikh Mohammed	L Cumani	L Piggott	Scottish Reel	Vin de France	8	6–4
1986	Sure Blade	Kris	Sheikh Mohammed	B Hills	B Thomson	Green Desert	Sharrood	7	9–2
1987	Half A Year	Riverman	John C Mabee	L Cumani	R Cochrane	Soviet Star	Risk Me	5	11–2
1988	Persian Heights	Persian Bold	HH Prince Yazid Saud	G A Huffer	Pat Eddery	Raykour	Caerwent	7	9–2
1989	Shaadi	Danzig	Sheikh Mohammed	M R Stoute	W R Swinburn	Greensmith	Scenic	5	6–4
1990	Shavian	Kris	Lord Howard de Walden	H Cecil	S Cauthen	Rock City	Lord Florey	8	11–1
1991	Marju	Last Tycoon	Hamdan Al Maktoum	J Dunlop	W Carson	Second Set	Hokusai	7	7–4
1992	Brief Truce	Irish River	Moyglare Stud Farms Ltd	D Weld	M Kinane	Zaahi	Ezzoud	8	25–1
1993	Kingmambo	Mr Prospector	S S Niarchos	F Boutin	C Asmussen	Needle Gun	Ventiquattrofogli	4	2–5
1994	Grand Lodge	Chief's Crown	Lord Howard de Walden	W Jarvis	M Kinane	Distant View	Turtle Island	9	6–1
1995	Bahri	Riverman	Hamdan Al Maktoum	J Dunlop	W Carson	Charnwood Forest	Vettori	9	11–4
1996	Bijou d'Inde	Cadeaux Genereux	J S Morrison	M Johnston	J Weaver	Ashkalani	Sorbie Tower	9	9–1
1997	Starborough	Soviet Star	Sheikh Mohammed	D Loder	L Dettori	Air Express	Daylami	8	11–2
1998	Dr Fong	Kris S	The Thoroughbred Corporation	H Cecil	K Fallon	Desert Prince	Duck Row	8	4–1
1999	Sendawar	Priolo	HH Aga Khan	A de Royer Dupre	G Mosse	Aljabr	Gold Academy	11	2–1
2000	Giant's Causeway	Storm Cat	Mrs John Magnier & M Tabor	A P O'Brien	M Kinane	Valentino	Medicean	11	7–2
2001	Black Minnaloushe	Storm Cat	Mrs John Magnier & M Tabor	A P O'Brien	J Murtagh	Noverre	Olden Times	11	8–1

THE QUEEN'S VASE (Group 3)

Distance: About 2 miles
For 3-year-olds.

First run in 1838 over 1 mile 4 furlongs as The Gold Vase. Extended to 2 miles 45 yards or 'about 2 miles' in 1839. Renamed in 1960. Prior to 1987 the race was open to 3-year-olds and upwards.

YEAR	WINNER	SIRE	OWNER	TRAINER	JOCKEY	SECOND	THIRD	RUNNERS	SP
1946	Look Ahead	Signal Light	Sir Humphrey de Trafford	Capt C Boyd-Rochfort	D Smith	Iona	Carassin	10	20–1
1947	Auralia	The Satrap	Mrs Alec Johnston	Reg Day	D Smith	Whiteway	Ford Transport	20	100–8
1948	Estoc	Jock	Marcel Boussac	C Semblat	R Bertiglia	Vulgan	Woodburn	20	7–2
1949	Lone Eagle	Isolator	William Woodward	Capt C Boyd-Rochfort	D Smith	Royal Empire	Fair Reproach	15	100–30
1950	Fastlad	Fastnet	Baron G de Waldner	P Carter	F Palmer	Rainfall	Consternation	19	100–6
1951	Faux Pas	Mieuxce	Mrs R Foster	J Lawson	E Smith	Snowdon	Shahanshah	15	6–1
1952	Souepi	Epigram	G R Digby	G R Digby	C Elliott	Kingsfold	Ksiri	21	100–7
1953	Absolve	Owen Tudor	Sir Malcolm McAlpine	V Smyth	L Piggott	Le Bourgeois	Rigoberto	21	20–1
1954	Prescription	Precipitation	Lord Rosebery	J Jarvis	E Smith	Karali	Friseur	14	6–1
1955	Prince Barle	Kingsway	Jabez Barker	J Lawson	E Mercer	Big Chief	Bless You	11	11–2
1956	French Beige	Bois Roussel	R F Dennis	H Peacock	G Littlewood	Rosati	Trovato	22	100–8
1957	Tenterhooks	Tenerani	Lord Allendale	Capt C Elsey	E Britt	Palor	Compromise	13	6–1
1958	Even Money	Krakatao	C H Palmer	M V O'Brien	A Breasley	Owen Glendower	Red Dragon	18	9–4
1959	Vivi Tarquin	Black Tarquin	Joseph McGrath	S McGrath	D Greening	Lemnos	Supreme Courage	12	100–8
1960	Prolific	Preciptic	Mrs C Evans	W Nightingall	D Keith	Farney Fox	Poetic Licence	18	5–2
1961	Black King	Nimbus	H J Joel	W Elsey	E Hide	Polyktor	Sagacity	10	100–8
1962	Pavot	Vimy	E R More O'Ferrall	P J Prendergast	J Sime	Parthaon	Tamper	14	10–1
1963	Hereford	Royal Challenger	Mrs W Macauley	H Murless	J Hunter	Credo	Apprentice	25	20–1
1964	I Titan	Ballymoss	Mrs V Hue-Williams	N Murless	M Giovannelli	Mahbub Aly	Minotaur	22	10–1
1965	Beddard	Quorum	R S Reynolds	H Murless	J Sime	Hillgrove	Zulu	24	9–1
1966	Bally Russe	Ballymoss	F R Hue-Williams	N Murless	A Breasley	Vrai	Gaulois	16	5–1
1967	The Accuser	Javelot	Lord Rotherwick	Major W R Hern	F Durr	Lead The Way	Burn The Candle	14	15–2
1968	Zorba II	Tantieme	C Clore	P J Prendergast	R Hutchinson	Hurry Hurry	Ophite	14	10–1
1969	Tantivy	Tanavar	N Hetherton	W Elsey	A Barclay	Baletta	Tirconail	15	15–8
1970	Yellow River	Elf Arrow	David Sung	A Breasley	T Carter	Greenloaning	Golden Love	16	20–1
1971	Parnell	St Paddy	E R More O'Ferrall	S Quirke	R Hutchinson	Ballyglitter	Windrush	20	7–1
1972	Falkland	Right Royal V	Lord Howard de Walden	H Cecil	G Starkey	Ribomio	Cicero's Court	10	9–2
1973	Tara Brooch	Tarqogan	Joseph McGrath	S McGrath	Pat Eddery	Piccolo Player	China Bank	13	10–1
1974	Royal Aura	Right Royal V	Mrs J Silcock	P Walwyn	Pat Eddery	Town Tyrant	Rekindle	13	11–2
1975	Blood Royal	Ribot	Mrs S Getty II	M V O'Brien	L Piggott	Coed Cochion	Moss Trooper	20	11–2
1976	General Ironside	Sea Hawk II	Garfield Weston	H Cecil	L Piggott	Valuation	Ormeley	14	11–8
1977	Millionaire	Mill Reef	Mrs D McCalmont	P Walwyn	Pat Eddery	Owen Glin	Japsilk	14	8–1
1978	Le Moss	Le Levanstell	C d'Alessio	H Cecil	G Baxter	Antler	Arapahos	12	7–4
1979	Buttress	Busted	HM The Queen	Major W R Hern	W Carson	Olympios	Palace Dan	13	3–1
1980	Toondra	Northfields	Lady Beaverbrook	M Jarvis	P Cook	Good Thyne	Simette	14	15–2
1981	Ore	Ballymore	Patrick Prendergast	K Prendergast	W Carson	Protection Racket	Krug	13	15–2
1982	Evzon	English Prince	Capt M Lemos	C Brittain	L Piggott	Santella Man	Karadar	14	16–1
1983	Santella Man	Nebbiolo	R Taiano	G Harwood	G Starkey	Karadar	Condell	17	11–1
1984	Baynoun	Sassafras	HH Aga Khan	R F Johnson Houghton	W Carson	Van Dyke Brown	Castle Rising	11	13–8
1985	Wassl Merbayeh	The Minstrel	Sheikh Ahmed Al Maktoum	H Thomson Jones	R Hills	Kublai	Maldoror	10	6–1
1986	Stavordale	Dance In Time	Mrs H T Jones	H Thomson Jones	M Roberts	Knights Legend	Reason to Be	13	33–1
1987	Arden	Ardross	Lord Howard de Walden	H Cecil	S Cauthen	Sergeyevich	Old Dundalk	9	7–2
1988	Green Adventure	Green Dancer	J Garcia-Roady	G Harwood	G Starkey	Moscow Society	Bold Stranger	14	6–4
1989	Weld	Kalaglow	Lord Howard de Walden	W Jarvis	B Raymond	Demawend	Polar Run	11	15–2
1990	River God	Val de L'Orne	Sheikh Mohammed	H Cecil	S Cauthen	Parting Moment	Kasayid	11	6–4
1991	Jendali	Nijinsky	Sheikh Mohammed	H Cecil	S Cauthen	Silver Rainbow	Le Corsaire	14	15–2
1992	Landowner	Kris	Sheikh Mohammed	J Gosden	R Cochrane	Belgran	Goldsmith's Hall	11	8–1
1993	Infrasonic	Dancing Brave	K Abdullah	A Fabre	Pat Eddery	Silverdale	Kassab	8	3–1
1994	Silver Wedge	Silver Hawk	Mrs Shirley Robins	G Lewis	M Hills	Ptoto	Summit	12	20–1
1995	Stelvio	Shirley Heights	Sheikh Mohammed	H Cecil	M Kinane	Double Eclipse	Pedraza	11	7–4
1996	Gordi	Theatrical	Allen Paulson	D Weld	M Kinane	Athenry	Persian Punch	14	7–1
1997	Windsor Castle	Generous	HRH Prince Fahd Salman	P Cole	T Quinn	Three Cheers	Book At Bedtime	11	9–2
1998	Maridpour	Shernazar	HH Aga Khan	Sir Michael Stoute	W R Swinburn	Laurentide	Capri	8	6–1
1999	Endorsement	Warning	Cliveden Stud	H Cecil	K Fallon	Time Zone	Compton Ace	11	5–1
2000	Dalampour	Shernazar	HH Aga Khan	Sir Michael Stoute	K Fallon	Dutch Harrier	Samsaam	13	3–1
2001	And Beyond	Darshaan	Maktoum Al Maktoum	M Johnston	K Darley	When In Rome	Aquarius	16	11–1

THE COVENTRY STAKES (Group 3)

Distance: 6 furlongs
For 2-year-olds

First run in 1890 over the 2-year-old course of about 6 furlongs. From 1907 to 1954 the race was run over 5 furlongs.

YEAR	WINNER	SIRE	OWNER	TRAINER	JOCKEY	SECOND	THIRD	RUNNERS	SP
1945	Khaled	Hyperion	HH Aga Khan	F Butters	G Richards	Sky High	Woodwind	8	9–1
1946	Tudor Minstrel	Owen Tudor	J A Dewar	F Darling	G Richards	Patrol	Firemaster	6	2–13
1947	The Cobbler	Windsor Slipper	Lt-Col Giles Loder	F Darling	G Richards	Belvedere	Sitacles	12	4–5
1948	Royal Forest	Bois Roussel	Lt-Col R Macdonald-Buchanan	N Murless	C Richards	Nimbus	Peter Flower	14	5–1
1949	Palestine	Fair Trial	HH Aga Khan	F Butters	G Richards	Zodiac	Geraphar	12	1–2
1950	Big Dipper	Signal Light	Mrs J F C Bryce	Capt C Boyd-Rochfort	W H Carr	Grey Sovereign	Lord Of Verona	10	2–1
1951	King's Bench	Court Martial	A J Tompsett	M Feakes	G Richards	Chavey Down	Prince d'Or	11	4–6
1952	Whistler	Panorama	HH Maharenee of Baroda	P Nelson	E Britt	Nearula	Shining Knight	7	2–5
1953	The Pie King	The Solicitor	Ray Bell	P J Prendergast	T Gosling	Darius	Man About Town	12	11–2
1954	Noble Chieftain	Nearco	Major L B Holliday	H Cottrill	F Barlow	Blue Blazes	Factory	8	11–8
1955	Ratification	Court Martial	Sir Malcolm McAlpine	V Smyth	W H Carr	Pirate King	Idle Rocks	7	100–30
1956	Messmate	Blue Peter	Lord Milford	J Jarvis	E Mercer	Racin' Plaid	Buskin	17	20–1
1957	Amerigo	Nearco	Lord Howard de Walden	J A Waugh	E Smith	Trimmer	Ballyrullah	10	7–4
1958	Hieroglyph	Heliopolis	Mrs J W Hanes	Capt C Boyd-Rochfort	W H Carr	Taboun	New Warrior	14	10–1
1959	Martial	Hill Gail	R N Webster	P J Prendergast	W Swinburn	Blast	Running Blue	13	11–10
1960	Typhoon	Honeyway	N S McCarthy	P J Prendergast	R Hutchinson	Blue Sails	Bold Lover	9	Evens
1961	Xerxes	Darius	Mrs D McCalmont	G Brooke	D Smith	Torero	Court Sentence	17	9–2
1962	Crocket	King Of The Tudors	D G Van Clief	G Brooke	D Smith	Happy Omen	King's Case	14	9–4
1963	Showdown	Infatuation	Mrs D Prenn	F N Winter	D Smith	Travel Man	Piccadilly	12	6–1
1964	Silly Season	Tom Fool	Paul Mellon	I Balding	G Lewis	Barrymore	Sandro	19	13–2
1965	Young Emperor	Grey Sovereign	Mrs Parker Poe	P J Prendergast	L Piggott	At-a-Venture	Bull Dancer	13	9–4
1966	Bold Lad	Bold Ruler	Beatrice Lady Granard	P J Prendergast	D Lake	Donated	Bosworth Field	16	4–6
1967	Mark Royal	Monet	B Schmidt-Bodner	P Norris	A Breasley	Star and Garter	Storm Bird	16	13–2
1968	Murrayfield	Match III	Mrs Peter Hastings	I Balding	G Lewis	Royal Smoke	Whistling Top	16	15–2
1969	Prince Tenderfoot	Blue Prince II	Mrs Parker Poe	P J Prendergast	W Williamson	Constitutional	Saintly Song	10	15–8
1970	Mill Reef	Never Bend	Paul Mellon	I Balding	G Lewis	Cromwell	Twelfth Night	5	4–11
1971	Sun Prince	Princely Gift	Michael Sobell	Major W R Hern	J Mercer	Avancer	Wishing Star	10	20–1
1972	Perdu	Linacre	A Holland	T Corbett	J Lindley	Netherkelly	Starboard Buoy	7	16–1
1973	Doleswood	Double Jump	F Tory	R Akehurst	F Durr	Dragonara Palace	Furry Glen	12	20–1
1974	Whip It Quick	Philemon	G van der Ploeg	W Marshall	G Lewis	Legal Eagle	Panomark	18	11–1
1975	Galway Bay	Sassafras	J R Mullion	I Balding	L Piggott	Super Cavalier	Tampa	10	2–1
1976	Cawston's Clown	Comedy Star	J Murrell	N Adam	M Thomas	Lordedaw	And Behold	12	11–2
1977	Solinus	Comedy Star	D Schwartz	M V O'Brien	L Piggott	Sharpen Your Eye	Swing Bridge	17	7–4
1978	Lake City	Annihilate 'Em	H Demetriou	H R Price	B Taylor	Ghazal	Moulin	20	7–1
1979	Varingo	Saulingo	PTP Plant Hire Ltd	H R Price	B Taylor	London Bells	Final Straw	18	11–8
1980	Recitation	Elocutionist	A Bodie	G Harwood	G Starkey	Motavato	Bel Bolide	13	11–1
1981	Red Sunset	Red God	P Burns	G Harwood	G Starkey	Chris's Lad	Bronowski	16	14–1
1982	Horage	Tumble Wind	A Rachid	M McCormack	Pat Eddery	Kafu	Stay Sharp	8	85–40
1983	Chief Singer	Ballad Rock	J C Smith	R Sheather	R Cochrane	Hegemony	Novello	14	20–1
1984	Primo Dominie	Dominion	Peter Wetzel	B Swift	J Reid	Star Video	Native Skier	8	4–7
1985	Sure Blade	Kris	Sheikh Mohammed	B Hills	B Thomson	Moorgate Man	Cliveden	12	3–1
1986	Cutting Blade	Sharpo	Mahmoud Fustok	L Piggott	C Asmussen	Polemos	Amigo Sucio	19	11–1
1987	Always Fair	Danzig	Maktoum Al Maktoum	M Stoute	W R Swinburn	Oakworth	Ship Of Fools	13	9–2
1988	High Estate	Shirley Heights	H J Joel	H Cecil	S Cauthen	Dancing Dissident	Sharp N' Early	9	10–11
1989	Rock City	Ballad Rock	A F Budge Ltd	R Hannon	W Carson	Wadood	Candy Glen	16	9–1
1990	Mac's Imp	Imp Society	Tamdown Ltd	W A O'Gorman	A Munro	Generous	Bold Nephew	13	2–1
1991	Dilum	Tasso	Prince Fahd Salman	P Cole	A Munro	Dr Devious	Casteddu	14	11–10
1992	Petardia	Petong	Mollers Racing	G Wragg	W R Swinburn	So Factual	Pips Pride	12	5–1
1993	Stonehatch	Storm Bird	R E Sangster	P Chapple-Hyam	J Reid	Polish Laughter	Wajiba Riva	6	Evens
1994	Sri Pekan	Red Ransom	HRH Sultan Ahmad Shah	P Cole	T Quinn	Moon King	Missel	16	6–1
1995	Royal Applause	Waajib	Maktoum Al Maktoum	B Hills	W R Swinburn	Russian Revival	South Salem	13	13–2
1996	Verglas	Highest Honor	A J F O'Reilly	K Prendergast	W J Supple	Daylight In Dubai	Deadly Dudley	15	9–1
1997	Harbour Master	Bluebird	Mrs John Magnier	A P O'Brien	C Roche	Desert Prince	Bold Fact	15	16–1
1998	Red Sea	Barathea	Prince Fahd Salman	P Cole	T Quinn	Be The Chief	Access All Areas	17	6–1
1999	Fasliyev	Nureyev	M Tabor & Mrs John Magnier	A P O'Brien	M Kinane	Sir Nicholas	Cornelius	18	15–8
2000	Cd Europe	Royal Academy	Circular Distributors Ltd.	M Channon	S Drowne	Bram Stoker	Modigliani	12	8–1
2001	Landseer	Danehill	M Tabor & Mrs John Magnier	A P O'Brien	J P Spencer	Firebreak	Meshaheer	20	20–1

THE JERSEY STAKES (Group 3)

Distance: 7 furlongs
For 3-year-olds

First run with this name in 1919. From 1848 the second-year race of the Triennial Stakes run over an extended 7 furlongs. Shortened in 1955.

YEAR	WINNER	SIRE	OWNER	TRAINER	JOCKEY	SECOND	THIRD	RUNNERS	SP
1946	Sayani	Fair Copy	Mme J Lieux	M J Lieux	R Poincelet	Wayward Belle	Edward Tudor	7	100–6
1947	Nebuchadnezzar	Nearco	Sir Percy Loraine	F Darling	G Richards	Rona	Slavian Ruler	8	4–6
1948	Hyperbole	Hyperion	James V Rank	N Cannon	T Weston	Hope Street	Woodflower	10	100–7
1949	Star King	Stardust	W Harvey	J C Waugh	D Smith	Moondust	Krakatao	9	9–2
1950	Double Eclipse	Hyperion	Lady Zia Wernher	Capt C Boyd-Rochfort	W H Carr	Emperor II	Rose Of Torridge	11	6–5
1951	Royal Serenade	Royal Charger	Mrs Geoffrey Kohn	H Wragg	C Elliott	Aristophanes	Salamat	5	3–1
1952	Kara Tepe	Hyperion	F G Robinson	G Colling	E Mercer	Monarch More	Merry Minstrel	11	100–8
1953	Rhinehart	Combat	Major E O Kay	D Candy	G Richards	Good Brandy	Propitiation	8	4–1
1954	Marshal Ney	His Highness	J J Cosgrove	W Byrne	W R Johnstone	Dyoko	Coronation Scot	9	100–9
1955	Windsor Sun	Windsor Slipper	Joseph McGrath	S McGrath	J Eddery	Sonorous	My Foot	11	100–8
1956	Adare	Panorama	J S M Cosgrove	M V O'Brien	W R Johnstone	Following Breeze	Water Snake / Lucero	15	8–1
1957	Quorum	Vilmorin	T H Farr	W Lyde	A Russell	Kings Barn	Fuel	7	4–6
1958	Faith Healer	Petition	W H Harrison	P Beasley	J Sime	Two Francs	Game Ball	13	11–2
1959	Welsh Guard	Royal Charger	Mrs J W Hanes	Capt C Boyd-Rochfort	W H Carr	Sallymount	Gang Warily	10	4–1
1960	Red Gauntlet	Nearula	H J Joel	T Leader	E Smith	Le Levanstell	Gilboa	13	100–8
1961	Favorita	Abernant	Mrs V Lilley	N Murless	L Piggott	Indian Conquest	Erudite	9	5–4
1962	Catchpole	King Of The Tudors	R F Dennis	G Brooke	D Smith	Abermaid	Featheredge	10	13–2
1963	The Creditor	Crepello	Lady Sassoon	N Murless	L Piggott	Brief Flight	Queen's Hussar	17	11–2
1964	Young Christopher	Royal Palm	James McShane	F Maxwell	L Piggott	Prince Hansel	Whistling Buoy	16	5–4
1965	Fortezza	Botticelli	R B Moller	H Wragg	F Durr	Go Shell	Hassan	26	100–6
1966	Vibrant	Vilmorin	Mrs George Lambton	E Lambton	P Robinson	All A'Light	Kibenka	14	4–1
1967	St Chad	St Paddy	Mrs Noel Murless	N Murless	G Moore	Broadway Melody	Mark Scott	11	11–2
1968	World Cup	Match III	J R Mullion	P J Prendergast	W Williamson	Town Crier	Paddy Me	10	15–8
1969	Crooner	Sammy Davis	Lord Rosebery	D Smith	J Gorton	Hotfoot	The Geostan	8	8–1
1970	Fluke	Grey Sovereign	R D Hollingsworth	J Oxley	G Duffield	Zingari	Miss Skyscraper	9	9–4
1971	Ashleigh	Ragusa	Mrs Parker Poe	P J Prendergast	W Williamson	Tula Rocket	Les Baux	5	13–8
1972	Proof Positive	Gulf Pearl	J H Whitney	J Tree	Pat Eddery	Anak Malaysia	Alonso	16	14–1
1973	Pitskelly	Petingo	David Robinson	M Jarvis	W Williamson	Fabvista	Apple King	11	15–2
1974	Red Alert	Red God	Bertram R Firestone	D Weld	J Roe	High Award	Step Ahead	17	6–1
1975	Gay Fandango	Forli	A Clore	M V O'Brien	L Piggott	Joking Apart	Hillandale	13	11–10
1976	Gwent	Welsh Pageant	A Villar	B Hobbs	G Lewis	Wolverlife	Scott Joplyn	12	11–2
1977	Etienne Gerard	Brigadier Gerard	P Philipps	M Stoute	P Cook	La Ville de Rire	Kifinti	13	25–1
1978	Camden Town	Derring-Do	Sir J Thorn	P Walwyn	Pat Eddery	Cosmopolitan	Padro	17	4–1
1979	Blue Refrain	Majority Blue	Mrs L Wood	C Benstead	B Rouse	Bolton Tom	Jeroboam	17	12–1
1980	Hard Fought	Habitat	L Holliday	M Stoute	L Piggott	Sunfield	Etoile de Paris	13	15–8
1981	Rasa Penang	Gay Fandango	U Wijewardene	R Armstrong	L Piggott	Star Pastures	Noalto	20	11–1
1982	Merlins Charm	Bold Bidder	R E Sangster	B Hills	S Cauthen	Silly Steven	Beldale Lustre	21	9–1
1983	Tecorno	Tentam	Countess M Esterhazy	Major W R Hern	W Carson	Persian Glory	Aragon	13	8–1
1984	Miss Silca Key	Welsh Saint	E Aldridge & Son Ltd	D Elsworth	B Rouse	Mystery Ship	Round Hill	16	15–1
1985	Pennine Walk	Persian Bold	Mrs S S Niarchos	J Tree	Pat Eddery	Miami Count	Heraldiste	19	9–2
1986	Cliveden	Valdex	Anthony Speelman	G Harwood	G Starkey	Brave Owen	Hard Round	20	9–1
1987	Midyan	Miswaki	Prince A A Faisal	H Cecil	S Cauthen	Linda's Magic	Deputy Governor	13	11–2
1988	Indian Ridge	Ahonoora	Mrs Anne Coughlan	D Elsworth	C Asmussen	Salse	Hibernian Gold	12	10–1
1989	Zilzal	Nureyev	Mana Al Maktoum	M Stoute	W R Swinburn	Russian Royal	Distant Relative	12	10–11
1990	Sally Rous	Roussillon	Sir Philip Oppenheimer	G Wragg	G Carter	Bold Russian	Qui Danzig	15	20–1
1991	Satin Flower	Shadeed	Sheikh Mohammed	J Gosden	S Cauthen	Dawson Place	Desert Sun	14	12–1
1992	Prince Ferdinand	King Of Spain	Miss J Winch	M McCormack	J Reid	Pursuit Of Love	Fair Cop	12	6–1
1993	Ardkinglass	Green Desert	Sir David Wills	H Cecil	W Ryan	Matelot	Abbey's Gal	15	10–1
1994	[Gneiss	Diesis	Matthew Oram	Mrs J Cecil	Paul Eddery		Dumaani	21	10–1
	River Deep	Riverman	Prince Fahd Salman	P Cole	T Quinn				20–1
1995	Sergeyev	Mulhollande	B T Stewart-Brown	R Hannon	R Hughes	Shahid	First Island	16	5–1
1996	Lucayan Prince	Fast Play	Lucayan Stud	D Loder	R Hughes	Ramooz	Bewitching	16	50–1
1997	Among Men	Zilzal	M Tabor & Mrs John Magnier	M Stoute	M Kinane	Kahal	Hornbeam	20	4–1
1998	Diktat	Warning	Sheikh Mohammed	D Loder	D Holland	Bold Edge	Lovers Knot	16	3–1
1999	Lots Of Magic	Magic Ring	P Valentine	R Hannon	Dane O'Neill	Enrique	Bertolini	12	33–1
2000	Observatory	Distant View	K Abdullah	J Gosden	K Darley	Umistim	Hunting Lion	19	11–2
2001	Mozart	Danehill	M Tabor & Mrs John Magnier	A P O'Brien	M Kinane	Aldebaran	Ratio	18	7–4

THE QUEEN MARY STAKES (Group 3)

Distance: 5 furlongs
For 2-year-old fillies

First run in 1921.

YEAR	WINNER	SIRE	OWNER	TRAINER	JOCKEY	SECOND	THIRD	RUNNERS	SP
1945	Rivaz	Nearco	HH Aga Khan	Frank Butters	C Elliott	Neolight	Romana	5	4–7
1946	Apparition	Blue Peter	Mrs R Macdonald-Buchanan	F Darling	G Richards	Lalita	Benane	14	11–8
1947	Masaka	Nearco	HH Aga Khan	Frank Butters	C Smirke	Open Sesame	Brillante II	18	4–1
1948	Coronation V	Djebel	Marcel Boussac	C Semblat	C Elliott	Valkyrie	Programme	28	7–2
1949	Diableretta	Dante	HH Aga Khan	Frank Butters	W R Johnstone	Quarterdeck	Danae	18	7–4
1950	Rose Linnet	Colombo	Mrs Alec Johnston	Reg Day	D Smith	Clutha	Sarah Madeline	16	10–1
1951	Primavera	Chamossaire	Lord Milford	J Jarvis	E Mercer	Golden Rapture	Stalina	20	100–6
1952	Devon Vintage	Devonian	R C Boucher	R J Colling	E Mercer	Omelia	Niccolite	23	100–8
1953	Sybil's Niece	Admiral's Walk	Lord Milford	J Jarvis	E Mercer	Prudence	Cordova II	24	100–6
1954	Bride Elect	Big Game	Major L B Holliday	H Cottrill	F Barlow	Aberlady	Dark Helen	16	6–1
1955	Weeber`	Panorama	J Olding	P Nelson	A Breasley	La Fresnes	Wennapa	16	10–1
1956	Pharsalia	Panorama	Major L B Holliday	H Cottrill	L Piggott	Colonel's Lady	Street Singer	19	100–7
1957	Abelia	Abernant	Col B Hornung	N Murless	L Piggott	Patroness	Liberal Lady	14	11–4
1958	A 20	Panorama	H W Clifton	F Sutherland	W Rickaby	Rose Of Medina	Sapphire	23	5–1
1959	Paddy's Sister	Ballyogan	Mrs J R Mullion	P J Prendergast	G Moore	Queensberry	Queen Of The Roses	21	15–8
1960	Cynara	Grey Sovereign	G A Oldham	G A Oldham	W H Carr	Crisper	Sweet Solera	17	Evens
1961	My Dream	King Of The Tudors	David Robinson	G Brooke	D Smith	Gay Mairi	Silken Glade	11	2–1
1962	Shot Silk	High Treason	Lt-Col D S Cripps	G Brooke	D Smith	Hera	Guinea Sparrow	14	100–8
1963	Lerida	Matador	Mrs R Macdonald-Buchanan	J A Waugh	J Lindley	High Powered	St Cecilia	15	9–2
1964	Brassia	Buisson Ardent	Arpad Plesch	M V O'Brien	J Purtell	Wind Song	Toffee Nose	17	7–2
1965	Visp	Nantallah	Edward B Benjamin	J F Watts	J Lindley	Procession	Loyalty	10	6–4
1966	Petite Path	Sovereign Path	R E Mason	R Mason	J Lindley	Broadway Melody	Floosie	13	33–1
1967	Sovereign	Pardao	R B Moller	H Wragg	R Hutchinson	Cease Fire	Sing Again	12	10–1
1968	Grizel	Grey Sovereign	Col W Stirling	P J Prendergast	W Williamson	Stung	Carsina	13	5–2
1969	Farfalla	Crocket	D G Van Clief	D Smith	A Murray	Starmount Belle	Humble Duty	13	13–2
1970	Cawston's Pride	Con Brio	L B Hall	F Maxwell	B Taylor	Areola	Flight Dancer	11	2–1
1971	Waterloo	Bold Lad	Mrs R Stanley	J W Watts	E Hide	Miss Christine	Takawin	11	9–2
1972	Truly Thankful	Majority Blue	G van der Ploeg	H R Price	A Murray	April Bloom	Latin Melody	14	14–1
1973	Bitty Girl	Habitat	David Robinson	M Jarvis	B Raymond	Chili Girl	Mrs Tiggywinkle	13	11–2
1974	Highest Trump	Bold Bidder	Lord Petersham	D Weld	J Roe	Amazing Maid	Tender Camilla	10	5–2
1975	Rory's Rocket	Roan Rocket	Mrs W Slaytor	P Ashworth	A Murray	Enchanted	Hayloft	18	33–1
1976	Cramond	Porto Bello	Mrs S Eldin	R Boss	J Mercer	Piney Ridge	Easy Landing	12	25–1
1977	Amaranda	Bold Lad	R B Moller	H Wragg	L Piggott	Noiritza	Princess Zena	13	4–6
1978	Greenland Park	Red God	Greenland Park Ltd	W Hastings-Bass	H White	Kilijaro	Devon Ditty	21	15–2
1979	Abeer	Dewan	K Abdullah	J Tree	W Carson	Teachers Pet	Smokey Lady	14	7–1
1980	Pushy	Sharpen Up	Lord Tavistock	H Cecil	J Mercer	Welshwyn	Nasseem	17	7–1
1981	Fly Baby	African Sky	Malden Farms Ltd	R Hannon	P Cook	Princess Seal	Quest	11	40–1
1982	Widaad	Mr Prospector	Maktoum Al Maktoum	M Stoute	W R Swinburn	Crime Of Passion	Annie Edge/Carolside (d ht)	16	13–8
1983	Night Of Wind	Tumble Wind	P Durkan	M McCormack	B Raymond	Netsuke	Sajeda	15	50–1
1984	Hi Tech Girl	Homeboy	Intercraft	P J Makin	G Starkey	Tumble Dale	Cameroun	17	16–1
1985	Gwydion	Raise A Cup	S S Niarchos	H Cecil	S Cauthen	Welsh Note	Kingscote	14	2–1
1986	Forest Flower	Green Forest	Paul Mellon	I Balding	Pat Eddery	Propensity	D'Azy	13	9–4
1987	Princess Athena	Ahonoora	H J Senn	D Elsworth	W Carson	Saintly Lass	Icefern	15	9–1
1988	Gloriella	Caerleon	John J McLoughlin	John J McLoughlin	J Reid	Bocas Rose	Honoria	12	8–1
1989	Dead Certain	Absalom	Commander G G Marten	D Elsworth	S Cauthen	Please Believe Me	Performing Arts	13	8–1
1990	On Tiptoes	Shareef Dancer	J W Rowles	J P Leigh	D McKeown	It's All Academic	Furajet	12	8–1
1991	Marling	Lomond	E J Loder	G Wragg	G Carter	Culture Vulture	Central City	14	11–4
1992	Lyric Fantasy	Tate Gallery	Lord Carnarvon	R Hannon	M Roberts	Mystic Goddess	Toocando	13	11–8
1993	Risky	Risk Me	Roldvale Ltd	R Hannon	W R Swinburn	Snipe Hall	Elrafa Ah	11	11–2
1994	Gay Gallanta	Woodman	Cheveley Park Stud	M R Stoute	W R Swinburn	Myself	Hoh Magic	16	16–1
1995	Blue Duster	Danzig	Sheikh Mohammed	D Loder	M Kinane	Dance Sequence	My Melody Parkes	12	7–4
1996	Dance Parade	Gone West	Prince Fahd Salman	P Cole	M Kinane	Dame Laura	Moonshine Girl	13	8–1
1997	Nadwah	Shadeed	Hamdan Al Maktoum	P Walwyn	R Hills	Crazee Mental	Daunting Lady	18	10–1
1998	Bint Allayl	Green Desert	Sheikh Ahmed Al Maktoum	M Channon	L Dettori	Pipalong	Coralita	17	2–1
1999	Shining Hour	Red Ransom	R E Sangster	P Chapple-Hyam	J Fortune	Rowaasi	Warrior Queen	13	20–1
2000	Romantic Myth	Mind Games	T G Holdcroft	T Easterby	K Darley	Al Ihsas	Little Firefly	20	4–1
2001	Queen's Logic	Grand Lodge	Jaber Abdullah	M Channon	S Drowne	Sophisticat	Roundtree	20	13–2

THE PRINCE OF WALES'S STAKES (Group 1)

Distance: 1 mile 2 furlongs
For 4-year-olds and upwards

First run in 1862. From 1862 to 1939 run over 1 mile 5 furlongs.
Renewed in 1968 over shorter distance. Open to 3-year-olds to 1999.

YEAR	WINNER	SIRE	OWNER	TRAINER	JOCKEY	SECOND	THIRD	RUNNERS	SP
1968	Royal Palace	Ballymoss	H J Joel	N Murless	A Barclay	Djehad		2	1–4
1969	Connaught	St Paddy	H J Joel	N Murless	A Barclay	Wolver Hollow	Stoned	5	11–10
1970	Connaught	St Paddy	H J Joel	N Murless	A Barclay	Hotfoot	Recalled	4	10–11
1971	Arthur	Henry the Seventh	Lady Rosebery	J Dunlop	R Hutchinson	Quayside	Credit Man	4	5–4
1972	Brigadier Gerard	Queen's Hussar	Mrs J Hislop	Major W R Hern	J Mercer	Steel Pulse	Pembroke Castle	7	1–2
1973	Gift Card	Dan Cupid	Countess Margit Batthyany	A Penna	L Piggott	Scottish Rifle	Warpath	5	7–2
1974	Admetus	Reform	Sir Michael Sobell	J Cunnington Jr	M Philipperon	Owen Dudley	Hail The Pirates	7	6–1
1975	Record Run	Track Spare	S Grey	G Pritchard-Gordon	Pat Eddery	Swell Fellow	Giacometti	6	12–1
1976	Anne's Pretender	Pretense	Sir Charles Clore	H R Price	L Piggott	Chil The Kite	Rose Bowl	7	100–30
1977	Lucky Wednesday	Roi Soleil	C A B St George	H Cecil	J Mercer	Rymer	Radetzky	5	5–6
1978	Gunner B	Royal Gunner	Mrs P A Barratt	H Cecil	J Mercer	Fluellen	Malecite	7	4–5
1979	Crimson Beau	High Line	H Spearing	P Cole	L Piggott	Lyphards Wish	Town And Country	7	11–2
1980	Ela-Mana-Mou	Pitcairn	S Weinstock	Major W R Hern	W Carson	Moomba Masquerade	Bonnie Isle	10	100–30
1981	Hard Fought	Habitat	L Holliday	M Stoute	W R Swinburn	Vielle	Magesteria	9	3–1
1982	Kind Of Hush	Welsh Pageant	A Shead	B Hills	S Cauthen	Lobkowiez	Castle Keep	7	4–1
1983	Stanerra	Guillaume Tell	F Dunne	F Dunne	B Rouse	Sabre Dance	Commodore Blake	11	7–1
1984	Morcon	Morston	Lord Rotherwick	Major W R Hern	W Carson	Hot Touch	Muscatite	5	11–8
1985	Bob Back	Roberto	Antonio Balzarini	M Jarvis	B Raymond	Pebbles	Commanche Run	4	33–1
1986	English Spring	Grey Dawn II	Paul Mellon	I Balding	Pat Eddery	Bedtime	Fair Of The Furze	9	14–1
1987	Mtoto	Busted	Sheikh Ahmed Al Maktoum	A Stewart	R Hills	Amerigo Vespucci	Gesedeh	10	7–2
1988	Mtoto	Busted	Sheikh Ahmed Al Maktoum	A Stewart	M Roberts	Broken Hearted	Highland Chieftain	4	8–15
1989	Two Timing	Blushing Groom	K Abdullah	J Tree	Pat Eddery	Beau Sher	Most Welcome	8	5–1
1990	Batshoof	Sadler's Wells	Muttar Salem	B Hanbury	Pat Eddery	Relief Pitcher	Terimon	8	2–1
1991	Stagecraft	Sadler's Wells	Sheikh Mohammed	M Stoute	S Cauthen	Zoman	Terimon	6	6–4
1992	Perpendicular	Shirley Heights	Lord Howard de Walden	H Cecil	W Ryan	Young Buster	Kooyonga	11	20–1
1993	Placerville	Mr Prospector	K Abdullah	H Cecil	Pat Eddery	Urban Sea	Emperor Jones	11	11–2
1994	Muhtarram	Alleged	Hamdan Al Maktoum	J Gosden	W Carson	Ezzoud	Chatoyant	11	6–4
1995	Muhtarram	Alleged	Hamdan Al Maktoum	J Gosden	W Carson	Eltish	Needle Gun	6	5–1
1996	First Island	Dominion	Mollers Racing	G Wragg	M Hills	Montjoy	Tamayaz	12	9–1
1997	Bosra Sham	Woodman	Wafic Said	H Cecil	K Fallon	Alhaarth	London News	6	4–11
1998	Faithful Son	Zilzal	Godolphin	S bin Suroor	J Reid	Chester House	Daylami	8	11–2
1999	Lear Spear	Lear Fan	Raymond Tooth	D Elsworth	M Kinane	Fantastic Light	Xaar	8	20–1
2000	Dubai Millennium	Seeking The Gold	Godolphin	S bin Suroor	J Bailey	Sumitas	Beat All	6	5–4
2001	Fantastic Light	Rahy	Godolphin	S bin Suroor	L Dettori	Kalanisi	Hightori	9	100–30

THE ROYAL HUNT CUP (Handicap)

Distance: 1 mile (Straight Mile)
For 3-year-olds and upwards

First run in 1843 over various distances of about 1 mile and over a measured mile from 1955.

YEAR	WINNER	SIRE	OWNER	TRAINER	JOCKEY	SECOND	THIRD	RUNNERS	SP
1945	Battle Hymn	Hyperion	J H Whitney	Capt C Boyd-Rochfort	P Maher	Sir Edward	The Solicitor	14	20–1
1946	Friar's Fancy	Wychwood Abbot	O V Watney	T Leader	E Smith	Slide On	Pooflix	16	15–2
1947	Master Vote	Atout Maitre	H Blagrave	H Blagrave	T Sidebotham	Whitehall	Admiral's Yarn	28	25–1
1948	Master Vote	Atout Maitre	H Blagrave	H Blagrave	W R Johnstone	Prince Peto	Star Witness	27	100–7
1949	Sterope	Mid-day Sun	J B Townley	P Beasley	J Caldwell	Impeccable	Pride Of India	29	100–6
1950	Hyperbole	Hyperion	James V Rank	N Cannon	A Breasley	Wat Tyler	Burpham	20	10–1
1951	Val d'Assa	Dante	Major D McCalmont	H Persse	N Sellwood	Fair Judgement	Cabbage Hill	23	100–6
1952	Queen Of Sheba	Persian Gulf	Major D McCalmont	H Persse	F Barlow	Brunetto	Aristophanes	29	100–7
1953	Choir Boy	Hyperion	HM The Queen	Capt C Boyd-Rochfort	D Smith	Brunetto	Hilltop	21	100–6
1954	Chivalry	Prince Chevalier	P Hatvany	T R Rimell	D Forte	King Of The Tudors	Desert Way	26	33–1
1955	Nicholas Nickleby	Niccolo Dell'Arca	J S Gerber	F Armstrong	W Snaith	Coronation Year	Comic Turn	22	50–1
1956	Alexander	Alycidon	HM The Queen	Capt C Boyd-Rochfort	W H Carr	Jaspe	Blue Robe	27	13–2
1957	Retrial	Court Martial	Lady Zia Wernher	Capt C Boyd-Rochfort	P Robinson	Midget II	Loppylugs	18	100–7
1958	Amos	Mossborough	Mrs Leonard Carver	S Mercer	P Boothman	Empire Way	Falls Of Shin	17	20–1
1959	Faultless Speech	Impeccable	H Wallington	H Wallington	G Lewis	Pall Mall	Small Slam	23	8–1
1960	Small Slam	Nicolaus	Phillip King	G Barling	R P Elliott	Mustavon	Pheidippides	26	28–1
1961	King's Troop	Princely Gift	Mrs Peter Hastings	P Hastings-Bass	G Lewis	Choice	Night II	39	100–7
1962	Smartie	March Past	R E Mason	R Mason	J Sime	China Clipper	Water Skier	31	22–1
1963	Spaniards Close	Solonaway	Mrs Ben Davis	F N Winter	L Piggott	Mystery	Nereus	38	25–1
1964	Zaleucus	Zarathustra	Major D McCalmont	G Brooke	D Smith	Gelert	Emerald Cross	30	100–7
1965	Casabianca	Never Say Die	Lt-Col J Hornung	N Murless	L Piggott	Weeper's Boy	Zaleucus	26	100–9
1966	Continuation	Ballyogan	S McGrath	S McGrath	J Roe	Steeple Aston	Midnight Marauder	30	25–1
1967	Regal Light	Sovereign Path	Mrs L G Lazarus	S Hall	G Sexton	Kibenka	Midnight Marauder	15	100–9
1968	Golden Mean	Taboun or Hill Gail	S H Lee	D Smith	F Durr	Owen Anthony	Straight Master	26	28–1
1969	Kamundu	Will Somers	J Banks	F Carr	L Piggott	Lorenzaccio	Private Side	24	7–1
1970	Calpurnius	St Paddy	C W Engelhard	J W Watts	G Duffield	Brabant	Deadly Nightshade	18	33–1
1971	Picture Boy	Monet	K C B Mackenzie	G Todd	J Wilson	Londesborough Boy	Owen Anthony	18	11–1
1972	Tempest Boy	Typhoon	Lt-Col P Hesse	J Sutcliffe	R Hutchinson	Leander	Bright Fire	20	20–1
1973	Camouflage	March Past	J Edwards	J Dunlop	D Cullen	Pontam	Spring Stone	20	14–1
1974	Old Lucky	Sherluck	N Hunt	B van Cutsem	W Carson	Fabled Diplomat	Anak Malaysia	30	8–1
1975	Ardoon	Track Spare	F Feeney	G Pritchard-Gordon	D Maitland	Lottogift	Black Rhino	18	9–1
1976	Jumping Hill	Hilary	G Pope jnr	N Murless	L Piggott	My Hussar	Yamadori	16	6–1
1977	My Hussar	Queen's Hussar	L Goldschlager	J Sutcliffe	W Carson	Andy Rew	Yamadori	15	10–1
1978	Fear Naught	Connaught	W Norton	J Etherington	M Wigham	Petronisi	Baronet	19	12–1
1979	Pipedreamer	Breeders Dream	Mrs J Brookes	H Candy	P Waldron	Greenhill God	Smartset	24	12–1
1980	Tender Heart	Prince Tenderfoot	Esal Commodities Ltd	J Sutcliffe	J Mercer	Lord Rochford	Smartset	22	13–2
1981	Teamwork	Workboy	A Ward	G Harwood	G Starkey	Greenwood Star	Princes Gate	20	8–1
1982	Buzzards Bay	Joshua	Mrs V McKinney	H Collingridge	J Mercer	Paterno	Tower Joy	20	14–1
1983	Mighty Fly	Comedy Star	Mrs V A Tory	D Elsworth	S Cauthen	Fandangle	Christmas Cottage	32	12–1
1984	Hawkley	Monsanto	S A B Dinsmore	P Haslam	Tyrone Williams	Teleprompter	Basil Boy	18	10–1
1985	Come On The Blues	Blue Cashmere	Mrs C Pateras	C Brittain	C Rutter	Advance	Scoutsmistake	27	14–1
1986	Patriarch	London Bells	Peter S Winfield	J Dunlop	T Quinn	Siyah Kalem	King's Head	31	20–1
1987	Vague Shot	Vaigly Great	A W Anthony	R Casey	S Cauthen	Granny's Bank	Gold Prospect	25	10–1
1988	Governorship	Dominion	R E A Bott (Wigmore St) Ltd	C Nelson	J Reid	Ghadbbaan	Burkan	26	33–1
1989	True Panache	Mr Prospector	K Abdullah	J Tree	Pat Eddery	Wood Dancer	Cuvee Charlie	27	5–1
1990	Pontenuovo	Kafu	Walter Mariti	D Elsworth	G Bardwell	Curtain Call	Pride Of Araby	32	50–1
1991	Eurolink The Lad	Burslem	Eurolink Computer Services Ltd	J Dunlop	J Reid	Operation Wolf	Pontenuovo	29	25–1
1992	Colour Sergeant	Green Desert	HM The Queen	Lord Huntingdon	D Harrison	Gymcrak Premiere	Dorset Duke	31	20–1
1993	Imperial Ballet	Sadler's Wells	R E Sangster	H Cecil	Pat Eddery	Royal Seaton	Philidor	30	20–1
1994	Face North	Fayruz	Normandy Developments	R Akehurst	A Munro	Lower Egypt	Sharp Review	32	25–1
1995	Realities	Cozzene	Roy Taiano	G Harwood	M Kinane	Darnay	Indian Fly	32	11–1
1996	Yeast	Salse	B Haggas	W Haggas	K Fallon	Tertium	Crumpton Hill	31	8–1
1997	Red Robbo	Red Ransom	Lucayan Stud	R Akehurst	O Peslier	Crown Court	Cadeaux Tryst	32	16–1
1998	Refuse To Lose	Emarati	J C Smith	J Eustace	J Tate	Fly To The Stars	Prince Of My Heart	32	20–1
1999	Showboat	Warning	R D Hollingsworth	B Hills	N Pollard	Plan-B	Refuse To Lose	32	14–1
2000	Caribbean Monarch	Fairy King	Pierpoint Scott & C H Scott	Sir Michael Stoute	K Fallon	John Ferneley	Persiano	32	11–2
2001	Surprise Encounter	Cadeaux Genereux	Ahmed Ali	E Dunlop	L Dettori	Big Future	Muchea	30	8–1

THE RIBBLESDALE STAKES (Group 2)

Distance: 1 mile 4 furlongs
For 3-year-old fillies

First run in 1950. Another unconnected race of this name was run from 1919 to 1939 and in 1948 and 1949.

YEAR	WINNER	SIRE	OWNER	TRAINER	JOCKEY	SECOND	THIRD	RUNNERS	SP
1950	La Baille	Verso II	Mohamed Bey Sultan	M Marsh	C Smirke	Lonely Maid	Plume II	9	15–2
1951	Chinese Cracker	Dante	Mrs G Blagrave	H Blagrave	A Breasley	Monrovia	Sea Drift	9	7–4
1952	Esquilla	Djebel	Marcel Boussac	C Semblat	W R Johnstone	Nicky Nook	Stream of Light	13	9–2
1953	Skye	Blue Peter	Lord Rosebery	J Jarvis	W Rickaby	Kerkeb	Brolly	12	4–1
1954	Sweet One	Honeyway	Lord Milford	J Jarvis	W Rickaby	Brilliant Green	Dust Storm	8	100–8
1955	Ark Royal	Straight Deal	R D Hollingsworth	G Colling	D Smith	Reel In	Chorus Beauty	11	2–1
1956	Milady	Sayajirao	Major H P Holt	M Marsh	C Smirke	Mamounia	Kyak	13	100–8
1957	Almeria	Alycidon	HM The Queen	Capt C Boyd-Rochfort	W H Carr	Blue Galleon	Donna Lydia	9	13–8
1958	None Nicer	Nearco	Major L B Holliday	Major W R Hern	S Clayton	Tantalizer	Amante	12	11–2
1959	Cantelo	Chanteur II	William Hill	Capt C Elsey	E Hide	La Coquenne	Dame Melba	8	5–4
1960	French Fern	Mossborough	Major H R Broughton	J A Waugh	G Lewis	No Saint	Green Opal	8	8–1
1961	Futurama	Borealis	G A Oldham	H Wragg	A Breasley	Verbena	Paris Princess	12	9–2
1962	Tender Annie	Tenerani	Mrs J F Bryce	P J Prendergast	G Bougoure	Desert Moss	Tendentious	15	5–4
1963	Ostrya	Hornbeam	Lord Howard de Walden	J A Waugh	J Lindley	Shadow	Cretencia	8	100–9
1964	Windmill Girl	Hornbeam	Lt-Col Sir Jeffrey Darrell	A Budgett	A Breasley	Fusil	Lochailort	15	9–4
1965	Bracey Bridge	Chanteur II	M W Wickham-Boynton	N Murless	L Piggott	Miba	Wimpole Street	9	5–1
1966	Parthian Glance	Parthia	Mrs W H D Riley-Smith	G Todd	R Hutchinson	Varinia	Gyropolis	13	11–2
1967	Park Top	Kalydon	Duke of Devonshire	B van Cutsem	R Maddock	St Pauli Girl	Plotina	12	9–2
1968	Pandora Bay	Pandofell	Major C H Nathan	G Barling	M Thomas	Exchange	Celina	9	11–4
1969	Sleeping Partner	Parthia	Lord Rosebery	D Smith	J Gorton	Nedda	Relcia	10	7–4
1970	Parmelia	Ballymoss	Lord Howard de Walden	N Murless	A Barclay	Pretty Puffin	Riberta	12	9–1
1971	Fleet Wahine	Fleet Nasrullah	R R Ohrstrom	H Thomson Jones	G Starkey	Melodina	Hunting Cap	10	9–1
1972	Star Ship	Dicta Drake	C A B St George	H R Price	A Murray	Carezza	Moire	7	13–8
1973	Miss Petard	Petingo	P Williams	R Jarvis	M Thomas	Mandera	Wimosa	9	12–1
1974	Northern Princess	Sir Ivor	S Yoshida	J Hindley	A Kimberley	Hors Serie	Elegant Tern	8	9–2
1975	Gallina	Raise A Native	Simon Fraser	M V O'Brien	L Piggott	Light Duty	Foiled Again	6	7–1
1976	Catalpa	Reform	Lord Howard de Walden	H Cecil	A Bond	Roses For The Star	My Fair Niece	7	16–1
1977	Nanticious	Northfields	Mrs Bertram R Firestone	D Weld	W Swinburn	Busaca	Miss Pinkie	9	15–2
1978	Relfo	Relko	Lord Granard	P J Prendergast	C Roche	Be Sweet	Cherry Hinton	12	12–1
1979	Expansive	Exbury	HM The Queen	Major W R Hern	W Carson	Senorita Poquito	Crystal Queen	7	11–2
1980	Shoot A Line	High Line	R Budgett	Major W R Hern	W Carson	North Forland	Fenney Mill	9	5–2
1981	Strigida	Habitat	Lord Howard de Walden	H Cecil	L Piggott	Rollrights	Overplay	9	5–1
1982	Dish Dash	Bustino	J Bryce	R Armstrong	B Raymond	Sing Softly	Tants	10	6–1
1983	High Hawk	Shirley Heights	Sheikh Mohammed	J Dunlop	W Carson	Current Raiser	Funny Reef	14	7–1
1984	Ballinderry	Irish River	K Abdullah	J Tree	T Ives	Sandy Island	Mpani	9	9–2
1985	Sally Brown	Posse	R H Cowell	M Stoute	W R Swinburn	Graecia Magna	Goody Blake	10	7–1
1986	Gull Nook	Mill Reef	Lord Halifax	J Dunlop	Pat Eddery	Mill On The Floss	Santiki	12	8–1
1987	Queen Midas	Glint Of Gold	Louis Freedman	H Cecil	W Ryan	Blessed Event	Port Helene	6	9–1
1988	Miss Boniface	Tap On Wood	P A Kelleway	P A Kelleway	C Asmussen	Highbrow	Dutchess Best	11	12–1
1989	Alydaress	Alydar	Sheikh Mohammed	H Cecil	S Cauthen	Roseate Tern	Nearctic Flame	6	4–1
1990	Hellenic	Darshaan	Lord Weinstock	M Stoute	W R Swinburn	Ivrea	Gharam	11	6–1
1991	Third Watch	Slip Anchor	P G Goulandris	J Dunlop	J Reid	Finance Dancer	Sought Out	14	20–1
1992	Armarama	Persian Bold	C T Olley	C Brittain	M Roberts	Niodini	Blushing Storm	8	5–2
1993	Thawakib	Sadler's Wells	Hamdan Al Maktoum	J Dunlop	W Carson	Iviza	Talented	8	5–2
1994	Bolas	Unfuwain	K Abdullah	B Hills	Pat Eddery	Gothic Dream	Pearl Kite	9	3–1
1995	Phantom Gold	Machiavellian	HM The Queen	Lord Huntingdon	L Dettori	Tillandsia	Musetta	7	5–1
1996	Tulipa	Alleged	Sheikh Mohammed	A Fabre	S Guillot	Key Change	Shemozzle	10	15–2
1997	Yashmak	Danzig	K Abdullah	H Cecil	K Fallon	Akdariya	Crown Of Light	9	8–1
1998	Bahr	Generous	Godolphin	S bin Suroor	L Dettori	Star Begonia	Rambling Rose	9	10–1
1999	Fairy Queen	Fairy King	Godolphin	S bin Suroor	L Dettori	Samoa	Alabaq	12	14–1
2000	Miletrian	Marju	Miletrian plc	M Channon	M Roberts	Teggiano	Interlude	9	10–1
2001	Sahara Slew	Seattle Slew	Lady O'Reilly	J Oxx	J Murtagh	Nafisah	Marani	14	14–1

THE NORFOLK STAKES (Group 3)

Distance: 5 furlongs
For 2-year-olds

First run in 1843 as the New Stakes over the 2-year-old course of about 6 furlongs. Race shortened in 1907. Renamed in 1973.

YEAR	WINNER	SIRE	OWNER	TRAINER	JOCKEY	SECOND	THIRD	RUNNERS	SP
1946	Petition	Fair Trial	Sir Alfred Butt	Frank Butters	H Wragg	Goldsborough	Migoli	10	7–4
1947	[Lerins* (d ht)	Djebel	HH Maharaja of Baroda	F Armstrong	E Britt		Howdah	12	8–13
	Delirium (d ht)	Panorama	J Coltman	J Leach	C Smirke				7–1
1948	Makarpura	Big Game	HH Maharaja of Baroda	F Armstrong	C Smirke	Golden Triumph	Nasr-ed-Din	22	100–30
1949	Master Gunner	Nasrullah	D S Kennedy	P Thrale	K Gethin	Reminiscence	Full Dress	12	11–10
1950	Bay Meadows	Denturius	B J Hilliard	H Wragg	A Wragg	Zucchero	Crocodile	10	4–1
1951	Bob Major	Tudor Minstrel	Lord Rosebery	J Jarvis	W Rickaby	Fairforall	Double Blue	10	2–5
1952	Blue Lamp	Blue Peter	Mrs C M Woodbridge	Reg Day	D Smith	Turbulence	Marche Militaire	14	10–1
1953	Hydrologist	Golden Cloud	Mrs A Brown	W Bellerby	J Thompson	Arabian Night	L'Avengro	14	10–1
1954	Tamerlane	Persian Gulf	Lord Porchester	N Bertie	G Richards	Le Dieu d'Or	Beethoven	9	7–2
1955	Gratitude	Golden Cloud	Major L B Holliday	H Cottrill	D Smith	Prince Of Greine	Lucero	7	11–8
1956	Skindles Hotel	Maharaj Kumar	F Blackall	P J Prendergrast	B Swift	Ennis	Ballyprecious	15	11–2
1957	Pall Mall	Palestine	HM The Queen	Capt C Boyd-Rochfort	W H Carr	Troubadour	Will Somers	8	6–1
1958	Masham	King Of The Tudors	A R Ellis	G Brooke	D Smith	Galivanter	Spithead	8	8–1
1959	Sound Track	Whistler	Duke of Norfolk	W Smyth	G Lewis	Godiva's Pink Flower	Golden Merle	5	1–5
1960	Floribunda	Princely Gift	Mrs J R Mullion	P J Prendergast	R Hutchinson	Praise	Foxstar	7	2–7
1961	Abermaid	Abernant	Sir Percy Loraine	H Wragg	L Piggott	Princely Strath	Prince's Gift	13	3–1
1962	Daybreak	Golden Cloud	Sir Adrian Jarvis	J Jarvis	R Hutchinson	Romantic	Tierra Del Fuego	10	13–8
1963	Ballymacad	Kelly	Duke of Norfolk	G Smyth	R Hutchinson	Dark Sovereign	Blue Marine	8	9–4
1964	*race abandoned*								
1965	Tin King	Tin Whistle	C W Engelhard	R F Johnson Houghton	L Piggott	Track Spare	Village Cross	8	4–7
1966	Falcon	Milesian	C W Engelhard	R F Johnson Houghton	L Piggott	Wolver Hollow	Above Water	8	11–8
1967	Porto Bello	Floribunda	Dr D A Fermont	S Ingham	G Lewis	Sovereign Service	Whiz	4	7–4
1968	Song	Sing Sing	B P Jenks	D Candy	J Mercer	Lord John	Silverware	12	8–1
1969	Tribal Chief	Princely Gift	J L Swift	B Swift	J Wilson	Blinking	The Brianstan	8	7–2
1970	Swing Easy	Delta Judge	J H Whitney	J Tree	L Piggott	Our Note	Communication	6	5–2
1971	Philip Of Spain	Tudor Melody	Sir R Macdonald-Buchanan	N Murless	G Lewis	Firefright	Deep Diver	5	9–4
1972	Cade's County	Continuation	D Freeman	E Cousins	G Cadwaladr	Golden Master	Saulingo	8	10–1
1973	Habat	Habitat	Dr C Vittadini	P Walwyn	Pat Eddery	Red Alert	Flashback	11	7–4
1974	Overtown	Raffingora	Sir H Calley	D Smith	E Eldin	Touch Of Gold	Split Infinitive	12	9–2
1975	Faliraki	Prince Tenderfoot	Mrs M A O'Toole	M O'Toole	L Piggott	Royal Boy	National Wish	10	6–1
1976	Godswalk	Dancer's Image	P Gallagher	C Grassick	D Hogan	Alpherat	The Andrestan	5	8–13
1977	Emboss	Tribal Chief	T Saud	R Boss	L Piggott	Deed Of Gift	Golden Libra	5	11–4
1978	Schweppeshire Lad	Decoy Boy	M Madden	M Stoute	G Starkey	Inshallah	Park Romeo	8	9–4
1979	Romeo Romani	Jacinto	H Demetriou	H R Price	B Taylor	Jawad	Widd	10	7–2
1980	Chummy's Special	Mummy's Pet	J Maxwell	G Hunter	G Starkey	Tax Haven	Pontin Lad	6	11–2
1981	Day Is Done	Artaius	B Firestone	D Weld	W R Swinburn	Prowess Prince	My Dear Fellow	8	5–2
1982	Brondesbury	Welsh Saint	A Foustok	W A O'Gorman	T Ives	Krayyan	Maariv	5	8–11
1983	Precocious	Mummy's Pet	Lord Tavistock	H Cecil	L Piggott	Indigo Jones	Clantime	5	4–11
1984	Magic Mirror	Nureyev	S S Niarchos	M V O'Brien	L Piggott	Kentucky Quest	Absent Chimes	4	11–8
1985	Marouble	Double Form	Countess of Lonsdale	C Nelson	J Mercer	Runaway	Moonlight Lady	10	20–1
1986	Sizzling Melody	Song	Mrs Mary Watt	Lord John FitzGerald	R Hills	Zaibaq	Dominion Royal	6	5–1
1987	Colmore Row	Mummy's Pet	Mrs F G Allen	W Jarvis	B Raymond	Classic Ruler	Gallic League	8	100–30
1988	Superpower	Superlative	Mrs P L Yong	W A O'Gorman	T Ives	Desert Dawn	Time To Go Home	10	Evens
1989	Petillante	Petong	Peter Newell	A Scott	R Hills	Drayton Special	Elapse	6	10–1
1990	Line Engaged	Phone Trick	I Karageorgis	D Elsworth	S Cauthen	Sylva Honda	Gold Futures	9	14–1
1991	Magic Ring	Green Desert	Prince Fahd Salman	P Cole	A Munro	Paris House	Power Lake	9	7–4
1992	Niche	Risk Me	Lord Carnarvon	R Hannon	L Piggott	Silver Wizard	Darbonne	9	9–1
1993	Turtle Island	Fairy King	R E Sangster	P Chapple-Hyam	J Reid	Gold Land	Redoubtable	8	3–1
1994	Mind Games	Puissance	Robert Hughes	J Berry	J Carroll	Shamanic	General Monash	6	5–2
1995	Lucky Lionel	Mt Livermore	Antonio Balzarini	R Hannon	L Dettori	Cayman Kai	Mubhij	9	11–1
1996	Tipsy Creek	Dayjur	Abdullah Ali	B Hanbury	W Ryan	Raphane	Muchea	10	7–2
1997	Tippitt Boy	Prince Sabo	Highgrove Developments Ltd	K McAuliffe	J Reid	Hopping Higgins	Arawak Cay	6	33–1
1998	Rosselli	Puissance	T G Holdcroft	J Berry	J Carroll	Sheer Viking	Monkston Point	15	10–1
1999	Warm Heart	Diesis	Sheikh Mohammed	J Gosden	L Dettori	Victory Day	Asanovo	13	7–2
2000	Superstar Leo	College Chapel	The Superstar Leo Partnership	W Haggas	T Quinn	Bouncing Bowdler	Pan Jammer	11	5–1
2001	Johannesburg	Hennessy	M Tabor & Mrs John Magnier	A P O'Brien	M Kinane	Waterside	Lord Merlin	10	11–8

* Lerins was renamed My Babu in 1948

THE GOLD CUP (Group 1)

Distance: 2 miles 4 furlongs
For 4-year-olds and upwards.

First run in 1807 over 2 miles. Distance extended in 1808. Run as the Emperor's Plate from 1845 to 1853. Open to 3-year-olds from 1807 to 1986. Geldings excluded from 1904 to 1985.

YEAR	WINNER	SIRE	OWNER	TRAINER	JOCKEY	SECOND	THIRD	RUNNERS	SP
1945	Ocean Swell	Blue Peter	Lord Rosebery	J Jarvis	E Smith	Tehran	Abbots Fell	10	6–1
1946	Caracalla II	Tourbillon	Marcel Boussac	C Semblat	C Elliott	Chanteur II	Basileus	7	4–9
1947	Souverain	Maravedis	F R Schmitt	H Delavaud	M Lollierou	Chanteur II	Field Day	6	6–4
1948	Arbar	Djebel	Marcel Boussac	C Semblat	C Elliott	Bayeux II	Roi de Navarre II	8	4–6
1949	Alycidon	Donatello II	Lord Derby	W Earl	D Smith	Black Tarquin	Heron Bridge	7	5–4
1950	Supertello	Donatello II	W Harvey	J C Waugh	D Smith	Bagheera	Alindrake	13	10–1
1951	Pan II	Atys	E Constant	E Pollet	R Poincelet	Colonist II	Alizier	11	100–8
1952	Aquino II	Tornado	HH Maharanee of Baroda	F Armstrong	G Richards	Eastern Emperor	Talma II	6	4–1
1953	Souepi	Epigram	G R Digby	G R Digby	C Elliott	Aram	Le Bourgeois	10	11–2
1954	Elpenor	Owen Tudor	Marcel Boussac	C Elliott	J Doyasbere	Silex II	Blarney Stone	11	100–8
1955	Botticelli	Blue Peter	Marchese Incisa della Rochetta	U Penco	E Camici	Blue Prince II	Elpenor	6	9–4
1956	Macip	Marsyas II	Marcel Boussac	C Elliott	S Boullenger	Bewitched III	Clichy	10	6–1
1957	Zarathustra	Persian Gulf	T J S Gray	Capt C Boyd-Rochfort	L Piggott	Cambremer	Tissot	9	6–1
1958	Gladness	Sayajirao	J McShain	M V O'Brien	L Piggott	Hornbeam	Doutelle	8	3–1
1959	Wallaby II	Fast Fox	Baron G de Waldner	P Carter	F Palmer	Alcide	French Beige	6	9–4
1960	Sheshoon	Precipitation	Prince Aly Khan	A Head	G Moore	Exar	Le Loup Garou	6	7–4
1961	Pandofell	Solar Slipper	H Warwick Daw	F Maxwell	L Piggott	Jet Stream	Prolific	10	100–8
1962	Balto	Wild Risk	M A Rueff	M Bonaventure	F Palmer	Sagacity	Prolific	7	7–4
1963	Twilight Alley	Alycidon	Lady Sassoon	N Murless	L Piggott	Misti IV	Taine	7	100–30
1964	*race abandoned*								
1965	Fighting Charlie	Tenerani	Lady Mairi Bury	F Maxwell	L Piggott	Waldmeister	Autre Prince	7	6–1
1966	Fighting Charlie	Tenerani	Lady Mairi Bury	F Maxwell	G Starkey	Biomydrin	Mintmaster	7	15–8
1967	Parbury	Pardal	Major H P Holt	D Candy	J Mercer	Meharl	Danseur	7	7–1
1968	Pardallo II	Pardal	Mme Leon Volterra	C Bartholomew	W Pyers	Samos	Petrone	9	13–2
1969	Levmoss	Le Levanstell	S McGrath	S McGrath	W Williamson	Torpid	Fortissimo	6	15–8
1970	Precipice Wood	Lauso	R J McAlpine	Mrs R Lomax	J Lindley	Blakeney	Clairon	6	5–1
1971	Random Shot	Pirate King	Mrs G S Benskin	A Budgett	G Lewis	Orosio	Charlton	10	11–1
1972	Erimo Hawk	Sea Hawk II	Y Yamamoto	G Barling	Pat Eddery	Rock Roi	Irvine	8	10–1
1973	Lassalle	Bon Mot	Z Yoshida	R Carver	J Lindley	Celtic Cone	The Admiral	7	2–1
1974	Ragstone	Ragusa	Duke of Norfolk	J Dunlop	R Hutchinson	Proverb	Lassalle	6	6–4
1975	Sagaro	Espresso	G A Oldham	F Boutin	L Piggott	Le Bavard	Kambalda	8	7–4
1976	Sagaro	Espresso	G A Oldham	F Boutin	L Piggott	Crash Course	Sea Anchor	7	8–15
1977	Sagaro	Espresso	G A Oldham	F Boutin	L Piggott	Buckskin	Citoyen	6	9–4
1978	Shangamuzo	Klairon	Mrs E Charles	M Stoute	G Starkey	Royal Hive	Hawkberry	10	13–2
1979	Le Moss	Le Levanstell	C d'Alessio	H Cecil	L Piggott	Buckskin	Arapahos	6	7–4
1980	Le Moss	Le Levanstell	C d'Alessio	H Cecil	J Mercer	Ardross	Vincent	8	3–1
1981	Ardross	Run The Gantlet	C A B St George	H Cecil	L Piggott	Shoot A Line	Ayyabaan	4	30–100
1982	Ardross	Run The Gantlet	C A B St George	H Cecil	L Piggott	Tipperary Fixer	El Badr	5	1–5
1983	Little Wolf	Grundy	Lord Porchester	Major W R Hern	W Carson	Khairpour	Indian Prince	12	4–1
1984	Gildoran	Rheingold	R E Sangster	B Hills	S Cauthen	Ore	Condell	9	10–1
1985	Gildoran	Rheingold	R E Sangster	B Hills	B Thomson	Longboat	Destroyer	12	5–2
1986	Longboat	Welsh Pageant	R D Hollingsworth	Major W R Hern	W Carson	Eastern Mystic	Spicy Story	11	Evens
1987	Paean	Bustino	Lord Howard de Walden	H Cecil	S Cauthen	Sadeem	Saronicos	8	6–1
1988	Sadeem	Forli	Sheikh Mohammed	G Harwood	G Starkey	Sergeyevich	Chauve Souris	13	7–2
1989	Sadeem	Forli	Sheikh Mohammed	G Harwood	W Carson	Mazzacano	Lauries Crusador	8	8–11
1990	Ashal	Touching Wood	Hamdan Al Maktoum	H Thomson Jones	R Hills	Tyrone Bridge	Thethingaboutitis	11	14–1
1991	Indian Queen	Electric	Sir Gordon Brunton	Lord Huntingdon	W R Swinburn	Arzanni	Warm Feeling	12	25–1
1992	Drum Taps	Dixieland Band	Yoshio Asakawa	Lord Huntingdon	L Dettori	Arcadian Heights	Turgeon	6	7–4
1993	Drum Taps	Dixieland Band	Yoshio Asakawa	Lord Huntingdon	L Dettori	Assessor	Turgeon	10	13–2
1994	Arcadian Heights	Shirley Heights	J Pearce	G Wragg	M Hills	Vintage Crop	Sonus	9	20–1
1995	Double Trigger	Ela-Mana-Mou	R W Huggins	M Johnston	J Weaver	Moonax	Admiral's Well	7	9–4
1996	Classic Cliche	Salse	Godolphin	S bin Suroor	M Kinane	Double Trigger	Nononito	7	3–1
1997	Celeric	Mtoto	Christopher Spence	D Morley	Pat Eddery	Classic Cliche	Election Day	13	11–2
1998	Kayf Tara	Sadler's Wells	Godolphin	S bin Suroor	L Dettori	Double Trigger	Three Cheers	16	11–1
1999	Enzeli	Kahyasi	HH Aga Khan	J Oxx	J Murtagh	Invermark	Kayf Tara	17	20–1
2000	Kayf Tara	Sadler's Wells	Godolphin	S bin Suroor	M Kinane	Far Cry	Compton Ace	11	11–8
2001	Royal Rebel	Robellino	P D Savill	M Johnston	J Murtagh	Persian Punch	Jardines Lookout	12	8–1

THE CORK AND ORRERY STAKES (Group 2)

Distance: 6 furlongs
For 3-year-olds and upwards

First run 1868 as The All-Aged Stakes over 1 mile. From 1871 to 1898 run over the 2-year-old course of about 6 furlongs and from 1899 over its present distance. Renamed The Cork and Orrery All-Aged Stakes in 1926. Open to 2-year-olds until 1937. Elevated to Group 1 status and renamed The Golden Jubilee Stakes in 2002.

YEAR	WINNER	SIRE	OWNER	TRAINER	JOCKEY	SECOND	THIRD	RUNNERS	SP
1946	Honeyway	Fairway	Lord Milford	J Jarvis	E Smith	Daily Mail	Fine Art II	6	5–6
1947	The Bug	Signal Light	N H Wachman	M Marsh	C Smirke	Cul-de-Sac	Closeburn	9	11–10
1948	Delirium	Panorama	J T Coltman	J Leach	C Smirke	Palm Vista	Falls of Clyde	9	7–4
1949	Solonaway	Solferino	R A Duggan	M C Collins	G Richards	Wonder Why	Paramount	7	100–30
1950	Abadan	Persian Gulf	Lt-Col Giles Loder	H Hartigan	G Richards	Combined Operations	Bob Cherry	5	9–4
1951	Bob Cherry	Bobsleigh	Lord Sefton	H Persse	N Sellwood	Luminary	Balbuzard	9	13–8
1952	Royal Serenade	Royal Charger	G M Bell	H Wragg	E Mercer	Agitator	Miss Winston	7	6–1
1953	Blood Test	Fair Trial	Lt-Col Giles Loder	N Murless	G Richards	Set Fair	Banri an Oir	5	8–1
1954	Key	Big Game	Mrs D M FitzPatrick	N Murless	G Richards	Westerlands Rosebud	Fair Jane II	8	5–4
1955	Trouville	Dogat	Lady Waterford	W Smyth	W Rickaby	Royal Palm	My Kingdom	5	11–4
1956	Grass Court	Court Martial	Mrs C Evans	K Cundell	W Elliott	Andante	Princesse Reta	8	7–4
1957	Matador	Golden Cloud	Stanhope Joel	J A Waugh	E Smith	Wasps Fifteen	Tudor Grand	6	13–8
1958	Right Boy	Impeccable	G A Gilbert	W Dutton	L Piggott	Alastair	Rampant	5	5–6
1959	Right Boy	Impeccable	G A Gilbert	P Rohan	L Piggott	Red Sovereign	Capuchon	9	11–4
1960	Tin Whistle	Whistler	B W Grainger	P Rohan	L Piggott	Sovereign Path	Title Deed	7	8–13
1961	Bun Penny	Hook Money	Stanhope Joel	R Fetherstonhaugh	D Smith	Irish Gambol	Loquacious	8	2–1
1962	Compensation	Gratitude	Mrs G Lambton	E Lambton	J Lindley	Top Song	Prince Tor	9	4–1
1963	El Gallo	Matador	C A B St George	N Murless	L Piggott	Turbo Jet	Scabbard	7	20–1
1964	*race abandoned*								
1965	Majority Blue	Major Portion	Mrs B Aitken	J Oxx snr	W Williamson	Prince Of Orange	Port Merion	13	100–8
1966	Current Coin	Hook Money	Hugh Leggat	J Oxx snr	J Roe	Quisling	Prince Of Orange	10	100–8
1967	Siliconn	Princely Gift	Conn Pollock	T Corbett	G Moore	Empress Sissi	Holborn	8	5–2
1968	Moutain Call	Whistler	I E Kornberg	B van Cutsem	L Piggott	Abbie West	Welshman	7	8–15
1969	Tudor Music	Tudor Melody	David Robinson	M Jarvis	F Durr	Balidar	Burglar	8	4–1
1970	Welsh Saint	St Paddy	J P Philipps	M V O'Brien	L Piggott	Keekerok	Joshua	4	15–8
1971	King's Company	King's Troop	B Firestone	G W Robinson	F Head	Ma Sheema	Arctic Frolic	11	6–1
1972	Parsimony	Parthia	E Holland-Martin	R F Johnson Houghton	W Carson	Pearl Star	Princess Bonita	6	8–1
1973	Balliol	Will Somers	D Prenn	J Winter	B Taylor	Dapper	April Bloom	9	100–30
1974	Saritamer	Dancer's Image	C A B St George	M V O'Brien	L Piggott	Blessed Rock	Nevermore	17	11–1
1975	Swingtime	Buckpasser	John A Mulcahy	M V O'Brien	W Carson	Street Light	Our Charlie	9	11–4
1976	Gentilhombre	No Mercy	T Robson	N Adam	P Cook	Be Tuneful	Pascualete	11	17–2
1977	He Loves Me	Sovereign Path	J Allbritton	J Hindley	J Mercer	Bold Fantasy	Wolverlife	15	20–1
1978	Sweet Mint	Meadow Mint	M Wright	N Meade	W Swinburn	Double Form	La Rosee	12	20–1
1979	Thatching	Thatch	R E Sangster	M V O'Brien	L Piggott	Rose Above	Back Bailey	17	6–1
1980	Kearney	Sandford Lad	Mrs D Macgillycuddy	G W Robinson	W R Swinburn	Sharpo	Valeriga	20	40–1
1981	The Quiet Bidder	Auction Ring	Heathavon Stables Ltd	R Hollinshead	W R Swinburn	Crews Hill	Integrity	16	11–1
1982	Indian King	Raja Baba	J Levy	G Harwood	G Starkey	Vaigly Star	Great Eastern	18	9–2
1983	Sylvan Barbarosa	Native Bazaar	Mrs B Wade	P Mitchell	B Rouse	Curravilla	Times Time	17	20–1
1984	Committed	Hagley	R E Sangster	D Weld	B Thomson	Celestial Dancer	Gabitat	15	3–1
1985	Dafayna	Habitat	HH Aga Khan	M Stoute	W Carson	Gabitat	Alpine Strings	12	8–1
1986	Sperry	Stanford	Yahya Nasib	P Walwyn	Paul Eddery	Cyrano de Bergerac	Bridesmaid	10	9–1
1987	Big Shuffle	Super Concorde	Moyglare Stud Farms Ltd	D Weld	M Kinane	Ongoing Situation	Handsome Sailor	11	8–1
1988	Posada	Homing	T D Holland-Martin	R F Johnson Houghton	M Roberts	Wing Park	Point Of Light	14	11–2
1989	Danehill	Danzig	K Abdullah	J Tree	W Carson	Nabeel Dancer	Savahra Sound	12	11–8
1990	Great Commotion	Nureyev	Maktoum Al Maktoum	A Scott	Pat Eddery	Dead Certain	La Grange Music	17	5–1
1991	Polish Patriot	Danzig	R A Kirstein	G Harwood	R Cochrane	Chicarica	Montendre	16	5–1
1992	Shalford	Thatching	D F Cock	R Hannon	M Roberts	Amigo Menor	Spanish Storm	17	3–1
1993	College Chapel	Sharpo	Mrs M V O'Brien	M V O'Brien	L Piggott	Keen Hunter	Dolphin Street	19	7–2
1994	Owington	Green Desert	Baron G von Ullman	G Wragg	M Hills	So Factual	Catrail	17	4–1
1995	So Factual	Known Fact	Godolphin	S bin Suroor	L Dettori	Lake Coniston	Nuriva	11	9–2
1996	Atraf	Clantime	Hamdan Al Maktoum	D Morley	W Carson	Catch The Blues	Watch Me	17	12–1
1997	Royal Applause	Waajib	Maktoum Al Maktoum	B Hills	M Hills	Blue Goblin	Catch The Blues	23	11–2
1998	Tomba	Efisio	J R Good	B Meehan	M Tebbutt	Dyhim Diamond	Andreyev	12	4–1
1999	Bold Edge	Beveled	Lady Whent and Friends	R Hannon	Dane O'Neill	Russian Revival	Vision of Night	19	16–1
2000	Superior Premium	Forzando	J C Parsons	R Fahey	J Murtagh	Sampower Star	Lend A Hand	16	20–1
2001	Harmonic Way	Lion Cavern	Mrs Alexandra J Chandris	R Charlton	S Drowne	Three Points	Freud	21	10–1

THE KING EDWARD VII STAKES (Group 2)

Distance: 1 mile 4 furlongs
For 3-year-old colts and geldings

First run in 1834 as The Ascot Derby; renamed in 1926. Until 1947 the race was for 3-year-olds; from 1948 it was for colts and fillies. From 1976 fillies were excluded. Geldings again eligible from 1978.

YEAR	WINNER	SIRE	OWNER	TRAINER	JOCKEY	SECOND	THIRD	RUNNERS	SP
1946	Field Day	Fastnet	Prince Aly Khan	Frank Butters	G Richards	Fleet Street	Fine Lad	8	5–2
1947	Migoli	Bois Roussel	HH Aga Khan	Frank Butters	G Richards	Wet Bob	Blandace	5	1–4
1948	Vic Day	Prince Rose	H Blagrave	H Blagrave	W R Johnstone	Folie II	Alycidon	14	13–2
1949	Swallow Tail	Bois Roussel	Lord Derby	W Earl	D Smith	Astale	Scottish Meridian	7	4–5
1950	Babu's Pet	Hyperion	HH Maharaja of Baroda	G Duller	T Burns	Prince Simon	Exodus	4	20–1
1951	Supreme Court	Persian Gulf or Precipitation	Mrs V Lilley	E Williams	C Elliott	Sybil's Nephew	Fraise du Bois II	9	6–4
1952	Castleton	Windsor Slipper	T H Carey	T H Carey	D Smith	Indian Hemp	Arctic Lad	10	100–6
1953	Skyraider	Airborne	Prince Aly Khan	A Head	R Poincelet	Chatsworth	Pearl Stud	9	13–2
1954	Rashleigh	Precipitation	C Steuart	N Murless	G Richards	Tarjoman	Blue Prince II	8	5–1
1955	Nucleus	Nimbus	Miss Dorothy Paget	C Jerdein	L Piggott	True Cavalier	Praetorian	10	4–1
1956	Court Command	Precipitation	Mrs V Lilley	N Murless	L Piggott	Hornbeam	Prince Moon	12	100–7
1957	Arctic Explorer	Arctic Prince	Lt-Col Giles Loder	N Murless	L Piggott	Brioche	Messmate	8	6–1
1958	Restoration	Persian Gulf	HM The Queen	Capt C Boyd-Rochfort	W H Carr	Capitaine Corcoran	All Serene	10	6–1
1959	Pindari	Pinza	HM The Queen	N Murless	L Piggott	Hieroglyph	Peterman	12	13–8
1960	Atrax	Pharis II	Marcel Boussac	H Nicholas	R Poincelet	Faust	Jet Stream	12	4–1
1961	Aurelius	Aureole	Mrs V Lilley	N Murless	L Piggott	Pinzon	Gailowind	10	11–4
1962	Gaul	Alycidon	Lord Sefton	P Hastings-Bass	G Lewis	Escort	Silver Cloud	9	20–1
1963	Only For Life	Chanteur II	Miss M Sheriffe	J Tree	J Lindley	Nadir Shah	Fighting Ship	7	3–1
1964	*race abandoned*								
1965	Convamore	Court Harwell	E R More O'Ferrall	R Smyth	J Mercer	Bally Russe	Alcade	12	13–2
1966	Pretendre	Doutelle	J A C Lilley	J Jarvis	P Cook	Crozier	Crisp And Even	8	1–2
1967	Mariner	Acropolis	R D Hollingsworth	J Oxley	G Starkey	Hopeful Venture	Dancing Moss	10	8–1
1968	Connaught	St Paddy	H J Joel	N Murless	A Barclay	Ribero	Karabas	5	1–2
1969	Vervain	Crepello	Major Victor McCalmont	P Nelson	E Hide	Paddys Progress	Baggala	6	10–1
1970	Great Wall	Crepello	David Sung	A Breasley	W Williamson	Saracen Sword	Charlton	5	9–4
1971	Seafriend	Sea Hawk II	Mrs J R Mullion	P J Prendergast	J Mercer	Selhurst	Hazard	7	3–1
1972	Lord Nelson	Nelcius	T Frost	G Todd	W Williamson	Loyal Guard	Yaroslav	6	16–1
1973	Klairvimy	Klairon	Mrs B Allen Jones	D Weld	R Parnall	Tepukei	Proverb	7	10–1
1974	English Prince	Petingo	Mrs V Hue-Williams	P Walwyn	Pat Eddery	Straight As A Die	Honoured Guest	6	8–11
1975	Sea Anchor	Alcide	R D Hollingsworth	Major W R Hern	J Mercer	Libra's Rib	Whip It Quick	8	4–1
1976	Marquis de Sade	Queen's Hussar	C A B St George	H R Price	B Taylor	Smuggler	Tierra Fuego	5	6–1
1977	Classic Example	Run The Gantlet	Col F Hue-Williams	P Walwyn	Pat Eddery	Leonato	Ad Lib Ra	10	14–1
1978	Ile de Bourbon	Nijinsky	A McCall	R F Johnson Houghton	J Reid	Stradavinsky	Obraztsovy	10	11–1
1979	Ela-Mana-Mou	Pitcairn	Mrs A Muinos	G Harwood	G Starkey	Man Of Vision	Hardgreen	9	11–10
1980	Light Cavalry	Brigadier Gerard	H J Joel	H Cecil	J Mercer	Saviour	Saint Jonathan	10	9–2
1981	Bustomi	Bustino	Lady Beaverbrook	Major W R Hern	W Carson	Admirals Heir	Baz Bombati	10	13–2
1982	Open Day	Northfields	Sir Michael Sobell	Major W R Hern	W Carson	Lords	Old Country	11	9–1
1983	Shareef Dancer	Northern Dancer	Maktoum Al Maktoum	M Stoute	W R Swinburn	Russian Roubles	Hawa Bladi	7	10–1
1984	Head For Heights	Shirley Heights	Sheikh Mohammed	Major W R Hern	W Carson	Kirmann	Commanche Run	10	5–1
1985	Lanfranco	Relko	C A B St George	H Cecil	S Cauthen	Mango Express	Infantry	10	13–8
1986	Bonhomie	What A Pleasure	Sheikh Mohammed	H Cecil	S Cauthen	New Trojan	Nisnas	13	9–4
1987	Love the Groom	Blushing Groom	Mrs V Gaucci del Bono	J Dunlop	Pat Eddery	Legal Bid	Shantaroun	8	7–1
1988	Sheriff's Star	Posse	Lavinia Duchess of Norfolk	Lady Herries	T Ives	Polar Gap	Kalakate	8	9–2
1989	Cacoethes	Alydar	Lady Harrison	G Harwood	Pat Eddery	Zayyani	Spring Hay	6	8–13
1990	Private Tender	Shirley Heights	Cliveden Stud	H Cecil	S Cauthen	Mukddam	Air Music	8	11–4
1991	Saddlers' Hall	Sadler's Wells	Lord Weinstock	M Stoute	L Piggott	Secret Haunt	Marcus Thorpe	9	7–1
1992	Beyton	Alleged	D F Cock	R Hannon	M Kinane	Jeune	Alflora	12	12–1
1993	Beneficial	Top Ville	Exors of Sir Robin McAlpine	G Wragg	M Hills	Winged Victory	Azzilfi	8	11–4
1994	Foyer	Sadler's Wells	Sheikh Mohammed	M Stoute	M Kinane	Pencader	Opera Score	8	7–2
1995	Pentire	Be My Guest	Mollers Racing	G Wragg	M Hills	Classic Cliche	Kalabo	8	4–1
1996	Amfortas	Caerleon	B H Voak	C Brittain	B Doyle	Desert Boy	Shantou	7	66–1
1997	Kingfisher Mill	Riverman	Lord Howard de Walden	Mrs J Cecil	Pat Eddery	Palio Sky	Musical Dancer	5	9–4
1998	Royal Anthem	Theatrical	The Thoroughbred Corporation	H Cecil	K Fallon	Kilimanjaro	Scorned	10	9–4
1999	Mutafaweq	Silver Hawk	Godolphin	S bin Suroor	L Dettori	Iscan	Red Sea	10	4–1
2000	Subtle Power	Sadler's Wells	The Thoroughbred Corporation	H Cecil	T Quinn	Zafonium	Roscius	7	7–4
2001	Storming Home	Machiavellian	Maktoum Al Maktoum	B Hills	M Hills	Snowstorm	Theatre Script	12	9–2

THE HARDWICKE STAKES (Group 2)

Distance: 1 mile 4 furlongs
For 4-year-olds and upwards

First run in 1879. Until 1949 the race was for 3-year-olds and upwards. From 1950 to 1977 geldings were excluded.

YEAR	WINNER	SIRE	OWNER	TRAINER	JOCKEY	SECOND	THIRD	RUNNERS	SP
1946	Priam II	Pharis II	Marcel Boussac	C Semblat	C Elliott	Anwar	Scarlet Emperor	4	4–11
1947	Nirgal	Goya II	Marcel Boussac	C Semblat	C Elliott	Claro	Highland Laddie	5	2–1
1948	Sayajirao	Nearco	HH Maharajah of Baroda	F Armstrong	C Smirke	Nirgal	Pearl Diver	3	13–8
1949	Helioscope	Hyperion	Lady Zia Wernher	Capt C Boyd-Rochfort	J Sime	High Stakes	Dogger Bank	8	20–1
1950	Peter Flower	Blue Peter	Lord Rosebery	J Jarvis	W Rickaby	Iron Duke	Spy Legend	4	6–5
1951	Saturn	Hyperion	Lord Derby	G Colling	D Smith	Pardal	Burnt Brown	5	9–2
1952	Dynamiter	Pharis II	Marcel Boussac	J Glynn	C Elliott	Sybil's Nephew	Tufthunter	4	7–2
1953	Guersant	Bubbles	Baron Guy de Rothschild	G Watson	P Blanc	Pharad II	Gay Time	4	Evens
1954	Aureole	Hyperion	HM The Queen	Capt C Boyd-Rochfort	E Smith	Janitor	Karali	4	8–11
1955	Elopement	Rockefella	Sir Victor Sassoon	N Murless	L Piggott	By Thunder		2	6–5
1956	Hugh Lupus	Djebel	Lady Ursula Vernon	N Murless	W R Johnstone	Hafiz II	Kurun	6	100–30
1957	Fric	Vandale	M Calmann	J Lawson	J Deforge	Pirate King	High Veldt	6	11–10
1958	Brioche	Tantième	W Humble	Capt C Elsey	E Britt	China Rock	True Code	5	7–2
1959	Impatient	Precipitation	Sir Harold Wernher	J Gosden	J Lindley	Restoration	Guersillus	5	10–1
1960	Aggressor	Combat	Sir Harold Wernher	J Gosden	J Lindley	Parthia	Barclay	5	7–2
1961	St Paddy	Aureole	Sir Victor Sassoon	N Murless	L Piggott	Vienna	Die Hard	4	4–9
1962	Aurelius	Aureole	Mrs V Lilley	N Murless	A Breasley	Hot Brandy	Dahabeah	4	8–13
1963	Miralgo	Aureole	G A Oldham	H Wragg	W Williamson	Best Song	Tender Annie	8	100–30
1964	*race abandoned*								
1965	Soderini	Crepello	L L Lawrence	S Ingham	G Lewis	Earldom	Bally Joy	9	3–1
1966	Prominer	Beau Sabreur	J R Mullion	P J Prendergast	D Lake	Rehearsed	I Say	6	4–1
1967	Salvo	Right Royal V	G A Oldham	H Wragg	R Hutchinson	Sodium	My Kuda	8	7–4
1968	Hopeful Venture	Aureole	HM The Queen	N Murless	A Barclay	Tapis Rose	Fortissimo	6	4–6
1969	Park Top	Kalydon	Duke of Devonshire	B van Cutsem	G Lewis	Chicago	Bringley	4	11–8
1970	Karabas	Worden II	Lord Iveagh	B van Cutsem	L Piggott	Intermezzo	Reindeer	5	11–8
1971	Ortis	Tissot	Dr C Vittadini	P Walwyn	D Keith	Pembroke Castle	Laurence	8	9–2
1972	Selhurst	Charlottesville	H J Joel	N Murless	G Lewis	Frascati	Homeric	5	11–4
1973	Rheingold	Faberge II	H Zeisel	B Hills	Y Saint-Martin	Attica Meli	Baragoi	4	1–5
1974	Relay Race	Relko	Sir R Macdonald-Buchanan	H Cecil	L Piggott	Buoy	Klairvimy	5	10–11
1975	Charlie Bubbles	Wolver Hollow	L Sainer	P Walwyn	Pat Eddery	Arthurian	Dibidale	11	12–1
1976	Orange Bay	Canisbay	Dr C Vittadini	P Walwyn	Pat Eddery	Bruni	Libra's Rib	5	9–2
1977	Meneval	Le Fabuleux	Mrs George F Getty II	M V O'Brien	L Piggott	Ranimer	Quiet Fling	7	2–1
1978	Montcontour	Luthier	Mrs H Hausmann	M Zilber	Y Saint-Martin	Dunfermline	Balmerino	8	25–1
1979	Obraztsovy	His Majesty	R E Sangster	H R Price	B Taylor	Noir et Or	Swiss Maid	6	9–4
1980	Scorpio	Sir Gaylord	G A Oldham	F Boutin	P Paquet	More Light	Noelino	7	2–1
1981	Pelerin	Sir Gaylord	Sir Philip Oppenheimer	H Wragg	B Taylor	Light Cavalry	Lancastrian	9	7–1
1982	Critique	Roberto	G Vanian	H Cecil	L Piggott	Glint Of Gold	Stanerra	8	7–2
1983	Stanerra	Guillaume Tell	F Dunne	F Dunne	B Rouse	Electric	Be My Native	10	4–1
1984	Khairpour	Arctic Tern	G J Chittick	R F Johnson Houghton	S Cauthen	Jupiter Island	Trakady	7	13–2
1985	Jupiter Island	St Paddy	Lord Tavistock	C Brittain	L Piggott	Seismic Wave	Raft	4	85–40
1986	Dihistan	Tyrnavos	HH Aga Khan	M Stoute	Pat Eddery	St Hilarion	Iroko	10	11–2
1987	Orban	Irish River	Prince A A Faisal	H Cecil	S Cauthen	All Haste	Moon Madness	4	11–4
1988	Almaarad	Ela-Mana-Mou	Hamdan Al Maktoum	J Dunlop	W Carson	Infamy	Moon Madness	8	6–1
1989	Assatis	Topsider	K Abdullah	G Harwood	Pat Eddery	Top Class	Emmson	4	4–11
1990	Assatis	Topsider	S Harada	G Harwood	R Cochrane	Ile de Nisky	Old Vic	7	50–1
1991	Rock Hopper	Shareef Dancer	Maktoum Al Maktoum	M Stoute	Pat Eddery	Topanoora	Spritsail	9	5–6
1992	Rock Hopper	Shareef Dancer	Maktoum Al Maktoum	M Stoute	Pat Eddery	Sapience	Luchiroverte	5	8–15
1993	Jeune	Kalaglow	Exors of Sir Robin McAlpine	G Wragg	R Cochrane	Red Bishop	Highland Dress	5	7–2
1994	Bobzao	Alzao	T G Mills	T G Mills	J Reid	Bob's Return	Wagon Master	11	11–1
1995	Beauchamp Hero	Midyan	E Penser	J Dunlop	J Reid	Midnight Legend	Bal Harbour	6	11–2
1996	Oscar Schindler	Royal Academy	Oliver Lehane	K Prendergast	M Kinane	Annus Mirabilis	Posidonas	8	7–4
1997	Predappio	Polish Precedent	Godolphin	S bin Suroor	Gary Stevens	Pilsudski	Whitewater Affair	10	6–1
1998	Posidonas	Slip Anchor	Athos Christodoulou	P Cole	Pat Eddery	Germano	Swain	7	15–2
1999	Fruits Of Love	Hansel	M Doyle	M Johnston	O Peslier	Royal Anthem	Sea Wave	8	12–1
2000	Fruits Of Love	Hansel	M Doyle	M Johnston	O Peslier	Yavana's Pace	Blueprint	9	9–2
2001	Sandmason	Grand Lodge	Plantation Stud	H Cecil	W Ryan	Zindabad	Mutafaweq	7	12–1

THE CORONATION STAKES (Group 1)

Distance: 1 mile (Old Mile)
For 3-year-old fillies

First run in 1840.

YEAR	WINNER	SIRE	OWNER	TRAINER	JOCKEY	SECOND	THIRD	RUNNERS	SP
1946	Neolight	Nearco	J A Dewar	F Darling	G Richards	Cama	Amboyna	7	15–8
1947	Saucy Sal	Atout Maitre	Mrs G Blagrave	H Blagrave	W R Johnstone	Netherton Maid	Missolonghi	9	20–1
1948	Fortuity	Colombo	J Musker	M Marsh	E Britt	Tudor Lady	Open Sesame	8	20–1
1949	Avila	Hyperion	HM The King	Capt C Boyd-Rochfort	M Beary	Solar Myth	Suntime	15	11–2
1950	Tambara	Nasrullah	HH Aga Khan	M Marsh	C Smirke	Happy Haven	Flying Slipper	7	6–5
1951	Belle Of All	Nasrullah	H S Tufton	N Bertie	G Richards	Djebellica	Camp Fire	11	15–8
1952	Zabara	Persian Gulf	Sir Malcolm McAlpine	V Smyth	K Gethin	Adjournment	Pharamis	7	6–5
1953	Happy Laughter	Royal Charger	D H Wills	J Jarvis	W Rickaby	Tessa Gillian	Tudor Goddess	7	7–4
1954	Festoon	Fair Trial	J A Dewar	N Cannon	J Mercer	Sybil's Niece	Aliscia	6	11–8
1955	Meld	Alycidon	Lady Zia Wernher	Capt C Boyd-Rochfort	W H Carr	Gloria Nicky	Mary Falconer	5	4–9
1956	Midget II	Djebe	M Pierre Wertheimer	A Head	W R Johnstone	Victoria Cross	Arietta	7	5–6
1957	Toro	Tudor Minstrel	HH Aga Khan	A Head	J Massard	Angelet	Sarcelle	11	3–1
1958	St Lucia	Alycidon	Lord Sefton	P Hastings-Bass	G Lewis	Yla	Persian Wheel	8	100–8
1959	Rosalba	Court Martial	J J Astor	R J Colling	J Mercer	Ginetta	Mirnaya	8	11–8
1960	Barbaresque	Ocarina	W F C Guest	W Clout	G Moore	Running Blue	Lady In Trouble	6	9–2
1961	Aiming High	Djebe	HM The Queen	N Murless	L Piggott	Opaline II	Ambergris	6	100–8
1962	Display	Rustam	Beatrice Lady Granard	P J Prendergast	G Bougoure	Mona Louise	Lovely Gale	8	3–1
1963	Fiji	Acropolis	Lady Halifax	J Oxley	G Starkey	Crevette	Honey Portion	7	7–2
1964	Ocean	Petition	R D Hollingsworth	J Oxley	G Starkey	Words And Music	Pourparler	6	7–1
1965	Greengage	Primera	R F Watson	Sir Gordon Richards	A Breasley	Night Off	Quitta II	8	5–4
1966	Haymaking	Galivanter	Clifford Nicholson	R F Johnson Houghton	J Mercer	Bravery	Glad Rags	8	100–7
1967	Fleet	Immortality	R C Boucher	N Murless	G Moore	Royal Saint	Whirled	8	15–8
1968	Sovereign	Pardao	R B Moller	H Wragg	R Hutchinson	Front Row	Pseudonym	6	3–1
1969	Lucyrowe	Crepello	L Freedman	P Walwyn	D Keith	Knighton House	Belitis	10	15–8
1970	Humble Duty	Sovereign Path	Jean Lady Ashcombe	P Walwyn	D Keith	Black Satin	Spotty Bebe	3	1–6
1971	Magic Flute	Tudor Melody	Lord Howard de Walden	N Murless	G Lewis	Seaswan	Favoletta	4	85–40
1972	Calve	Bold Ruler	Lord Granard	P J Prendergast	L Piggott	Waterloo	Miss Paris	7	12–1
1973	Jacinth	Red God	Lady Butt	B Hobbs	J Gorton	Silver Birch	Melodramatic	9	15–8
1974	Lisadell	Forli	John A Mulcahy	M V O'Brien	L Piggott	Himawari	Matuno God	8	7–2
1975	Roussalka	Habitat	N Phillips	H Cecil	L Piggott	Tender Camilla	Highest Trump	11	9–1
1976	Kesar Queen	Nashua	Ravi N Tikkoo	A Breasley	Y Saint-Martin	Guichet	Clover Princess	8	7–2
1977	Orchestration	Welsh Pageant	Major V McCalmont	A Maxwell	Pat Eddery	Lady Capulet	No Cards	10	12–1
1978	Sutton Place	Tyrant	Mrs T Donahue	D Weld	W Swinburn	Ridaness	Baccalaureate	14	14–1
1979	One In A Million	Rarity	Helena Springfield Ltd	H Cecil	J Mercer	Topsy	Yanuka	13	10–11
1980	Cairn Rouge	Pitcairn	D Brady	M Cunningham	A Murray	Quick As Lightning	Our Home	8	6–5
1981	Tolmi	Great Nephew	G Cambanis	B Hobbs	E Hide	Happy Bride	Nasseem	10	4–1
1982	Chalon	Habitat	M Riordan	H Cecil	L Piggott	Grease	Dancing Rocks	8	9–4
1983	Flame Of Tara	Artaius	Miss P O'Kelly	J Bolger	D Gillespie	Favoridge	Magdalena	6	11–2
1984	Katies	Nonoalco	T P Ramsden	M J Ryan	P Robinson	Pebbles	So Fine	10	11–2
1985	Al Bahathri	Blushing Groom	Hamdan Al Maktoum	H Thomson Jones	A Murray	Top Socialite	Soprano	7	4–6
1986	Sonic Lady	Nureyev	Sheikh Mohammed	M Stoute	W R Swinburn	Embla	Someone Special	7	8–15
1987	Milligram	Mill Reef	Helena Springfield Ltd	M Stoute	W R Swinburn	Shaikiya	Martha Stevens	6	4–5
1988	Magic Of Life	Seattle Slew	S S Niarchos	J Tree	Pat Eddery	Inchmurrin	Ravinella	8	16–1
1989	Golden Opinion	Slew O' Gold	Sheikh Mohammed	A Fabre	C Asmussen	Magic Gleam	Guest Artiste	12	7–2
1990	Chimes Of Freedom	Private Account	S S Niarchos	H Cecil	S Cauthen	Hasbah	Heart Of Joy	7	11–2
1991	Kooyonga	Persian Bold	M Haga	M Kauntze	W O'Connor	Shadayid	Gussy Marlowe	8	3–1
1992	Marling	Lomond	E J Loder	G Wragg	W R Swinburn	Culture Vulture	Katakana	7	8–11
1993	Gold Splash	Blushing Groom	J Wertheimer	Mme C Head	G Mosse	Elizabeth Bay	Zarani Sidi Anna	5	100–30
1994	Kissing Cousin	Danehill	Sheikh Mohammed	H Cecil	M Kinane	Eternal Reve	Mehthaaf	10	13–2
1995	Ridgewood Pearl	Indian Ridge	Mrs Anne Coughlan	J Oxx	J Murtagh	Smolensk	Harayir	10	9–2
1996	Shake The Yoke	Caerleon	S Brunswick	E Lellouche	O Peslier	Last Second	Dance Design	7	Evens
1997	Rebecca Sharp	Machiavellian	A E Oppenheimer	G Wragg	M Hills	Ocean Ridge	Sleepytime	6	25–1
1998	Exclusive	Polar Falcon	Cheveley Park Stud	Sir Michael Stoute	W R Swinburn	Zalaiyka	Winona	9	5–1
1999	Balisada	Kris	A E Oppenheimer	G Wragg	M Roberts	Golden Silca	Wannabe Grand / Valentine Waltz (d ht)	9	16–1
2000	Crimplene	Lion Cavern	Sheikh Marwan Al Maktoum	C Brittain	P Robinson	Princess Ellen	Bluemamba	9	4–1
2001	Banks Hill	Danehill	K Abdullah	A Fabre	O Peslier	Crystal Music	Tempting Fate	13	4–1

THE WOKINGHAM STAKES (Handicap)

Distance: 6 furlongs

For 3-year-olds and upwards

First run in 1813.

YEAR	WINNER	SIRE	OWNER	TRAINER	JOCKEY	SECOND	THIRD	RUNNERS	SP
1945	Portamara	Portlaw	D Morris	J Beary	D Smith	Honeyway	Sir Edward	10	20–1
1946	The Bug	Signal Light	N H Wachman	G Wellesley	C Smirke	Commissar	Chateau Madrid	21	7–1
1947	Lucky Jordan	Panorama	Mrs G Gilroy	A Boyd	J Sirett	Val de Grace	La Scala	24	33–1
1948	White Cockade	Orthodox	R L Glasspool	T Leader	J Sirett	Final Score	Clarion III	32	33–1
1949	The Cobbler	Windsor Slipper	Lt-Col Giles Loder	N Murless	G Richards	Irish Dance	Colorado Star	35	4–1
1950	Blue Book	Court Martial	H E Morriss	M Marsh	E Britt	Angelico	Spartan Sacrifice	24	100–6
1951	Donore	Fair Trial	Sir Humphrey de Trafford	Capt C Boyd-Rochfort	W H Carr	Spartan Sacrifice	Byland	23	100–9
1952	Malka's Boy	Nasrullah	H E Elvin	W Nightingall	L Piggott	Orgoglio	Hyacinthus	22	100–6
1953	Jupiter	The Phoenix	Lord Lambton	P Beasley	J Sirett	Donore	Spring Day	22	22–1
1954	March Past	Petition	Mrs G Trimmer-Thompson	K Cundell	W Rickaby	Military Court	Stone Fox	16	15–2
1955	The Plumber's Mate	Vigorous	Lord Ashcombe	H Smyth	D Keith	Polish Lancer	Kenmore	19	25–1
1956	Light Harvest	Signal Light	Col D Foster	J A Waugh	J Sime	Cockrullah	Eccleston Street	28	100–6
1957	Dionisio	My Babu	P Bull	Capt C Elsey	E Britt	Bigibigi	Light Harvest	8	5–1
1958	Magic Boy	Magic Red	Lt-Commander Dawson Miller	M Bolton	D Greening	Autonomy	Earl Marshal	22	20–1
1959	Golden Leg	Golden Cloud	Edwin McAlpine	M Pope	R P Elliott	Anxious Lady	Logarithm	29	33–1
1960	Silver King	Grey Sovereign	J Phang jnr	S Hall	J Sime	Sovereign Path	Dawn Watch	29	15–2
1961	Whistler's Daughter	Whistler	T S Lucas	S Hall	J Sime	Little Redskin	Frieze's Winna	28	10–1
1962	Elco	King's Bench	Capt T E Langton	D Whelan	W Williamson	Demerara	Rins Of Clyde	35	20–1
1963	Marcher	March Past	R Zelker	D Hanley	R Hutchinson	Spring Wheat	Creole	27	100–8
1964	*race abandoned*								
1965	Nunshoney	Welsh Abbot	G C Todd	G Beeby	D East	Silver Churn	Audience	25	33–1
1966	My Audrey	Pall Mall	Mrs D Rosenfield	E Cousins	G Cadwaladr	Air Patrol	Barrymore	33	20–1
1967	Spaniards Mount	Monet	B Schmidt-Bodner	J Winter	D Smith	Lunar Princess	Vibrant	19	100–6
1968	Charicles	Bleep Bleep	P Bull	E Lambton	D East	Gemini Six	Directory	21	100–7
1969	Sky Rocket	Warfare	A B Pope	M Pope	Pat Eddery	Spaniards Inn	Bunto	21	20–1
1970	Virginia Boy	Polly's Jet	B Schmidt-Bodner	D Smith	D McKay	Koala	Sweet Revenge	28	100–9
1971	Whistling Fool	Whistling Wind	B Schmidt-Bodner	D Smith	D McKay	Golden Tack	Sweet Revenge	21	11–2
1972	Le Johnstan	El Gallo	S Powell	J Sutcliffe jnr	G Lewis	Prince Of Dunoon	Golden Tack	17	9–1
1973	Plummet	Falcon	M Myers	J E Sutcliffe	W Carson	Welsh Warrior	Fallowfield	21	11–1
1974	Ginnies Pet	Compensation	J Jackson	J E Sutcliffe	L Piggott	Western Run	Hovis	22	7–1
1975	Boone's Cabin	Forli	R E Sangster	M V O'Brien	L Piggott	Tolspring	Blue Star	20	6–1
1976	Import	Porto Bello	Major G Cayzer	W Wightman	M Thomas	Caljobo	Ribramble	12	4–1
1977	Calibina	Caliban	E Badger	P Cole	G Baxter	Last Tango	Kintore	13	14–1
1978	Equal Opportunity	Birdbrook	P Wentworth	P Arthur	R Curant	Overseas Admirer	Scott Joplyn	24	20–1
1979	Lord Rochford	Tudor Music	B Shine	B Swift	S Raymont	Marching On	Kintore	28	16–1
1980	Queen's Pride	Royben	Mrs L d'Ambrumenil	P Cole	G Baxter	King Of Spain	Columnist	29	28–1
1981	Great Eastern	Jukebox	Mrs A Struthers	J Dunlop	W Carson	Enchantment	Ferriby Hall	29	16–1
1982	Battle Hymn	Music Boy	Mrs D Abbott	G Harwood	A Clark	Camisite	Murillo	24	14–1
1983	Melindra	Goldform	Miss A Winfield	D Elsworth	A McGlone	Milk Heart	Morse Pip	27	7–1
1984	Petong	Mansingh	T G Warner	M Jarvis	B Raymond	Amarone	Milk Heart	28	11–1
1985	Time Machine	Connaught	T Harty	P Hughes	W Carson	Bridge Street Lady	Al Trui	30	10–1
1986	Touch Of Grey	Blakeney	T M Jennings	D Thom	M Thomas	Manimstar	Perfect Timing	28	20–1
1987	Bel Byou	Try My Best	Prince Fahd Salman	P Cole	T Quinn	Dorking Lad	Miss Primula	29	11–2
1988	Powder Blue	He Loves Me	Stewart McColl	P J Makin	T Ives	Norgabie	Slip and Stick	30	28–1
1989	Mac's Fighter	Hard Fought	M McDonnell	W A O'Gorman	C Asmussen	A Prayer For Wings	Bertie Wooster	27	16–1
1990	Knight of Mercy	Aragon	M W Grant	R Hannon	Pat Eddery	Amigo Menor	Hana Marie	28	16–1
1991	Amigo Menor	Whistling Deer	Frank Glennon	D J G Murray-Smith	C Rutter	Local Lass	Cantoris	29	14–1
1992	Red Rosein	Red Sunset	J S Gittins	Capt J Wilson	G Carter	Double Blue	Kayvee	29	33–1
1993	Nagida	Skyliner	Mrs U D Toller	J A R Toller	J Weaver	Cumbrian Waltzer	Arabellajill	30	11–1
1994	Venture Capitalist	Never So Bold	Stanley E Lever	R Hannon	J Reid	Law Commission	No Extras	30	20–1
1995	Astrac	Nordico	C J Titcomb	R Akehurst	S Sanders	Alzianah	Brave Edge	30	14–1
1996	Emerging Market	Emarati	Philip Wroughton	J Dunlop	K Darley	Prince Babar	Double Bounce	29	33–1
1997	Selhurstpark Flyer	Northiam	Chris Deuters	J Berry	P Roberts	Danetime	Bollin Joanne	30	25–1
1998	Selhurstpark Flyer	Northiam	Chris & Antonia Deuters	J Berry	C Lowther	Dancethenightaway	Superior Premium	29	16–1
1999	Deep Space	Green Desert	Maktoum Al Maktoum	E Dunlop	G Carter	Halmahera	Young Josh	30	14–1
2000	Harmonic Way	Lion Cavern	Mrs Alexandra Chandris	R Charlton	R Hughes	Tussle	Strahan	29	12–1
2001	Nice One Clare	Mukaddamah	Oremsa Partnership	J W Payne	J Murtagh	Ellens Academy	Seven No Trumps	30	7–1

PRINCIPAL FLAT RACES OUTSIDE ROYAL MEETING

THE KING GEORGE VI AND QUEEN ELIZABETH DIAMOND STAKES (Group 1) *Sponsored by the De Beers Group.*

Distance: 1 mile 4 furlongs

For 3-year-olds and upwards

First run in 1951 to mark the Festival of Britain.

YEAR	WINNER	SIRE	OWNER	TRAINER	JOCKEY	SECOND	THIRD	RUNNERS	SP
1951	Supreme Court	Persian Gulf or Precipitation	Mrs T Lilley	E Williams	C Elliott	Zucchero	Tantième	19	100–9
1952	Tulyar	Tehran	HH Aga Khan	M Marsh	C Smirke	Gay Time	Worden II	15	3–1
1953	Pinza	Chanteur II	Sir Victor Sassoon	N Bertie	G Richards	Aureole	Worden II	13	2–1
1954	Aureole	Hyperion	HM The Queen	Capt C Boyd-Rochfort	E Smith	Vamos	Darius	17	9–2
1955	Vimy	Wild Risk	M P Wertheimer	A Head	R Poincelet	Acropolis	Elopement	10	10–1
1956	Ribot	Tenerani	Marchese Incisa della Rochetta	U Penco	E Camici	High Veldt	Todrai	9	2–5
1957	Montaval	Norseman	R B Strassburger	G Bridgland	F Palmer	Al Mabsoot	Tribord	12	20–1
1958	Ballymoss	Mossborough	J McShain	M V O'Brien	A Breasley	Almeria	Doutelle	8	7–4
1959	Alcide	Alycidon	Sir Humphrey de Trafford	Capt C Boyd-Rochfort	W H Carr	Gladness	Balbo	11	2–1
1960	Aggressor	Combat	Sir Harold Wernher	J Gosden	J Lindley	Petite Etoile	Kythnos	8	100–8
1961	Right Royal V	Owen Tudor	Mme J Couturie	E Pollet	R Poincelet	St Paddy	Rockavon	4	6–4
1962	Match III	Tantième	M F Dupre	F Mathet	Y Saint-Martin	Aurelius	Arctic Storm	11	9–2
1963	Ragusa	Ribot	J R Mullion	P J Prendergast	G Bougoure	Miralgo	Tarqogan	10	4–1
1964	Nasram II	Nasrullah	Mrs Howell E Jackson	E Fellows	W Pyers	Santa Claus	Royal Avenue	4	100–7
1965	Meadow Court	Court Harwell	G M Bell	P J Prendergast	L Piggott	Soderini	Oncidium	12	6–5
1966	Aunt Edith	Primera	Lt-Col J Hornung	N Murless	L Piggott	Sodium	Prominer	5	7–2
1967	Busted	Crepello	Stanhope Joel	N Murless	G Moore	Salvo	Ribocco	9	4–1
1968	Royal Palace	Ballymoss	H J Joel	N Murless	A Barclay	Felicio II	Topyo	7	4–7
1969	Park Top	Kalydon	Duke of Devonshire	B van Cutsem	L Piggott	Crozier	Hogarth	9	9–4
1970	Nijinsky	Northern Dancer	C W Engelhard	M V O'Brien	L Piggott	Blakeney	Crepellana	6	40–85
1971	Mill Reef	Never Bend	Paul Mellon	I Balding	G Lewis	Ortis	Acclimatization	10	8–13
1972	Brigadier Gerard	Queen's Hussar	Mrs J Hislop	Major W R Hern	J Mercer	Parnell	Riverman	9	8–13
1973	Dahlia	Vaguely Noble	N Bunker Hunt	M Zilber	W Pyers	Rheingold	Our Mirage	12	10–1
1974	Dahlia	Vaguely Noble	N Bunker Hunt	M Zilber	L Piggott	Highclere	Dankaro	10	15–8
1975	Grundy	Great Nephew	Dr C Vittadini	P Walwyn	Pat Eddery	Bustino	Dahlia	11	4–5
1976	Pawneese	Carvin	D Wildenstein	A Penna	Y Saint-Martin	Bruni	Orange Bay	10	9–4
1977	The Minstrel	Northern Dancer	R E Sangster	M V O'Brien	L Piggott	Orange Bay	Exceller	11	7–4
1978	Ile de Bourbon	Nijinsky	A McCall	R F Johnson Houghton	J Reid	Acamas	Hawaiian Sound	14	12–1
1979	Troy	Petingo	Sir Michael Sobell	Major W R Hern	W Carson	Gay Mecene	Ela-Mana-Mou	7	2–5
1980	Ela-Mana-Mou	Pitcairn	S Weinstock	Major W R Hern	W Carson	Mrs Penny	Gregorian	10	11–4
1981	Shergar	Great Nephew	HH Aga Khan	M Stoute	W R Swinburn	Madam Gay	Fingals Cave	7	2–5
1982	Kalaglow	Kalamoun	A Ward	G Harwood	G Starkey	Assert	Glint Of Gold	9	13–2
1983	Time Charter	Saritamer	R Barnett	H Candy	J Mercer	Diamond Shoal	Sun Princess	9	5–1
1984	Teenoso	Youth	E B Moller	G Wragg	L Piggott	Sadler's Wells	Tolomeo	13	13–2
1985	Petoski	Nijinsky	Lady Beaverbrook	Major W R Hern	W Carson	Oh So Sharp	Rainbow Quest	12	12–1
1986	Dancing Brave	Lyphard	K Abdullah	G Harwood	Pat Eddery	Shardari	Triptych	9	6–4
1987	Reference Point	Mill Reef	Louis Freedman	H Cecil	S Cauthen	Celestial Storm	Triptych	9	11–10
1988	Mtoto	Busted	Sheikh Ahmed Al Maktoum	A Stewart	M Roberts	Unfuwain	Tony Bin	10	4–1
1989	Nashwan	Blushing Groom	Hamdan Al Maktoum	Major W R Hern	W Carson	Cacoethes	Top Class	7	2–9
1990	Belmez	El Gran Senor	Sheikh Mohammed	H Cecil	M Kinane	Old Vic	Assatis	11	15–2
1991	Generous	Caerleon	Prince Fahd Salman	P Cole	A Munro	Sanglamore	Rock Hopper	9	4–6
1992	St Jovite	Pleasant Colony	Mrs Virginia Kraft Payson	J Bolger	S Craine	Saddlers' Hall	Opera House	8	4–5
1993	Opera House	Sadler's Wells	Sheikh Mohammed	M Stoute	M Roberts	White Muzzle	Commander In Chief	10	8–1
1994	King's Theatre	Sadler's Wells	Sheikh Mohammed	H Cecil	M Kinane	White Muzzle	Wagon Master	12	12–1
1995	Lammtarra	Nijinsky	Saeed Maktoum Al Maktoum	S bin Suroor	L Dettori	Pentire	Strategic Choice	7	9–4
1996	Pentire	Be My Guest	Mollers Racing	G Wragg	M Hills	Classic Cliché	Shaamit	8	100–30
1997	Swain	Nashwan	Godolphin	S bin Suroor	J Reid	Pilsudski	Helissio	8	16–1
1998	Swain	Nashwan	Godolphin	S bin Suroor	L Dettori	High-Rise	Royal Anthem	8	11–2
1999	Daylami	Doyoun	HH Aga Khan	S bin Suroor	L Dettori	Nedawi	Fruits Of Love	8	3–1
2000	Montjeu	Sadler's Wells	M Tabor	J E Hammond	M Kinane	Fantastic Light	Daliapour	7	1–3
2001	Galileo	Sadler's Wells	Mrs J Magnier & M Tabor	A P O'Brien	M Kinane	Fantastic Light	Hightori	12	1–2

THE QUEEN ELIZABETH II STAKES (Group I)
Distance: 1 mile (Old Mile)
For 3-year-olds and upwards

First run in 1955. Geldings have been eligible since 1976.

YEAR	WINNER	SIRE	OWNER	TRAINER	JOCKEY	SECOND	THIRD	RUNNERS	SP
1955	Hafiz II	Nearco	HH Aga Khan	A Head	R Poincelet	Golden Planet	My Smokey	8	9–4
1956	Cigalon	Sayani	Comte L de Kerouara	M d'Okhuysen	S Boullenger	Klairon	Hugh Lupus	11	8–1
1957	Midget II	Djebe	Pierre Wertheimer	A Head	A Breasley	Bellborough	El Relicario	7	5–6
1958	Major Portion	Court Martial	H J Joel	T Leader	E Smith	Babur	Blockhaus	4	1–3
1959	Rosalba	Court Martial	J J Astor	R J Colling	J Mercer	Sallymount	Crystal Palace	6	5–2
1960*	Sovereign Path	Grey Sovereign	R E Mason	R Mason	W H Carr	Release	Djebel Traffic	4	13–8
1961	Le Levanstell	Le Lavandou	Joseph McGrath	S McGrath	W Williamson	Etoile	Eagle	6	20–1
1962	Romulus	Ribot	C W Engelhard	R F Johnson Houghton	W Swinburn	Cyrus	Eagle	7	7–4
1963*	The Creditor	Crepello	Lady Sassoon	N Murless	L Piggott	Spree	Lock Hard	9	5–4
1964	Linacre	Rockefella	F More O'Ferrall	P J Prendergast	L Piggott	Derring-Do	Feather Bed	5	11–10
1965	Derring-Do	Darius	Mrs H H Renshaw	A Budgett	A Breasley	Ballyciptic	Minor Portion	6	9–4
1966	Hill Rise	Hillary	G A Pope	N Murless	L Piggott	Silly Season	Tesco Boy	6	7–2
1967	Reform	Pall Mall	Michael Sobell	Sir Gordon Richards	A Breasley	Track Spare	St Chad	4	6–5
1968	World Cup	Match III	J Mullion	P J Prendergast	W Williamson	Wolver Hollow	Lorenzaccio	5	7–2
1969	Jimmy Reppin	Midsummer Night II	Mrs Sidney Bates	J Sutcliffe jnr	G Lewis	Connaught	Crooner	6	13–8
1970	Welsh Pageant	Tudor Melody	H J Joel	N Murless	A Barclay	Gold Rod	Prince de Galles	5	100–30
1971	Brigadier Gerard	Queen's Hussar	Mrs J Hislop	Major W R Hern	J Mercer	Dictus	Ashleigh	3	2–11
1972	Brigadier Gerard	Queen's Hussar	Mrs J Hislop	Major W R Hern	J Mercer	Sparkler	Redundant	4	4–11
1973	Jan Ekels	Derring-Do	A E Bodie	G Harwood	J Lindley	Pompous	Loyal Manzer	5	5–1
1974	*race abandoned*								
1975	Rose Bowl	Habitat	Mrs C W Engelhard	R F Johnson Houghton	W Carson	Gay Fandango	Anne's Pretender	5	9–2
1976	Rose Bowl	Habitat	Mrs C W Engelhard	R F Johnson Houghton	W Carson	Ricco Boy	Dominion	8	13–8
1977	Trusted	Crepello	Lavinia Duchess of Norfolk	J Dunlop	W Carson	Air Trooper	Radetzky	7	20–1
1978	Homing	Habitat	Lord Rotherwick	Major W R Hern	W Carson	Stradavinsky	Caro Bambino	11	9–2
1979	Kris	Sharpen Up	Lord Howard de Walden	H Cecil	J Mercer	Foveros	Jellaby	7	8–11
1980	Known Fact	In Reality	K Abdullah	J Tree	W Carson	Kris	Gift Wrapped	7	3–1
1981	To-Agori-Mou	Tudor Music	Mrs A Muinos	G Harwood	L Piggott	Kittyhawk	Cracaval	6	5–4
1982	Buzzards Bay	Joshua	Mrs V McKinney	H Collingridge	W R Swinburn	Noalcoholic	Achieved	10	50–1
1983	Sackford	Stop The Music	A E Bodie	G Harwood	G Starkey	Adonijah	Montekin	9	11–2
1984	Teleprompter	Welsh Pageant	Lord Derby	J W Watts	W Carson	Katies	Sackford	6	11–2
1985	Shadeed	Nijinsky	Maktoum al Maktoum	M Stoute	W R Swinburn	Teleprompter	Efisio	7	9–4
1986	Sure Blade	Kris	Sheikh Mohammed	B Hills	B Thomson	Teleprompter	Efisio	7	6–5
1987	Milligram	Mill Reef	Helena Springfield Ltd	M Stoute	Pat Eddery	Miesque	Sonic Lady	5	6–1
1988	Warning	Known Fact	K Abdullah	G Harwood	Pat Eddery	Salse	Persian Heights	8	9–4
1989	Zilzal	Nureyev	Mana Al Maktoum	M Stoute	W R Swinburn	Polish Precedent	Distant Relative	5	Evens
1990	Markofdistinction	Known Fact	Gerald Leigh	L M Cumani	L Dettori	Distant Relative	Green Line Express	10	6–1
1991	Selkirk	Sharpen Up	George Strawbridge jnr	I Balding	R Cochrane	Kooyonga	Shadayid	9	10–1
1992	Lahib	Riverman	Hamdan Al Maktoum	J Dunlop	W Carson	Brief Truce	Selkirk	9	8–1
1993	Bigstone	Last Tycoon	D Wildenstein	E Lellouche	Pat Eddery	Barathea	Kingmambo	9	100–30
1994	Maroof	Danzig	Hamdan Al Maktoum	R W Armstrong	R Hills	Barathea	Bigstone	9	66–1
1995	Bahri	Riverman	Hamdan Al Maktoum	J Dunlop	W Carson	Ridgewood Pearl	Soviet Line	6	5–2
1996	Mark Of Esteem	Darshaan	Godolphin	S bin Suroor	L Dettori	Bosra Sham	First Island	7	100–30
1997	Air Express	Salse	Mohamed Obaida	C Brittain	O Peslier	Rebecca Sharp	Faithful Son	9	9–1
1998	Desert Prince	Green Prince	Lucayan Stud	D Loder	O Peslier	Dr Fong	Second Empire	7	100–30
1999	Dubai Millennium	Seeking The Gold	Godolphin	S bin Suroor	L Dettori	Almushtarak	Gold Academy	4	4–9
2000	Observatory	Distant View	K Abdullah	J Gosden	K Darley	Giant's Causeway	Best Of The Bests	12	14–1
2001	Summoner	Inchinor	Godolphin	S bin Suroor	R Hills	Noverre	Hawkeye	8	33–1

* Run at Newbury

THE FILLIES' MILE STAKES (Group I)
Distance: 1 mile
For 2-year-old fillies

Sponsored by Meon Valley Stud

First run in 1973 as The Green Shield Stakes.

YEAR	WINNER	SIRE	OWNER	TRAINER	JOCKEY	SECOND	THIRD	RUNNERS	SP
1973	Escorial	Royal Palace	HM The Queen	I Balding	L Piggott	Evening Venture	Gaily	11	7–4
1974	*race abandoned*								
1975	Icing	Prince Tenderfoot	Lady Iveagh	P Prendergast	C Roche	Bedfellow	Gilding	6	5–1
1976	Miss Pinkie	Connaught	H J Joel	N Murless	L Piggott	Dunfermline	Triple First	8	5–1
1977	Cherry Hinton	Nijinsky	R Moller	H Wragg	L Piggott	Tartan Pimpernel	Watch Out	8	10–11
1978	Formulate	Reform	Mrs D Butter	H Cecil	J Mercer	Odeon	Rimosa's Pet	9	5–4
1979	Quick As Lightning	Buckpasser	Ogden Mills Phipps	J Dunlop	W Carson	Vielle	Sharp Castan	9	9–1
1980	Leap Lively	Nijinsky	Paul Mellon	I Balding	J Matthias	Exclusively Raised	Fiesta Fun	7	9–2
1981	Height Of Fashion	Bustino	HM The Queen	Major W R Hern	J Mercer	Stratospheric	Zinzara	8	15–8
1982	Acclimatise	Shirley Heights	J Hambro	B Hobbs	A Murray	Dancing Meg	Alligatrix	8	3–1
1983	Nepula	Nebbiolo	Sulaiman Al-Qemlas	G A Huffer	B Crossley	Nonesuch Bay	Circus Plume	8	3–1
1984	Oh So Sharp	Kris	Sheikh Mohammed	H Cecil	L Piggott	Helen Street	Morning Devotion	8	6–5
1985	Untold	Final Straw	R H Cowell	M Stoute	W R Swinburn	Moonlight Lady	Sue Grundy	9	6–4
1986	Invited Guest	Be My Guest	Kinderhill Corporation	R W Armstrong	S Cauthen	Mountain Memory	Shining Water	12	8–11
1987	Diminuendo	Diesis	Sheikh Mohammed	H Cecil	S Cauthen	Haiati	Ashayer	7	2–1
1988	Tessla	Glint Of Gold	C A B St George	H Cecil	Pat Eddery	Pick Of The Pops	Rain Burst	8	5–2
1989	Silk Slippers	Nureyev	R E Sangster	B Hills	M Hills	Moon Cactus	Fujaiyrah	8	10–1
1990	Shamshir	Kris	Sheikh Mohammed	L Cumani	L Dettori	Safa	Atlantic Flyer	12	11–2
1991	Culture Vulture	Timeless Moment	C Wright	P Cole	T Quinn	Mystery Play	Party Cited	8	5–2
1992	Ivanka	Dancing Brave	Ali Saeed	C Brittain	M Roberts	Ajfan	Iviza	8	6–1
1993	Fairy Heights	Fairy King	Frank W Golding	N Callaghan	C Asmussen	Dance To The Top	Kissing Cousin	11	11–1
1994	Aqaarid	Nashwan	Hamdan Al Maktoum	J Dunlop	W Carson	Jural	Snowtown	9	11–2
1995	Bosra Sham	Woodman	Wafic Said	H Cecil	Pat Eddery	Bint Shadayid	Matiya	6	10–11
1996	Reams Of Verse	Nureyev	K Abdullah	H Cecil	M Kinane	Khassah	Sleepytime	8	5–1
1997	Glorosia	Bering	Robert Smith	L M Cumani	L Dettori	Jibe	Exclusive	8	10–1
1998	Sunspangled	Caerleon	M Tabor & Mrs John Magnier	A P O'Brien	M Kinane	Calando	Edabiya	8	9–1
1999	Teggiano	Mujtahid	Abdullah Saeed Bul Hab	C Brittain	L Dettori	Britannia	My Hansel	6	11–8
2000	Crystal Music	Nureyev	Lord Lloyd-Webber	J Gosden	L Dettori	Summer Symphony	Hotelgenie Dot Com	9	4–1
2001	Gossamer	Sadler's Wells	Gerald Leigh	L M Cumani	J P Spencer	Maryinsky	Esloob	7	4–5

THE ROYAL LODGE STAKES (Group 2)

Distance: 1 mile (Old Mile)
For 2-year-old colts and geldings

Sponsored in 2001 by Hackney Empire.
First run in 1948. A race of this name was run in July 1946 and 1947 over 5 furlongs. Fillies were eligible until 1977.

YEAR	WINNER	SIRE	OWNER	TRAINER	JOCKEY	SECOND	THIRD	RUNNERS	SP
1948	Swallow Tail	Bois Roussel	Lord Derby	W Earl	D Smith	Burnt Brown	Nasr-ed-Din	8	11–4
1949	Tabriz	Tehran	HH Aga Khan	Frank Butters	G Richards	Linesman	Paracios	5	5–2
1950	Fraise du Bois II	Bois Roussel	HH Aga Khan	H Wragg	C Smirke	Stokes	Cortil	5	7–2
1951	Khor-Mousa	Persian Gulf	Mrs S T Tate	P Thrale	K Gethin	Nearque	Indian Hemp	5	100–7
1952	Neemah	Migoli	HH Aga Khan	M Marsh	C Smirke	Pinza	Canardeau	4	5–2
1953	Infatuation	Nearco	Sir Malcolm McAlpine	V Smyth	G Richards	Wylye Valley	Tarjoman	9	100–30
1954	Solarium	Hyperion	J Ortiz-Patino	F Armstrong	W Snaith	Port St Anne	Lonely Hills	12	6–1
1955	Royal Splendour	Pardal	Mrs Geoffrey Kohn	W Nightingall	A Breasley	Woodruff House	Clarification	4	5–2
1956	Noble Venture	Nearco	HH Begum Aga Khan	H Wragg	E Mercer	Brioche	Arctic Explorer	10	3–1
1957	Pinched	Pinza	Sir Victor Sassoon	N Murless	L Piggott	Miner's Lamp	Lacydon	6	Evens
1958	Cantelo	Chanteur II	William Hill	Capt C Elsey	E Hide	Last Line	Pindari	7	5–4
1959	St Paddy	Aureole	Sir Victor Sassoon	N Murless	L Piggott	Goose Creek	Jet Stream	5	11–4
1960*	Beta	Alycidon	Lord Rosebery	J Jarvis	E Larkin	Dual	Orbit	10	9–4
1961	Escort	Palestine	J J Astor	R J Colling	J Mercer	Heron	Aznip	12	9–2
1962	Star Moss	Mossborough	Major H R Broughton	J A Waugh	E Smith	Coliseum	Merchant Venturer	9	5–1
1963*	Casabianca	Never Say Die	Col B Hornung	N Murless	L Piggott	Desaix	Oncidium	12	4–1
1964	Prominer	Beau Sabreur	J R Mullion	P J Prendergast	G Bougoure	Never A Fear	Rehearsed	13	3–1
1965	Soft Angels	Crepello	Lady Sassoon	N Murless	L Piggott	Sodium	Glad Rags	11	5–2
1966	Royal Palace	Ballymoss	H J Joel	N Murless	L Piggott	Slip Stitch	Starry Halo	5	6–4
1967	Remand	Alcide	J J Astor	Major W R Hern	L Piggott	Riboccare	Attalus	7	13–8
1968	Dutch Bells	Poaching	G J van der Ploeg	H R Price	A Murray	Adropejo	Murrayfield	4	100–7
1969	Domineering	Determine	George A Pope jnr	N Murless	A Barclay	Sandal	Dubrava	8	13–2
1970	Seafriend	Sea Hawk II	Mrs J R Mullion	P J Prendergast	J Mercer	Harland	Selhurst	12	9–2
1971	Yaroslav	Santa Claus	Mrs V Hue-Williams	N Murless	G Lewis	Home Guard	Young Arthur	7	8–13
1972	Adios	Silly Season	G Weston	N Murless	G Lewis	Noble Decree	Sharp Edge	12	10–1
1973	Straight as a Die	Never Bend	B Jenks	B Hills	F Durr	Angerstein	Wrongly Down	13	16–1
1974	*race abandoned*								
1975	Sir Wimborne	Sir Ivor	Mrs A Manning	M V O'Brien	L Piggott	Coin Of Gold	Spade Guinea	6	4–6
1976	Gairloch	Roan Rocket	Miss V Hermon-Hodge	H R Price	B Taylor	Pampapaul	Hot Grove	6	6–1
1977	Shirley Heights	Mill Reef	Lord Halifax	J Dunlop	G Starkey	Bolak	Hawaiian Sound	8	10–1
1978	Ela-Mana-Mou	Pitcairn	Mrs A Muinos	G Harwood	G Starkey	Troy	Lyphard's Wish	8	10–1
1979	Hello Gorgeous	Mr Prospector	D Wildenstein	H Cecil	J Mercer	Star Way	Rontino	4	5–4
1980	Robellino	Roberto	Mrs J McDougald	I Balding	J Matthias	Recitation	Gielgud	8	4–1
1981	Norwick	Far North	A E Bodie	G Harwood	J Mercer	Silver Hawk	Lobkowiez	9	12–1
1982	Dunbeath	Grey Dawn II	M Riordan	H Cecil	L Piggott	Lyphards Special	The Noble Player	9	5–2
1983	Gold And Ivory	Key To The Mint	Paul Mellon	I Balding	S Cauthen	Rousillon	Trojan Fen	5	25–1
1984	Reach	Kris	HRH Prince Faud Salman	P Cole	T Quinn	Khozaam	Royal Harmony	8	15–2
1985	Bonhomie	What A Pleasure	Sheikh Mohammed	H Cecil	S Cauthen	Water Cay	Silvino	7	2–1
1986	Bengal Fire	Nishapour	N H Phillips	C Brittain	M Roberts	Deputy Governor	Balakirev	9	14–1
1987	Sanquirico	Lypheor	C A B St George	H Cecil	S Cauthen	Undercut	Alwuhush	10	8–11
1988	High Estate	Shirley Heights	H J Joel	H Cecil	M Roberts	Samoan	Frequent Flyer	5	4–6
1989	Digression	Seattle Slew	K Abdulla	G Harwood	Pat Eddery	Bridal Toast	Air Music	9	4–1
1990	Mujaazif	Alydar	Maktoum Al Maktoum	M Stoute	W R Swinburn	Jahafil	Stone Mill	8	11–2
1991	Made Of Gold	Green Forest	Ecurie Fustok	M Moubarak	A Cruz	Mack The Knife	Twist And Turn	8	4–1
1992	Desert Secret	Sadler's Wells	Maktoum Al Maktoum	M Stoute	Pat Eddery	Geisway	Lost Soldier	10	12–1
1993	Mister Baileys	Robellino	G R Bailey Ltd	M Johnston	L Dettori	Concordial	Overbury	9	100–30
1994	Eltish	Cox's Ridge	K Abdullah	H Cecil	Pat Eddery	Stiletto Blade	Juyush	8	7–4
1995	Mons	Deploy	Mrs E H Vestey	L M Cumani	L Dettori	More Royal	Jack Jennings	8	7–2
1996	Benny The Dip	Silver Hawk	Landon Knight	J Gosden	W R Swinburn	Desert Story	Besiege	8	9–4
1997	Teapot Row	Generous	Duke of Devonshire	J A R Toller	S Sanders	Prolix	City Honours	8	9–1
1998	Mutaahab	Dixieland Band	Hamdan Al Maktoum	E Dunlop	R Hills	Glamis	Desaru	6	5–1
1999	Royal Kingdom	Fairy King	M Tabor & Mrs John Magnier	A P O'Brien	M Kinane	Best Of The Bests	Kingsclere	6	10–11
2000	Atlantis Prince	Tagula	Lucayan Stud	S P C Woods	L Dettori	Turnberry Isle	Hill Country	8	11–2
2001	Mutinyonthebounty	Sadler's Wells	M Tabor & Mrs John Magnier	A P O'Brien	J P Spencer	Tholjanah	Parasol	9	16–1

** Run at Newbury*

THE DIADEM STAKES (Group 2)

Distance: 6 furlongs
For 3-year-olds and upwards

Sponsored by Betdaq.

First run in 1946.

YEAR	WINNER	SIRE	OWNER	TRAINER	JOCKEY	SECOND	THIRD	RUNNERS	SP
1946	The Bug	Signal Light	N H Wachman	M Marsh	C Smirke	Poolfix	Honeyway	4	5–4
1947	Djelal	Djebel	Marcel Boussac	C Semblat	C Elliott	Happy Night	Clarion III	6	5–1
1948	Combined Operations	Fair Trial	R Foster	J Lawson	T Burns	Squander Bug	Falls Of Clyde	3	2–5
1949	Solonaway	Solferino	R A Duggan	A Smyth	G Richards	Luminary	Damnos	3	6–5
1950	Abadan	Persian Gulf	Lt-Col Giles Loder	N Murless	G Richards	Luminary	Fair Fallow	3	30–100
1951	Ki Ming	Ballyogan	Ley On	M Beary	A Breasley	Royal Serenade		2	2–1
1952	Set Fair	Denturius	C W Bell	W Nightingall	E Smith	Agitator	Wallace's Tower	4	13–2
1953	Rose Coral	Rockefella	Lady Elizabeth Basset	G Brooke	D Smith	Set Fair	Oleandrin	6	3–1
1954	Set Fair	Denturius	C W Bell	W Nightingall	A Breasley	March Past	Dumbarnie	5	11–4
1955	Pappa Fourway	Pappageno II	Mrs E Goldson	W Dutton	W H Carr	Trouville		2	2–5
1956*	King Bruce	Fair Trial	Walter C Tarry	P Hastings-Bass	A Breasley	Verrieres	Matador	4	100–7
1957	Arcandy	Archive	Mrs M V Linde	G Beeby	T Gosling	Game Hide	Drum Beat	4	7–4
1958	Jack & Jill	Delirium	Emile Littler	W Nightingall	S Clayton	Welsh Abbot	Stanmar	5	20–1
1959	Jack & Jill	Delirium	Emile Littler	W Nightingall	W H Carr	Anxious Lady	Galivanter	7	6–1
1960*	Zanzibar	King's Bench	Capt P Dunne	J Oxley	W Rickaby	Shamrock Star	Deer Leap	3	15–8
1961	Satan	Buisson Ardent	A Biddle	T Shaw	J Mercer	Ritudyr	Skymaster	5	100–8
1962	La Belle	Vilmorin	Lady Noble	H Wragg	W Williamson	Featheredge	Daisy Belle	13	10–1
1963*	Sammy Davis	Whistler	Jocelyn Hambro	G Brooke	D Smith	Secret Step	Windscale	6	4–1
1964	Ampney Princess	Wilwyn	Mrs Joanne Wood	H Hannon	F Durr	Weeper's Boy	Dondeen	13	25–1
1965	Majority Blue	Major Portion	Mrs B Aitken	J Oxx snr	W Williamson	Merry Madcap	Compensation	12	3–1
1966	Lucasland	Lucero	J U Baillie	J A J Waugh	E Eldin	Dondeen	Current Coin	13	7–2
1967	Great Bear	Star Gazer	Lady Sarah Fitzalan-Howard	J Dunlop	R Hutchinson	Desert Call	Quy	8	11–2
1968	Secret Ray	Privy Councillor	A G Cornish	D Smith	A Barclay	Great Bear	Mountain Call	4	11–2
1969	Song	Sing Sing	H J Joel	D Candy	J Mercer	Burglar	Tudor Music	6	7–4
1970	Realm	Princely Gift	R C Boucher	J Winter	B Taylor	Welsh Saint	Fluke	4	11–8
1971	Abergwaun	Bounteous	C A B St George	M V O'Brien	L Piggott	Apollo Nine	Sweet Revenge	7	15–2
1972	Home Guard	Forli	Mrs C W Engelhard	M V O'Brien	L Piggott	Parsimony	Shoolerville	8	4–5
1973	Boldboy	Bold Lad	Lady Beaverbrook	Major W R Hern	J Mercer	Balliol	Perdu	5	100–30
1974	Saritamer	Dancer's Image	C A B St George	M V O'Brien	L Piggott	New Model	Boldboy	5	11–10
1975	[Roman Warrior (d ht)	Porto Bello	J Brown	N Angus	J Seagrave		Be Tuneful	8	5–2
	Swingtime (d ht)	Buckpasser	J Mulcahy	M V O'Brien	L Piggott				9–4
1976	Honeyblest	So Blessed	J Slade	D Smith	G Baxter	Be Tuneful	Royal Boy	7	8–1
1977	Gentilhombre	No Mercy	J Murrell	N Adam	P Cook	Scarcely Blessed	Mandrake Major	6	7–4
1978	Creetown	Tower Walk	R Galpin	R Sheather	R Street	Springhill	Vaigly Great	14	20–1
1979	Absalom	Abwah	Mrs C Alington	Ryan Jarvis	L Piggott	Abdu	Petty Purse	6	9–4
1980	Sovereign Rose	Sharpen Up	Mrs P Pearce	Major W R Hern	W Carson	King Of Spain	Pace Jean	9	7–1
1981	Moorestyle	Manacle	Moores International Furnishings	R Armstrong	L Piggott	Crews Hill	Dalsaan	10	Evens
1982	Indian King	Raja Baba	J Levy	G Harwood	G Starkey	Soba	Blue Singh	12	7–4
1983	Salieri	Accipiter	C A B St George	H Cecil	L Piggott	Silverdip	Soba	12	9–4
1984	Never So Bold	Bold Lad	E D Kessly	R W Armstrong	S Cauthen	Fortysecond Street	Habibti	9	85–40
1985	Al Sylah	Nureyev	Hamdan Al Maktoum	H Thomson Jones	A Murray	Dafayna	Gabitat	8	9–1
1986	Hallgate	Vaigly Great	Hippodromo Racing	Miss S E Hall	G Starkey	Gwydion	Firm Landing	12	11–4
1987	Dowsing	Riverman	K Abdullah	J Tree	Pat Eddery	Governor General	Serve N' Volley	17	8–1
1988	Cadeaux Genereux	Young Generation	Maktoum Al Maktoum	O J Douieb	Pat Eddery	Point Of Light	Chummy's Favourite	13	9–2
1989	Chummy's Favourite	Song	Michael Hill	N Callaghan	L Dettori	Silver Fling	Dancing Dissident	11	40–1
1990	Ron's Victory	General Holme	J S Moss	A J Falourd	F Head	Northern Goddess	Tadwin	14	13–2
1991	Shalford	Thatching	D F Cock	R Hannon	A Cruz	Montendre	Satin Flower	16	10–1
1992	Wolfhound	Nureyev	Sheikh Mohammed	J Gosden	S Cauthen	Lochsong	Montendre	11	4–1
1993	Catrail	Storm Cat	Sheikh Mohammed	J Gosden	M Roberts	Marina Park	Zarani Sidi Anna	9	10–11
1994	Lake Coniston	Bluebird	Highclere Thoroughbred Racing Ltd	G Lewis	Pat Eddery	First Trump	Thousla Rock	11	85–40
1995	Cool Jazz	Lead On Time	Saeed Manana	C Brittain	C Nakatani	Young Ern	Branston Abby	15	33–1
1996	Diffident	Nureyev	Godolphin	S bin Suroor	L Dettori	Lucayan Prince	Leap for Joy	12	12–1
1997	Elnadim	Danzig	Hamdan Al Maktoum	J Dunlop	R Hills	Monaassib	Averti	14	4–1
1998	Bianconi	Danzig	Mrs John Magnier & M Tabor	A P O'Brien	J Murtagh	Russian Revival	Averti	9	7–1
1999	Bold Edge	Beveled	Lady Whent and Friends	R Hannon	Dane O'Neill	Munjiz	Show Me The Money	11	12–1
2000	Sampower Star	Cyrano de Bergerac	Godolphin	S bin Suroor	L Dettori	Tayseer	Trinculo	11	7–4
2001	Nice One Clare	Mukaddamah	Oremsa Partnership	J W Payne	J Murtagh	Orientor	Bahamian Pirate	15	6–1

** Run at Kempton Park*

PRINCIPAL NATIONAL HUNT RACES

THE LONG WALK HURDLE (Grade 1)
Distance: 3 miles 1½ furlongs
For 4-year-olds and upwards

Sponsored by Cantor Sport.
First run in 1965 over 3 miles 2 furlongs.
Distance reduced from 1990.

YEAR	WINNER	SIRE	OWNER	TRAINER	JOCKEY	SECOND	THIRD	RUNNERS	SP
1965	Minute Gun	Mossborough	W Shand Kydd	W Shand Kydd	R Pitman	Moleskin	Regal John	26	100–8
1966	Sir Edward	Crepello	R Heaton	H R Price	J Gifford	Brig	Minute Gun	18	7–2
1967	*race abandoned*								
1968	*race abandoned*								
1969	Candid Camera	Alcide	R F P Ross	E Goddard	J Guest	Colonel Imp	October	22	100–8
1970	Rouge Autumn	Autumn Gold	Bryan P Jenks	T F Rimell	K B White	Zadok	Dresden Grey	20	9–2
1971	St Patrick's Blue	St Paddy	P Aunger	D Tatlow	W Smith	Fleet Fox	The Spaniard	12	7–2
1972	Highland Abbe	Jock Scot	Mrs K Hankey	L Kennard	Mr R Smith	Bourdon	Coral Diver	8	11–1
1973	Soloning	Solon Morn	Mrs C Thornton	F T Winter	R Pitman	Carbury's Prince	Mac's Birthday	10	9–2
1974	Go Bingo	Bing II	G Reed	S Hall	D Munro	Mac's Birthday	Good Prospect	6	9–4
1975	Lanzarote	Milesian	Lord Howard de Walden	F T Winter	J Francome	Prince Eleigh	Orosio	7	4–9
1976	*race abandoned*								
1977	John Cherry	Stage Door Johnny	M Ritzenberg	H Thomson Jones	S Smith Eccles	Pueblo	Good Prospect	10	11–8
1978	Kelso Chant	Shackleton	Mrs M Richardson	B Wilkinson	S Charlton	Gaffer	Chumson	14	10–1
1979	John Cherry	Stage Door Johnny	M Ritzenberg	H Thomson Jones	S Smith Eccles	Islander	Mountrivers	12	6–1
1980	Derring Rose	Derring-Do	P Savill	F T Winter	J Francome	John Cherry	Siege King	9	7–1
1981	*race abandoned*								
1982	Mayotte	Little Buskins	B Davies	R Holder	P Richards	Here's Why	Luxuriate	12	15–8
1983	Crimson Embers	Cheval	Mrs S W Smart	F Walwyn	S Shilston	Kintbury	Goldspun	11	14–1
1984	Kristenson	Menelek	Mrs Ursula Fantasia	R F Fisher	M Williams	Nialan	Crimson Embers	12	7–2
1985	Misty Dale	Dalesa	David Rose	Mrs J Pitman	P Tuck	Kristenson	Rose Ravine	8	9–4
1986	Out Of The Gloom	Netherkelly	Paul Green	R Hollinshead	P Scudamore	Sheer Gold	Ibn Majed	5	4–1
1987	Bluff Cove	Town Crier	Dickins Ltd	R Hollinshead	R Dunwoody	Miss Nero	Sabin du Loir	10	14–1
1988	French Goblin	Beau Charmeur	Maurice E Pinto	J T Gifford	Peter Hobbs	Gaye Brief	Tewit Castle	10	3–1
1989	Royal Athlete	Air Trooper	Gary Johnson	Mrs J Pitman	D Gallagher	Mrs Muck	Pragada	11	33–1
1990	Floyd	Rolleo	M V Walsh	D Elsworth	G Bradley	Ryde Again	Boscean Chieftain	8	10–1
1991	*race abandoned*								
1992	Vagog	Glint Of Gold	M A Swift	M Pipe	M Foster	Burgoyne	Shuil Ar Aghaidh	9	15–2
1993	Sweet Duke	Iron Duke	Andy Mavrou	N Twiston-Davies	C Llewellyn	Burgoyne	Avro Anson	9	7–2
1994	Hebridean	Norwick	P A Deal	N Henderson	A Maguire	Dorans Pride	What A Question	8	100–30
1995	Silver Wedge	Silver Hawk	E S & W V Robins	O Sherwood	J Osborne	Putty Road	Top Spin	10	7–1
1996	Ocean Hawk	Hawkster	M Archer & Mrs J Broadhurst	N Twiston-Davies	C Llewellyn	Trainglot	Pleasure Shared	6	100–30
1997	Paddy's Return	Kahyasi	P O'Donnell	F Murphy	N Williamson	Pridwell	Bimsey	7	8–1
1998	Princeful	Electric	Robert Hitchins	Mrs J Pitman	R Dunwoody	Deano's Beano	Ocean Hawk	11	11–4
1999	Anzum	Ardross	The Old Foresters Partnership	A King	R Johnson	Deano's Beano	Count Campioni	6	4–1
2000	Baracouda	Alesso	Roger Barby	F Doumen	F Doumen	Deano's Beano	Celtic Native	9	11–4
2001	Baracouda	Alesso	J P McManus	F Doumen	T Doumen	Ballet-K	Carlovent	5	2–5

THE TOTE SILVER CUP HANDICAP 'CHASE (Listed Race)
Distance: 3 miles ½ furlong
For 5-year-olds and upwards

First run in 1965 as the SGB Handicap 'Chase.

YEAR	WINNER	SIRE	OWNER	TRAINER	JOCKEY	SECOND	THIRD	RUNNERS	SP
1965	Vultrix	Vulgan	H Dare	F Cundell	S Mellor	Happy Arthur	Peacetown	7	6–4
1966	Arkle	Archive	Anne, Duchess of Westminster	T Dreaper	P Taaffe	Sunny Bright	Vultrix	5	1–3
1967	*race abandoned*								
1968	*race abandoned*								
1969	Straight Fort	Straight Deal	G Ansley	T Dreaper	P Taaffe	Beau Champ	Flyingbolt	7	7–2
1970	Glencaraig Lady	Fortina	P Doyle	F Flood	R Coonan	Even Keel	Two Springs	10	4–1
1971	Spanish Steps	Flush Royal	E Courage	E Courage	W Smith	Charles Dickens	Royal Toss	12	4–1
1972	Soloning	Solon Morn	Mrs C Thornton	F T Winter	R Pitman	Spanish Steps	Mocharabuice	16	6–1
1973	Mocharabuice	Autumn Gold	Mrs R Carew Pole	T Forster	G Thorner	Helmsman	French Colonist	9	7–1
1974	Rough House	Songedor or Ritudyr	Mrs R Brown	T F Rimell	J Burke	Land Lark	Money Market	14	11–1
1975	What A Buck	Royal Buck	Lord Vestey	D Nicholson	J King	Royal Relief	Bula	9	9–2
1976	*race abandoned*								
1977	Midnight Court	Twilight Alley	Mrs O Jackson	F T Winter	J Francome	Master Spy	Formula	8	6–5
1978	Grand Canyon	Oakville	D Samuel	D Kent	R Barry	Approaching	Coolishall	10	15–8
1979	Raffi Nelson	Saucy Kit	Mrs P Fry	N Henderson	S Smith Eccles	Flashy Boy	Master Spy	6	5–2
1980	Henry Bishop	Crown lease	Sir R Wates	J T Gifford	R Champion	Venture To Cognac	Silent Valley	4	7–1
1981	*race abandoned*								
1982	Captain Emani	Mon Capitaine	F Emani	M Dickinson	R Earnshaw	Earthstopper	Sea Captain	8	11–8
1983	The Mighty Mac	Master Owen	Jane Lane	M Dickinson	Mr D Browne	Another Breeze	Approaching	7	13–8
1984	Canny Danny	Le Coq d'Or	P Norton	J FitzGerald	M Dwyer	Fortina's Express	Greenwood Lad	7	6–4
1985	Door Latch	Cantab	H J Joel	J T Gifford	R Rowe	West Tip	Burrough Hill Lad	8	11–4
1986	Door Latch	Cantab	H J Joel	J T Gifford	R Rowe	Sign Again	Cross Master	12	6–1
1987	Cavvies Clown	Idiot's Delight	Mrs J Ollivant	D Elsworth	R Arnott	Gold Bearer	Claude Monet	12	10–1
1988	Ballyhane	Crash Course	H J Joel	J T Gifford	Peter Hobbs	Sun Rising	Castle Warden	5	13–8
1989	Solidasarock	Hardboy	Les Randall	R Akehurst	L Harvey	Panto Prince	Brown Windsor	12	33–1
1990	Man O' Magic	Manado	James D Greig	K Bailey	M Perrett	Karakter Reference	Okeetee	6	5–1
1991	*race abandoned*								
1992	Captain Dibble	Crash Course	Mrs R Vaughan	N Twiston-Davies	C Llewellyn	Miinnehoma	Rowlandsons Jewels	8	7–1
1993	Young Hustler	Import	G M MacEchern	N Twiston-Davies	C Llewellyn	Latent Talent	Fighting Words	8	11–8
1994	Raymylette	Le Moss	Lady Lloyd-Webber	N Henderson	M Fitzgerald	Dubacilla	Lord Relic	8	3–1
1995	Unguided Missile	Deep Run	D E Harrison	G Richards	R Dunwoody	Rough Quest	Unholy Alliance	9	7–2
1996	Go Ballistic	Celtic Cone	Mrs B J Lockhart	J G M O'Shea	A P McCoy	Unguided Missile	Major Bell	9	4–1
1997	Cool Dawn	Over The River	The Hon. Miss D Harding	R H Alner	A Thornton	Harwell Lad	Call It A Day	6	5–2
1998	Torduff Express	Kambalda	Two Plus Two	P Nicholls	N Williamson	Callisoe Bay	King Lucifer	7	9–2
1999	Tresor de Mai	Grand Tresor	Joe Moran	M Pipe	A P McCoy	Spendid	Sounds Like Fun	9	10–1
2000	Legal Right	Alleged	Russell McAllister	J J O'Neill	N Williamson	Royal Predica	Smarty	7	7–1
2001	Shooting Light	Shernazar	J M Brown & M J Blackburn	M Pipe	A P McCoy	Siberian Gale	You're Agoodun	9	5–2

THE VICTOR CHANDLER HANDICAP 'CHASE (Grade 2)
Distance: 2 miles
For 5-year-olds and upwards

First run in 1989 after the inaugural race scheduled for 1988 was abandoned.

YEAR	WINNER	SIRE	OWNER	TRAINER	JOCKEY	SECOND	THIRD	RUNNERS	SP
1988	*race abandoned*								
1989	Desert Orchid	Grey Mirage	R Burridge	D Elsworth	S Sherwood	Panto Prince	Ida's Delight	5	6–4
1990	Meikleour	Reliance II	Mrs A C Leggat	J FitzGerald	D Byrne	Feroda	Panto Prince	10	10–1
1991	Blitzkrieg	General Ironside	J P McManus	E J O'Grady	T Carmody	Young Snugfit	Katabatic	5	11–4
1992	Waterloo Boy	Deep Run	M R Deeley	D Nicholson	R Dunwoody	Young Snugfit	Sure Metal	8	6–4
1993	Sybillin	Henbit	Marquesa de Moratalla	J FitzGerald	M Dwyer	Deep Sensation	Fragrant Dawn	11	9–2
1994*	Viking Flagship	Viking	Roach Foods Ltd	D Nicholson	R Dunwoody	Egypt Mill Prince	Billy Bathgate	4	3–1
1995	Martha's Son	Idiot's Delight	P J Hartigan	Capt T A Forster	R Farrant	Egypt Mill Prince	Coulton	8	3–1
1996	Big Matt	Furry Glen	T Benfield & W Brown	N Henderson	M Fitzgerald	Martin's Lamp	Dancing Paddy	8	8–1
1997**	Ask Tom	Strong Gale	B T Stewart-Brown	T Tate	R Garritty	Clay County	Big Matt	8	9–4
1998	Jeffell	Alias Smith	T Bailey	A L T Moore	C O'Dwyer	Celibate	Or Royal	9	13–2
1999**	Call Equiname	Belfort	M Coburn & P K Barber	P Nicholls	R Thornton	Get Real	Celibate	7	15–2
2000	Nordance Prince	Nordance	Pinks Gym and Leisure Wear Ltd	Miss V Williams	A P McCoy	Flagship Uberalles	Celibate	10	13–8
2001	Function Dream	Strong Gale	Scart Stud	Mrs M Reveley	A Ross	Cenkos	Exit Swinger	10	2–1
2002	Turgeonev	Turgeon	D F Sills	T Easterby	R McGrath	Wave Rock	Davoski	8	9–2

* Run at Warwick
** Run at Kempton Park

MONARCHS AND OFFICIALS
IN ASCOT HISTORY

MONARCHS

1702-1714	Anne
1714-1727	George I
1727-1760	George II
1760-1820	George III
1820-1830	George IV (Regent from 1811)
1830-1837	William IV
1837-1901	Victoria
1901-1910	Edward VII
1910-1936	George V
1936	Edward VIII
1936-1952	George VI
1952-	Elizabeth II

MASTERS OF THE BUCKHOUNDS

1711-1712		Sir William Wyndham, Baronet
1712-1715		George, 3rd Earl of Cardigan
1715-1727		no Masters of the Buckhounds appointed
1727-1732		Colonel Francis Negus
1733-1737		Charles Bennett, 2nd Earl of Tankerville
1737-1744	(1st incumbency)	Ralph Jennison, Esq
1744-1746		George Montague Dunk, 3rd Earl of Halifax
1746-1757	(2nd incumbency)	Ralph Jennison, Esq
1757-1782		John, 2nd Viscount Bateman
1782		George Bussey, 4th Earl of Jersey
1783-1806		John Montagu, 5th Earl of Sandwich
1806-1807		William Charles Keppel, 4th Earl of Albemarle
1807-1823		Charles, 2nd Marquess of Cornwallis
1823-1830		William Wellesley-Pole, Lord Maryborough
1830-1834		Thomas William, 2nd Viscount Anson and 1st Earl of Lichfield
1834-1835		George Stanhope, 6th Earl of Chesterfield
1835-1839		William George, 16th Earl of Erroll
1839-1841		George William Fox Kinnaird, 9th Baron Kinnaird
1841-1846	(1st incumbency)	The Earl of Rosslyn
1846-1848		Granville George Leveson-Gower, 2nd Earl Granville
1848-1852	(1st incumbency)	John George Brabazon Ponsonby, 6th Earl of Bessborough
1853	(2nd incumbency)	The Earl of Rosslyn
1854-1858	(2nd incumbency)	John George Brabazon Ponsonby, 6th Earl of Bessborough
1858-1859		John William Montagu, 7th Earl of Sandwich
1859-1866	(3rd incumbency)	John George Brabazon Ponsonby, 6th Earl of Bessborough
1866	(1st incumbency)	Richard Edmund St. Lawrence Boyle, 9th Earl of Cork and Orrery
1866-1868		Charles John, Lord Colville of Culross, 10th Baron
1868-1874	(2nd incumbency)	Richard Edmund St. Lawrence Boyle, 9th Earl of Cork and Orrery
1874-1880		Charles Philip Yorke, 5th Earl of Hardwicke
1880-1885	(3rd incumbency)	Richard Edmund St. Lawrence Boyle, 9th Earl of Cork and Orrery
1885-1886		John Henry De La Poer-Beresford, 5th Marquess of Waterford
1886		Charles Harbord, 5th Baron Suffield
1886-1892	(1st incumbency)	George William Coventry, 9th Earl of Coventry
1892-1895		Thomas Lister, 4th Baron Ribblesdale
1895-1900	(2nd incumbency)	George William Coventry, 9th Earl of Coventry
1900-1901		Charles Crompton William Cavendish, 3rd Baron Chesham

THE KING'S REPRESENTATIVES AT ASCOT

1901-1934	Victor Albert Francis Charles Spencer, 1st Viscount Churchill
1934-1945	Lord Hamilton of Dalzell
1945-1952	Bernard Marmaduke Fitzalan-Howard, 16th Duke of Norfolk

THE QUEEN'S REPRESENTATIVES AT ASCOT

1952-1972	Bernard Marmaduke Fitzalan-Howard, 16th Duke of Norfolk
1972-1982	John Henry Guy Nevill, 5th Marquess of Abergavenny
1982-1997	Colonel Sir Piers Bengough
1997-	Peregrine Andrew Morny Cavendish, Marquess of Hartington

THE CHANGING SHAPE OF ASCOT RACECOURSE

Racing at Ascot began in 1711 on 'the round heat' – the course which, with various realignments over the centuries, forms the basis of the round track we know today. The Old Mile was established in the mid-1750s, and the first Straight Mile in 1785. So the plan of the course in 1810 – based on the map reproduced on page 49 – has a degree of familiarity for modern Ascot racegoers. It should be noted that what we would now think of as the paddock bend was farther to the west, and significantly sharper, than it is today: indeed, the semi-circle of trees at the roundabout end of No. 1 Car Park today marks where the outer curve of the course was during the nineteenth century. The part of the track running down to Swinley Bottom in the 1810 plan has a dog-leg where the course went near the Buckhounds' kennels, and the course at Swinley Bottom itself is a short straight rather than (as is now the case) a sweeping curve. The Straight Mile (which actually accommodated a maximum race distance of 7 furlongs 166 yards) is to the south of the road (nowadays named New Mile Road). By 1860 the run down to Swinley Bottom is

straight (the change had been made in 1825), the run up from Swinley Bottom is more regular, the home turn is less sharp, and the stand area features a greater number of permanent buildings. By 1910 the straight has been realigned to allow for an easier bend beyond the winning post, and for the track itself to be moved a little to the north to allow more room for stands. Note also the chute to the west of the paddock area: this was built in 1862 to accommodate the start for races over 1 mile 5 furlongs. Fifty years later in 1960 the shape of the course shows major alterations in three areas. In 1948 and 1949 the paddock bend was transformed into a smooth curve (and the chute done away with) and Swinley Bottom was likewise altered to make a smooth curve, and a new Straight Mile was constructed north of the road (though racing did not move to the new Straight Mile until the 1955 season). The 2000 plan shows the area of the National Hunt courses (first used in 1965) on the inner of the Flat course, as well as the outline of the new stands built in the early 1960s. (The distance of one and a half miles is still formally known as the Swinley Course.)

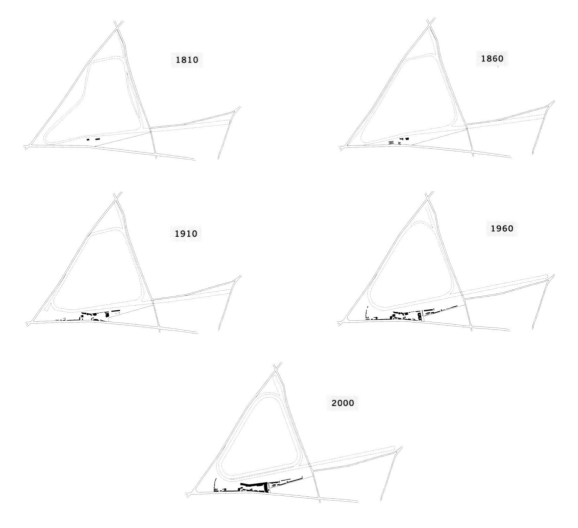

AUTHOR'S NOTE

The preface to *Royal Ascot* by George James Cawthorne and Richard S. Herod, published in 1902, begins:

In these pages the authors believe they are presenting the first complete history of the Ascot Race Meeting that has ever been compiled. They have, of course, referred to all the standard works relative to the subject, and have also fortunately been in a position which allowed them free access to records which are closed to the general public. Moreover, in many instances, information which they could not otherwise have obtained has been most courteously placed at their disposal by private individuals. To these their best thanks are due.

Change the phrase 'the first complete history of the Ascot Race Meeting' to 'the first official history of Ascot racecourse', and one hundred years later the paragraph applies equally to the present volume.

By 2002 the 'standard works' are the Cawthorne and Herod book itself, plus two major modern histories which have appeared in the last thirty years. *Royal Ascot* by the late Dorothy Laird, published in 1976, is particularly strong on the social aspects of the Royal Meeting, while *Royal Ascot* by Richard Onslow, published in 1990, is – as one would expect from such a distinguished Turf historian – a mine of information on the horses and the characters who have made the story of Ascot so absorbing.

Note that *Royal Ascot* is the title of each of those three 'standard works'. Ascot in the twenty-first century is about much more than just the Royal Meeting – wonderful as that occasion is, for racing aficionado and socialite alike – and the present book is the first to combine the history of the royal fixture with an appropriate description of the development of racing away from it.

To convey the true range of the Ascot experience, the words of those who have enjoyed it first hand – jockeys, owners, trainers, diarists, monarchs, journalists (but sadly no horses) – have whenever possible been commandeered. A comprehensive bibliography of works which have been consulted would be tedious, but it may be useful to note that among the principal sources mined have been:

- horses: the indispensable *Racehorses* annuals published by Timeform; *Pretty Polly: An Edwardian heroine* by Michael Tanner; *Brown Jack* by R. C. Lyle; *Teleprompter and Co.: The story of the English Flat-race gelding* (for Trelawny) by Michael Tanner; *Park Top: A romance of the Turf* by the Duke of Devonshire; *The Story of Mill Reef* by John Oaksey; *The Brigadier* (on Brigadier Gerard) by John Hislop; *The Grey Horse: The true story of Desert Orchid* by Richard Burridge;
- jockeys: *Genius Genuine* by Sam Chifney; *Tod Sloan by Himself* by Tod Sloan; *My Story* by Gordon Richards; *Donoghue Up!* by Steve Donoghue; *Lester* by Lester Piggott; *Five Times Champion* by Doug Smith; *Queen's Jockey* by Harry Carr; *Winner's Disclosure* by Terry Biddlecombe; *Scobie* by Scobie Breasley; *The Race of My Life* (for pieces by Pat Eddery, Joe Mercer and Frankie Dettori), edited by Sean Magee; *Good Horses Make Good Jockeys* by Richard Pitman; *To be a Champion* by Pat Eddery; *Frankie Dettori* by John Karter; *The Magnificent Seven* (on Frankie Dettori's big Ascot day) by Graham Sharpe;

- trainers: *Men and Horses I Have Known* by George Lambton; *The Captain* (on Cecil Boyd-Rochfort) by Bill Curling; *On the Level* by Henry Cecil; *Handy All the Way* by Peter Walwyn; *Crossing the Line* by Charlie Brooks;
- royalty and racing: *Bred in the Purple* by Michael Seth-Smith; *All the Queen's Horses* by Bill Curling; *Royal Thoroughbreds: A history of the Royal Studs* by Arthur Fitzgerald; *Royal Racing* by Sean Smith;
- diaries and autobiographies: *The Journals of Jonathan Swift*; *The Girlhood of Queen Victoria: A Selection from Her Majesty's Diaries* (edited by Viscount Esher); *The Letters of Queen Victoria* (edited by G. E. Buckle); *The Diaries of Charles Greville* (edited by Strachey and Fulford); *Far from a Gentleman* by John Hislop; *Sods I Have Cut on the Turf* by Jack Leach; *Calling the Horses* by Peter O'Sullevan;
- reference: *Biographical Encyclopaedia of British Flat Racing* by Roger Mortimer, Richard Onslow and Peter Willett.

The number of people whose efforts have in one way or another contributed to the publication of this book would just about fill the old Five Shilling Stand, but a select few should be singled out.

Sally Aird undertook the bulk of the historical research at an early stage and produced an extraordinary amount of raw material – and provided invaluable assistance throughout the later phases of the writing.

Emily Hedges has been a heroic picture researcher, finding an array of wonderful images of Ascot over three centuries and then – at least as long as the phone conversation lasted – resisting the temptation to scream when the author called with yet another last-minute arcane request ('Can you find a photo of Brown Jack eating cheese?').

At Ascot, special thanks are due to the Marquess of Hartington, Douglas Erskine-Crum, Claire Endersby and Audrey Bundock for all manner of help, while Paul Roberts of Turnberry Consulting has driven the project forward with an enthusiasm of which Queen Anne herself would have been envious.

Phillip Jones, Chris and Mary Pitt and Robert Cooper cheerfully donned their anoraks to comment in learned detail on early drafts, and a particular vote of thanks is due to David Oldrey, whose extraordinary knowledge of racing history has made a huge contribution to this book. It is due to his erudition that the colour of horses such as Eclipse and Aureole is here 'chesnut' rather than the more common (and historically erroneous) 'chestnut'.

Those who have worked on the production phase of the book should congratulate themselves that it has been produced to a very tight schedule without any raised voices (or fists). Particularly grateful thanks go to Mari Roberts for copy-editing and to Hazel Orme for proof-reading and for doggedly trying to explain the difference between *that* and *which*; to Carole McDonald at designsection, for her design and for her patience; and at Methuen to Peter Tummons, Max Eilenberg and Margot Weale. The benevolent spider at the centre of a delicate web has been Vicki Traino, Methuen's production manager, without whom you would not be reading these words.

Sean Magee
May 2002

PICTURE CREDITS

Picture Researcher: Emily Hedges

The Ascot Authority should like to thank the following sources for their kind permission to reproduce the illustrations in this book: